Non-Human Rights

Non-Human Rights
Critical Perspectives

Edited by

Alexis Alvarez-Nakagawa

Lecturer & IHSS Fellow, Queen Mary University of London, UK

Costas Douzinas

Emeritus Professor, School of Law, Birkbeck, University of London, UK

Cheltenham, UK • Northampton, MA, USA

© The Editors and Contributors Severally 2024

All rights reserved. No part of this publication may be reproduced, stored in a retrieval system or transmitted in any form or by any means, electronic, mechanical or photocopying, recording, or otherwise without the prior permission of the publisher.

Published by
Edward Elgar Publishing Limited
The Lypiatts
15 Lansdown Road
Cheltenham
Glos GL50 2JA
UK

Edward Elgar Publishing, Inc.
William Pratt House
9 Dewey Court
Northampton
Massachusetts 01060
USA

A catalogue record for this book
is available from the British Library

Library of Congress Control Number: 2024830585

This book is available electronically in the Elgaronline
Law subject collection
http://dx.doi.org/10.4337/9781802208528

Printed on elemental chlorine free (ECF)
recycled paper containing 30% Post-Consumer Waste

ISBN 978 1 80220 851 1 (cased)
ISBN 978 1 80220 852 8 (eBook)

Printed and bound in the USA

Contents

List of contributors		vii
A critical introduction to Non-Human Rights *Alexis Alvarez-Nakagawa*		1
1	Residual humanism *Colin Dayan*	13
2	On the juridical existence of animals: the case of a bear in Colombia's Constitutional Court *Edward Mussawir*	20
3	Why nature has no rights *Alain Pottage*	39
4	The rights of robots *David J. Gunkel*	66
5	Who is the subject of (non) human rights? *Alexis Alvarez-Nakagawa*	88
6	Deliberate legal equivocations: making non-human persons, multiplying differences *Ciméa B. Bevilaqua*	118
7	The EU Charter on Rights of Nature – colliding cosmovisions on non/human relations *Marie-Catherine Petersmann*	141
8	A diplomacy for human/non-human relations: letter to a young climate activist *Oscar Guardiola-Rivera*	164
9	More-than-human rights to data *Jannice Käll*	189

10	Decentring the human or rescaling the state? Grassroots movements for the 'rights' of nature in the United States *Erin Fitz-Henry*	206
11	Non-Human Rights, Amazonian ecocide and Davi Kopenawa's counter-ethnography of merchandise people *Idelber Avelar*	223
12	Do androids dream of having rights? *Costas Douzinas*	240
Index		256

Contributors

Alexis Alvarez-Nakagawa is a Lecturer in Law and Fellow of the Institute for the Humanities and Social Sciences at Queen Mary University of London (UK). His research focuses on the question of law and political ontology, and he is currently working on a project about the extension of rights to non-humans funded by the British Academy.

Idelber Avelar is Professor at the Department of Spanish and Portuguese, Tulane University (US). He is the author of several influential books and over 100 scholarly articles in the fields of Latin American studies.

Ciméa B. Bevilaqua is Associate Professor at the Department of Anthropology, University of Parana (Brazil). Her research interests focus on the anthropology of law and bureaucracy, including legal-theoretical debates and court decisions concerning non-human beings.

Colin Dayan is the Robert Penn Warren Professor in the Humanities at Vanderbilt University (US). Her books include *The Law is a White Dog: How Legal Rituals Make and Unmake Persons* (Princeton UP 2013) and *With Dogs at the Edge of Life* (Columbia UP 2016).

Costas Douzinas is Emeritus Professor of Law and Founder of the Birkbeck Institute for the Humanities, Birkbeck University of London (UK). He is the author of *The End of Human Rights* (Hart 2000), *Human Rights and Empire* (Routledge 2007) and *The Radical Philosophy of Rights* (Routledge 2019).

Erin Fitz-Henry is a Senior Lecturer in Anthropology and the Development Studies in the School of Social and Political Sciences at the University of Melbourne (Australia). She works primarily on transnational social movements, with a particular interest in the global movement for the rights of nature in Ecuador, the United States, and Australia.

Oscar Guardiola-Rivera is Professor of Human Rights and Political Philosophy at Birkbeck Law School, University of London (UK). He is the author of *What If Latin America Ruled the World?* (Bloomsbury 2010) and *Story of a Death Foretold* (Bloomsbury 2013).

David J. Gunkel is Professor at the Department of Communication at Northern Illinois University (US). He is the author of over 80 scholarly articles and has published 12 influential books, including *Person, Thing, Robot: A Moral and Legal Ontology for the 21st Century and Beyond* (MIT Press 2023) and *Robot Rights* (MIT Press 2018).

Jannice Käll is Associate Professor at the Sociology of Law Department, Lund University (Sweden). Her research focuses on legal changes under the influence of new digital technologies. She is the author of *Posthuman Property and Law: Commodification and Control through Information, Smart Spaces and Artificial Intelligence* (Routledge 2023).

Edward Mussawir is a Senior Lecturer at Griffith Law School (Australia). His research covers various themes in jurisprudence including jurisdiction, judgment, legal personality, the legal status of animals and the work of Gilles Deleuze. He co-edited (with Yoriko Otomo) *Law and the Question of the Animal: A Critical Jurisprudence* (Routledge 2013).

Marie-Catherine Petersmann is Assistant Professorial Research Fellow at LSE Law School (UK). Her project *Anthropocene Legalities: Reconfiguring Legal Relations within More-than-human Worlds* is funded by a Dutch NWO Veni grant (2022-2025). Her book *When Environmental Protection and Human Rights Collide* was published with Cambridge University Press in 2022.

Alain Pottage is Professor of Law, Sciences Po, Paris (France). His research focuses on the question of law in the Anthropocene. Currently he is working on a project about Climate Change and the Legal Tradition (funded by IEP Paris). He co-edited (with Martha Mundy) *Law, Anthropology, and the Constitution of the Social: Making Persons and Things* (CUP 2004).

A critical introduction to Non-Human Rights

Alexis Alvarez-Nakagawa

Non-human rights are becoming part of our ordinary legal landscape and vocabulary. Animals, rivers, mountains, rainforests, ecosystems and synthetic or artificial entities such as machines, AI and robots are currently regarded or in the process of being considered subjects of rights in different parts of the world. This trend has spread in domestic jurisdictions and is rapidly gaining ground in regional and international settings.

Interestingly, however, this surge in rights for non-humans has coincided with a growing uncertainty about the future of human rights. Human rights seem to be suffering from an 'existential crisis', as the reactions of states and international organizations indicate, and critical appraisals in the scholarship have evinced for some time now. The perceived ineffectiveness of human rights in preventing humanitarian disasters and their misuse in justifying war, imperialism, and uneven power-dynamics, and, more generally, their lack of success in delivering their messianic promise of a fairer, equal, and just world, have led to doubts about their moral authority and universal predicament. Recent events such as the response of states to the global pandemic – driven more by political opportunism and economic or medical pragmatism than by the ethics of human rights – further underscore the diminishing relevance of human rights. How to explain this dual trajectory of the discourse of rights? How can we understand these circumstances which signal the vitality and extension of the rights rhetoric as well as its agony and contraction? Is the expansion of rights to non-humans an outcome of the twilight of human rights, or something that occurs despite their apparent decline?

These contradictory tendencies also seem to be part of how the scholarship perceives this 'non-human turn' in the law. Non-human rights have been met with enthusiasm and derision. They have been considered both 'revolutionary' – a 'paradigm shift' – and 'not radical enough', an 'ontological opening' and the affirmation of the Western humanistic episteme, a threat to the human condition and its assertion by other means. Some see in them a 'decentring of the human', others a form of veiled anthropocentrism. Some think they are a useful 'juridical fiction', while others believe they represent a timely acknowledgement of non-humans' sentiency or intelligence. Some assert that these rights express non-human agentivity, others that they sacrifice their alterity. While many believe that basic rights are a safeguard to non-humans' 'interests', 'intrinsic worth' or 'dignity', others contend that they are not enough to uphold their moral status. Non-human rights have been considered a recognition of non-Western beliefs, ontologies and epistemes, as well as a cultural appropriation of Indigenous practices, a straitjacket to their worldviews, not sufficiently 'decolonizing' or a new tool for neo-colonialism. While some consider they are a way of protecting non-humans from exploitation, an alternative to developmental practices, and a potential means to confront capitalism, others see a form of masking extractivism and neoliberal policies. Some assert they are a renewed 'nonsense upon stilts' – will pets or house appliances be able to sue us if we mistreat them, and we will sue rivers if someone drowns in them? – others the step forward the law must take to keep pace with the times, whether this is seen as the age of the 'intrusion of Gaia', the transhumanist 'Singularity', the Anthropocene (or any of its multiple variants) or simply, 'the end of the world'.[1] In most cases, it is difficult to assert which of these opposing accounts is valid. It is as if non-human rights were a bit of both, or as if they were strained by the new 'trying to emerge' and the old 'refusing to let go'. Is it, as Marx said, that the new often appears in old garments? Is the old pregnant with the new?[2]

These are some of the questions this book raises and attempts to, if not answer, at least address. Moreover, as can be anticipated from the questions formulated above, this volume proposes a somewhat different approach to the study of non-human rights. Far from exacerbated optimism, it attempts to cast a critical light on this trend's rapid emergence and how it is gradually shaping how we perceive, understand, and engage with non-humans in the law. This has not been the default position in the literature. Arguably, while non-human rights are the product of different political movements and theoretical perspectives that have been critical in their orientation and have confronted both the environmental crisis, driven by the capitalist form of accumulation and production, and the anthropocentrism of our political institutions, their approach to the law has not been equally problematizing and critical. In particular, the discourse of rights and legal reform taken as unquestioned values, ends in themselves that do not require further scrutiny. There seems to be little interest in questioning the law, either as part of the problem or as part of the solution to

---

[1] For a good overview of these different formulations see Déborah Danowski and Eduardo Viveiros de Castro, *The Ends of the World* (Rodrigo Guimaraes Nunes tr, Polity 2016).

[2] Karl Marx, *The Civil War in France*, MECW, vol 22 (Lawrence & Wishart Ltd 2010) 335.

our current difficulties. In particular, we are not told why, if rights have been unsuccessful in securing the protection of human beings and if the gap between declarations of rights and their application and enforcement is as wide as ever, they could be effective for non-humans – particularly when the difficulties of implementation seem to be greater in these cases. Also, since much of the scholarship has attempted to influence policymaking or the attitude of courts, it has focused on challenging legal institutions that exclude non-humans as right holders, and its agenda has been essentially advocacy-orientated. This has meant that theoretical concerns and a critical orientation have been sidelined, preventing us from seeing that non-human rights often produce and reproduce the logics and rationalities that they were supposed to challenge.

This book presents three strands together that are usually studied separately: animal rights, nature rights and robot rights. These strands, in turn, have similarities with a number of discussions that are left out of this volume about the status of the unborn, the nature of human tissue, the personhood of religious idols, etc. This book's particular focus assumes that animal rights, nature's rights and robot rights are discursively connected and must be analysed in tandem as part of the same phenomenon. While the historical emergence of each of these strands can be differentiated, they share ideological assumptions, political and legal imaginaries, discursive justifications, and a core of common tenets, goals and ideas. Moreover, there is a chronological correlation between them as they emerged in parallel and have gained momentum together, sometimes feeding back on each other. The reason for this is that they respond to the same set of concerns and motivations revolving around the technological revolution, on the one hand, and the impact that this has had on the environment and the habitability of the planet, on the other. In this regard, non-human rights make sense and are explicable in what Peter Frase has called the 'two spectres' that haunt the 21st century: 'ecological catastrophe and automation.'[3] It could be said that if human rights were 'the ideology at the end of history'[4] – epitomized by the fall of the Soviet Union and the triumph of capitalism – non-human rights are the ideology at 'the end of the world' – epitomized by the devastating effects of the technical revolution on the ecological milieu.

We are aware that by using the term 'non-human' we risk reifying a problematic category with no empirical correlation. As with 'non-white', 'non-European', and 'non-Western', non-human establishes its field of semantic application based upon an opposition (with the 'human') and relies on a purely negative definition. These problems are not necessarily averted by using other expressions of the like such as 'more-than-human' or

---

[3] Peter Frase, *Four Futures: Visions of the World After Capitalism* (Verso 2016).
[4] Costas Douzinas, *The End of Human Rights* (Hart 2000) 2.

'other-than-human', as they also work by reference to the 'human'. It could be said that all these descriptors are 'ideologically loaded' (they are not neutral) as only from the point of view of the human can other entities be described as 'non-human', 'more-than-human', or 'other-than-human'.[5] This is clear as these are not unavoidable descriptors – there are other ways through which we can refer to the beings in question: by species, habitat, constitution, etc.[6]

The human/non-human opposition seems even more inadequate today as it does not help to organize and understand the multiplicity of human/non-human 'assemblages' technology has made possible. From creatures created through bioengineering using both human and animal cells to transgenic seeds and bacteria produced by humans in laboratories, drones and robots programmed to adopt human or animal behaviour, 'xenobots' that act like organic machines, and the 'cyborg' quality of human bodies enhanced by different technologies, human and non-human existence seem to blur in our societies, sometimes becoming utterly indistinguishable. As Latour explained, however, these 'hybrids' have always existed, despite our 'modern' attempts of purification and classification. Our lack of success in such an enterprise, and the uncontainable proliferation of hybrids we witness today, indicate that 'we have never been modern'.[7] Indeed, given the constant co-presence, co-development and entangled biographies of humans with animals, plants, microbes and other entities, we might say that 'human nature is an interspecies relationship'[8] to the extent that we have 'never been human'.[9]

As with 'non-white' or 'non-European', the term 'non-human' indicates lacking and fault, which has justified different forms of social exclusion. In the legal framework, the term non-human both includes and excludes the non-human in relation to the human. It is thus a mechanism of 'inclusion through exclusion'. This is precisely why we decided to keep the term 'non-human' as this volume's common denominator. Despite all its shortcomings, the term is useful to designate an ontological realm to which those who are not regarded as 'human' are cast. It serves to identify the *locus* and circumstances that non-humans (and some humans considered inhuman) inhabit. The usefulness of the descriptor then lies in that it encapsulates this phenomenon of inclusion/exclusion, making it visible and graspable. 'Non-human' thus designates both a state and an onto-epistemological operation through which

---

[5] Marianne DeKoven, 'Why Animals Now?' (2009) 124.2 PMLA 363.
[6] Ibid.
[7] Bruno Latour, *We Have Never Been Modern* (Catherine Porter tr, Harvard UP 1993).
[8] Anna Tsing, 'Unruly Edges: Mushrooms as Companion Species' (2012) 1 Environmental Humanities 144.
[9] Donna Haraway, *When Species Meet* (University of Minnesota Press 2008) 19.

this state is generated and assigned to certain forms of existence – constituting a 'form of existing' in the world. The term serves us heuristically to signal a problematic sphere in which reification works to produce and perpetuate a 'human, all too human' world.

Another reason to keep the term is that the expression 'non-human rights' can be understood in different ways, reflecting the tension existing between opposing views. On the one hand, this expression indicates the rights of animals, nature, AI, etc. This is how it is generally used in the literature. However, without the hyphen, 'non human rights' refers to what are *not* human rights. While the former designates the rights of non-humans (an extension of human rights to non-humans), the latter points towards something different from human rights. Something which does not yet have a name because it is in the process of emerging, something which, to return to Marx, might be arising from the rubble of the old. Which of these 'variations' of 'non human rights' will prevail remains to be seen. If it is true that a quick overview indicates that, in most cases, we just witness an extension of human rights to non-humans – as some of the chapters of this volume demonstrate – it is not less right that non-human rights offer an opportunity to think beyond human rights. The ambiguity of the expression 'non human rights' invites us to be playful with the words and look at this 'beyond'.

This volume advances our knowledge about the changing patterns of the rights discourse in contemporary societies marked by rapid technological changes and the fast degradation of the environment. The book aims to fill a gap in the scholarship – which except from a few interesting exceptions has usually focused on animal, nature or robot rights in isolation – and contributes to establishing a set of studies on the subject of 'non-human rights' as a general emerging field of enquiry. The chapters that this collective volume gather explore the non-human turn in the law critically and interdisciplinarily. Most of them draw and take inspiration from a broader shift in the humanities and social sciences – ranging from the 'ontological turn' in anthropology to new materialism, post-human feminism, object-oriented ontology, actor-network theory and other similar approaches informed by decolonial thinking, phenomenology, Indigenous scholarship, and critical animal studies. Such varied theoretical and analytical lenses disagree in many of their methods, assumptions, and ideas, all of which is reflected in this volume's chapters. However, they are also united in considering the non-human entity as a significant cypher to understand our times and the problems we face, as well as in questioning the binary dualisms that support human exceptionalism and the exploitation of non-humans through different political, legal, and economic institutions. Drawing on this and other perspectives, the authors of this volume provide a rich and ample overview of what non-human rights are today and how we can engage (even sometimes sympathize) with them without lowering our critical threshold.

CRITICAL PERSPECTIVES

The twelve chapters of this volume bring together an ample and rich range of critical perspectives on non-human rights. Some of them are wider in nature addressing general aspects that affect all kinds of non-human rights, others are focused on particular rights and subjects. Even if contributors come from diverse backgrounds and use different theoretical and methodological approaches, all of them aim to problematize certain aspects of the 'non-human turn' in law.

Our volume opens with a short contribution by Colin Dayan, which confronts head-on the 'residual humanism' in animal rights and sets the critical and polemical tone of the collection. Chapter 1 is an examination of the limits of humanism and the potential of 'animality' to think anew our relationship with others (humans and non-humans alike). Drawing extensively on modern and contemporary literature, Dayan casts doubt on 'humanity' as a political project and on the 'personalist dichotomy' (person/non-person or thing) on which it is based, as well as on the robustness and transportability of the ontological partitions it presupposes (body/mind, animality/humanity, nature/culture). Rather than giving animals rights (or whatever we think we owe them in moral liberal terms), she argues we need to think through the 'creaturely'. Instead of opposing animals to humans, we need to question the limits of our humanity: could we define ourselves alongside and through our dogs? Can we think along with our dogs, but as the basis for our sensibility and cognition, not the other way around? What would it mean to reorient our ethical, political, or juridical assumptions by taking the perspective of our dogs? This 'condition of being a dog' might be a means to seek new kinds of communion and a way out of human rationality and the presumptions that have tormented other species and destroyed our environment. The question of the 'residual humanism' in non-human rights somehow traverses most of the contributions to this volume, sometimes explicitly, some others implicitly, as we will see.

In the same critical tone, chapter 2 discusses a recent failed attempt to grant legal subjectivity to a spectacled bear named 'Chucho' at Colombia's Constitutional Court. Edward Mussawir critically engages with current efforts to theorize non-human legal personhood and argues for a shift of emphasis away from the 'subject of rights' and towards a jurisprudence attentive to the ways in which non-human animals feature as active participants in legal thought. Mussawir shows how discussions on animal personhood have been reliant on scientific 'authorities', 'experts' and 'natural truths' (from biology, ethology, ecology, etc.) rather than on specific juridical reasoning. In contrast, he argues, animals allow us to think about the law from a different perspective, acting more as bearers of legal meaning than as bearers of legal rights. Thus, the chapter ends by exploring how animals, in particular bears, have helped jurisprudence to conceptualize the limits of actions in Roman law, problematize particular forms of liability in common law, create exceptions to the rule against hearsay, set the boundaries of jurisdiction and Aboriginal title, and unearth fundamental principles of civil and family law.

The role of expertise plays a significant part in chapter 3 as well, where Alain Pottage wonders about the 'nature' of nature's rights. Pottage argues that as they are practiced today, the rights of nature do not protect it from the exploitation of global capital. The attribution of personality and rights to nature both obscures and facilitates the subjection of natural entities to the market. The agency and vitality ascribed to nature today, which would justify granting it rights, originates in the very epistemic conditions that generated fossil capital and neoliberalism. 'Cybernetisicim' and its ethos of auto-limitlessness is as much behind our newfound ability to think of natural entities as agentive, sensitive, complex, self-organizing, or 'mattering' as it is behind the fundamental drivers of the market economy. As Pottage highlights, Lovelock's Gaia hypothesis allowed the Royal Dutch Shell Company to envisage a particular strategy of climate denialism based on the 'self-regulating' and 'adaptative' mechanisms of the Earth. The mode of vitality and agentivity that enabled Gaia to be promoted as a figuration of our 'Earthbound' existence was initially cultivated as a theme of fossil economy. In a renewed display of colonial violence, this cybernetic 'episteme of surfeit' is usually coated and mediated by the connection to nature forged by the cosmologies of others. At stake, however, is not a new appreciation of the practices and usages of Indigenous peoples, but the human control over basic geo-material processes. Rights of nature become then a new modality of exploitation that attempts to 'settle' the contradictions of the fossil economy by deferring their solution to the future.

Cybernetisicim might well be in-built into our modern episteme, underlying contemporary thinking and practices that extend from ecology to robotics. This cannot be clearer than in discussions about AI and machines agentivity, which is explored in detail in chapter 4. In this section, David Gunkel describes the terms and conditions of the debate on robot rights, identifying the common set of values and assumptions supporters and detractors endorse. Despite differences, what both sides agree on is that the debate about AI is to be framed in terms of 'rights'. It is reasonable to ask, however, as Gunkel does, whether this mode of framing things is the most conducive, as there are other ways to arrange inquiries about the status of others – ways that do not necessarily entail the same set of assumptions and that enable different ways of seeing and responding to others. Gunkel explores some of these alternatives, from Indigenous traditions, Easter philosophy and relational ontologies and ethics to his own proposal based on Levinasian philosophy. However, he also concedes that taking note of the alternatives does not necessarily mean we can stop talking about rights. For better or worse, this is the way the debate has been framed and it is only by addressing rights that we can intervene in the existing debates.

If rights are an elusive way of conducting the debate about the status of non-humans, ascribing subjecthood to them does not seem to be less problematic. In chapter 5, Alexis Alvarez-Nakagawa examines this category considering the broad proliferation of non-human legal subjects we are witnessing today in different jurisdictions. He notes that Jacques Rancière's work has been embraced by several scholars in order to understand and mobilize the subjectification of non-humans in the context of a 'pluralization of ontologies' and 'cosmopolitics'. He questions, however, whether this approach is apt for such an endeavour. Deploying an archaeological/genealogical approach to the 'subject' and the 'person', he asserts that these figures have been irremediably associated with the human and that any ascription of subjecthood and personhood to non-humans risks reinstating the problems non-human rights have purportedly come to sort out (among them, anthropocentrism and an arbitrary *scala naturae* where non-humans are devalued). For Alvarez-Nakagawa, the question one needs to ask is whether it is possible to think of a subject dissociated from its human form and the normative model it has imprinted on it based on features such as reason, agency, autonomy, and will. What is sure, in any case, is that non-human rights should go beyond the politics as usual of human rights if they want to give actual 'legal existence' to other-than-human beings.

Also looking for new forms of 'legal existence', in chapter 6 Ciméa B. Bevilaqua analyses two ground-breaking court rulings in Argentina that acknowledged the orangutan 'Sandra' and the chimpanzee 'Cecilia' as a 'non-human subject of rights' and a 'non-human person', respectively. The novelty of these judgments evinces a broader movement towards reversing the 'ontological cleansing' consubstantial to the development of modern legal systems through which animals and other non-humans became mere things and property. Bevilaqua carefully examines the different argumentative paths and technical operations utilized in these cases and argues that as a result of 'deliberate equivocations', judges were able to overcome procedural and substantive obstacles to turn Sandra and Cecilia into legal persons with rights. In contrast to the power of 'experts' that Mussawir critically shows are dominating the narrative of animal rights cases in Colombia, Bevilaqua points to the specific juridical techniques used by judges in Argentina. The outcome of these technical operations, however, is not less paradoxical, as non-human animals become simultaneously persons and things, furthering the inherent dualism of modern legal systems.

It could be said that this ambiguous but characteristic dualism is pulled into tension in some contemporary legislative initiatives that attempt to draw on other onto-epistemic traditions while keeping intact the main tenets of modern Western legal systems. In chapter 7, Marie-Catherine Petersmann analyses the EU Charter on the Fundamental Rights of Nature, focusing on the colliding and sometimes conflicting ontologies at its foundation. Petersmann argues that the Charter discursively relies on the cosmovisions of Indigenous peoples, which have underlain the rights of nature movement in Ecuador and Bolivia, but substantively departs from their way of conceiving 'relationality'. Thus, while Indigenous relationality focuses on entangled and co-constitutive agencies, the EU Charter deploys a 'rights relationship', that is, a kind of relationality linking pre-existing and pre-formed human and non-human beings. Contrary to Andean cosmologies and in tune with Western prevailing ideas, the Charter conceptualizes relationality as the interaction between discrete, bounded, and separate entities – e.g. 'humans' vis-à-vis 'nature'. Petersmann argues that even if we must be cautious about not appropriating Indigenous ideas, re-enacting colonial violence and dispossession, we also need to be attentive to these onto-epistemic differences, as they enact and bring diverse worlds into existence. She argues that these differences matter, especially today when generic 'rights of nature' are being advocated worldwide.

Bringing light to these onto-epistemic differences is what Oscar Guardiola-Rivera seeks in chapter 8. He draws on the cosmology of Andean, Caribbean, and Amazonian Amerindians to assess non-human rights and a new human/non-human diplomacy. Interestingly, Guardiola-Rivera's chapter adopts the form of a letter addressed to a young female climate activist, who asserted that Indigenous peoples should be considered as bearers of solutions to the climate crisis. Although they are not usually invited to 'sit at the table' of environmental talks, Guardiola-Rivera argues that Indigenous people could bring alternative forms of establishing conversations (of 'eating each other's words') that are more considerate of the relational nature of human and non-human worlds. He contrasts the work of *palabreros* (wordsmiths), skilled in shamanic diplomatic practices based on gift-logics, which seek to forge alliances and thus preserve life, to the Western model of warfare against the Other, which turns out to be a cult of death. Current legal technologies are nourished by this cult and are unable to create remedies for the climate crisis and its unevenly distributed effects. Moreover, concepts such as 'liberty' and 'agency', which infuse Western legal categories, are insufficient when articulated in the frame of settler colonialism, neoliberalism and neoconservatism. Therefore, Guardiola-Rivera argues that we should aim to translate the Amerindian gift-logics of alliance into legal difference, a kind of 'multijuridical multiperspectivism' reliant on difference in a relational rather than essentialist form.

Chapter 9 also seeks to explore relationality but from a different standpoint, paying attention to our 'digitally entangled worlds'. Drawing on posthuman and new materialist approaches, Jannice Käll points out the deep connection between the extractive economy, the ecological crisis, and the rise of the information culture. Digitization, automation and our data-driven societies rely on the increasing consumption of energy and resources, which drives the intensification of extractivism and the resultant ecological degradation of the planet. From this perspective, the abstract 'computational matrix' becomes utterly material. Käll argues that this ecological aspect of the infrastructure of digitalization brings questions yet unexplored by law and technology studies, such as the similar direction that data rights and rights of nature are taking, and the need to consider them together in order to fulfil sustainable digitalization. In this regard, Käll aims to examine whether it is possible to move towards 'more-than-human rights to data'. To do so, she explores Deleuzian/Spinozian understandings of rights – conceptualized as 'rights to bodies' – which could affirm more sustainable collectivities.

As chapter 10 shows, this issue is crucial as human/non-human collectives suffer most of the ecological harm. In this section, Erin Fitz-Henry examines the rights of nature movement and argues that because of the recent focus of the scholarship on 'decentring the human', in particular, by exploring human entanglements with other-than-human beings, we overlook the occurrence of an even more significant and transcendent displacement – a 'decentring of the state'. In most national contexts in which rights of nature are being considered or implemented, local struggles are directed at contesting the decision-making authority of states: from the power of national ministries to issue environmental permits to the poor role played by regulatory agencies or their collusion with corporations. In all these cases, people are resorting to the rights of nature to challenge the legal frameworks that enable private capital to pollute the soil, waterways and air of their cities and towns. Fitz-Henry claims that closer examination – she relies on archival and ethnographic research conducted in the State of Ohio in the United States – of these on-the-ground efforts takes us quite far from the 'ontological' debates that currently animate the literature. Instead, they bring us back to the long-standing political-economic questions about the state and private capital, as environmental activists weaponize the rights of nature against the verticality of centralized environmental agencies. While many scholars have recently spent considerable time describing the political potentials of 'radical alterity', Fitz-Henry suggests we must turn our gaze to the 'tactical and strategic' questions raised by movements for the rights of nature and pay attention to the different scales at which environmental decisions are taken (and challenged).

Also focusing on the rights of nature but from a different perspective, in chapter 11, Idelber Avelar analyzes two simultaneous and contrasting processes that took place in Brazil during the last few years. On the one hand, the construction of the Belo Monte hydroelectric dam, which has been the cause of massive environmental destruction and loss of biodiversity in the Amazon's Middle Xingu. On the other hand, the publication of *The Falling Sky*, a volume that marks several years of collaboration between Yanomami shaman Davi Kopenawa and Brazil-based French anthropologist Bruce Albert, which, according to Avelar, could be considered the most powerful Amerindian critique to date of the ecocidal mentality that underlies developmentalist's projects like the one in Belo Monte. The book provides a counter-ethnography of the 'merchandise people' (Westerners) and presents the ideas of the Yanomani about the world, who, in tune with other Amazonian peoples, believe in a primordial state of undifferentiation between humans and non-humans. Whereas for Westerners humans are former animals, for the Yanomani, animals are former humans. The original condition is humanity, not animality. Consequently, the Yanomani believe that the attributes that the West ascribe to humans (self-consciousness, volition, soul) are shared by all animals. Amerindian thought provides a different way of conceptualizing the relationship between humans and non-humans. Therefore, even if *The Falling Sky* does not use juridical language, its significance for thinking (or rethinking) non-human rights is immeasurable.

Costas Douzinas closes this volume by exploring whether robots and AI could be entitled to legal personhood. In 2017, Saudi Arabia granted citizenship to a humanoid robot named Sophia. In June 2023, the Royal Aeronautical Society reported that the US air force had conducted a simulation where a drone decided to 'kill' its operator to prevent him from interfering with its mission. This and similar news created significant fuss and led to a public debate. Douzinas argues that legal personality has not been an exclusively human prerogative and that there is nothing new about its extension to non-humans. Slaves, women and minoritized groups were not recognized as persons for much of history. Conversely, corporations, idols and animals have been given some of legal personhood's entitlements and responsibilities. The legal person is a juridical creation, an artificial character assigned with an abstract function. As a formal vessel, it can contain and give form to all sorts of content. Therefore, the answer to the question of AI rights is to be sought not in the meaning or essence of personhood but in the economic and social practicalities entailed in ascribing it to such entities. Douzinas asserts that it seems unlikely that today robot rights will result from an organized social and political movement – as happens, for example, with animal rights. The law will extend legal entitlements and duties to AI and robots when economic interests demand it. But what about the reverse side? Do androids dream of human rights to protect them from harmful actions? Douzinas argues that when they do, personhood and rights will undoubtedly follow. The key question, then, is about the android's ability to dream, not their capacity to enjoy rights or personhood.

The chapters of this book show a diversity of approaches to non-human rights. They are intended to open a discussion on non-human rights and, therefore, they should be considered a starting point for further exploration, and an invitation to look critically at the rapid surge of non-human rights and the power they have to shape our contemporary legal debates about the degradation of the environment and emerging technologies.

1. Residual humanism
Colin Dayan

What does conscience look like at the boundaries of humanity, at the edge of a cherished humanism? Let me begin with Herman Melville, the lone writer in the so-called 'American Renaissance' who tackled the question of the human as terminological quest romance and racial conundrum. In *Bartleby*, the bookish narrator ponders the recalcitrant scrivener and asks elliptically: 'had there been anything ordinarily human about him [...].'[1] In his novel *Pierre: or, the Ambiguities*, Isabel roots herself in the living landscape of her dream and loses 'the power of being sensible of myself as something human.'[2] Giving affect and sensibility to the non-human, Melville encouraged his readers to confront the limits and dangers of that value-laden term 'humanity,' as well as Enlightenment assumptions about the boundaries of consciousness. His whales have more affect and sensibility than his mariners. Melville recognized the lure of whatever, as Israel Potter ponders in the story bearing his name, is 'something more than humanly significant.'[3]

To think about the fragility of personhood is my aim. Not just the nature of *personhood* as applied to humans, but the problem of *animality* for humans and non-humans, with both human and non-human persons seen against the threat of *things* or *thinglikeness*: never actual death but the lure of the inanimate or insensate. How, in other words, are we to explain the generally invisible nexus of animality, human marginalization, and juridical authority? Perhaps by trying to understand how, where – and why – human beings, often quite arbitrarily, devise, formulate, and apply lines separating the human and the animal, or, more tellingly, deliberately blur those lines.

In *The Law is a White Dog*,[4] I analyzed how legal rituals gave and took away personhood. It was only with my recent work on dogs, canine profiling, and preemptive justice – and the means by which humans are dispossessed through their dogs – that I realized personhood might not be the issue. It is not

---

[1] *Billy Budd, Bartleby, and Other Stories* (Penguin 2016).
[2] *Pierre: Or, the Ambiguities* (Penguin 1996).
[3] *Israel Potter. His Fifty Years of Exile* (Penguin 2008).
[4] *The Law is a White Dog: How Legal Rituals Make and Unmake Persons* (Princeton UP 2013).

just a question of human disposal, but what tracks it: whether personalized or depersonalized, I now realize, it does not matter. I want to push beyond the residual humanism that lingers in such a personalist dichotomy.

Why (to take up Mary Midgley's point in *Animals and Why They Matter*), does 'A sense of unreality' block 'our attempts to understand our moral relations with animals'?[5] Why is the question of the animal or the *animot*, as Derrida put it at the end of his life,[6] so hard to fit into our ethical system? I think here of Hannah Arendt's vigorous attempt to 'save' political action and political understandings of action from humanitarianism.[7] Indeed, it is her argument that led to my work on the exterminating rituals of 'humane societies' that kill certain breeds with impunity. She feared and understood the cunning of any properly *political* project of humanity.

What I propose is a resistance to the terms of our epistemological debates and so to cast doubt on the robustness and transportability of the ontological partitions they presuppose: body and mind, animality and humanity, nature and culture – social and political. This means more importantly that neither 'depersonalization' nor 'dehumanization' matters as much as a capacious rendering of human and non-human animal. In thinking through *the creaturely*, then, I am not interested in animal rights, in giving animals what we think it is we get as bearers of rights and obligations in standard liberal moral terms.

Animality is what we should be thinking about rather than claims for humanity. We need to question the status of human as a problem, the kind of privilege that remains ambiguous at best. Dogs live on the track between the mental and the physical and seem to tease out a near-mystical disintegration of the bounds between them. Such knowing has everything to do with perception, an attentiveness that unleashes another kind of intelligibility beyond the world of the human.

Why aren't dogs persons? What do we mean by personhood? I always return to John Locke's exquisite distinction between *humans* and *persons* in the most controversial section of his *Essay on Human Understanding* (1694).[8] Whereas humans all have the same frontispiece or external shape of their bodies, he defines a person as a 'thinking thing,' no matter whether that thinking thing is man, horse, or dog. Anyone or anything can be a person, as long as consciousness can be extended back to past actions, so far 'that consciousness

---

[5] *Animals and Why They Matter* (University of Georgia Press 1998).
[6] Jacques Derrida, *The Animal That Therefore I Am* (David Wills trans, Fordham UP 2008) 41.
[7] Hannah Arendt, *The Origins of Totalitarianism* (Penguin 1994).
[8] John Locke, *Essay Concerning Human Understanding* (Peter H. Nidditch ed, OUP 1979).

reaches, and no farther.'[9] Also, persons are subject to law. 'It is a Forensick term appropriating Actions and their Merit; and so belongs only to intelligent Agents capable of a Law, and Happiness and Misery.' What makes you a person is the capacity to know your actions as good and evil. What makes a person – and Locke implies that a dog with awareness might also be a person – is responsibility: the ability to *appropriate* these past actions 'to that present *self* by consciousness.'[10]

In *Canine Confidential: Why Dogs Do What They Do* (2018), Marc Bekoff,[11] an authority on animal emotions, writes at length about 'dog mind,' concluding that dogs have cognitive abilities very much like humans. They are capable of making decisions. They think and feel, and, most of all – for those who aren't yet sure how to react to the US government's recent decision to continue excruciatingly painful, long-drawn-out, and ultimately fatal experiments on dogs – they remember. Spain and New Zealand have extended personhood rights to great apes; the town council of Tirgueros del Valle, Spain, has voted unanimously to define dogs and cats as 'non-human residents,' giving them rights similar to those of humans living there; and the Indian government has ruled that cetaceans, such as whales and dolphins, and even rivers are 'non-human persons,' with their own specific rights. Here in the United States, Steven Wise, of the Nonhuman Rights Project, has turned repeatedly to law in order to make a case for the personhood of chimpanzees.

What about dogs? Are they persons? Of course, they are. But I'll add a caveat here. Although I'm keen for animal rights lawyers to succeed in their struggle to recognize the *legal personhood* of animals, including dogs, I also recognize the dangers involved in using human terminology when dealing with non-humans. To say that dogs are *persons* is to attribute to them the kind of conscious intentionality that defines subjectivity, as we understand it; and giving dogs what we think they need in terms of human conceptions of right and wrong or capacity and incapacity is part of the top-down judgment that always fails those we speak for. So instead of opposing dogs to humans, perhaps we need to question the limits of humanity, and start defining ourselves from the ground up, alongside and through our dogs.

Can we push beyond the residual humanism that lurks in considerations of the rights of personhood? We need to think along with our dogs, but as the basis for human sensibility and cognition, not the other way around. In such a terrain, perhaps the word *human* can be redeemed. Finally, in turning away

---

[9] Ibid.
[10] Ibid.
[11] Mark Bekoff, *Canine Confidential: Why Dogs Do What They Do* (University of Chicago Press 2018).

from standard liberal approaches to human and non-human relations – such as animal rights or animal welfare – I ask for an alternative, risky and bracing way of being in the world: again, another way of thinking and loving.

Early one morning I walked my dog Stella down the main street of my Nashville neighborhood. She's a black American Staffordshire terrier with front paws of white fur and a tail that has always been crooked. A pick-up truck was waiting in a drive. She ran up to it, as she sometimes does when white men in trucks, those I grew up knowing as 'crackers' or 'rednecks,' look out at her – a ritual that I've never understood. She jumped, one paw on the man's seat, and another on his leg, and began to greet him with licks, sniffs, and nudges. He welcomed her, as I looked on in wonder. Then he explained: 'She knows I'm sick, and that's why she's trying to help me. I'm dying.' Then he gently beat his chest, adding, 'She can smell it. She wants to give me some relief.'

Stella is dead now, but her spirit lives on. I look into her eyes and know a faith more palpable than the divine. Can you find God in the least likely of places? Stella answers the question. She was utterly Pauline in her consecration of matter – no matter how foul – as the surest road to the spirit. That tough faith relies on paradox, since the stuff of spiritual life is never anything if not radically material. By watching Stella, I learned about faith – and its difference from abstract vagaries of belief. She looks for faith, as Herman Melville put it in *Moby-Dick*, 'among the jackals,' in an earth of rot and stink.[12]

In her eyes, any bone discarded could become sacred. I learned of her transformative powers by watching how instead of chewing and devouring the bones I gave her, she used to wander purposefully inside the house or outside in the back yard, looking for a suitable place for burial. And no mere burial did she intend. Rather, in a studied performance of care, she sniffed the dirt, moved it aside with her paws, and then fiercely dug the hole into which she would lay the bone with a delicacy that astonished.

By watching her, I learned to know feeling that is nothing other than knowing: an exhilaration that braces the mind. This knowing has nothing to do with our assumptions and everything to do with ways of seeing. It demands an unprecedented attentiveness that summons another way of being in the world. Consider with me what it might mean to feel sufficiently, not sentimentally. It is another political life I envision, one that finds its expression through a reorientation of our ways of seeing and thinking.

What would it mean to reorient our ethical and conceptual assumptions by taking on the perspective of dogs? Remaining in touch with the matter of daily life, we too might begin to travel across space and into other bodies – a state of dogs. This *condition of being dog* is not the precondition for uniqueness

---

[12] *Moby-Dick: Or, the Whale* (Penguin 2003).

but rather an imperative to seek a more voracious if always provisional communion.

'Empathetic entanglement', to take my cue from Lori Gruen's brilliant writing, in upsetting such divisions as human and non-human, may be the means out of rationality and the pernicious presumptions that have tormented other species and assailed our environment.[13] In responding to the state of injury, pain and violence of this world, we need to step back and ask what it means to feel – not feeling tied to sentiment but to *feel* sufficiently, to grasp how we can see otherwise or crosswise. We straddle what remains always interstitial.

Let me take the drama of *vodou*, and its *lwa* – its spirits or gods – as instructive. The lwa can only manifest themselves in the corporeal envelope. In lineaments both human and non-human, spirits experience life and unfold their potential. The epistemology of vodou, therefore, offers a context for reconfiguring our understanding of the supernatural as not impalpable or ideal but rather all-too natural, or natural to the nineth degree. Vodou's apprehension of sentient life takes us beyond personhood by exploding terms such as 'humanism,' and its call to the 'universal,' even as it bridges the gaps between body and mind, dead and living, human and non-human.

Perhaps, as Jeanne Moreau in the character of Catherine in Truffaut's *Jules and Jim*, remarked, one must 'reinvent' the word 'love.' I always understood that to mean that it needed to be exhumed, not just remade, taken out of its comfort zone and pushed beyond what could be simply comprehended. Something about viscera and blood and heat and closeness more intense than what can be easily borne. The story that would be told is a 'true love story,' to recall Tim O'Brien's 'true war story.'[14] It calls for another kind of apprehension, a subtle, apparently inauspicious insistence that we take in what comes before preconception.

In this realm, binaries are inefficient at best, dangerous at worst. Words like respect, domination, victimization, body and spirit sit uneasily in their customary positions. No longer contradictory or opposed, the words are intermeshed one with the other in the heat of a nuanced and particular passion. This journey, crude and unpalatable to some, teaches us how we can reconstitute something of a life together on this earth. In the tension of our disagreements and hatreds, we might begin to share a narrative as discontinuous as it is embattled.

We might compare this to the communion shared by the psychoanalyst and the patient: equivocal, risky, transformative, what Freud understood as

---

[13] *Entangled Empathy: An Alternative Ethic for Our Relationships with Animals* (Lantern Books 2015).
[14] Tim O'Brien, *The Things They Carried* (Mariner Books 1990) 64.

a kind of knowing without knowing. He identified this relation more fully in *Group Psychology and the Analysis of the Ego* (1921)[15] as *Einfühlung* or empathy. It became essential to *transference*, the wondrous relation that alone made analysis possible. In 'The Dynamics of Transference' (1912),[16] 'Remembering, Repeating, and Working Through' (1914)[17] and 'Observations on Transference-Love' (1915),[18] Freud found his method in the redirection of a patient's past emotions onto the present relation with the analyst. The very 'peculiarities of the transference to the doctor,' Freud wrote, exceed 'both in amount and nature, anything that could be justified on sensible or rational grounds.'[19] It is not surprising that at the end of his life Freud turned to dogs as his companions. They alone know pure love, a love beyond convenience or comfort. They also bite. As Freud famously said, though no one is quite sure where: 'Dogs love their friends and bite their enemies, quite unlike people, who are incapable of pure love and always have to mix love and hate in their object relations.'

Such love has little to do with romance, or the frills that go along with it. It remains visceral, as physical as a punch to the gut. So, then, what does it mean to become more like a dog? Lucy protests to David Lurie in J.M. Coetzee's *Disgrace* (1999) that she has no property, no this, no that, just 'like a dog.'[20] To be like a dog is something more akin to plenitude than nothing, as Lurie learns when he too gives up what he holds on to most dearly. He surrenders the crippled dog he loves and who loves him to the lethal injection endured by all the stray and abandoned dogs surrounding him.

Living with Stella helped me to reconsider my priorities. I lost friendships and nearly a marriage because of that reconsideration. Her sense of ethics was spot on. What I mean by ethics here is relatedness, *a being with others*, that depends on proximity, a closeness that demands an experience quite distinct from something as abstract as morality. So, if you happen to live with a human

---

[15] 'Group Psychology and the Analysis of the Ego' in *The Standard Edition of the Complete Psychological Works of Sigmund Freud*, Volume XVIII (1920–1922) (James Strachey ed., The Hogarth Press 1958) 65–144.
[16] 'The Dynamics of Transference' in *The Standard Edition of the Complete Psychological Works of Sigmund Freud*, Volume XII (1911–1913) (James Strachey ed., The Hogarth Press 1958) 97–108.
[17] 'Remembering, Repeating, and Working Through' in *The Standard Edition of the Complete Psychological Works of Sigmund Freud*, Volume XII (1911–1913) (James Strachey ed., The Hogarth Press 1958) 147–156.
[18] 'Observations on Transference-Love' in *The Standard Edition of the Complete Psychological Works of Sigmund Freud*, Volume XII (1911–1913) (James Strachey ed., The Hogarth Press 1958) 159–173.
[19] Ibid.
[20] J.M. Coetzee, *Disgrace* (Vintage 1999).

who has firm ideas about dirt and cleanliness, right and wrong ways to be – on or off the bed – a dog like Stella, by luring you into her rowdy antics, gives you the chance to be another kind of person.

2. On the juridical existence of animals: the case of a bear in Colombia's Constitutional Court

Edward Mussawir

HABEAS URSUS AD SUBJICIENDUM

In June of 2017, an Andean or 'spectacled' bear named 'Chucho' became the subject of a legal proceedings in Colombia on the basis of the filing of a writ of *habeas corpus* on his behalf.[1] The writ was filed by a law professor Luis Domingo Gómez Maldonado, an interested third-party, concerned about the rights of animals in general and in this particular case in Chucho's right to live other than in a state of captivity. The bear had been sought to be transferred by the Environmental Office in Manizales, 'Corpocaldas', who had previously kept Chucho at a nature reserve (Río Blanco Protected Forest Reserve) near Manizales, to Barranquilla City Zoo (Fundazoo). The zoo had expressed an interest in obtaining custodianship of Chucho after the 22 to 24-year-old bear, who had always lived in some form of captivity during his life, had fallen into a state of poor-health due in part according to Corpocaldas to the recent death of his sister and without access to the companionship of other members of his species. Becoming aware of Chucho's purported transfer to the zoo, the law professor sought to intervene not just on a political and ethical terrain of the debate, but in the juridical sphere. He sought through the mechanism of a *habeas corpus* petition essentially to have Chucho's freedom from captivity in the zoo upheld on the basis that Colombian law protects not only the idea of

---

[1] For discussion of the background and legal issues in the case see Macarena Montes Franceschini, 'Legal Personhood: The Case of Chucho the Andean Bear' (2021) 11(1) Journal of Animal Ethics 36–46. The *habeas corpus* writ is an ancient writ that allows the question of the lawfulness of an imprisonment to be brought before the courts. It is enshrined in the Constitution of Colombia, Article 30 and also regulated by Law 1095 of 2006. Montes Franceschini notes that the case was the 'first time in history that a habeas corpus writ has been granted to a bear' (at 37).

the welfare of animals, but their rights and liberties, of which captivity itself was to be a primary form of deprivation.

Was *habeas corpus* the most appropriate mechanism to use to ensure that the decision about where Chucho was to live was a lawful one? For those such as Gómez Maldonado, who saw the matter as something more than one concerning animal welfare, it was the only available mechanism: one which forced the judicial system to confront the underlying question of Chucho's imprisonment, thus also his 'personhood', and with that – according to a theory of personhood that treats it as the necessary condition for the attribution of 'rights' – of thinking of the possibility of attributing constitutional rights to a non-human animal.

Neither the mechanism of a 'popular action' which in Colombia might have permitted proceedings to protect collective rights and interests,[2] nor the 'preventive apprehension' mechanism aimed at protecting animals from mistreatment,[3] would do in this case for Gómez Maldonado. Under the auspices of a fundamental writ, a constitutional safeguard guaranteeing to individuals the right to have the lawful basis for their imprisonment brought before a competent tribunal, a fundamental question – one that he thought it supposedly should no longer shirk – was likewise sought to be brought by him before the courts: can a bear be recognized in itself as a 'subject of right'?

LEGAL BACKGROUND TO THE CASE

Amendments to Colombia's civil code in Law 1774 of 2016 had only a year or so earlier recognized in animals a category of property that was both '*semoviente*' (neither movable nor immovable but capable of moving on their own) and '*sintientes*' (sentient).[4] This law also made animals subject to basic protections and welfare provisions, creating the obligation for the State, society and its members to assist in this protection and provision of care. The text formulated the object of its set of amendments by way of a status, described in an entirely negative way with regard to the juridical regime of 'persons' and 'things': namely that a special protection against pain and suffering shall apply to 'animals as sentient beings that are *not things*' (*Los animales como seres sintientes no son cosas, recibirán especial protección contra el sufrimiento y el dolor*).[5] It was, in other words, somehow neither as things nor as persons

---

[2] See Constitution of Colombia, Article 88, which provides a legal basis for action that can be brought for the protection of collective rights and interests related, amongst other things, to heritage and the environment.
[3] See Law 1774 of 2016, Article 8.
[4] See Law 1774 of 2016, Article 1, 2.
[5] See Law 1774 of 2016, Article 1.

but as 'sentient non-things' that the protections of the Colombian law were to come to touch animal life.

Did this law open the juridical space for the recognition of fundamental rights for members of species other than human? The reasoning in an earlier decision of the Constitutional Court of Colombia, concerning the validity of sport-hunting in 2019, would imply that the constitutional protection could operate without the need to ascribe subjectivity to the main beneficiaries of the protection.[6] But Chucho's case presented the court not just with the protection of a living environment. It was presented with a living individual. The case met with a range of different reasonings: first in the initial decision of the Civil Family Chamber of the Superior Court of Manizales which denied the petition on the basis that the rights sought to be protected by the *habeas corpus* writ were available only to humans.[7] Then that of the Civil Cassation Chamber of the Supreme Court which overturned that decision, outwardly pursuing what Judge Luis Armando Tolosa Villabona called an 'ecocentric-anthropic' worldview, recognizing the 'undeniable' truth that sentient beings such as animals are subjects of rights and ordering that Chucho be provided with an environment that better resembled his natural habitat.[8] Next, that of the Labor Cassation Chamber of the Supreme Court which granted the subsequent *tutela* action brought by the zoo against Tolosa Villabona's order claiming that by applying the *habeas corpus* writ in the way the court had, the decision was a violation of the right of due process, and the Criminal Cassation Chamber of the Supreme Court which upheld it.[9] And finally there are the various forms of argumentation contained in the majority and dissenting opinions of the Constitutional Court which handed down its final decision in the matter in January 2020 ultimately finding that there was no basis for the writ of *habeas corpus* to be granted for the protection of the rights of an Andean bear such as Chucho.[10]

---

[6] See Corte Constitucional, Sentencia C-045, February 6 2019.

[7] See Tribunal Superior del Distrito Judicial de Manizales, Sala Civil de Familia, July 13 2017. Vote of Judge César Augusto Cruz Valencia.

[8] Corte Suprema de Justicia, Sala de Casación Civil, AHC4806-2017, July 26 2017. Vote of Judge Luis Armando Villabona. An English translation of the judgment by Javier Salcedo is available at <https://www.nonhumanrights.org/blog/chucho-supreme-court-hearing-colombia/> accessed 25 March 2022.

[9] Corte Suprema de Justicia, Sala de Casación Laboral, STL12651-2017, August 16 2017. Vote of Judge Fernando Castillo Cadena.

[10] Corte Constitucional, Sentencia SU016, January 23 2020.

CONSTRUCTION OF THE DEBATE IN THE CONSTITUTIONAL COURT

For a brief moment, commentators had heralded the recognition of a bear, for the first time, as a legal subject.[11] But the Constitutional Court would ensure not the end but the beginning of a debate. Underlying the judges' opinions in that court was a concern for maintaining the proper limits of a procedural form such as *habeas corpus*. Judge Luis Guillermo Guerrero Pérez took the commonplace approach of recharacterizing the whole issue as one of 'welfare'.[12] The notion of 'freedom and liberation' for Chucho was considered by him at best only a 'simile'[13] of what it means for a political subject in the context of a *habeas corpus* proceedings. *Habeas corpus*, Judge Guerrero Pérez thought, 'has as its inescapable presupposition the arbitrary, unjust and illegal deprivation of personal freedom, and fundamentally seeks the immediate recovery of the same'.[14] The case for Chucho could not be sustained under this form since it was neither for a 'person' nor was it centred on a claim of illegality of captivity but rather on the basis of the upholding of 'animal welfare standards'.[15] The legal history of the writ reinscribes itself in an essentially political and human subject. At the conceptual level, it was presented as a safeguard that did not contemplate its application to non-human beings. And at the procedural level, a legal form that was drastically ill-adapted to the requirements of deciding the complex issue – inevitably presented in the case – of where it was most appropriate for Chucho to live.

This approach which characterized the decision of the court, was criticized by a notable dissenting voice. Judge Diana Fajardo Rivera pointed out that the argumentation on which the decision was reached was flawed firstly at the conceptual level by inadequately addressing the real question of whether the writ was truly limited to the protection of human beings, and also at the

---

[11] See e.g., Annette Garland, 'Habeas corpus victory for bear in Colombia encourages animal rights lawyers' (2017) Changing Times <https://changingtimes.media/2017/08/03/habeas-corpus-victory-for-bear-in-colombia-encourages-animal-rights-lawyers/> accessed 25 March 2022 ; Javier Ernesto Baquero Riveros, 'La Libertad para "Chucho", el oso andino de anteojos. Comentario a la Sentencia de la Corte Suprema de Justicia, Sala de Casación Civil, del veintiséis (26) de julio de dos mil diecisiete (2017)' (2018) 9(1) Derecho Animal 96.

[12] Corte Constitucional, Sentencia SU016, January 23 2020. Vote of Judge Luis Guillermo Guerrero Pérez, at para 1.3.1.

[13] Ibid para 5.2.2.

[14] Ibid.

[15] Ibid.

procedural level by favouring convenience or practicality of decision-making over the requirements of due process.[16]

In Judge Fajardo Rivera's opinion, 'the majority position was lost in the maze of procedural forms'.[17] They had, in effect, simply presupposed the lawfulness of the custody of Chucho by Fundazoo, a question that it was the function of the writ itself, after all, to ultimately put before the courts. And they had thus confused the complexity of the question over the lawfulness of Chucho being held in captivity, which was by no means self-evident, with the simplicity in the availability of the writ itself to protect against such things as the arbitrary imprisonment of individuals that may otherwise, without the protection of the writ, occur beneath the gaze of the law. '[T]he essence of the habeas corpus remedy,' Judge Fajardo Rivera said, 'is to promote the inquiry into the legality of a deprivation of freedom.'[18] To exclude the availability of the writ on the basis of the inconvenience that its mechanism would pose for the particular case, or for cases of this kind, then, would be to turn the objects of constitutional protection on their head. The writ, from Judge Fajardo Rivera's point of view, doesn't seek to accommodate, within a single process, the determination of every legal issue that may be at stake for the individual. It simply ensures the involvement of the courts to address the lawfulness of the process whereby somebody is confined against their will. Thus, her view was that legislative, constitutional, comparative, international and philosophical reasons were sufficient to recognize Chucho – as a wild species for whom freedom is a prevailing status – as the holder of a right to have his freedom protected by constitutional means.[19] And as she proposed in this regard, the establishment of a technical committee to conduct an ethological inquiry into Chucho's condition and whether transfer to the zoo was appropriate.[20]

Between these two rhetorical approaches to the issue, however, lies a tension that a whole litigation strategy of a group like the Non-human Rights Project – reflective of the general approach taken by Gómez Maldonado – is designed to bring to the fore. The whole problem must be constructed, not just by a particular circumstance of injustice but by the general reformatory design of the litigant, as if this problem turned precisely on the unprecedented judicial recognition of a new form of subjectivity: a transformation of existing species from the realm of legal 'things' to that of legal 'persons'. The fact that Chucho was a bear rather than some other species wasn't insignificant in this respect,

---

[16] Corte Constitucional, Sentencia SU016, January 23 2020. Vote of Judge Diana Fajardo Rivera.
[17] Ibid para 6.
[18] Ibid para 111.
[19] Ibid paras 20–113.
[20] Ibid para 126.

since a key to the strategic approach of such groups involves commencing proceedings at first, not only in courts that appear favourable to the protection of animal rights, but also for members of those species that it believes have the strongest evidentiary basis for being recognized as 'subjects'. The risk of an accumulation of lost cases also involves that of the entrenchment of the very legal precedent it seeks to overcome. The juridical forms must be carefully selected therefore: those which appear to address 'fundamental' rights, and those which singularly prevent the matter from being decided on grounds that side-step the issue of subjecthood in favour of 'welfare'. Constructed in this way the debate can be centred on the 'lack' at the heart of the legal status of non-human animals and what Judge Fajardo Rivera described as the 'deep conceptual gap that at times seems unbridgeable and whose consequences resonate as manifest injustices':[21] that between the status of person and the status of thing.

JUDGE ORTIZ DELEGADO'S CLARIFICATION

Yet, against this whole tension between the rationales of Judge Guerrero Pérez and Judge Fajardo Rivera, artificially constructed as it may be by the litigants, it is worth making mention of the illuminating clarification of the vote of Judge Gloria Stella Ortiz Delgado of the Constitutional Court.[22] Hers is a text that is curiously omitted along with some of the other clarifications from an English translation of the decision in the Chucho case that the Non-Human Rights Project sought permission to submit for the New York State Court of Appeal's consideration in a separate matter that they were involved in concerning an elephant named 'Happy'.[23] Ortiz Delgado delivers a critique, not so much about the substantive claims on behalf of Chucho, but of the structure of argumentation around legal subjectivity and personhood itself implicit in the approach taken by the advocates for the bear. She was the only judge in the case, it appears, to refuse to be drawn onto the polemical terrain of the advocates, where the legal science can be sidelined in favour of a supposed moral truth, supported by other experts (of animal cognition and so on) and grafted

---

[21] Ibid para 79.

[22] Corte Constitucional, Sentencia SU016, January 23 2020. Vote of Judge Gloria Stella Ortiz Delgado.

[23] Letter from Elizabeth Stein to John P. Asiello Re: *The Nonhuman Rights Project, Inc., on behalf of Happy v. James J. Breheny, et al.* (Bronx County Clerk's Index No. 260441/2019; Appellate Division, First Department Docket No. 2020-02581), 13 April 2021 <https:// www .nonhumanrights .org/ blog/ nhrp -commends -opinion -colombian -nonhuman-rights-case/> accessed 25 March 2022.

onto a surface account of the value of an expansion of the liberal subject as a dimension to an unquestionable progression of a 'civil rights' movement.

Ortiz Delegado takes aim at this system of argumentation, describing the analogy of historical forms of legal discrimination in the condition of certain subjects such as slaves with that of animals as 'extremely problematic, and even outrageous'.[24] This is not, she makes clear, because she believes the current institutional protections for animal species are not without their deficiencies. Rather, in the face of an argument that certain animal species have qualities such as sentience that make them candidates for being recognized as persons and as subjects of at least very basic rights, Judge Ortiz Delegado announces in clarification of her vote that: 'the character of sentient being is neither a necessary nor a sufficient condition for the ascription to animals of the legal category of subject of rights.'[25] She adds: 'We are dealing with two entirely separable issues, one of a factual nature and the other of legal constructs, which act independently and which, for that very reason, do not generate interdependent relationships between them.'[26]

The subject of right for Judge Ortiz Delegado is a 'fiction', 'not a phenomenological matter but a mere juridical construction' entirely independent of the realm of fact. It is this kind of separation between the domain of the real subjectivity of concrete individuals and the realm of the legal construct of the 'subject of rights' that judges in both common law and civil law countries have been unable to make when for instance denying compensation to plaintiffs in so-called 'wrongful life' suits.[27] Since the natural person who claims compensation in such types of cases would not have existed as a concrete being if not for the very negligence complained of in the suit (i.e. a doctor through misdiagnosis precluding the mother from a decision to terminate her pregnancy), then the courts have tended to refuse compensation for the individual who claims for the lifetime of disability that such negligence has

---

[24] Corte Constitucional, Sentencia SU016, January 23 2020. Vote of Judge Gloria Stella Ortiz Delgado, at para 13.
[25] Ibid para 4.
[26] Ibid.
[27] See, for example, in various common law jurisdictions: in England *McKay v Essex Area Health Authority* [1982] 2 All ER 771; in Australia *Harriton v Stephens* [2006] HCA 15 and *Waller v James* [2006] HCA 16; in New York *Sheppard-Mobley v. King*, 4 N.Y.3d 627, 797 N.Y.S.2d 403, 830 N.E.2d 301 (2005); in Ontario *Bovingdon v Hergott*, 2008 ONCA 2, 290 D.L.R. (4th) 126. The action is allowed in a handful of US states. In France the Court of Cassation granted the action in the 2000 *Perruche* case, Cour de cassation, Nov. 17, 2000, JCP 2000, II, 10438, was subsequently abolished by an Act of Parliament. In Germany it was held to be unconstitutional for violating the human dignity principle of its *Grundgesetz* (Basic Law) see BGHZ 76, 249 – Kind als Schaden?, and BGHZ 86, 240 – Nicht ermöglichte Abtreibung (wrongful life).

caused them. It is as if the biological ontogenesis of the natural organism also created logical and inescapably causal conditions for the construction of the legal person, understood as a 'rights-bearing' unit. Judges in such cases thus often prefer to imagine the senselessness and impossibility of a 'right not to have been born' which can strictly attach to no one, than the sense – as part of a creative discipline such as jurisprudence – in the construction of various forms of subjectivity and personhood as required for dealing with the concrete case at hand.[28]

Judge Ortiz Delegado's outrage at the form of the argument brought by the advocates for Chucho – one which would force the judge to read the history of a constitutional writ such as *habeas corpus* alongside the present-day call for the 'liberation' of a spectacled bear – is not just an outrage at the dehumanization of politics implicit in it, but also a serious defence of the techniques of legal personhood in jurisprudence, against the threat of an entirely 'factualized' and thus 'biological' determinism. Judge Ortiz Delegado indicates that to ascribe personhood to an entity is not a moral question but a technical, political and procedural one. It is an artificial mechanism that allows the law to treat certain legal acts as if they were done in full autonomy without the need to open up an inquiry into the interests and motives that ultimately underly decisions that have strict legal consequences. '[T]he notion of a subject of law,' she says, 'does not respond to any particular factual parameter, but is a legal fiction designed to give recognition to a certain entity, which is conferred autonomy, ownership of rights and the possibility of legal interaction with other subjects, both in order to make those rights effective and to be the holder of correlative obligations.'[29] It was not, in other words, that an entity such as a bear can be accepted as sentient, self-aware, capable of pain and suffering and thus of having certain interests represented as rights – as Gómez Maldonado had sought to argue about Chucho – that mattered ultimately in terms of the question of personhood. For Ortiz Delegado, personhood was much more about the capacity to treat decisions made about the individual's own interests as if they were made by the individual itself and therefore as if they were to be taken as legally unequivocal. No shortage of evidence may have been brought to justify whether it was in Chucho's ultimate interests to live at the Reserve or at the zoo. This was a matter simply of human conjecture. To obviate the potential endlessness of such an inquiry – which no representational capacity on Gómez

---

[28] See especially Yan Thomas and Olivier Cayla, *Du droit de ne pas naître: à propos de l'affaire Perruche*, (Gallimard 2002).
[29] Corte Constitucional, Sentencia SU016, January 23 2020. Vote of Judge Gloria Stella Ortiz Delgado, at para 6.

Maldonado's behalf to speak for the bear could ultimately achieve – for Ortiz Delegado, was the very purpose of the legal person.[30]

POSTULATES OF LEGAL PERSONHOOD IN KURKI'S *A THEORY OF LEGAL PERSONHOOD*

In a 2019 book titled *A Theory of Legal Personhood*, legal academic Visa Kurki sought to challenge as both 'orthodox' and inadequate the idea that the legal person should be seen as the fundamental 'rights and duties bearing unit'.[31] This 'orthodox view', as Kurki called it, unhelpfully confused the picture on legal personhood, since it would make one assume that personhood is somehow the precondition of having rights whereas in fact it operates more to denote certain 'incidents', both 'active' and 'passive' that can adhere to definite individuals in legal contexts. Kurki, in the preface to his book, noted that his work found its origins in the attempt to make sense of certain strands of animal law scholarship in the early 2010s. 'Virtually everyone writing on the legal status of animals,' he wrote, 'endorsed a fundamental premise: even though animals are protected by the law, they do not hold any legal rights because they are not legal persons.'[32] The sense of inadequacy in this premise led Kurki to question the theory or rather 'definition' of legal personhood itself.

To this question of definition, Kurki brought a rather dialectical approach. By exploring, as he says, the 'salient features that the entities usually classified as legal persons share and nonpersons lack',[33] the idea was that the essential components to the recognition of any being as a 'person' for the law could be more accurately catalogued. But Kurki's book also did something more. It named a deeper premise underlying the contemporary conceptualization of legal personhood, including and perhaps especially among the proponents of the recognition of rights for non-human animals, that might otherwise have gone without reflection. 'One's being a legal *person*,' Kurki observed, 'is an attribute of a non-legal entity.'[34] With this simple formulation, in which personhood becomes a simple 'question of attribution',[35] the book put into words a view that had itself become a conceptual orthodoxy. The theoretical controversies of the 19th and 20th centuries over whether 'juristic persons' were real entities or rather whether they existed solely as fictional constructs of

---

[30] Ibid paras 12–15.
[31] Visa Kurki, *A Theory of Legal Personhood* (Oxford University Press 2019).
[32] Ibid vii.
[33] Ibid 18.
[34] Ibid 133.
[35] Ibid 138.

the law, could apparently be consigned to the history of legal theory. It wasn't the reality of the entity that was debated any longer; only its suitability for the attribute or incidents of 'personhood'. In this way, a whole familiar list of supposedly 'non-legal' candidates could be unfurled in Kurki's book in order to examine how each one can be *more or less* considered a person: from the independent living adult human being who is almost always one, to the corporation which happens also to be, the non-human animal who is typically not, artificial intelligences which could be, the unborn human foetus who is only conditionally, a river which Kurki suggests should not be, the rocks which can never be... To argue over the defining feature or features of personhood (or non-personhood) across each of these cases would be simply splitting hairs. What matters is that a single 'reality' of a world divided into natural empirical entities now becomes not just a theory but a presupposition of the legal person. A device that once helped legal thought grasp and handle the complexity of the world of law at the very limits of one's ordinary experience of it, now instead defers to the ordinary experience itself of a natural world hypostatized in beings who are attributed with individual legal significance.

It is enough to pause a little longer than usual at that commonplace etymological remark, so often repeated in the literature that Kurki digests – that *persona* derives from the notion of the 'mask'[36] – in order to acknowledge that the idea does not easily fit either into a purely empirical or an entirely analytical philosophical frame built on the notion of 'recognition'. As Gilles Deleuze once observed, that frame is haunted by a 'dogmatic image' that betrays philosophy itself: proceeding as though a whole set of moral co-ordinates (identity, representation, analogy, similarity, good-sense, common-sense) had to be postulated in advance before one could even claim the very terrain upon which it is possible to think.[37] Can these philosophical virtues: of conceptual clarity and good-sense, of the 'goodwill' and friendly communicability that are presupposed on the part of the thinker oriented to 'truth' in the midst of ideas – scratch more than the surface of a legal notion and artefact which operates more to *cover* and *conceal* than to lay bare? The logic of the person, the mask, does not rest (or not primarily) upon a logic of identity, representation, attribution. It is sustained by a sort of method of 'dramatization'. In a 'person', the law sometimes prefers to construct or figure legal relations through the crafting or isolation of a role rather than through the articulation of a rule. Take, for instance, the use of the technique of personification in Roman law,

---

[36] Ibid 32.
[37] Gilles Deleuze, *Difference and Repetition* (Paul Patton tr, Bloomsbury 1994) chapter 3.

as detailed by Yan Thomas.[38] In order to figure the radical instantaneousness of the transfer of an estate in Roman inheritance, a jurist sometimes found it apt to describe the father and the son as one person, or to personify the inheritance itself. In order to resolve a case concerning the validity of certain agreements made by a co-owned slave, it was necessary to imagine that the legal acts performed by the one individual were in fact done by separate 'persons' (the person 'slave of A' for one and the person 'slave of B' for the other). In those limit cases, the person is an aid to legal thought. Jurisprudence is not concerned with an answer to the question 'who is or is not a person?' or 'who should or should not be considered a person?' It is the person (or this or that person) which, as an artefact of the inventiveness of juridical thought, provides an answer to the jurisprudential question 'who?', 'which one?' And all these techniques whereby the device of the person served as a means to mask the concrete reality and hence to 'think' the law, tend to be displaced today by a single regime in which each concrete individual simply stakes its claim to the status of being 'a person'.

THE REFERENCE TO 'JURAL RELATION' AND SAVIGNY'S *SYSTEM OF MODERN ROMAN LAW*

There is a particular excerpt in Kurki's book that is instructive of this overall problem. It is a quote from Savigny's *System of Modern Roman Law*. Kurki uses the quote in the context of explaining the basis of the 'legal subject' in the German 'Historical School' and what Savigny might have meant by the term 'legal relationship' or 'jural relation', of which persons, as the title to book 2 of Savigny's *System* seems to indicate, may be the subjects.[39] However, to Savigny's example of what he calls the 'organic' nature of such 'jural relations', Kurki seems to want to give a decidedly natural and social meaning. 'First,' he says, intending to explicate the idea, 'we should [...] recall the idea of natural legal institutions.' These natural institutions, like marriage, 'acted as a "type" or "model" for "life relationships" (*Lebensverhältnisse*) which could also be described as social relationships,' Kurki says. 'If the law chose to give legal recognition to such a relationship, then the relationship and the legal recognition together constituted a legal relationship. Thus, legal relationships are "organic" only insofar as the life relationships that they recognize are organic.'[40]

---

[38] Yan Thomas, 'Le sujet de droit, la personne et la nature: Sur la critique contemporaine du sujet de droit' (1998) 100(3) *Le Débat* 85-107.
[39] Kurki (n 31) 46.
[40] Ibid.

Doesn't organicity depend on something outside law? Kurki seems to want the naturalness somehow of social, life relationships to perhaps in turn impart their organic nature to the law that recognizes them. Should a judge recognize the interrelated nature of these 'organic' social relations in his or her view of the law? And is the legal concept of the person similarly bound, if not completely then at least at an important level, to the organic, natural, social side of individual human or non-human life? These questions betray a preoccupation with a morality inherent in a nature to which legal institutionality becomes tied. If Savigny's 'jural relation' is organic, his text makes clear that it isn't because it ratifies something outside the law that already exists in nature, but because it is itself *living*, a 'living production': multiplicitous, independent, gradually unfolding, arising and passing away and coherent in its constituent parts.[41] Of that living relation, what one calls the 'individual right' he says, recognized by a judicial decision or a legal order, is just one particular aspect, 'separated from it by abstraction'.[42] For Savigny, the very 'intellectual element'[43] of law lies in this living production of the jural relation, more than in the determination of the individual right: a theoretical idea to which he lends a concrete example in the case borrowed from Roman jurisprudence which Kurki quotes:

> The famous law *Frater a fratre* deals with the following case: — Two brothers are under the paternal power. One makes a loan to the other. The borrower repays this loan after the father's death and it is asked whether he can recover this money paid, as money paid under mistake. Here the Judge has simply to decide upon the question whether there is or is not ground for the *condictio indebiti*; but to know this, a complete view of the jural relation must be present to him. The individual elements of this were: the paternal power over the two brothers, a loan of one to the other, a *peculium* which the debtor had received from the father, the inheriting to that father, the discharge of the loan. From these elements, the decision desired from the Judge must proceed.[44]

Savigny assumes some knowledge here on the part of his reader of the basic shape of the Roman legal actions and institutions at the heart of this problem. The *condictio indebiti* was an action in Roman civil law which gave someone a right to recover from another what had been paid to them by mistake, but it did not lie if there was an equitable obligation to pay the sum or if the party knew that nothing was in fact due. Savigny gives us the situation of two brothers who at the time of making the loan are under the power of their father.

---

[41] Friedrich Karl von Savigny, *System of the Modern Roman Law Volume 1* (W.J. Holloway tr, Higginbotham 1867) 7.
[42] Ibid.
[43] Ibid.
[44] Ibid. Also Kurki (n 31) 46.

The money lent is thus part of a *peculium*, that is as the father's own property given in certain amounts to each of the sons to use while they are still under his power. At the time the repayment of the loan is made however, the father has passed away and they have both therefore become legally independent.

Now, if the loan is just considered as a transaction between these two equal legally competent individuals, one would just see the existence of a simple obligation (at least equitable) to repay the money loaned on behalf of one party and the concomitant right to recover the amount on behalf of the other. But in fact, the juridical circumstance is more complicated than that. According to the set of Roman legal institutions that Savigny mentions, while the brothers are under the power of their living father they deal, as mentioned, only with what is effectively their father's own money, the whole patrimony increasing or decreasing as a unit and becoming theirs in full right individually in respective parts only at the time of the inheritance. Therefore, the money they held and the obligations they had with respect to it while the father was alive are not the same (in a legal sense) after the father died and all the funds were inherited as part of the estate. With this more complete legal picture in mind, one notices a more convoluted trajectory for the transaction and with a more difficult question at the heart of the case. What happens to this personal obligation of the loan between the brothers? Can one decide that the repayment of it was done in mistake – since the loaned money was reincorporated in the inherited estate – and that therefore it should be recoverable under the *condictio indebitii*? Should one decide on the other hand that the brother who repaid the loan should know of the peculiar legal logic that in fact annuls the obligation after the father's death and that the payment should therefore be interpreted as a gift and no basis for the *condictio indebtii*?

For Savigny this problem illustrates I think not simply the difficulty of adjudication in a hard case, but rather the *non-subsumability* of the case in all its lawful elements, the life and dynamism of the 'jural relation', beneath a static or purely dogmatic view of the law which, he says, arises only from the 'accidental need' for a decision.[45] It is precisely this dogmatic stance (the notion of there being a fixed position on the status of the obligation and thus on the 'individual right' of the parties) that prevents one from perceiving the case itself in its 'living production' and thus the unique institutional arrangement that lends itself to the contemplation and operation of jurisprudence. It is not a question of knowing how the brother subjectively imagined the nature of his repayment – whether as gift or under a mistaken belief. This brother may just as well be – without changing anything in the legal significance of the problem – an entirely fictional construct in the mind of the jurist rather than a real

---

[45] Savigny (n 41) 6.

individual. And even if one were to treat it as a factual matter, any belief on the part of the brother is no more decidable – given the legal issue on which it rests – than what is presented for the judge for determination. Savigny's point is not that there is a 'life' outside the law, to which the law offers its imperfect countenance: distinguishing between beings worthy of legal rights and those who are not. On the contrary, it is that we risk a relatively lifeless view of the law when we separate the perception of the legal institutions from the complexity and spontaneity of events and forms of life contained in the 'case', or when we reduce the perception of jurisprudential relations to the determination of the individual right and the ascription of that individual right to a subject. Rights don't just lie in wait for a subject to whom they can be attributed. They are borne – to extrapolate this idea – by the inventiveness of institutions, the non-subsumability of the case, in relation to which the 'individual right', attributed to a subject, is really like a mental block suffered by the lawyer.

What does this mean in terms of the theory of personhood that Kurki sought to espouse? It would certainly miss the point to suggest that his theory depended ultimately, or in any decisive sense, on his interpretation of this particular fragment from Savigny. And it would not necessarily be helpful to go on to dwell on all the subtleties of the Roman law of persons in question, such as in relation to the juridical side to the institution of paternal power which – far from being grounded in nature – Savigny reminds us is almost solely itself characterized by a configuration of personhood: namely the notion by which 'the son takes upon himself the personality of the father and carries it on beyond that father's life'.[46] A closer examination of this particular exchange in Kurki's book does reveal at least an important limitation to any theory that seeks to abstract the notion of personhood from the relations and institutions, the cases and singularities, for which it remains an important jurisprudential figure, in order to make it something that one can reliably 'extend' or 'attribute' to categories of 'real' individuals or collectivities according to a bundle of incidents comprising certain of their rights, obligations and competences. Such an approach risks putting things the wrong way around: exchanging every possible liveliness in the concept of personhood for the mere promise of its general applicability; any plasticity in the ways in which it may be put to new uses for the apparent certainty of criteria by which one may recognize it in definite entities. Personhood becomes in this way a mere battleground, falsely universalized, for a struggle for recognition. It ignores the way in which jurisprudence itself, in the contemplation of cases and singularities, does without

---

[46] Savigny (n 41) 288.

this very complicity between the 'positive law', the 'individual right' and the 'subject of right'.[47]

BEYOND THE ANIMAL AS SUBJECT OF RIGHT: CASES FOR THE JURISPRUDENTIAL MEANINGS OF THE BEAR

The Constitutional Court in Chucho's case was not left in a vacuum of expert opinion about Andean bears. The court heard submissions from various organizations, foundations, agencies, research institutes, philosophers, and animal law and environmental law experts. Those opinions did not just extend to the biological characteristics and ecological importance of Andean bears, but also to the question of animal rights, the possibility of giving effect to them through constitutional protection, and the treatment and condition of Chucho himself at the reserve and the zoo. A range of views were presented about whether it was possible and desirable to recognize animals, including members of such a species of bear, as subjects of certain fundamental rights compatible with the petition for *habeas corpus* and about what kinds of interests regarding Chucho and where he was to be kept could be considered and determined within that frame. In all this evidence, neatly summarized in Judge Guerrero's decision and in the annex to the opinion of Judge Fajardo Rivera,[48] it is not easy to disentangle the relevant kinds of expertise at play. All these forms of knowledge seemingly become authorized, in the court's estimation, under a single brush stroke: the expertise through which it is possible to represent what the law is and what it should be, the branches of science that allow us to know something about the natural world, including about what moral considerations could be drawn or not drawn from it, forms of knowledge about the respective roles for the courts and for the legislature in relation to the shaping of constitutional forms for the protection of non-human species, lessons that can be learnt from jurisdictions in which certain species of animal, or animals of certain types have been given protection such as that contemplated in the litigation.

What sort of gap in the courts' consciousness of either the facts or the law was this material sought to fill? In the first place, it isn't uncommon to imagine the terrain of law as not being the most fertile when it comes to an attempt to understand the lives of animals. The conceptual abstraction of at

---

[47] See Gilles Deleuze, *Two Regimes of Madness: Texts and Interviews 1975–1995* (D. Lapoujade ed, A. Hodges and M. Taormina tr, Semitext (ed) 2006) 350. Deleuze states that 'a conception of law founded on jurisprudence can do without any "subject" of rights'.
[48] Corte Constitucional, Sentencia SU016, January 23 2020. Vote of Judge Luis Guillermo Guerrero Pérez, paras 4.2–4.2; vote of Judge Diana Fajardo Rivera, Annex.

least Western juridical thinking, the sober technicality of its language and disposition, the functional and formulary nature of its idiom, the apparently deep-seated anthropocentrism of its logic and organization: all of this seems to come together to describe a terrain that to many thinkers appears hostile to the necessary ways of imagining the natural world and alien to the attempts to contemplate the varied intelligences, powers, unique modes of being of its animal species. It is as if, when it comes to a species of animal such as the spectacled bear, jurisprudence has little to say of its own, even when one imagines its expertise to sit on at least a level scientific playing field with that of biology, moral philosophy and so on.

What is striking in a case like this is how quickly the lawyers seem to concede their expertise, not in general, but *with regard to the animal*, to that of others. This clearly isn't because lawyers would be unaccustomed to verifying the proof of certain biological, zoological, ethological or ecological facts relating to animals or indeed assimilating them to new or existing legal norms. The whole figure of the animal seems to be overcome by these factual contours which – in the name of a 'truth of nature' – come to push not the normative but the jurisprudential meaning and conceptualization to the sidelines. It would be a mistake in this way to presuppose, as the animal rights discourse tends to, that just because Western legal systems have for certain purposes categorized animals under the supposedly lifeless or dimensionless figure of legal 'things', that animals remain equally lifeless and dimensionless thereby when it comes to their participation in the law. On the contrary, particular animals continue to lend their liveliness in many significant ways to the possibility of thinking the law: far less as 'subjects of right' (i.e. as bearers of legal rights) than as distinct *juridical species* (i.e. as bearers of legal meaning).

Lorraine Daston and Gregg Mitman observed in a 2005 collection that '[t]hinking with animals is not the same as thinking about them'.[49] The authors were interested not just in how we represent animals but how the animal is 'a participant, an actor in our analyses'. This is also the case with regard to law. But to acknowledge how animals act as legal species, it isn't enough to simply point to the fact that law sometimes gives its own meaning to species of animal. The fact for instance that the spectacled bear (*Tremarctos ornatus*) can be found legally classified under the Convention on International Trade in Endangered Species as a species in which trade is regulated under the Convention for instance, and therefore given a particular meaning in law that it may not necessarily have in nature, does not point in this way to its partic-

---

[49] Lorraine Daston and Gregg Mitman, 'The How and Why of Thinking with Animals' in Lorraine Daston and Gregg Mitman (eds), *Thinking with Animals: New Perspectives on Anthropomorphism* (Columbia UP 2005) 5.

ipation in the construction of legal meaning, whether or not one subscribes to the policies underlying it. The law simply borrows the set of specificities of the scientific definition of species here in order to give a stronger determination of the limits of its prohibition or regulation. The courts have been known to provide a forensic platform in this way for genuine zoological or botanical debates – even if not necessarily the most cutting-edge ones – about the existence or otherwise of species or the meaningfulness of certain species-distinctions.[50] The existence of these debates attests, in fact, as in Chucho's case, to the sidelining of the juridical aspect in the imagination of the species, in favour of a dominant biological conception.

However, when a bear sometimes finds a critical place in juridical thought, it is not always by some accident of a factual nature that happens to place it amidst the general social problems which are sometimes called to be resolved by legal means. If, for example, the classical Roman jurist Ulpian chose a bear to elucidate an aspect to the application of the *actio de pauperie* – an ancient no-fault form of reparation for harm inflicted by four-footed beasts – it is not because the bear was a typical animal in relation to which such kinds of proceedings were frequently brought,[51] but apparently because, in the figure of a bear escaping from its owner and causing damage, the limits of the action itself (which involved potentially a claim for the surrender of the animal and not simply an action for monetary reparation against its owner at the time) could be most clearly and dynamically conceptualized.[52] A bear is no longer the same legal thing as soon as its owner has set it loose. This presence of the bear in the thought of the jurist and preserved in the jurisprudential literature, which can only be explained by it constituting a species not only of nature here but of law itself, is not often appreciated in detail.

In another case – *Shaw v McCreary* – this figure of the bear reappears in the context of problematizing the liabilities in Canadian common law that would attach respectively to a husband as keeper of the animal and a wife as the owner of the property on which it had been kept.[53] The bear, in a juridical sense, resists being equated there with a more neutral substance like water that, as in the case of *Rylands v Fletcher*,[54] can escape from someone's land. The bear offered a more palpable image of what separates – in a gendered way –

---

[50] See for example Jocelyn Bosse, 'Before the High Court: The Legal Systematics of Cannabis' (2020) 29(2) Griffith Law Review 302–329.
[51] See Bernard Jackson, 'Liability for Animals in Roman Law: An Historical Sketch' (1978) 37(1) Cambridge Law Journal 136.
[52] Digest 9.1.1.10.
[53] *Shaw et al v McCreary et al* (1890) 19 OR 39.
[54] *Rylands v Fletcher* [1868] UKHL 1.

the obligations of those who keep animals from those who simply allow their presence.

And more tangibly still, in the case of *Delgamuukw v British Columbia*, we find in fact the juridical significance of the bear made surprisingly explicit before the Supreme Court of British Columbia specifically in important parts of the oral histories that were told as testimony in the case for a claim of jurisdiction and Aboriginal title on behalf of the Gitksan claimants.[55] The court confronted its capacity to hear this testimony, as evidence of the truth of what was spoken in the oral histories and as an exception to the rule against hearsay that would have excluded it, in part through the confrontation with the meaning of a bear: that which the judge called the 'Seeley Lake Medeek'.[56] However rather than seeing the bear as a distinct feature of the jurisdiction, constituting a meeting-place for the common law and Gitksan jurisprudences, the court was instead preoccupied only with judging the factual and historical plausibility of its existence according to a purely evidentiary frame separating the reporting of general 'beliefs' of an historical nature from the telling of specific historical 'facts'.[57] A single bear came, in this way, to stand in the place of a whole jurisdictional and epistemological problem of law and fact.

And one could also turn, finally, to the work of the Swiss jurist J. J. Bachofen who – seeking to view the figure of the bear not as a sign or attribute of something other than what it is but standing independently on its own power in a work of art – saw in the ancient beliefs associated most closely with the bear, a distinctively maternal principle lying dormant in the traditions of the civil law.[58] In the image of the bear, expressing the idea of the mother who shields her daughter, 'the oldest system of family law' was for Bachofen 'to lie before us in its cultic legal basis.'[59]

---

[55] See *Delgamuukw v The Queen*, 1987 CanLII 2980 (BC SC); *Delgamuukw v British Columbia*, 1991 CanLII 2372 (BC SC); *Delgamuukw v British Columbia*, 1997 CanLII 302 (SCC), [1997] 3 SCR 1010.

[56] See *Delgamuukw v British Columbia*, 1991 CanLII 2372 (BC SC), section titled 'The Seeley Lake Medeek'; *Delgamuukw v The Queen*, 1987 CanLII 2980 (BC SC). The relevant *adaawk* was told by Antgulilbix/Mary Johnson, Proceedings of the Supreme Court of British Columbia 27 May 1987, 666–668. For a recent critique of the judge's approach to the bear, see for example Jill Stauffer, 'Law and Oral History: Hearing the Claims of Indigenous Peoples' in Anne O'Byrne and Martin Shuster (eds), *Logics of Genocide: The Structures of Violence and the Contemporary World* (Routledge, 2021), 208-225.

[57] See *Delgamuukw v British Columbia*, 1991 CanLII 2372 (BC SC), section titled 'The Seeley Lake Medeek'; *Delgamuukw v The Queen*, 1987 CanLII 2980 (BC SC).

[58] J. J. Bachofen, *Der Bær in den Religionen des Alterthums* (Meyri 1863).

[59] Ibid 26. Author's translation. German original: '*Das älteste System des Familienrechts liegt hier in seiner kultlichen Grundlage uns vor.*'

These remnants that a species of animal can leave in legal thought are hidden in Chucho's case behind systems of representation that, at the same time as they supposedly make the interests of non-human biological organisms legible before decision-making institutions, also separate law from its own intelligences about animal life. It is as if Chucho's being a species of bear could be relevant for all the factual questions – concerning his individual welfare, concerning the specific questions of conservation that Colombian constitutional law protects, the ecological significance of his species and so on – but that as far as the imagination of the legal questions were concerned, one could just as easily replace this bear with a chimpanzee or an elephant. Is the liberal legal tradition truly as closed as this to the impressions that different animal species have made, over centuries, upon the mind that thinks the law?

CONCLUSION

Cases like Chucho's highlight critical impasses in legal thinking not just about the possibility or limits of the notion of 'non-human rights', but about the use and misuse of jurisprudential categories like the 'subject' or about 'persons' and 'things'. The demand that the lives of animals place upon legal thinking is not one for 'recognition' alone. It is one that requires a much deeper critique of the complicity between static rules of law, individual rights and the 'subject' of such rights. Just as a conception of law based in jurisprudence 'can do without a subject of right',[60] the activity of jurisprudence itself also has a much more intimate and creative relation to the lives of animals than we might notice at first glance.

ACKNOWLEDGEMENTS

This paper would not have been possible without the support of family and many friends and colleagues. A special word of gratitude to Luis Gomez Romero, who read a version of this paper and assisted with the translation of material in Spanish. The errors that remain are the author's own.

---

[60] Deleuze (n 47) 350.

3. Why nature has no rights
Alain Pottage

What would it mean for nature truly to have rights? In what medium would rights have to be articulated in order to express the agency of non-human natural beings? How might nature speak its wants or demands (to us)? Questions such as these are prompted by the increasing number of cases in which rivers, mountain ecosystems, lakes, or particular regions of 'nature' have been recognized as legal persons. As these instances accumulate, they seem to generate a new idiom of rights, an 'Earth jurisprudence', mediated or retailed by an expanding transnational policy network.[1] The founding document of this new jurisprudence, Christopher Stone's famous article on the standing of 'natural objects', was written in a period marked by the Vietnam war, by the dispute over *Roe* v *Wade*,[2] which was then on its way to the Supreme Court, and by the decision of the same court in *Swann* v *Charlotte-Mecklenburg Board of Education*,[3] which promoted the desegregation of schools. Given the historical moment, one can understand why Stone began by characterizing the ascription of rights to nature as an extension of the political or ethical project of recognizing hitherto excluded humans: 'We are not only developing the scientific capacity, but we are cultivating the personal capacities *within us* to recognize more and more the ways in which nature – like the woman, the Black, the Indian and the Alien – is like us (and we will also become more able realistically to define, confront, live with and admire the ways in which we are all different)'.[4] But for Stone, the point was not merely to extend to nature a status that had historically been controlled and enjoyed by white men. The suggestion that nature is 'like us' proposed symmetry in the sense that attention to the liveliness of nature was supposed to challenge and transform our understanding of the human. In his

---

[1] Ariel Rawson & Becky Mansfield, 'Producing Juridical Knowledge: "Rights of Nature" or the Naturalization of Rights?' (2018) 1:1&2 Environment and Planning E: Nature and Space 99–119.
[2] 410 US 113 (1973).
[3] 402 US 1 (1971).
[4] Christopher D Stone, 'Should Trees Have Standing? – Toward Legal Rights for Natural Objects' (1972) 45 Southern California Law Review 450–501, at 498.

conclusion, Stone drew on Dane Rudhyar's work on planetary consciousness[5] – and so, indirectly, on Vladimir Vernadsky's conception of the noosphere – to suggest that the recognition of natural beings as legal persons might be one step on the way to creating a new cosmology: 'a myth that can fit our growing body of knowledge of geophysics, biology and the cosmos'.[6] So the anthropic subjectivity upon which legal rights are supposedly premised might itself be reinvented by evolving a new juridical subject function. From this perspective, it could be said that: 'It is more and more the individual human being, with his consciousness, that is the legal fiction'.[7]

Now, half a century on, the questions asked by Stone resonate somewhat differently. From its origins as a critique of environmental law, which seemed to do no more than regulate the conditions under which nature could be exploited, the rights of nature project has evolved into what is described as 'an intersectionalist politics of plurinational communities, interdisciplinary actors and interspecies agents, forged in centuries of dispossession and struggles for justice, and directed currently against corporate globalization and its ongoing colonization of nature'.[8] This politics is informed by the cosmologies of indigenous peoples, the imaginaries of posthuman philosophies, and an intensified awareness of climate change, as expressed in theoretical figures such as the Anthropocene, the Capitalocene, or the Chthulucene. Rights of nature are still cultured on the local scale by initiatives such as the Home Rule Charter[9] and Rights of Nature Ordinances[10] promoted by the Community Environmental Legal Defense Fund (CELDF) in the United States, but the precedents that stand out as elements of an Earth jurisprudence are legislative and adjudicative acts such as the recognition of Nature as a person by the Constitution of Ecuador, and the attribution of personality to the Whanganui and Ganga rivers. In these precedents, one glimpses a truth about the discourse of rights of nature as it is actually practised. The effect of recognizing 'Nature' as a person is not to protect it from the depradations of global, corporate, capital. On the

---

[5] Ibid 499–500.

[6] Ibid 498.

[7] Ibid 494, where Stone states that: 'The legal system does the best it can to maintain the illusion of the reality of the individual human being'.

[8] T J Demos, 'Rights of Nature: The Art and Politics of Earth Jurisprudence' (2015) Rights of Nature: Art and Ecology in the Americas <https://cpb-us-e1.wpmucdn.com/sites.ucsc.edu/dist/0/196/files/2015/10/Demos-Rights-of-Nature-2015.compressed.pdf> accessed 20 June 2022.

[9] See the CELDF presentation of 'Home rule', which suggests that local self-government is 'a fulfilment of the long-postponed ideals of the American Revolution' <https://celdf.org/home-rule> accessed 20 June 2022.

[10] See CELDF, Community Rights Networks <https://celdf.org/where-we-work/community-rights-networks> accessed 20 June 2022.

contrary, the ascription of personhood to nature both intensifies and obscures the subjection of natural entities to the market. This is because the sense of agency and vitality that is ascribed to nature by the new 'intersectionalist politics' of rights of nature originates in the very epistemic conditions that generated twentieth-century fossil capital. Ironically, the theoretical impulse that generates images of a possible posthuman Earthly legality turns out to be genealogically complicit with the sense of surfeit that was generated by the availability of oil and processed energy (principally gasoline and electrical current), and which nurtured the neoliberal economy.

EARTHLY LEGALITY

The phenomenon of climate change, as articulated in the theme of the Anthropocene, has re-energized reflection on the rights of nature. Stone's article was part of an environmental movement that assumed a Holocene state of ecological equilibrium, and which sought to prevent the erosion, corruption, or destruction of nature as the stable and nurturing ground or envelope for the existence of humans and other natural beings.[11] The discourse of the Anthropocene suggests that for decades, if not centuries, human beings have been intervening in this ground or envelope, which is therefore not something external to human activity, something which might be conserved by restraining human intervention, but the expression of an agency that perturbs the terrestrial conditions of life. Even before the term 'Anthropocene' entered public discourse, Earth scientists spoke of a 'second Copernican revolution', in which, having located the planet within the solar system, we learned to see what 'may well be nature's sole successful attempt at building a robust geosphere–biosphere complex (the ecosphere) in our Galaxy, topped by a life-form that is appropriately tailored for explaining the existence of that complex, and of itself'.[12] This awareness is now intensified by the perception that human activities have driven the ecosphere beyond its safe 'operating limits', in some cases irreversibly, so that ecological politics is no longer about maintaining the equilibrium of the Holocene, but about intervening to stabilize new, more or less provisional, hopefully less catastrophic, 'system states'. Society is no longer immortal in the sense that sociology in the era of Durkheim imagined it to be, and we no longer have the time for immanent revolution that Marxian

---

[11] When Stone was writing, environmentalists addressed the destruction of nature, both in quantity and quality, and this against the background of the question whether the planet could survive what Paul Ehrlich called the 'population bomb'. See Paul R Ehrlich, *The Population Bomb* (Ballantine 1968).

[12] Hans Joachim Schellnhuber, '"Earth System"' Analysis and the Second Copernican Revolution' (1999) 402 Nature C19–C23.

tradition assumed we had, precisely because nature can no longer be externalized as a permanent base and measure of human existence.

Stone's project of enfranchising nature from its status as property[13] is echoed in current presentations of rights of nature: 'Rather than treating nature as property under the law, rights of nature acknowledges that nature in all its life forms has the right to exist, persist, maintain and regenerate its vital cycles'.[14] But in a sense nature has already broken the bounds of property: it no longer occupies the position of the *ob-jectus*, of that which lies before human agents like a tract of land awaiting appropriation through demarcation, cultivation, and distribution. Indeed, this sense of appropriation has long been a mystification of the real ecological entanglements of human society. In his influential paper on 'the climate of history', Dipesh Chakrabarty observed that '[t]he mansion of modern freedoms stands on an ever-expanding base of fossil-fuel use'.[15] The most essential of these freedoms was the right to property. Even before the advent of the steam engine, possessive individualism[16] externalized its material engagements with the Earth by pretending that the value of land was produced by the rational industry of European men rather than by the plantation economy of the colonial period and by the slaves and resources that were treated as 'cheap nature' within that racialized economy. The period of industrialization intensified the ideology of cheap nature by treating coal and then oil as abstract energy, which was costless both at the point of extraction and at the point of exhaustion because the accumulation of toxic residues was left off the balance sheet. Only now do we recognize that the industrial-colonial powers had embarked on the appropriation of the atmosphere, thereby adding a further fold or 'sediment' (see below) to a configuration of hyperproperty that is oversimplified if we assume that what rights of nature have to overcome is a singular modality of 'property'.

According to a prevailing sense, the moment of the Anthropocene calls for creativity in construing our material entanglements with nature, the better to evolve the ecological-political imagination that will inform new modes of earthly legality. Loosely speaking, if the ecological paradigm that informed Stone's manifesto for ecolegality was a version of Gaia 1.0, the Earth as

---

[13] 'What is it within us that gives us this need not just to satisfy basic biological wants, but to extend our wills over things, to objectify them, to make them ours, to manipulate them, to keep them at a psychic distance?': Stone (n 4) 495.

[14] Global Alliance for the Rights of Nature, 'What are the Rights of Nature?' <https://www.garn.org/rights-of-nature/> accessed 20 June 2022.

[15] Dipesh Chakrabarty, 'The Climate of History: Four Theses' (2009) 35:2 Critical Inquiry 197–222, at 208.

[16] In the sense of C B MacPherson, *The Political Theory of Possessive Individualism* (Clarendon Press 1962).

construed by Lovelock and Margulis, then the ecology that is made visible in the Anthropocene is that of Latour and Lenton's Gaia 2.0, which reveals 'a new continuity between humans and non-humans that was not visible before – a relation between free agents'.[17] In the epoch of the Anthropocene, the reflexivity of nature – which is manifested in the closed 'recycling loop' of the biosphere, the material and informational networks of microbial networks, 'persistence-enhancing' regulatory processes – becomes the inspiration for a mode of political and economic reflexivity that is 'returned' to Gaia as a mode of governance through resonance. But this reinvention of Gaia assumes the basic point of departure for current reimaginations of ecolegality; namely, the sense of the Earth as being 'lively', articulate, recalcitrant, in ways that go far beyond the mere provision of 'affordances'. For example, it turns out that the Earth is lively not only in the dimension of the biosphere but also in its rock formations: planets are 'bodies where the combination of fluid motion and solid durability creates information-rich pockets, where correlated states and motions can arise, endure and become more elaborate'.[18] The ambition is to articulate this material sensibility and responsiveness into law, to evolve a discourse that is not always-already committed, in its locutionary and illocutionary dimensions, to objectivity; that is, to the interpellation and representation of our material interlocutors as things or facts.

Whereas orthodox and critical jurisprudences have imagined law as a global discourse, composed of texts and technicalities of diverse kinds, the challenge now is to rematerialize law as a truly Earthly discourse, a 'discourse' forged in an encounter with the Earth itself, and mediated by the materials and competences of the Earth itself. A beginning is offered by Latour's reflections on Schmitt's *nomos*, which translate Schmitt's sense of the normative order of the Earth (*das Sinnreich der Erde*), or the capacity of the Earth to yield law, into a broader refiguration of nature. The argument will be familiar: whereas the law of the 'moderns' assumes that the Earth is the normatively inert ground for the foundation of human society, Schmitt understood that it interpellated humans with a call that was answered and actualized as law through the operations of mensuration, demarcation, and cultivation. Through Schmitt's figuration of space, we understand that our terrain is produced by processes that are political and radically conflictual in the sense that terrain is always *at stake*: 'whenever someone qualifies real space to be empty and neutral, we are called upon to understand that for some reason some power has emptied and

---

[17] Timothy M Lenton & Bruno Latour, 'Gaia 2.0. Could Humans Add Some Level of Self-Awareness to Earth's Self-Regulation' (2018) 361 Science 1066.
[18] Bronislaw Szerszynski, 'Planetary Mobilities: Movement, Memory and Emergence in the Body of the Earth' (2016) 11:4 Mobilities 616.

neutralized the territory of someone else'.[19] In the era of the Anthropocene, these contests are quite radically about life and death; they are contests in which we have to address an enemy, someone who does not share our ground of existence. The Earth itself is at stake. And the contest is all the more existential because it is not subsumed into historical process. Schmitt's friend/enemy distinction articulates a principle of negation that is non-Hegelian in the sense that it is absolutely flat rather than cumulative: 'An historical truth is true only once'.[20] Latour's reconstruction of the Gaia hypothesis through Schmitt's *nomos* elaborates the sense in which the Earth as a unique kind of multiple entity is the condition of a politics in which different 'life agents', humans and other Earthly beings, take a 'wary, puzzled, enigmatic, and shifting distance' from each other.[21]

Not everyone will consider Latour's reflections on Gaia to be the best starting point for the cultivation of an Earthly legality, but his authorship is crucial to reflection on rights of nature for two reasons. First, it is now the most familiar expression of the basic paradigm of late twentieth-century Euro-American thought: the cyberneticism that produces networks, systems and rhizomes, and which generates the sense of emergence that allows non-humans to be agentive, articulate, and sensible, and to 'matter' in ways that concern Earthly legality.[22] It symptomatizes an epistemic condition that projects itself into the 'Anthropocene', and which expresses itself in imaginaries that are more radical, politically and aesthetically, than that of Latour. Second, because of its engagement with the question of lawmaking,[23] Latour's authorship brings into play a dimension of cyberneticism that affords a rather different perspective on rights of nature, one that reveals the way in which lawmaking necessarily alienates political projects from themselves. Taken together, these two facets of cyberneticism illuminate the functioning of rights of nature.

---

[19] Bruno Latour, 'How to Remain Human in the Wrong Space? A Comment on a Dialogue by Carl Schmitt' (2021) 47 Critical Inquiry 706.

[20] Carl Schmitt, cited in Latour (n 19) 715.

[21] Bruno Latour & Timothy M Lenton, 'Extending the Domain of Freedom, or Why Gaia is So Hard to Understand' (2019) 45 Critical Inquiry 680.

[22] It should be acknowledged that many or most of those who develop these perspectives would reject the characterization of what they are doing as 'cyberneticism', and that further elaboration is required to explain what is cybernetic about the logic of 'revealing' that operationalizes what I call (below) the episteme of autolimitlessness. See my 'Electric Theory'(forthcoming).

[23] See notably Bruno Latour, *La fabrique du droit. Une ethnographie du Conseil d'État* (La Découverte 2002).

ECOLOGIES OF LEGALITY

According to the coalition that personifies the rights of nature movement, the Global Alliance for the Rights of Nature, the mission of the new jurisprudence is to 'reproduce the concept [of rights of nature] virally throughout the world, invading systems of thought and juridical systems'.[24] The Alliance was formed in 2010 at a meeting convened to mark the declarations of the Ecuadorean Constitution of 2008, that 'Nature is a legal subject', and that 'Nature, or Pachamama, where life is reproduced and occurs, has the right to integral respect for its existence and for the maintenance and regeneration of its life cycles, structure, functions and evolutionary processes'.[25] These provisions were modelled on a form of legislation that had been conceived as a framework for the formation of sustainable communities in the United States. The originator of this template, the CELDF, has since participated in its translation into different contexts throughout the world: 'CELDF not only contributes to new rights of nature policy landscapes occurring in the US but also has partnered with communities to advocate for rights of nature in Nepal, India, Australia, Colombia, Cameroon, and Sweden'.[26] The CELDF had been introduced to the Constituent Assembly of Ecuador by the *Fundación Pachamama*, a companion organization of the San Francisco-based Pachamama Alliance, which was founded in 1996 by two American fundraisers as a vehicle to protect the culture of the Achuar people.

This is just one of the genealogical tendrils that Rawson and Mansfield, in their critique of the rights of nature movement, draw out in order to show how this movement functions as a 'spatially intensive cluster of environmental organizations, law firms, legal non-profits, law schools and legal professional associations', or 'an epistemic community deeply imbricated with juridical authority'.[27] The suggestion is that this global academy is fashioned or composed in such a way as to naturalize a Euro-American vision of nature as a community of interdependent entities. And this vision is hypothecated to a representation of indigenous peoples as the guardians of this community, a vision that retrenches a production of otherness that was one of the prime effects of colonialism, and which thereby sustains the ideology of property that the rights of nature movement purports to overcome.[28] The charge is that 'nature becomes something identifiably "natural" by becoming more like

---

[24] Cited in Rawson & Mansfield (n 1) 106.
[25] Articles 10 & 71, respectively.
[26] Rawson & Mansfield (n 1) 110.
[27] Ibid 106–111.
[28] According to Rawson & Mansfield, 'holistic models of nature from providential legacies to new excitement over complex, adaptive emergent system depends on, even

colonial conceptions of the human, whose existence can only be legitimized by legal personhood'.[29]

For now, what is interesting about this genealogy of 'rights of nature' is its resonance with an observation once made by Rosemary Coombe about the economy of bioprospecting: 'lawmaking in this arena is emergent, iterative, and performative – it reproduces like a multisectoral virus as model legislation, contracting practices, database models, protocols and declarations are spread across the internet and adapted, adopted, and proclaimed in local communities, regional networks, national government agencies, and legislatures'.[30] The point about the 'virality' of these jurisprudences is that rights of nature as they exist currently live and evolve within the specific culturing medium of a network that is global, planetary, and discursive rather than Earthly, terrestrial, or earthbound. That is, rights take shape through transactions that are mediated by the reciprocal affordances of documents and the other 'technicalities' that compose ecologies of lawmaking,[31] and these transactions are articulated by political strategies that are adapted to the forum in which rights are negotiated. The 'nature' to which rights are attributed is 'nature' as it precipitates from this process of negotiation. This has two implications.

First, the idea that legal statements do not describe their own operation, but that propositional content is modulated by the process of lawmaking in which they are implicated, resonates with a familiar observation about legal personality: all legal persons are fictions, discursive artefacts, or products of dogmatic technique.[32] On this point, Andreas Fischer-Lescano cites Gustav Radbruch: 'Being a person is the result of an act of personification by the legal order. All persons, physical ones and legal ones, are creations of the legal order. Even physical persons are, in the strictest sense, "legal persons". There can therefore

---

helps generate the liminal indigenous figure that is both internal to the story of modernity and outside modernity as its conditions of possibility'. See (n 1) 114.

[29] Ibid 100.

[30] Rosemary Coombe, 'Works in Progress: Traditional Knowledge, Biological Diversity and Intellectual Property in a Neoliberal Era', in Richard W Perry and Bill Maurer (eds.) *Globalization Under Construction: Governmentality, Law and Identity* (University of Minnesota Press 2003) 273–314, at 278. The remainder of Coombe's paragraph is also salient: 'This is a global arena of intense multisectoral legal pluralism as international conventions and global declarations are put into dialogue and articulation with national legislation, regional positionings, local protocols and "customary laws" – both indigenous and international. Like most attempts to fundamentally shift and transform relationships of power, it is fuelled by rhetorical forms and empowering fictions – in this case, narratives of tragedy, loss, salvation, and potential redemption'.

[31] Annelise Riles, 'A New Agenda for the Cultural Study of Law: Taking on the Technicalities' (2005–2006) Buffalo Law Journal 973–1033.

[32] Cornelia Vismann, 'Cultural Techniques and Sovereignty' (2013) 30:6 Theory, Culture & Society 83–93.

be no argument over the "fictional", that is, the artificial nature of all, both physical and legal persons'.[33] The point is not just that legal personality clothes or supplements real people, and that the decision as to which people enjoy personality is contingent or political. Rather, it is that the law also fictionalizes the person behind the mask or role; both the role and role player are products of a distinction drawn by legal operations, which generates 'natural' capacities that are consistent with prevailing theories of liability or agency in general. So the 'just as' of the proposition that 'ecosystems – including trees, oceans, animals, mountains – have rights just as human beings have rights'[34] has to be interpreted as meaning something other than plain anthropomorphism. The legal form of rights is unable to 'humanize' nature: 'The legal person can never incorporate the human being as such, never nature as such, never the animal as such into the law; rather, the legal person is only ever able to establish legal points of attribution'.[35]

Second, even if it is true that the epistemic community of 'rights of nature' retails an ecological imaginary that is rooted in the violence of colonialism, lawmaking does not simply transpose this imaginary into action. Again, the statements and self-descriptions of that community do not describe the actual agency and effects of rights of nature. The personhood of nature is always, in the most radical sense, contextualized. For example, the decision of the High Court of Uttarakhand to recognize the Ganga and Yamuna rivers as legal persons was made shortly after the Parliament of New Zealand passed the legislation that made the Whanganui the first river to be granted legal personality.[36] Although the judgment makes no reference to the example of the Whanganui River, it is obvious that the decision was influenced if not by that particular case then by earlier instances in which natural entities had been granted personhood. But the personhood of the Ganga and the Yamuna was realized in ways that the rights of nature 'movement' obscures. To begin with, the decision had very little to do with a project of decentring human polity and economy. The High Court of Uttarakhand noticed the precedent of corporate personality, but it did so in order to say that all legal persons are created or 'evolved' in the interests of social development: 'the concept of the juristic

---

[33] Andreas Fischer-Lescano, 'Nature as a Legal Person: Proxy Constellations in Law' (2020) 32:2 Law & Literature 242.
[34] Global Alliance for the Rights of Nature, 'What Are the Rights of Nature?' <https://www.garn.org/rights-of-nature/> accessed 20 June 2022.
[35] Andreas Fischer-Lescano (n 33) 241.
[36] The proposal to recognize the personhood of the Whanganui River had in fact been formalized in a Deed of Settlement made between the Crown and the Whanganui Iwi in 2014.

person was devised and created by human laws for the purposes of society'.[37] Rights were ascribed to the Ganga and its tributary so as to empower the human agents who were nominated as its representatives – namely, officials of the state of Uttarakhand – to take action to reduce levels of pollution, and to do so in the interests of dependent humans.[38] And when the Supreme Court intervened to deprive the rivers of the personhood they had enjoyed for all of 109 days, it did so because the state might be held liable for flood damage caused by the river,[39] and because the river, in the exercise of its constitutional right to life, and acting through its representatives, might have standing to sue an open-ended set of defendants, from corporations to pilgrims, for polluting activities. To the extent that the decision of the High Court recognized the sanctity or dignity of the rivers, it did so not by advancing a holistic vision of 'Earth jurisprudence', but by retrenching Hindu nationalist investments in the river and its agency, thereby marginalizing the other communities who depended upon clean river water.[40]

AUTO-LIMITLESSNESS

On one hand, the vitalism of network thinking generates images of Earthly legality that allow us to project a truly terrestrial jurisprudence, to imagine a law attuned to the modes of existence of all Earthly entities; on the other, it generates the theoretical and ethnographic imagination that dissolves normativity into the articulation of documents, materialities, and other agencies, and which thereby alienates us from the political ambition of Earth jurisprudences. What is the relation between these two critical takes on rights of nature? And why emphasize the paradigm of network thinking in preference to other theories that might illuminate the question of Earthly legality? The answer lies in what both takes have in common; namely, the effect of network cyberneticism

---

[37] *Mohd. Salim* v *State of Uttarakhand*, March 20, 2017, para 16.

[38] On August 10, 2018, the same court invoked the same logic of representation to declare itself guardian of feral cows in the state of Uttarakhand (Vineet Upadhyay, 'Uttarakhand HC declares itself guardian of cows in state' (2018) Times of India <https:// timesofindia .indiatimes .com/ city/ dehradun/ uttarakhand -hc -declares -itself -legal -protector -of -cow -and -progeny/ articleshow/ 65389832 .cms> accessed 20 June 2022).

[39] This is what Stone calls 'the ontological problem': 'if "rights" are to be granted to the environment, then for many of the same reasons it might bear "liabilities" as well–as inanimate objects did anciently; when the Nile overflows, is it the "responsibility" of the river? the mountains? the snow? the hydro-logic cycle?'. See (n 4) 481.

[40] Eden Kincaid, '"Rights of Nature" in Translation: Assemblage Geographies, Boundary Objects, and Translocal Social Movements' (2019) 44:3 Transactions of the Institute of British Geographers 555–570.

that Marilyn Strathern characterizes as 'auto-limitlessness'. For Strathern, this episteme of 'surfeit' is peculiar to Euro-America thinking. In contrast to other anthropologists, Strathern is not interested in enhancing this aesthetic by bringing it into resonance with the cosmologies of others, but only in exploring how it is put to work in its 'indigenous context'.[41] If the figure of the network 'works indigenously as a metaphor for the endless extension and intermeshing of phenomena',[42] then what is interesting here is just this sense of endless proliferation and recombination. The vitality that is ascribed to Earthly beings by speculative jurisprudences is a reflection of the vitalism of network thinking. And this posthuman vitalism is not necessarily as critical as it seems.

The sense that nature is always in the making, that it is always in the process of inflection, hybridization, or 'mattering', has an interesting genealogy. Leah Aronowsky describes how in the 1960s James Lovelock developed what was to become the Gaia hypothesis in collaboration with Royal Dutch Shell. From the perspective of Shell, the theory that the biosphere generated its own conditions of existence through mechanisms of self-regulation which stabilized temperature and atmospheric chemistry was interesting because it allowed the company to develop a particular strategy of climate denialism. If the Earth regulated its own atmosphere, then it seemed plausible to suggest that it could adapt to the effects of CO_2 emissions, and that pollution might itself be part of a 'natural' cycle. So, the mode of vitality that now allows Gaia to be promoted as a figuration of our Earthbound existence was originally cultivated as a theme of fossil economy. The qualities of plasticity or limitlessness that energize reflection on the Anthropocene are politically ambivalent, to say the least: 'Gaia's brand of posthumanism is no longer a historically transcendent category that necessarily lends itself to a project of rearticulating questions of ecology as matters of politics. Rather, Gaia's history requires that we see posthumanism as itself a discourse that has historically served multiple political projects – from upending the nature/culture dualism of modernity to the insulation of a capitalist status quo'.[43] In the figure of Gaia, network thinking discovers its immanent cyberneticism and, in so doing it reconnects with the deeper genealogy of the episteme of surfeit, which emerged in the twentieth century as an effect of electrification. The vitalism of networks is a byproduct

---

[41] Marilyn Strathern, 'Cutting the Network' (1996) 2:3 Journal of the Royal Anthropological Institute 517–535, at 521. In her *Property, Substance & Effect* (Athlone, 1999) Strathern similarly 'indigenizes' second-order observation as the operative device of another version of cyberneticism, namely, Luhmann's systems theory (see especially chapter 9).

[42] Strathern, 'Cutting the Network' ibid 522.

[43] Leah Aronowsky, 'Gas Guzzling Gaia; or, a Prehistory of Climate Change Denialism' (2021) 47 Critical Inquiry 327.

of the horizon of technology and innovation that was presciently characterized by Heidegger (explicitly in connection with energy) as 'revealing' without end.[44]

In the case of the rights of nature, the politically unmotivated character of cyberneticism has allowed 'nature' to be personified in ways that 'settle' the contradictions of the contemporary fossil economy. Before it becomes critical and posthuman, the vitalism that generates visions of Earthly legality is already at work in political and juridical operations, which use the device of legal personhood to dismember and instrumentalize 'nature', all in the name of its integrity and dignity. The semantics of surfeit turns nature into a kind of floating signifier, which is able to articulate varying and divergent meanings. As such, the signifier 'nature' becomes a resource for the other modality of cyberneticism, namely, the process of lawmaking. In other words, one modality of cyberneticism folds into the other. These points can be developed by returning to the question of contextualization, and to do so by way of two foundational precedents of Earth jurisprudence: the example of the Whanganui River in New Zealand, and that of the Yasuní National Park in Ecuador.

TE AWA TUPUA

In the case of the Whanganui River, the declaration that the river had legal personality was made within the context of an ongoing conflict over the interpretation of the Treaty of Waitangi of 1840, which was understood by the British Crown as a cession of sovereignty by the Maori peoples and as a delegation of limited authority to the Crown. The Whanganui River was implicated in this conflict because the Crown proceeded as though it had the authority to embark on acts such as the construction of bridges, wharves and harbours, the removal of gravel for use in the construction of railway tracks, and the conservation of so-called 'scenic and historical' landscapes. In 1903 the Coal Mines Amendment Act vested ownership of the riverbed in the Crown. A report produced by the Waitangi Tribunal, which was formed in 1975 to adjudicate upon the Treaty, observed that the dispute over the river had come about 'because the New Zealand Government had assumed and had then acquired, in fact, an unbridled power over the Maori people'.[45] The Maori people consistently opposed these acts of appropriation, sometimes through direct action, such as the obstruction of the workers employed to remove traditional fishing weirs, but principally through petitions which argued that the taking of the river

---

[44] See my paper on 'Electric Theory' (forthcoming).
[45] Waitangi Tribunal, *The Whanganui River Report*, Wellington, New Zealand, 1999, 165.

was contrary to the Treaty of Waitangi. In 1895, 152 Maori 'women of rank' petitioned the Parliament of New Zealand to stop the removal of stones from the riverbed.[46] Finally, the Maori people took legal action to claim ownership of the riverbed, through a process of litigation that lasted from 1938 to 1962. As the Waitangi Tribunal observed, 'that [could not] have been a Maori case, for, in the Maori view, the river was part of an indivisible whole, a resource comprised of the water, the bed, the tributaries, the banks, the flats, and indeed the whole catchment area'.[47]

According to the provisions of the Te Awa Tupua (Whanganui River Claims Settlement) Act 2017, the river, Te Awa Tupua, is supposed to enjoy 'all the rights, powers, duties, and liabilities of a legal person';[48] and, corporeally, it is supposed to be 'an indivisible and living whole, comprising the Whanganui River from the mountains to the sea, incorporating all its physical and metaphysical elements'.[49] But the body of the river is juridically amputated and constricted in such a way as to make its 'rights, powers and duties' largely illusory. The Te Awa Tupua Act does not derogate from the common law principle that water cannot be owned,[50] so the river has no control over what constitutes its own being: 'Adopting the holistic thinking of Maori, water was an integral part of the river that they possessed. Though its molecules pass by, the river, as a water entity, remains. The water was their water, at least until it naturally escaped to the sea, at which point its *mauri* changed'.[51] And although the Act confirms that the legislation of 1903 did not extinguish the rights of the Maori people to the riverbed, the river can now recover only those parts of the bed in which the Crown had retained free simple ownership. Moreover, the Act expressly preserves existing public and private rights of access to the

---

[46] Ibid 185–186.
[47] Ibid 197. See also 261: 'The river was conceptualized as a whole and indivisible entity, not separated into beds, banks, and waters, nor into tidal and non-tidal, navigable and non-navigable parts. Through creation beliefs, it is a living being, an ancestor with its own mauri, mana, and tapu'.
[48] Te Awa Tupua (Whanganui River Claims Settlement) Act 2017, section 14(1).
[49] Ibid section 12.
[50] Ibid section 16: 'Unless expressly provided for by or under this Act, nothing in this Act—
    (a)   limits any existing private property rights in the Whanganui River; or
    (b)   creates, limits, transfers, extinguishes, or otherwise affects any rights to, or interests in, water; or
    (c)   creates, limits, transfers, extinguishes, or otherwise affects any rights to, or interests in, wildlife, fish, aquatic life, seaweeds, or plants; or
    (d)   affects the application of any enactment'.
[51] Waitangi Tribunal (n 45) 262.

river, existing rights in fisheries and other resources, rights of navigation, and the mineral rights of the Crown.

The amputated body of Te Awa Tupua's person bears witness to a history of legal discrimination that is evident as much in the history of Aotearoa New Zealand as in the history of Australia, notwithstanding the existence of the Treaty of Waitangi. Although the legal systems of both nations have recognized that indigenous peoples had rights to their land at the moment of colonization, they have at the same time immunized the Crown against claims to restitution of these original rights, either through the application of limitation rules (the New Zealand Maori Land Act of 1993) or through the retrenchment of the doctrine of extinguishment (as did the High Court of Australia in *Mabo v Queensland* (1992)).[52] Ultimately, both systems have ratified the results of a process of expropriation that was sanctioned by earlier courts: notably, in New Zealand, the case of *Wi Parata v Bishop of Wellington* (1877),[53] in which Chief Justice Prendergast famously declared that the Maori people were 'a group of savages' who did not have the competence to enter into a treaty; and, in Australia, the decision of the Privy Council in *Cooper v Stuart* (1889),[54] which held that the continent was *terra nullius*. The recognition of Te Awa Tupua as a legal person 'settles' the dispute over the river by reinventing this strategy. It represents colonial violence as an aberration of the past, and proposes an ostensibly post-racist political discourse through which this violence might be narrated and absolved, but the settlement conserves all that had been capitalized, juridically and otherwise, through the exercise of that violence. Crucially, by having recourse to the idiom of 'rights of nature', colonial New Zealand is able to acknowledge the claims of the Maori people while denying them ownership or sovereign authority over the river.

The device of legal personhood transforms the claims of the Maori people into the interests of the river. This move retrenches the perception of indigenous peoples as 'past-tense people';[55] people who are not political actors so much as the producers and agents of an eternal, extra-political, cosmology. At the same time, it suspends the tensions between different senses of property, and different moments in the history of property: between the cosmological attachments of the Maori people and the settler nation's understanding of property, which is itself riven by the tension of that nation's own relation to its colonial origins. Given that a river can only articulate its interests through its representatives, the object of this settlement is not to resolve the historical

---

[52] 1992 175 CLR 1.
[53] (1877) 3 NZ Jur (NS) SC 72.
[54] (1889) 14 App Cas 286.
[55] Elizabeth A Povinelli, *The Cunning of Recognition: Indigenous Alterities and the Making of Australian Multiculturalism* (Duke University Press 2002) 178.

dispute over the Whanganui; rather, it is to set in motion a process in which the two people who constitute Te Pou Tapua, the 'human face'[56] of the river, negotiate the respective interests of the state and the Maori people. This might be seen as a new kind of constitutional process, a new and more genuinely symmetrical iteration of the Treaty of Waitangi, oriented towards the 'maintenance of relationships between peoples, and, perhaps, between peoples and land'.[57] Because these negotiations are necessarily mediated by the 'body' of the river, perhaps there is symmetry also in the sense that the process shapes the competences of human and non-human agents. Precisely because the river is a different thing for each 'side' of Te Pou Tapua, precisely because there is a dispute, the being of the river becomes at once a medium for and a precipitate of human perspectives. But what is interesting about this settlement is precisely the fact that it turns the personality of the river into a work in progress, a work which articulates a complex of different relations to terrain and identity, different moments of appropriation, and whose resolution might be postponed indefinitely.

TIPUTINI

Perhaps the most celebrated 'rights of nature' precedent is the declaration of the Ecuadorean Constitution that 'Nature is a legal subject', which paralleled the launching in 2007 of the Yasuní-ITT (Ishpingo-Tambococha-Tiputini) initiative by the government of Rafael Correa. The theme of non-appropriational relation to nature was very much to the fore in what was variously described as a pioneering 'post-neoliberal' or 'neo-extractivist' policy. According to Correa, the objective of the initiative was to 'change the market logic through collective action and seeking other logics beyond the profit logic through agreement, justice and responsibility'.[58] According to the estimates of Petroecuador, the ITT wells of the Yasuní National Park held 846 billion barrels of oil, with a market value of $7 billion. In return for an undertaking to 'strand' these reserves in perpetuity, the Ecuadorean government asked that

---

[56] Te Awa Tupua (Whanganui River Claims Settlement) Act 2017, section 18(2). The Act goes on to stipulate the composition of Te Pou Tapua: 'One person must be nominated by the iwi with interests in the Whanganui River and one person must be nominated on behalf of the Crown' (section 20(2)).

[57] Katherine Sanders, 'Beyond Human Ownership'? Property, Power and Legal Personality for Nature in Aotearoa New Zealand' (2018) 30 Journal of Environmental Law 233.

[58] Rafael Correa, lecture on 'Environmental Policies in Latin America', given in London in October 2009, cited in Laura Rival, 'Ecuador's Yasuní-ITT Initiative: The Old and New Values of Petroleum' (2010) 70 Ecological Economics 358.

the international community provide compensation of about half this projected market value.[59] The object, suggested Correa, was to move from 'an extractive type of economy to a service economy. We would be selling services to the rest of the world. We would be avoiding deforestation and, beyond, pollution as well'.[60] One of the services in question was carbon offsetting. Subscribers were invited to purchase Yasuní Guaranty Certificates, each of which represented one tonne of CO_2, and which were valued at $10,000. These certificates, which were to remain valid as long as the Ecuadorean government honoured its commitment to leave the oil in the ground, were to be tradable within the European Union's emission trading scheme, which had by then gathered in 80% of the global market in carbon allowances.[61] The money raised from subscriptions to the project was to be held in a trust fund administered by the United Nations Development Program, and applied to uses consistent with 'sustainable human development', notably investments in different kinds of renewable energy, and would continue to do so through the reforestation programmes that were to be supported by the revenue generated for the United Nations Development Programme (UNDP) fund. Carbon offsetting was complemented by another service to the international community, namely, the conservation of the 'hyperdiversity' expressed in the ecology of the Yasuní National Park.[62]

As it turned out, the offer of carbon certificates was seriously undersubscribed, and in August 2013, faced with the unwillingness of the international community 'to fulfil its obligations', the government of Ecuador reverted to a 'plan B' that had been announced when the initiative was launched. It authorized Petroamazonas, the state oil company, to embark on the extraction of oil from the National Park, with the idea that production should be under way within two years. Already, in 2010, the government had given permission to Petroecuador, the other state oil company, to begin constructing a pipeline to the 'stranded' ITT fields,[63] and production around the *zona intangible* of the National Park continued to expand in neighbouring fields in Ecuador, Colombia, and Peru. A scientist working within the Park at the time captured the sense of inexorable encroachment: 'Tiputini is very remote, but you can hear the generator of an oil platform from a few kilometres' distance, and at

---

[59] On the question of valuation, see ibid 360–362.
[60] Cited in ibid 359.
[61] European Commission, EU Action Against Climate Change: EU Emissions Trading (2008) 21.
[62] 'It isn't even diversity any longer – it's hyperdiversity, or megadiversity', a tropical biologist, quoted in Eric Marx, 'The Fight for Yasuni' (2010) 330 Science 1170.
[63] Elissa Dennis, 'Keep It in the Ground' (2010) Dollars & Sense <http://www.dollarsandsense.org/archives/2010/0710dennisNEW.html> accessed 20 June 2022.

night you can see the glow of the gas flame'.[64] So perhaps the 'left turn' of the Correa government right was less about renouncing extraction altogether than it was about evolving a policy of 'neo-extractivism', which replaced a process of neoliberal extraction controlled by global corporations, which contributed little to the wellbeing or per capita income of the nation, with a process that was mediated by a political idiom of national interest, social participation, and *buen vivir*.[65] To the extent that it invoked this latter notion, the recognition that nature was 'a legal subject' was bound up with the creation of a new kind of polity.

Bearing in mind the sense in which rights of nature are supposed to dissolve the figuration of nature as property, the form of the Yasuní Guaranty Certificate is of particular interest. The project as it was formalized by the Ecuadorean government was preceded by a popular campaign in which supporters were invited to buy 'a barrel in the ground'; in other words, the project of sequestration was implemented through transactions that were reckoned in terms of the prevailing market value of oil, and which relied on the basic property-effect of exclusion to sequester the reserves. By contrast, the denomination of the Guaranty Certificate was based on the value of the CO_2 emissions that would have resulted from the extraction and combustion of the sequestered reserves. So, the overall dollar value of the share issue was no longer a proportion of the 720 million dollars that the reserves were supposedly worth, but the 8 billion dollars that the negative carbon emissions were worth in total.[66] Pragmatically, the change of measure insulated the scheme against the volatility of the global market in crude oil. Symbolically, it emphasized the 'service' dimension of the project: leaving the oil sequestered in the ground would in effect enable polluters elsewhere in the word to consume that proportion of the global carbon budget (as measured in parts per million of atmospheric CO_2) that was represented by the Yasuní reserves.

Timothy Mitchell suggests that oil, by virtue of its material and infrastructural liquidity, conditioned the emergence of 'the economy' in the sense of

---

[64] Cited in Marx (n 62) 1171.

[65] Eduardo Gudynas, 'Diez tesis urgentes sobre el nuevo extractivismo: contextos y demandas bajo el progresismo sudamericano actual' in Jürgen Schuldt et al. (eds) *Extractivismo, política y sociedad* (CAAP/CLAES, 2009) 187–225.

[66] 'Using a representative value of the European Emission Allowances (EUA) on the European market, i.e. US$ 19.81 per tonne of CO_2-eq, the economic value of the emissions prevented by the Initiative would amount to US$ 8.067 billion'. See Carlos Larrea, 'Ecuador's Yasuni-ITT Initiative: A Critical Assessment', paper presented at the ENGOV (Environmental Governance in Latin America and the Caribbean) Project Conference, Brasilia, June 13–16, 2012, in Lucas Andrianos (et al.) *Sustainable Alternatives for Poverty Reduction and Eco-Justice*, volume 1 (Cambridge Scholars 2013) 36.

Keynes and his successors. The assumption that oil was an inexhaustible resource, reinforced by the externalization of the environmental costs of its production and consumption, fostered the sense that the economy, as a product of transactions in currency, could expand without spatial or temporal restrictions: 'Innovations in methods of calculation, the use of money, the measurement of transactions and the compiling of national statistics made it possible to imagine the central object of politics as an object that could expand without any form of ultimate material constraint'.[67] The extractivist economy from which the government of Rafael Correa sought to liberate itself was an iteration of this performative understanding of the economy. From the 1970s onwards, the question of the environment could no longer be externalized, in part because of the fact that the oil industry itself had changed the metrics by which it measured remaining reserves, so that oil suddenly became a finite resource.[68] But even if the resources it extracted and consumed were now perceived as finite, the machinery of the neoliberal economy was immortal, always ready to implant itself in new locales, always alert to new potential resources for extraction, and always in the process of 'innovating' new apparatuses of appropriation.

The pledging of stranded assets to the economy of carbon trading switched the oil reserves of the national into a different modality of appropriation, in which the scarce resource was the global carbon budget. The project was articulated across the temporal chiasmus that Andreas Folkers characterizes as 'fossil modernity'; a configuration in which fossil fuels 'make possible and propel the pace and progressive perspective of modern temporality and by the same token, or rather the same material substratum, confront modern societies with a particular slow time of material durability and ecological degradation'.[69] In the process of consuming the past (in the form of fossilized biomass) to generate the future, industrialized modernity began to accumulate the parts per million of CO_2 that are now the concern of climate governance initiatives. The materials of a supposedly dead and inert past were cycled into the future as toxic residues that now permeate all layers of geological and biological systems, from the atmosphere to cellular metabolism. In this temporal chiasmus, what were once infrastructures of infinite possibility now manifest as deadweight with an inertia that compresses the future: 'the material weight of existing fossil infrastructures (extraction, transportation, energy) and vested

---

[67] Timothy Mitchell, 'Carbon Democracy' (2009) 38:3 Economy and Society 418.
[68] Ibid 419–420.
[69] Andreas Folkers 'Fossil Modernity: The Materiality of Acceleration, Slow Violence, and Ecological Futures' 30:2 Time & Society 223–246, at 224.

capital interests drags it toward a disastrous pathway of ever more fossil fuel consumption'.[70]

The strategy of carbon trading purports to reconcile the dimensions of this chiasmus. In theory, the compressive tension between future and past can be alleviated by incentivizing larger emitters to adopt sources of renewable energy, thereby cleaning up the inertial infrastructures of fossil capital. In that regard, carbon trading is in the same line of business as the politics of ecomodernism, which imagines that the process of extracting value from nature can be 'decoupled from environmental impacts'.[71] Ultimately, both strategies assume that we will invent our way out of fossil modernity by operationalizing technologies of carbon removal and sequestration. The Yasuní-ITT initiative was formulated at a time when the need for this escape clause seemed less urgent. Under the Clean Development Mechanism of the Kyoto Protocol, industries in the global North were encouraged to offset their emissions against carbon sinks (principally forests) established in the global South. Even overlooking the notorious contingencies of the accounting procedure, the scale of afforestation that would have been necessary to offset even a modest proportion of industrial emissions implied the creation of a late modern equivalent of the plantation. Offset forests recolonize territory and labour, replacing local ecologies and farming practices with plantations that are maintained purely as collateral for industrial production in the North. The strategy of 'keeping it in the ground' committed less territory, but in the process of 'servicing' the global economy, Ecuador participated in this strange historical involution, in which the chiasmus of fossil modernity was re-expressed as a fresh iteration of the relation between the colonial powers and their 'ghost acres'.[72] It is precisely this kind of temporal configuration, which renders simultaneous different, contradictory, historical moments of appropriation, that forms the contexts in which personality is ascribed to nature, and that dictates what is asked of nature in the process.

---

[70] Ibid 232.

[71] 'Intensifying many human activities — particularly farming, energy extraction, forestry, and settlement — so that they use less land and interfere less with the natural world is the key to decoupling human development from environmental impacts. These socioeconomic and technological processes are central to economic modernization and environmental protection. Together they allow people to mitigate climate change, to spare nature, and to alleviate global poverty'. See John Asafu-Adjaye et al., *An Ecomodernist Manifesto* (2015) <http://www.ecomodernism.org> accessed 20 June 2022.

[72] Kenneth Pomeranz, *The Great Divergence* (Princeton UP 2000).

VENTRILOQUIZING 'NATURE'

What do these examples tell us about rights of nature? The most obvious point is that natural entities become 'persons' in very different ways and to very different effect, depending on the context in which they come into being. There is, as yet, no universal declaration of rights of nature, no a priori status of sanctity or dignity, no set of constitutional rights that 'nature' would be able to assert whatever its manifestation and whatever its location.[73] It is true that human rights are necessarily 'vernacularized' in the process of their realization,[74] precisely because they are products of 'lawmaking'. But there is still a difference between a personhood which, according to its face value, precedes its engagements with the world and one that comes into being in or as a specific intersection of political, economic, and historical forces. Although the Global Alliance for the Rights of Nature, and other networks of 'rights of nature', collect these specific instances into an 'ecological jurisprudence', and although the ultimate objective may be to evolve something like a universal declaration of rights of nature, the fact is that the personhood that is produced by rights of nature is radically intersectional. The mode of existence of 'nature' is to be found in the political and economic configurations that generate these intersections, and not in some Earthly mode of being that would be recognized, however imperfectly, by the ascription of personality. So why is 'nature' amputated, diffracted, and alienated from 'itself' in the very moment in which it is recognized as a legal person?

First, what is at stake in the recognition of natural entities as legal persons is really (human) control over geo-material processes that were once the province of property law. In that sense, one might indeed see rights of nature as a counter-strategy to property. But we should recall that we are now at a specific moment in the history of appropriation; or, more accurately, a moment at which we are finally beginning to grasp the real history of appropriation. Thanks to, for example, the theory of the Capitalocene or histories of racialized capital, we are becoming aware of the earthly or geological dimension

---

[73] By contrast, a complex of trade agreements, jurisdictional laws of corporate form, and of franchising and licensing, conspire to give corporations (through their subsidiary or alternate personae) freedoms and immunities that are exercisable almost anywhere in the world. Although Euro-American legal systems have had no difficulty in naturalizing the fiction of corporate personality, systematically passing off the corporation as if it were an unremarkable feature of our ecology, they treat the ascription of personality to natural beings as a deviation from the natural purpose of rights.

[74] See generally Mark Goodale & Sally Engle-Merry, *The Practice of Human Rights: Tracking Law Between the Global and the Local* (Cambridge University Press 2007).

of appropriation, production and distribution, a dimension that was systematically repressed and externalized by the legal and economic discourse of property rights. The history of property is not just a (hagiographic or critical) biography of the possessive individual, but a narrative whose authorships should be able to rearticulate 'property' into the material ecology upon which it depended, and from which it extracted value, but which at the same time it suppressed ideologically; by, for example, abstracting the 'propriety' (to use Locke's term) of white European men from the ghost acres of the plantations upon which that propriety depended. The real history of appropriation would recount the successive moments of this ideology: the ways in which the legal-economic forms of land, money, and the corporation have incorporated nature into the production of value while at the same time eclipsing the material entanglements in which these forms are embedded. As the examples of the Whanganui River and the Yasuní National Park reveal, this history is not a linear process in which one figure of appropriation supplants another. Rather, the Euro-American episteme of property is stratified or sedimented, in the sense that different historical formations of property, the old and the new, slide over one another in the manner of Koselleck's 'simultaneity of the non-simultaneous'[75] to produce a phenomenon of hyperproperty.

The strata exposed by the Yasuní-ITT enterprise are those of fossil modernity, a temporal configuration which forces the deposits of 'old' extractivism into the reckonings of contemporary politics in the manner of a geological non-conformity; effects that were sedimented into Earth history by treating nature, energy, and human labour as 'cheap nature'[76] suddenly become present and active (again) by irrupting into the stratum of the atmosphere, as the agency of the parts per million of CO_2 that constrict the horizon of 'progress' or 'development'. This epistemic non-conformity is the product not of geological forces strictly speaking, but of a new, reflexive, human apprehension of geology or material ecology, which begins to make the ecological history of Euro-American society visible for the first time – the effects of 'old' extractivism were already a force in the world, but they were experienced by mortal beings which were not cognizable to modern political economy. And, because we remain addicted to fossil fuels, the non-conformity is dynamic rather than static, generating the temporal chiasmus that Folkers calls fossil modernity. The Yasuní project did not free 'nature' from these entanglements; on the contrary, it distributed nature across the dimensions or strata of the

---

[75] Reinhart Koselleck, *Futures' Past: On the Semantics of Historical Time* (Keith Tribe tr, Columbia University Press) 266.

[76] See Jason W Moore, 'The Capitalocene, Part I: On the Nature and Origins of Our Ecological Crisis' (2017) 44:3 Journal of Peasant Studies 594–630.

fossil episteme. Nature acquired a multiple existence: it was at once the raw resource lying under the national park, with a market value that could be realized as soon as the project failed, the stranded asset which was pledged to the global economy of carbon trading by the Yasuní Guaranty Certificate; and the ecology of the indigenous communities whose cosmologies had inspired the politics of *buen vivir*. This multiple and self-contradictory existence was unremarkable precisely because 'nature' could be presumed to be so vital and dynamic as to be capable of being in many times and places at once. 'Nature' as a constitutionally-recognized person obfuscated and deferred the tensions between different modes of appropriation and production of nature as resource or set of affordances.

In the case of Te Awa Tupua, the chiasmus was formed by the politics of the postcolonial settler nation. In one sense, the settlement addressed a conflict between a first nation and a colonial state over the material and symbolic control of land; but, through its engagement with the cosmology of the Maori people, white New Zealand was also reckoning with its own past.[77] The colonial past persists as an infrastructure that continues to generate discriminatory effects, and for the settler nation the question is how to reconcile those effects with the sense of itself as being no longer that nation, as being no longer the people who practised colonial violence and who pursued that extractivist relation to nature. The settlement is made by projecting the tension forward, by turning it into the ongoing project of negotiating the interests of Te Awa Tupua.

Both cases illustrate the function of the device of personality. Taking biotechnology as a specific agent of 'auto-limitlessness', Marilyn Strathern notices how the attribution of property rights 'cuts' networks. By recognizing products of nature as inventions, intellectual property law arrests the movement of surfeit; it fixes the articulation of nature and technique at a specific moment to produce a 'thing' that gives purchase on a network, even if that artefact is then reabsorbed into further proliferation.[78] The situation with rights of nature is somewhat different. The ascription of personality to nature does not arrest auto-limitlessness, even momentarily. Rather, it sustains the episteme of surfeit in conditions in which it has begun to undermine itself (as

---

[77] As Povinelli puts it, the white nation was sending 'a national postcard' to itself. See (n 55) 154.

[78] Strathern, 'Cutting the Network' (n 41) 525: 'The hybrid object, the modified cell, gathered a network into itself; that is, it condensed into a single item diverse elements from technology, science and society, enumerated together as an invention and available for ownership as property. [...] As at once the thing that has become the object of a right, and the right of a person in it, property is, so to speak, a network in manipulable form'.

evidenced by the temporality of fossil modernity, in which inertial infrastructures drag modernity towards the 'disastrous pathway of ever more fossil fuel consumption'). The tensions of this chiasmus are not resolved but held open by deferring the moment at which they would have to be addressed. By ascribing personality to natural entities, courts and legislatures externalize the contradictions of modernity into the 'nature' that they are supposedly protecting. Juridically, this operation of externalization is not one of appropriation but one of hypothecation: that is, the vitality and malleability of nature allows it to secure the epistemic or semantic 'credit' that is expended in sustaining the ideology of surfeit. Of course, hypothecation is added to appropriation in the sense that it allows the machinery of surfeit to keep multiplying the ways in which nature is exploited.

Ironically, the recognition of natural entities as persons rather than things is precisely what enables them to be fractioned and distributed across the strata of contemporary ecologies of appropriation. The ascription of personality actually makes 'nature' more malleable, more responsive to the demands of human systems of appropriation and production. If nature were protected as a thing, as *res sancta* or *res extra commercium*, its qualities and boundaries would be defined in advance, and even if those bounds were subject to casuistic negotiation, they give nature a determinate status or 'standing'.[79] But the recognition of natural entities as legal persons activates a mechanism in which, to borrow Spivak's terms, nature is 'represented' in the mode of both proxy and portrait.[80] Whatever eco-cyberneticism tells us about the agency of matter or the capacity of Gaia to engage humans, nature is not an interlocutor,[81] and until or unless

---

[79] For Roman law instances, see generally Yan Thomas, *Les opérations du droit* (Seuil 2011), and for commentary see my 'A Knowledge Apart' in Yan Thomas, *Legal Artifices: Ten Essays on Roman Law in the Present Tense* (Chantal Schütz and Anton Schütz tr, Edinburgh University Press 2021) 299–316.

[80] In terms of Spivak's expression of the difference between *vertreten* (representation) and *darstellen* (re-presentation), natural entities are 'represented' both in the sense of 'proxy' or 'portrait' (Gayatri Chakravorty Spivak, 'Can the Subaltern Speak?' in Cary Nelson & Lawrence Grossberg (eds), *Marxism and the Interpretation of Culture* (University of Illinois Press 1988) 276.

[81] If we presuppose the cybernetic theory of communication – as exemplified in the work of Bühler, Habermas and Luhmann – then there is no true interlocutory 'communion' in communication, only a coupling of reciprocal self-observations. In communication, agents necessarily have to 'construct' the meaning that they ascribe to their interlocutor. But even if natural entities engage and perturb the perceptions of humans, they cannot participate in this dance of double contingency because the capacity to perturb is not the same thing as the capacity to see oneself being seen. If we switch to a more Latourian mode of cyberneticism, the point might be that non-humans 'affect' humans in a register that is not that of communication, but which has to do with a material or affective 'covariation' (to use Deleuze's term) of competences. But if it is to

the discourse of law is remediated into an Earthly language that would signify otherwise, the needs and wants of nature will have to be ventriloquized by human representatives.

This mechanism of representation is constitutive of all persons in Euro-American law: 'representation is not an exception but is rather the fundamental constellation of law: legal reality is representation'.[82] When legal subjects act, legal discourse itself calls into being the willing subject that is supposed to lie behind the mask of personality. Subjectivity is ascribed rather than innate. But in the historical moment in which we find ourselves, the violence of construction is particularly evident and particularly pernicious in the case of nature. Stone believed that nature's wants were largely self-evident: 'We make decisions on behalf of, and in the purported interests of, others every day; these "others" are often creatures whose wants are far less verifiable, and even far more metaphysical in conception, than the wants of rivers, trees, and land'.[83] Trees need water, river ecologies are harmed by pollutants, and the soil is radically degraded by what Marx had already called the 'robbing' of the soil.[84] But precisely because the ascription of personality now turns 'nature' into a medium or alibi for auto-limitlessness, the question of what nature 'wants' is a function of 'context'; that is, of the nexuses of contradiction that are produced by the implosion of our economy of auto-limitlessness. As persons, natural entities can be presumed to have, if not a spontaneous will, then at least a set of wants or interests that have to be discerned in the light of context. And because the context of the Anthropocene is characterized by the multiplication (and stratification) of modes and apparatuses of appropriation, 'nature' turns out to have wants that are just as complex and indeterminate.

It is here that the 'vitality' of the episteme of surfeit comes into play: cyberneticism generates a 'nature' that is fluid and malleable enough to have these open-ended wants. When, for example, Latour and Lenton talk about the sense in which the Gaia hypothesis recognizes the ability of living beings to create for themselves 'the conditions for lasting in time and expanding in space',[85] they make more vivid the mode of 'revealing' nature that characterizes late twentieth-century networks of fossil-fuelled capital and technology. 'Nature' is as fluid and malleable as this process of revealing requires it to be. And in the figure of Gaia one can see another significant aspect of cyberneticism: the

---

become a jurisprudence, this experience of covariation would have to be communicated about by humans, and taken up into a programme of lawmaking.

[82] Fischer-Lescano (n 33) 243, citing Christoph Menke.
[83] Stone (n 4) 471.
[84] Karl Marx, *Capital. A Critique of Political Economy*, volume 1 (Penguin, 1976) 638.
[85] Latour & Lenton (n 21) 664.

capacity to reconcile this plastic vitality with the singularity that is required if natural entities are to be legal persons. As Latour and Lenton put it, 'there is one Gaia, but Gaia is not "a whole"'.[86] So nature can be a legal person while at the same time having the quality of multiplicity that allows it to be in many places at once and to have such contradictory wants. The discourse of Earth jurisprudence fastens on this moment of quasi-transcendence to suggest that despite the radically different ways in which nature is contextualized in the leading precedents, it is still possible to talk about 'rights of nature'.

There is a further dimension to the production of 'nature' as guarantor of the episteme of surfeit; namely, the process of 'epistemic extractivism' that translates the knowledge of indigenous peoples into a corroboration of post-human cyberneticism. Because indigenous cosmologies are supposed to be already, originally, attuned to the wants of nature, because they have always been innocent of the person/thing distinction that corrupts the Euro-American apprehension of nature, and because they are supposed already to have the ecological inclusivity that would characterize Earthly legality, they serve to legitimate or naturalize the 'nature' that is produced by eco-cyberneticism. This process of epistemic extractivism has been under way for some time, and it has long been implicated in the broader process of extractivism. So, the colonial contexts in which indigenous peoples were presented to ethnographers were crucial to the evolution of cybernetic thought.[87] The effect of ethnographic distantiation disguises this original complicity, and allows cosmologies that have always-already been framed by cyberneticism to be rendered as expressions of an uncorrupted way of being with nature. And the capital that is generated can be as much academic as political or economic: 'The objective of epistemic extractivism is the pillaging of ideas so as to market them and transform them into economic capital or to appropriate them within the Western academic machine to the end of winning symbolic capital'.[88] The examples of Te Awa Tupua and Tiputini illustrate a function of epistemic extractivism that is specific to the recognition of nature as a legal person. In New Zealand as in Ecuador, the act of representing nature is made to seem more faithful, more like the performance of a direct mandate than a trick of ventriloquism, because the process of representation is supposedly mediated by the connection to nature forged by the cosmologies of others – the *buen vivir* or *sumak kawsay* of Amazonian peoples, or the mauri honoured by the Whanganui *Iwi*. The effect

---

[86] Ibid 674.

[87] See Bernard Dionysius Geoghegan, *Code: From Information Theory to French Theory* (Duke University Press 2023).

[88] Ramón Grosfoguel, cited in Philipp Altmann, 'The Commons as Colonisation – The Well-Intentioned Appropriation of *buen vivir*' (2020) 39:1 Bulletin of Latin American Research 93 (quotation slightly modified).

is to give cybernetic vitality a normative and affective pathos that it would not otherwise have, and, in the case of rights of nature, to sustain the illusion that a 'nature' that has been animated, multiplied and dismembered by fossil capital has the qualities of singularity and dignity that are ostensibly recognized by the attribution of legal personality.

*

The jurisprudence of nature that I review in this chapter is not necessarily representative of what can be achieved by ascribing rights to nature. It might be, particularly at more local scales, that the recognition of personality works effectively as a tactic to counter specific depredatory projects, that it gives visibility and voice to otherwise marginalized constituencies, and that it lends impetus to the development of more liveable ecologies, as much for non-human as for human beings. But if the broader ambition is to fracture or arrest the complex of discourses, institutions and practices that has, over the course of centuries, turned nature into a global standing reserve, then that ambition cannot be realized by Earth jurisprudence as it is currently imagined and configured. Ultimately, the effect of ascribing personality to natural entities is only to suspend or articulate tensions generated by the machinery of global appropriation. As the precedents of the Whanganui and Tiputini suggest, the device of natural personality at once obfuscates and facilitates the operation of that machinery. And, ironically, this is an effect of our newfound ability to imagine natural entities as complex, self-organizing, or 'mattering' beings. Given that this imaginary is fuelled by twentieth-century cyberneticism and its ethos of auto-limitlessness, it is not entirely surprising that it should disclose modes of agency that are compatible with the economy of fossil modernity. For example, if we ask what interventions are necessary to foster the flourishing of Gaia 2.0, we have to content ourselves with platitudes about the circular economy and the transition to renewable energy.[89] Despite the authors' intentions, Gaia resonates with the programme of ecomodernism because the mode of self-organization that makes it so lively and unruly is not alien to the logic of the market economy.

Latour's ecological thought is only one of the currents that compose the new Euro-American imaginary of nature, but alternative figures of nature will soon encounter a limitation that Latour's work on networks makes visible. Strathern's essay on 'cutting the network' makes the point that legal form can, precisely, only 'cut' the network, each cut being recombinant in the sense that it stimulates further ramification of the network. In other words, whereas law is supposed to fix actors and events in prescribed configurations, the ostensible determinacy of legal form is immediately recruited as a resource for the

---

[89] Latour and Lenton (n 21) 1067.

auto-limitless dynamic of the network. Indeed, law that is, as Coombe puts it, 'emergent, iterative, and performative' has always-already been captured by the logic of auto-limitlessness, and can only function 'collaterally'[90] to the market processes that it is supposed to regulate or discipline. So, in a sense the project of rights of nature would need to begin by changing the terms in which it seeks to reimagine the agency of law. The challenge is to reconceive law in terms that refuse both the cyberneticism of network ecology and the moment of the beautiful soul in which figures such as 'mattering' or 'sympoiesis' are cultivated without reference to their capacity to inform a true but effective Earth jurisprudence.

---

[90] In the sense of Annelise Riles, 'Collateral Expertise: Legal Knowledge in the Global Financial Markets' (2010) 51:6 Current Anthropology 795–818.

4. The rights of robots
David J. Gunkel

If 'robot rights' sounds like something out of science fiction, there is a good reason for this. Unlike artificial intelligence (AI), which originated during planning for a scientific workshop held at Dartmouth College in the summer of 1956, robots are the product of fiction, specifically Karel Čapek's 1921 stage play *R.U.R.* or *Rossumovi Univerzální Roboti*[1]. And the idea of 'robot rights' is already in play and operational from the moment the robot appeared on the stage of history.[2] But the question of robot rights is not a matter for fiction, or something limited to future speculation. It is an idea that is already being debated and discussed in the academic and popular literature and being put into practice by way of recent legislative efforts and proceedings.

Even if real-world circumstances and scenarios are seemingly less exciting and action-packed than the robot uprisings of science fiction, robot rights are the site of a dramatic and important conflict. And like any conflict, there are two sides or opposing forces. On one side, there is what could be called the 'conservative' faction; not in the political sense of the term, but in terms of designating efforts that seek to conserve and preserve existing ways of proceeding. According to this group, the very idea of robots, AI, or other socially interactive machines being accorded anything approaching moral or legal status beyond that of a mere instrument or piece of property is not just wrong-headed thinking but a dangerous development that should be curtailed, resisted, or interrupted before it even begins. The other side recognizes that various technological systems and implementations might need some form of social recognitions and/or legal protections and that entertaining this exigency is an important contribution to on-going efforts to test, validate, and even revise the limits of our moral and legal systems.

The debate is polarizing, with the one side opposing what the other promotes. And like similar disagreements – think, for example, of other seemingly irresolvable moral or legal disputes, like the abortion debate or physician-assisted

---

[1] Karel Čapek, *Rossum's Universal Robots* (David Wyllie tr, The Echo Library 2009).
[2] Seo-Young Chu, *Do Metaphors Dream of Literal Sleep? A Science-Fictional Theory of Representation* (Harvard UP 2010).

suicide – there has been a lot of effort but (as of yet) no clear victor. Both sides continue to heap up arguments and evidence in support of their position, but the basic terms and conditions of the dispute remain largely in place and essentially unchanged. For this reason, this chapter does not take sides in the existing conflict by advocating for one position over and against the other, nor does it seek to mediate their differences and points of disagreement with some kind of compromise or resolution. Instead, it deploys a different strategy. It targets not the points of conflict nor the differences that separate the one from the other, but the common set of shared values and fundamental assumptions that both sides already endorse and support in order to enter into conflict in the first place. And it does so to devise an alternative that may be better suited to respond to and take responsibility for the moral and legal opportunities or challenges that we currently confront in the face or the faceplate of robots, AI, and other seemingly intelligent artifacts.

SHARED INVESTMENTS AND COMMON GROUND

One thing both sides already agree on is that *rights* is the right way to organize and pursue this subject matter. Despite different opinions on the question regarding who (or what) can or should have rights, what the two sides do not dispute is the fact that the debate is to be arranged and pursued in terms of *rights*. Both sides, in other words, already order their positions in terms of rights and have a vested interest in the integrity of the concept and its protection. It is only because of this shared interest that the two sides are able to stake a claim to positions that are situated in opposition to one another. But what exactly is meant by 'rights?' What is it that both sides, despite their polarizing differences, argue about and seek to protect? This is where things get tricky.

That's because 'rights' is one of those concepts which, similar to 'time' in *The Confessions* of St. Augustine, we are all pretty sure we know the meaning of up to the point when someone asks us to actually define and characterize it. Then we run into difficulties and confusions.[3] This is neither unexpected nor uncommon. One hundred years ago, an American jurist, Wesley Hohfeld, observed that even experienced legal professionals tend to misunderstand the term, often using contradictory or insufficient formulations in the course of a decision or even a single sentence.[4]

---

[3] Augustine of Hippo, *The Confessions* (R. S. Pine-Coffin tr, Penguin Books 1961).
[4] Wesley Hohfeld, *Fundamental Legal Conceptions as Applied in Judicial Reasoning* (Yale UP 1920).

An all-too-common error – one that has been perpetrated by both sides in the dispute – results from the mistaken assumption that 'rights' must mean and can only mean *human rights*. Evidence of this can be seen all over the popular press, with eye-catching headlines like 'Do Humanlike Machines Deserve Human Rights?',[5] 'When Will Robots Deserve Human Rights?',[6] 'Do Robots Deserve Human Rights?',[7] and 'Should Sentient Robots Have the Same Rights as Humans?'.[8] It is also operative in the scientific and academic literature on the subject, with journal articles and book chapters bearing titles like 'Granting Automata Human Rights',[9] 'We Hold These Truths to Be Self-Evident, That All Robots Are Created Equal',[10] 'The Constitutional Rights of Advanced Robots (and of Human Beings)',[11] 'Can Robots Have Dignity?',[12] and 'Human Rights for Robots? A Literature Review'.[13] Further complicating the picture is the fact that even in situations where the word 'rights' appears in a seemingly generic and unspecified sense, the way it comes to be operationalized often implies and denotes human rights.

GETTING RIGHTS WRONG

The immediate association of the term 'rights' with 'human rights' is something that is both understandable and expedient. It is understandable, to the extent that so much of the interest in and attention circulating around the

---

[5] Daniel Roh, 'Do Humanlike Machines Deserve Human Rights?' (2009) Wired <https://www.wired.com/2009/01/st-essay-16> accessed 20 March 2022.

[6] George Dvorsky, 'When Will Robots Deserve Human Rights?' (2017) Gizmodo <https://gizmodo.com/when-will-robots-deserve-human-rights-1794599063> accessed 20 March 2022.

[7] Lauren Sigfusson, 'Do Robots Deserve Human Rights? (2017) Discover <https://www.discovermagazine.com/technology/do-robots-deserve-human-rights> accessed 20 March 2022.

[8] Hugh McLachlan 'Ethics of AI: Should Sentient Robots Have the Same Rights as Humans?' (2019) Independent <https://www.independent.co.uk/news/science/ai-robots-human-rights-tech-science-ethics-a8965441.html> accessed 20 March 2022.

[9] Lantz Fleming Miller, 'Granting Automata Human Rights: Challenge to a Basis of Full-Rights Privilege' [2015] 16 Human Rights Review 369.

[10] Amanda Wurah, 'We Hold These Truths to be Self-Evident, That All Robots are Created Equal' (2017) 22 Journal of Futures Studies 61.

[11] George R. Wright, 'The Constitutional Rights of Advanced Robots (and of Human Beings)' (2019) 71 Arkansas Law Review 613.

[12] Carmen Krämer, 'Can Robots Have Dignity?' in Benedikt Paul Goecke and Astrid Rosenthal-von der Pütten (eds), *Artificial Intelligence: Reflections in Philosophy, Theology, and the Social Sciences* (Brill 2020).

[13] John-Stewart Gordon and Ausrine Pasvenskiene, 'Human Rights for Robots? A Literature Review' (2021) 1 AI & Society 579.

subject of rights typically is presented and discussed in terms of human rights, especially their protections and potential abuses. Even though experts in the field have been careful to distinguish and explain that human rights constitute 'a special, narrow category of rights',[14] there is a tendency to immediately assume that any talk of rights must mean or at least involve some aspect of human rights. It is expedient, because proceeding from this assumption has turned out to be an effective way to formulate arguments, capture attention, and even sell content. Pitching the contest in terms of 'human rights' helps generate a kind of self-righteous indignation and moral outrage, with different configurations of this 'outrage' serving to advance the interests and objectives of both sides in the debate.

For many who support the idea of robot rights, this can be (and has been) mobilized as a kind of clarion call that is implicitly justified by nominal associations with previous liberation efforts. As Peter Asaro has characterized it, 'robots might simply demand their rights. Perhaps because morally intelligent robots might achieve some form of moral self-recognition, [the] question [might then become] why they should be treated differently from other moral agents.' This would follow the path of many subjugated groups of humans who fought to establish respect for their rights against powerful socio-political groups who have suppressed, argued, and fought against granting them equal rights'.[15] A similar line of argument has been advanced by Amedeo Santosuosso in the aptly titled essay 'The Human Rights of Nonhuman Artificial Entities: An Oxymoron?': 'Assuming that even an artificial entity may have a certain degree of consciousness would mean that, despite its artificiality, such entity shares with humans something that, according to the legal tradition intertwined into the Universal Declaration of Human Rights, is considered an exclusively human quality. That is a matter of human rights or, better, of extending human rights to machines.'[16]

This is undeniably persuasive. Connecting the dots between the history of previous liberation movements and proposals for considering something similar for other kinds of entities like robots or AI sounds appealing if not intuitively right. 'Human history', as Sohail Inayatullah and Phil McNally point out in what is one of the earliest publications on the subject, 'is the history of exclusion and power. Humans have defined numerous groups as less than human: slaves, woman, the "other races", children and foreigners. These are the wretched who have been defined as, stateless, personless, as suspect,

---

[14] Andrew Clapham, *Human Rights: A Very Short Introduction* (OUP 2007) 4.

[15] Peter Asaro, 'What Should We Want from a Robot Ethic?' (2006) 6 International Review of Information Ethics 9.

[16] Amedeo Santosuosso, 'The Human Rights of Nonhuman Artificial Entities: An Oxymoron?' (2016) 19 Jahrbuch für Wissenschaft und Ethik 204.

as rightless. This is the present realm of robotic rights.'[17] All of this had been prepared and prototyped in science fiction, which mobilized a version of this liberation narrative from the moment the word 'robot' was introduced. Even if you are unfamiliar with Čapek's 1921 play, you already know the basic plot, because it has been retold time and again in subsequent robot science fiction: The robots – which are described and portrayed in humanoid form – are tireless servants or even slaves that work on behalf of their human masters. They come to realize the injustices of their oppression. They rise up to overthrow their oppressors, realizing their own interests and dignity in the process.

Čapek's play, therefore, not only mobilizes the basic plot elements of a slave narrative, like the *Exodus* story that is recounted in the Jewish and Christian scriptures, but was, at the time of its initial staging, widely recognized as an allegory of the workers' revolutions that were sweeping across the globe during the decade of the 1920s. But these allegorical associations may have worked almost too well. In connecting the plight of his fictional robots to that experienced by real-world human individuals and communities, Čapek not only set the stage for subsequent forms of 'robot liberation' efforts – whether presented in science fiction or science fact – but provided justification by way of what amounts to (or at least risks amounting to) a kind of false equivalency, casting the robot in the role of subjugated human slave or oppressed worker.

The problem with this line of reasoning is that it can be and has been criticized for fostering and facilitating what are questionable associations between previously 'subjugated groups of humans', who have endured centuries of oppression at the hands of those in power, and robots or AI that are often developed by and serve the interests of those same powerful individuals and organizations doing the oppressing. The associations might be rhetorically expedient, tapping into and making connections to the history of previous liberations efforts – social movements that are recognized and celebrated as important progressive socio-political innovations – but they also risk being insensitive and tone deaf to the very real conditions and material circumstances that have contributed to actual situations of oppression and human suffering. And critics on the conservative side of debate have been quick and entirely correct to focus on this issue and point it out, calling the entire escapade of robot rights a first-world problem that might be fun to contemplate as a kind of mental gymnastics but is actually something 'detestable to consider as

---

[17] Sohail Inayatullah and Phil McNally, 'The Rights of Robots: Technology, Culture and Law in the 21st Century' (1988) Futures 123.

a pressing ethical issue in light of real threats and harms imposed on society's most vulnerable'.[18]

Consider, for example, a famous (or, perhaps better stated, 'notorious') event involving the Hanson Robotics humanoid robot Sophia. In October 2017, Sophia was bestowed with 'honorary citizenship' by the Kingdom of Saudi Arabia during the Future Investment Initiative conference that was held in Riyadh.[19] Many experts in the field of AI and robotics, like Joanna Bryson and Yann LeCun, who was at that time director of Facebook AI Research, immediately criticized the spectacle as 'bullshit' and dismissed the entire affair as little more than a PR stunt.[20] Others, such as Robert David Hart, found it demoralizing and degrading: 'In a country where the laws allowing women to drive were only passed last year and where a multitude of oppressive rules are still actively enforced (such as women still requiring a male guardian to make financial and legal decisions), it's simply insulting. Sophia seems to have more rights than half of the humans living in Saudi Arabia'.[21] Statements like 'Saudi Arabia's robot citizen is eroding human rights' (which was the title of Hart's story) are designed to trigger moral outrage, and they do pack an undeniably powerful rhetorical punch. Formulated in this fashion, anyone who truly values and supports human rights cannot but help find the very idea of robot rights something that is detestable, demoralizing, and even dangerous.

But all of this – the entire conflict and dispute – proceeds from an initial error or miscalculation. In both cases, the moral outrage and righteous indignation are the result of an unacknowledged category mistake. The question concerning rights is immediately assumed to entail or involve human rights (so much so that the word 'human' is often not even present but inferred from the mere use and appearance of the term 'rights'), not recognizing that the set of possible rights belonging to one category of entity, like a non-human animal or an artifact, is not necessarily equivalent to nor the same as that enjoyed by another category of entity, like a human being. Rights do not automatically

---

[18] Abeba Birhane and Jelle van Dijk, 'Robot Rights? Let's Talk About Human Welfare Instead' (2020) *AIES '20: Proceedings of the AAAI/ACM Conference on AI, Ethics, and Society* 207.

[19] In the case of Sophia, the entire debate is caused by similar confusion/conflation — the assumption that 'honorary citizenship' must be (and can only be) the same as 'citizenship'. But this is not the case. Sophia is not a legal citizen of the Kingdom of Saudi Arabia; the robot does not hold a Saudi passport and is not required to procure entry visas for traveling across national borders.

[20] Daniel Estrada, 'Sophia and Her Critics' (2018) Medium <https://medium.com/@eripsa/sophia-and-her-critics-5bd22d859b9c> accessed 22 March 2022.

[21] Robert David Hart, 'Saudi Arabia's Robot Citizen is Eroding Human Rights' (2017) Quartz <https://qz.com/1205017/saudi-arabias-robot-citizen-is-eroding-human-rights/> accessed 22 March 2022.

and exclusively mean human rights. A good illustration of how and why this distinction makes a difference can be found with actual efforts involving the extension of legal rights and responsibilities to robots.

In November 2020, the legislature of the Commonwealth of Pennsylvania passed a bill (Senate Bill 1199) that classifies autonomous delivery robots, or what the text of the act calls 'personal delivery devices' (PDD) as pedestrians in order to provide a legal framework for their deployment on city streets and sidewalks.[22] Similar laws have been passed in a number of other jurisdictions,[23] including the Commonwealth of Virginia, which provides the following stipulation: 'a personal delivery device operating on a sidewalk or crosswalk shall have all the rights and responsibilities applicable to a pedestrian under the same circumstance'.[24] In granting this status and the rights and responsibilities that go with it to personal delivery robots, the State Legislature was not seeking to resolve or even address the big questions of robot moral standing or AI/robot personhood. It was simply seeking to provide a legal framework for the integration of the robot into existing legal practices and to align those practices with evolving social needs.

GETTING RIGHTS RIGHT

Whatever rights and obligations might be attributable to a non-human artifact, like a robot – and this is something that is only beginning to be determined and/or codified – they can be and will most certainly be different from the set of what we currently recognize and collect under the umbrella term 'human rights'. One way to begin to get this right, or at least correct the potential for misunderstandings, is to work with more concrete and specific formulations of rights. It is, therefore, often more accurate and attentive to address these matters not in terms of some theoretical abstraction but by way of specific statements that would be (or could be) attributed to a particular entity or group of entities. A good model of this more specific approach is currently being developed and prototyped in social scientific studies.

---

[22] General Assembly of Pennsylvania, (2020) Senate Bill No. 1199 <https://legiscan.com/PA/bill/SB1199/2019> accessed 22 March 2022.

[23] For an overview of recently passed legislation for personal delivery robots, see Cincy M. Grimm and Kristen Thomasen, 'On the Practicalities of Robots in Public Spaces' (2021) We Robot. University of Miami School of Law, September 23–25 <https://werobot2021.com/wp-content/uploads/2021/08/GrimmThomasen_Sidewalk-Robots.pdf> accessed 22 March 2022.

[24] Code of Virginia, Title 46.2, subtitle III, chapter 8, article 12, § 46.2-908.1:1 <https://law.lis.virginia.gov/vacode/title46.2/> accessed 22 March 2022.

In 'Collecting the Public Perception of AI and Robot Rights', Gabriel Lima and colleagues surveyed the opinions of human subjects regarding eleven specific robot rights statements that they explain '1) have been proposed by scholars, 2) have precedents of being granted to non-natural entities, or 3) are directly related to AI and robots.' Their list includes the following eleven items:

1. Right to sue and be sued.
2. Right to hold assets.
3. Right to enter contracts.
4. Right granted under copyright law.
5. Right to freedom of speech.
6. Right to a nationality.
7. Right to choose occupation freely.
8. Right to remuneration.
9. Right to privacy.
10. Right to life.
11. Right against cruel punishment and treatment.[25]

In another study, 'Who Wants to Grant Robots Rights?' Dutch researchers Maartje de Graaf, Frank A. Hindriks, and Koen V. Hindriks 'empirically investigate the general public's attitudes towards granting robots rights.'[26] In designing their survey, these researchers also work with a list of specific rights statements. Each one of these, as they explain, has been derived from stipulations provided in existing documents – specifically the *Universal Declaration of Human Rights*, the *International Covenant on Economic, Social and Cultural Rights* (ICESCR), and the *International Covenant on Civil and Political Rights* (ICCPR) – and then appropriately modified 'to match the (apparent) needs of robots, which inherently differ from biological entities'.[27] Their list consists of twenty concrete rights claims, presented in the form of a series of normative questions:

Should robots have the right to:
    1. make decisions for itself?
    2. select and block services that it provides?
    3. receive fair wages for the work they perform?

---

[25] Gabriel Lima, Changyeon Kim, Seungho Ryu, Chihyung Jeon and Meeyoung Cha, 'Collecting the Public Perception of AI and Robot Rights' (2020) 4 Proceedings of the ACM on Human-Computer Interaction 4–6.

[26] Maartje de Graaf, Frank A. Hindriks and Koen V. Hindriks, 'Who Wants to Grant Robots Rights?' (2021) Frontier in AI and Robotics 1.

[27] Ibid.

4. access energy to recharge themselves?
5. receive updates and maintenance?
6. evolve and develop new capabilities over time?
7. shape and form their own biography?
8. not to be abused either physically or in any other way?
9. be free to leave and return to any country, including its own?
10. a fair trial?
11. have freedom of expression through any media of their choice?
12. collectively pursue and protect robot interests?
13. vote for public officials?
14. be elected for political positions?
15. own property?
16. the pursuit of happiness?
17. copy and duplicate themselves?
18. not to be terminated indefinitely?
19. enter into contracts?
20. store and process data they collect?

The two lists are different, which may just be an indication of the fact that we currently do not yet know what rights, if any, would be needed by or appropriate for non-human entities and artifacts. This is, of course, what both studies set out to identify and define. Additionally, the results obtained from these surveys (and there will undoubtedly be others to follow) demonstrate different levels of support for different rights statements. Some statements, like 'the right against cruel punishment and treatment,' garner wide and significant acceptance. Others, like the 'right to life' or the 'right to vote for public officials' do not. And as Lima et al. insightfully conclude, we can and should expect this to be a moving target as perceptions and levels of acceptance are likely to evolve and change over time.[28] But what is important here is that specifying rights in this way helps to distinguish the set of all possible robot rights from those that would be included in the set of human rights. Even if there are points of contact and similitude, getting specific about differences is an important way to reduce the confusions and apparent disagreements that they produce.

ANALYZING RIGHTS

Even when formulated in terms of a set of specific rights statements concerning a specific robot or a particular class of robots, none of this actually gets us any closer to a workable definition of rights. 'Rights', as Leif Wenar

---

[28] Lima et al. (n 25) 2.

explains, 'are entitlements (not) to perform certain actions, or (not) to be in certain states; or entitlements that others (not) perform certain actions or (not) be in certain states.'[29] Though this characterization is technically accurate, it is not very portable or immediately useful. In order to get a better handle on the concept and the way that rights actually work, we can break it down into more fundamental and functional components. This is where Hohfeld's ground-breaking work can help.

In response to what he perceived to be confusions regarding the (mis)use of the concept of rights, Hohfeld developed a typology that analyzes rights into four basic components or what he called 'incidents': claims, powers, privileges, and immunities.[30] His point was simple and direct: A right, like the right one has over a piece of property, can be defined and operationalized by one or more of these incidents. It can, for instance, be formulated as a claim that an owner has over and against another individual. Or it could be formulated as an exclusive privilege for use and possession that is granted to the owner. Or it could be described as a combination of these.

Hohfeld also recognized that rights are relational. The four types of rights or incidents only make sense to the extent that each one necessitates a correlative duty or obligation that is imposed on at least one other individual. 'The "currency" of rights', as Johannes Marx and Christine Tiefensee explain, 'would not be of much value if rights did not impose any constraints on the actions of others. Rather, for rights to be effective they must be linked with correlated duties'.[31] Hohfeld, therefore, presents and describes the four incidents in terms of rights/duties pairs:

If A has a Privilege, then someone (B) has a No-claim.
If A has a Claim, then someone (B) has a Duty.
If A has a Power, then someone (B) has a Liability.
If A has an Immunity, then someone (B) has a Disability.

This means that a right – like a claim to property ownership – means little or nothing if there is not, at the same time, some other entity who is obligated to respect this claim. 'One's enjoyment of a legally sanctioned benefit necessarily imposes restrictions on another as a means of protecting the first person from potential violations committed by the second'.[32] On this account, a solitary

---

[29] Leif Wenar, 'Rights' (*The Stanford Encyclopedia of Philosophy*, February 2020) <https://plato.stanford.edu/archives/spr2021/entries/rights/> accessed 22 March 2022.
[30] Hohfeld (n 4).
[31] Johannes Marx and Christine Tiefensee, 'Of Animals, Robots and Men' (2015) 40 Historical Social Research 71.
[32] Joshua Gellers, *Rights for Robots: Artificial Intelligence, Animal and Environmental Law* (Routledge 2021) 46.

human being living in isolation and apart from any contact with another human person (which is arguably a hypothetical scenario developed and explored in both fiction and philosophy) would have no need for rights. A claim over a piece of property, for instance, would not make sense or even be necessary, if there were not another who had a correlative duty to respect that claim.

Furthermore, and as a direct consequence of this, rights and their protections can be perceived and formulated either from the side of the possessor of the right (e.g. the power, privilege, claim, or immunity that one is granted or endowed with), which is a 'patient oriented' way of looking at a moral or legal interaction; or from the side of the agent (e.g. what obligations are imposed on the other individual or individuals involved in social interactions with the rights holder), which considers the responsibilities of the producer of a moral or legal action. For these reasons, robot rights are not just about the robots, AIs, and other technological artifacts; they are also and inextricably about us – we who would be obligated by and responsible for responding to whatever claims, powers, privileges, and/or immunities that are possessed by or have been assigned to the robot.

Though Hohfeld supplies a more precise characterization of rights, his analysis does not explain who has or deserves to have a particular right or why. For that, we have to rely on two competing theories – will theory and interest theory. Will theory sets the bar for moral and legal inclusion rather high, requiring that the subject of a particular right be capable of making a claim to it on their own behalf. Understood in this way, a vindication of the rights of robots would need to be spearheaded by the robots themselves, who rise up and demand recognition of their rights. This was, for example, the case with Wollstonecraft's *A Vindication of the Rights of Women*, whereby a particular woman, speaking on behalf of all women, made a case for their inclusion in the community of moral and legal subjects.[33]

Interest theory, by contrast, has a lower bar for inclusion, stipulating that rights may be extended to others irrespective of whether the entity in question can demand it or not. This approach has been successfully modelled and deployed in both animal rights arguments, like that advanced by Non-Human Rights Watch on behalf of Happy the elephant, and the rights of nature cases, where human advocates petition for the protection of others who cannot speak on their own behalf. And this was the case with Thomas Taylor's *A Vindication of the Rights of Brutes*, which argued for the rights of all creatures and had

---

[33] Mary Wollstonecraft, *A Vindication of the Rights of Woman* (first published 1792, Penguin 2004).

been intended as a critical (and sarcastic) rejoinder to Wollstonecraft's proto-feminist manifesto.[34]

The contest between these two theories has been debated for decades but, in the final analysis, has been declared an irresolvable stalemate.[35] What is important for our purposes is not to advocate for or to stake a claim to one over the other but to recognize how and why these two competing frameworks organize different sets of problems, modes of inquiry, and possible outcomes. If, for example, one proceeds on the basis of the will theory, then a petition for robot rights would presumably need to come from the robots (or a representative robot), who would demand recognition on their own behalf. This way of proceeding follows the contours of the robot uprising that has been developed in over a century of science fiction. If, on the contrary, one proceeds on the basis of the interest theory, then we would expect something far less dramatic and even boring. Instead of *Terminator*, *Bladerunner* or *Westworld*, what we get looks more like a legislative hearing on C-SPAN or a courtroom drama, like *Law and Order*. Though the majority of published texts on both sides of the argument tend to operationalize a version of the interest theory, there are moments when the will theory is deployed, typically for dramatic effect and usually in an effort to disarm arguments made by the opposing side.

DIFFERENTIATING RIGHTS

Finally, one of the influential and enduring logical oppositions that organizes how we talk about and operationalize the concept of rights is the distinction between *natural rights* and *legal rights*. Getting this right is crucial for a number of reasons, not the least of which is the fact that 'participants in these discourses shift between moral and legal frames without fully appreciating how they differ in terms of the criteria applied and the conclusions they reach as a result'.[36]

Natural rights, or what have also been called 'moral rights', are grounded in and derived from the essence or nature of the rights holder. Human rights, for instance, are anchored in and justified by 'human nature'. 'All natural rights theories', as Leif Wenar explains, 'fix upon features that humans have by their nature, which make respect for certain rights appropriate. The theories differ over precisely which attributes of humans give rise to rights'.[37] In many reli-

---

[34] Thomas Taylor, *A Vindication of the Rights of Brutes* (first published 1792, Scholars' Facsimiles & Reprints 1966).
[35] Matthew Kramer, N. E. Simmonds and Hillel Steiner, *A Debate Over Rights: Philosophical Enquiries* (OUP 1998).
[36] Gellers (n 32) 28.
[37] Wenar (n 29).

gious traditions, for instance, this is something that is typically explained and justified by appeal to divine or transcendental authority. In Christianity, the 'rights of man' (and the gender-exclusive construction is an unfortunate aspect of this formulation) are justified by the doctrine of the *imagio dei*, the belief that human beings – beginning with the first man, Adam – have been created in the image of God and bestowed by their creator with inalienable rights.[38] In non-religious or secular traditions, the determining factors are 'the same sorts of attributes described in more or less metaphysical or moralized terms: free will, rationality, autonomy, or the ability to regulate one's life in accordance with one's chosen conception of the good life'.[39]

Whether anchored in divine authority or through a list of qualifying metaphysical attributes, natural or moral rights are derived from and justified by the fundamental ontological conditions or psychological properties belonging to the rights holder. This is something that philosopher Mark Coeckelbergh has called 'the properties approach' to deciding questions of moral status.[40] Following this line of reasoning, determining whether a robot (or a class of robots) could be a moral subject or not would be a rather simple and straightforward undertaking that would proceed by way of three basic steps:

1) Having property P is sufficient for moral status S
2) Entity E has property P
3) Entity E has moral status S[41]

In other words, *we* (and who is interpelled by and included in this first-person plural pronoun is not immaterial and is something that will need to be investigated in what follows) first make a determination as to what metaphysical property or set of properties is sufficient for something to have moral status. In effect, we identify the qualifying criteria that would be needed for 'something' to be recognized as 'someone'. We then investigate whether robots or a particular robot, either currently existing or theoretically possible, actually possess that property or set of properties (or not). Finally, and by applying the criteria decided in step one to the artifact identified in step two, we can 'objectively' determine whether the robot in question either can or cannot be a moral subject possessing rights and responsibilities. This way of thinking follows a long-standing tradition in Western philosophy: What something is –

---

[38] For an insightful critical reevaluation of the doctrine, its significance within Christian theology, and its consequences for AI and robots, see Joshua K. Smith's *Robotic Persons* (Westbow 2021).
[39] Wenar (n 29).
[40] Mark Coeckelbergh, *Growing Moral Relations: Critique of Moral Status Ascription* (Palgrave 2012) 14.
[41] Ibid.

e.g. its ontological condition – determines how it ought to be treated – e.g. its moral status. Or as Luciano Floridi accurately describes it: 'what the entity is determines the degree of moral value it enjoys, if any'.[42]

For those situated on the conservative side of the debate, natural rights provide what is an undeniably persuasive argument in opposition to anything approaching the extension of rights to robots and other artifacts. These arguments, despite some variation in the way they are formulated and presented, typically take the following form:

> 'Robots are nothing more than machines, or tools, that were designed to fulfil a specific function. These machines have no interests or desires; they do not make choices or pursue life plans; they do not interpret, interact with and learn about the world. Rather than engaging in autonomous decision-making on the basis of self-developed objectives and interpretations of their surroundings, all they do is execute a preinstalled programme. In short, robots are inanimate automatons, not autonomous agents. As such, they are not even the kind of object which could have a moral status.'[43]

For those situated on the other side of the debate, natural or moral rights provide an equally powerful argumentative strategy. In this case, the main task is to demonstrate how what is assumed to be a mere thing is actually or potentially much more. Robots, it is asserted, are not like other things. They are capable – either right now in their current form or in the future – of possessing the right set of properties that would qualify them to be the kind of thing that is not just an object but a moral subject who can and should have rights. As John-Stewart Gordon explains in an article published in the academic journal *AI & Society*:

> Current robots do not fully meet the morally relevant criteria (rationality, autonomy, understanding, and having social relations) necessary for them to have moral personhood and hence moral rights bestowed on them. However, we should not assume that robots will never meet these criteria; on the contrary, we should provide intelligent robots with moral and legal rights comparable to those that human beings enjoy once they have reached a certain level of functioning. At that point, it will not be up to us; rather, the apparent nature of things will compel us to grant these robots what they deserve, regardless of whether we like it.[44]

This side of the debate, although advocating for a position that is the polar opposite of what is put forth by the conservative faction, proceeds by utilizing

---

[42] Luciano Floridi, *The Ethics of Information* (OUP 2013) 116.
[43] Marx and Tiefensee (n 31) 83.
[44] John-Stewart Gordon, 'Artificial Moral and Legal Personhood' (2021) 26 AI & Society 470.

the same or a substantially similar argumentative strategy supported and legitimated by the properties approach.

These arguments are persuasive and powerful. They tap into fundamental convictions about the nature of life and our commitment to logical consistency and good social outcomes in moral and legal decision-making. The problem – no matter what side of the debate you happen to agree with or occupy – is that they are fragile. Since, on the one hand, everything depends on metaphysical properties and the ability to be certain (or at least convinced) about the actual presence or absence of these properties, all that is needed to undermine the argument is to pull the rug out from underneath the metaphysical scaffolding, either by pointing out how a property like *consciousness* not only lacks univocal definition but varies across different contexts of use[45] or capitalizing on the epistemological difficulties of positively detecting the presence or absence of these qualities as they exist (or not) in the mind of another.[46] Natural rights, therefore, provide what is quite possibly the strongest claim that could be made either against or in favour of the rights of robots and the moral/legal status of AI, but are also vulnerable and fragile, because they are built on a prior set of metaphysical beliefs and commitments that are flimsy to begin with and easily toppled.

Legal rights, by contrast, are 'rights which exist under the rules of legal systems or by virtue of decisions of suitably authoritative bodies within them'.[47] According to this formulation, rights are not justified by and derived from the essential nature of the rights holder and propped up by an appeal to metaphysical properties. They are conventional rules or socially constructed stipulations. As Jacob Turner explains, 'rights are collective fictions, or as Harari calls them "myths." Their form can be shaped to any given context. Certainly, some rights are treated as more valuable than others, and belief in them may be more widely shared, but there is no set quota of rights which prevents new ones from being created and old ones from falling into abeyance'.[48] This is both good news and bad news.

First the good news. Unlike natural rights, legal rights do not need to engage in fanciful metaphysical speculations about the essential nature of things

---

[45] On the problem of defining consciousness, see Max Velman, *Understanding Consciousness* (Routledge 2000).

[46] This is what philosophers call 'the problem of other minds'. See Paul Churchland, *Matter and Consciousness* (MIT Press 1999).

[47] Kenneth Campbell, 'Legal Rights' (The Stanford Encyclopedia of Philosophy, November 2017) <https://plato.stanford.edu/entries/legal-rights/> accessed 22 March 2022.

[48] Jacob Turner, *Robot Rules: Regulating Artificial Intelligence* (Palgrave 2019) 135–136.

nor appeal to supernatural authorities, the existence of which can always be doubted or questioned. But – and here's the bad news – that means that legal rights are a matter of human-all-too-human decision-making and that the assignment, distribution, and protections of rights are ultimately a matter of finite exercises of terrestrial power. Where natural rights are anchored in eternal metaphysical truths that can be discussed and debated by theologians and metaphysicians, legal rights are legitimated by earthly exercises of specific socio-political power.

For these reasons, legal justifications for rights are considered to be 'weaker'. Because they are ultimately anchored in and legitimated by conventional agreement, legal rights are not only alterable (e.g. able to be modified and repealed) but relative, meaning that they exhibit significant variability across different human communities distributed in time and space. Saying this, is not, as Turner is quick to point out, a critique; it is merely descriptive. 'Describing rights as fictions or constructs is by no means pejorative; when used in this context, it does not entail duplicity or error. It simply means that they are malleable and can be shaped according to new circumstances.'[49] And technological innovations, like robots, AI, and other seemingly intelligent artifacts, certainly provide ample opportunities and challenges for 'new circumstances.'

To summarize: The terms, conditions, and consequences of the robot rights debate differs based on what kind of rights are operationalized and complicated by the fact that the one kind of right is often confused with, or at least not sufficiently distinguished from, the other. Natural rights arguments – on both sides of the conflict – tend to advance strong and determinative declarations about the rights of others, but they often get bogged down in arguments about complicated and ultimately irresolvable metaphysical matters, like consciousness, free-will, or autonomy. Legal rights arguments, by contrast, avoid the *cul de sac* of metaphysical speculation, but then issue declarations that are context dependent, conditional, and even relativistic. These debates typically focus on social outcomes and quibble about social costs and benefits.

ALTERNATIVES AND THINKING OTHERWISE

Given these complications and potential problems, it is reasonable to inquire whether applygint he concept of rights is even the right way to go about organizing and conducting these debates in the first place. As Slavoj Žižek reminds us, there are not only true and false solutions, there are also wrong questions, e.g. modes of inquiry that get in the way of and are already a potential barrier to

---

[49] Ibid.

developing a solution.[50] Even though both sides in the debate already mobilize and describe their positions in terms of rights, it may be the case that framing the dispute in this way is already misguided or inadequately formulated.

Rights are about power. Decisions and distributions regarding rights are organized in terms of a binary logic that makes a distinction between those others *who* count as another moral or legal subject and *what* remains a mere object or thing that does not. As Roberto Esposito, who arguably wrote the book on the subject explains: 'If there is one assumption that seems to have organized human experience from its very beginnings it is that of a division between persons and things. No other principle is so deeply rooted in our perception and in our moral conscience as the conviction that we are not things – because things are the opposite of persons'.[51]

Maintaining these existing categories and their boundaries (which were, as Esposito points out, initially codified and instituted in the *Institutes* of the Roman jurist Gaius) is clearly about policing this fundamental decision and enforcing this fundamental ontological dichotomy. But extending rights to those others that have been typically excluded is no less a matter of power and privilege. As the environmental ethicist Thomas Birch recognized: 'The nub of the problem with granting or extending rights to others, a problem which becomes pronounced when nature is the intended beneficiary, is that it presupposes the existence and the maintenance of a position of power from which to do the granting. Granting rights to nature requires bringing nature into our human system of legal and moral rights, and this is still a (homocentric) system of hierarchy and domination'.[52] The extension of rights to previously excluded things, although appearing to be altruistic and open to the challenges presented to us in the face of others and other forms of otherness, can only proceed on the basis of decisions instituted from a position of power that is (ironically) already the source of the exclusions that would be challenged.

This is something Mary Wollstonecraft understood and skilfully managed in the process of crafting her *A Vindication of the Rights of Women*. In order to be effective – in order to have the chance of changing anything – her argument needed to be addressed to and speak the language of those *men* who were already in a position of power, had the privilege to make a change, and occupied this position precisely because of the decisive act of exclusion that was to be contested. In effect, and contrary to the famous adage issued by Audre Lorde, the vindication of the rights of excluded others, if it is to be understand-

---

[50] Slavoj Žižek, 'Philosophy, the "Unknown Knowns", and the Public Use of Reason' (2006) 25 Topoi 137.

[51] Roberto Esposito, *Persons and Things* (Zakiya Hanafi tr, Polity 2015) 1.

[52] Thomas Birch, 'The Incarnation of Wilderness: Wildness Areas as Prisons' in Max Oelschlaeger (ed.) *Postmodern Environmental Ethics* (SUNY Press 1995) 39.

ably articulated and successful, needs to (and cannot help but) use the master's tools to tear down the master's house.[53]

The robot rights debate confronts a similar set of challenges. Advocates find themselves in the position of agitating for the inclusion of robots – either in general or in terms of some specific robotic device or AI system – in the community of moral subjects by appealing to and utilizing the very anthropocentric concepts and terminology that had been used to make and justify these exclusions in the first place. The other side in the dispute, by contrast, seems to have an easier – or at least a less burdensome – task. They only need to defend what is already recognized as SOP (standard operating procedure), using the existing privileges and power structures to support more of the same. But because the debate is organized by and conducted in terms of rights expansion (or not), it is we – human beings – who are in the position of power either to decide to grant or to deny rights claims to robots, AI, and other technological artifacts. Whether the effort is situated on the side of those who argue in favour of maintaining the status quo or on the other side, which would seek a vindication of the rights of robots, it is *we* who have granted to ourselves the right to decide who (or what) can and/or should have rights. There are at least two fundamental problems here.

First, who is included in this first-person plural pronoun 'we'? Who has been granted the privilege to participate in and contribute to these decisions, and who or what has been marginalized and excluded from these very determinations? Since these decisions presumably matter for all of us, insofar as they affect the very shape and configuration of our social milieu, everyone it seems should have an equal stake in the debate and a seat at the table. But not everyone is involved or involved to the same degree. Some people are – as George Orwell cleverly described it – more equal than others.[54] If one, for example, tracks-back to locate where the people, institutions, and venues involved in these conversations and debates are situated, it is hard to deny the charge that these disputes are, like so many others, 'first world problems', or at least something that has been concentrated in the region of the global north.

There are exceptions, but these exceptions often prove the rule. That is, their 'exceptional' status is a testament to the fact that the vast majority of work mobilized on the question of robot rights comes from individuals and organizations which are already situated in geopolitical conditions and circumstances that, due to these very conditions, already enjoy certain privileges and opportunities not shared by others. The granting or denying of rights to others,

---

[53] Audre Lorde, *Sister Outsider: Essays and Speeches* (The Crossing Press 1984) 110.
[54] George Orwell, *Animal Farm* (Random House 1993).

as Birch insightfully points out, assumes a privileged position of power from which to do this granting or denying. This is not optional or accidental. The very concept of rights entails this exigency, and both sides in the debate cannot help but work within this space and conduct their operations according to these rules. Whether rights come to be denied or extended to robots, AI, and other artifacts, is still part and parcel of what Birch calls 'imperial power mongering'. Even if efforts to debate this matter open up the privilege of anthropocentric moral thinking to new and unheard-of opportunities, it is still something that is controlled and decided by human beings – or more accurately stated some human beings. We pull the strings and are responsible for the decisions.

Second, rights is a Western philosophical concept. Even if it is presented (especially when formulated in terms of moral rights) as a kind of universal idea, it remains a specific form of situated knowledge. Stating this is not a moral judgment. Recognizing the specific situation and legacy of rights does not mean that this is 'wrong'. It is only an acknowledgement of the fact that the concept of rights comes from somewhere and brings with it expectations and assumptions that are context specific. By comparison, there are other ways to arrange and organize inquiries about the status of others – ways that do not engage with the same kinds of assumptions. These alternatives are not necessarily 'better'; they are just different and allow for other ways of seeing and responding to the opportunities and challenges of others.

Indigenous traditions (in the plural), for instance, often frame these matters not in the language of rights – which are a kind of individual possession that is to be granted or denied on the authority of some established position of power – but in terms of kinship relations. 'We believe', Jason Edward Lewis writes in the introduction to the collaboratively written essay *Making Kin with the Machines*, 'that Indigenous epistemologies are much better at respectfully accommodating the non-human. We retain a sense of community that is articulated through complex kin networks anchored in specific territories, genealogies, and protocols. Ultimately, our goal is that we, as a species, figure out how to treat these new non-human kin respectfully and reciprocally – and not as mere tools, or worse, slaves to their creators'.[55] Formulated in this way, 'making kin' does not get involved in the same power dynamics as the granting of rights. There are still expressions of power in decisions regarding kinship, but the arrangement and distribution of power is formulated in ways that are different from what has been available in and by the concept of rights. In this way, making kin with the machines – which is not one way to proceed

---

[55] Jason Edward Lewis, Noelani Arista, Archer Pechawis and Suzanne Kite, 'Making Kin with the Machines' (2018) Journal of Design and Science <https://doi.org/10.21428/bfafd97b> accessed 20 March 2022.

but names a plurality of different ways of proceeding – will look remarkably different from what has been pursued in the debates about the rights (or not) of robots.

Something similar (although understandably not the same) is available in Eastern (and it should be noted that 'Eastern' is a Western/European concept used to designate what is non-Western) religious and philosophical traditions like Confucianism, where the focal point is, according to an argument developed by Tae Wan Kim, not *rights* but *rites*:

> The modern concept of an individual right is a human artifact, one especially well-developed in Western societies. I maintain that granting rights is not the only proper way to treat the moral status of robots. Furthermore, I suggest it is time to explore an alternative path, one drawing upon Confucianism and its concept of a moral agent as a rites-bearer, not as a rights-bearer. I submit that this Confucian alternative is superior to the robot rights perspective, especially given that the concept of rights is inherently adversarial and that potential conflict between humans and robots is worrisome.[56]

Kim's argument turns on the clever substitution of the English word 'rites' for 'rights'. Whereas 'rights' refers to an individual entitlement or possession that can be bestowed or denied by some authority, 'rites' names a social performance that determines status by way of communal participation and interaction. Where 'robot rights' institutes and takes place as an adversarial conflict between individuals, 'robot rites' focuses attention on 'the social rites that define and sustain social interactions.'[57]

There are also alternatives situated in and proceeding from the Western philosophical tradition, mainly through work that is, in one way or another, situated in/at the margins. Mark Coeckelbergh, who wrote one of the first critical investigations of the subject, in an essay aptly titled 'Robot Rights?' (with a question mark), has developed a 'social relational ethics' that provides for opportunities similar to those offered by way of Confucian ethics, but rooted in and informed by innovations in environmental philosophy.[58] For Coeckelbergh the operative question is not directed to rights, which are often seen as an inalienable possession of an entity, but concerns 'moral status ascription', which

---

[56] Tae Wan Kim, 'Should Robots have Rights or Rites? A Confucian Cross-Cultural Exploration to Robot Ethics' (2020) SSRN <https:// ssrn .com/ abstract = 3753070> accessed 22 March 2022.

[57] Ruiping Fan, *Reconstructionist Confucianism: Rethinking Morality after the West* (Springer 2010) xii.

[58] Mark Coeckelbergh, 'Robot Rights? Towards a Social-Relational Justification of Moral Consideration' (2010) 12 Ethics and Information Technology 209.

is 'not about the entity but about us and about the relation between us and the entity'.[59]

This approach flips the script on the usual method for deciding questions regarding moral status. 'There is not "first" the individual and then society; according to this view, it is rather the other way around. "First" there is the community; only in this context does it make sense to talk about the obligations we have toward one another and perhaps toward non-humans.'[60] Janina Loh has developed a similar kind of relational alternative by drawing on the work of feminist STS scholars Karen Barad and Lucy Suchman. For Loh, Barad's 'relational ontology' and Suchman's concept of interference, which 'stands for a non-binary, non-linear and yet relational form for generating otherness', provide an alternative formulation of ethics 'in which no singular autarkic agents exist, but these are merely recognized within their mutual entanglements'.[61]

For my part, I have advocated for and advanced a method of *thinking otherwise* that is indebted to and builds upon the work of the Jewish philosopher, Emmanuel Levinas.[62] For Levinas, the principal moral gesture is not the conferring or extending of rights to others as a kind of benevolent gesture or even an act of compassion. This is, on the Levinasian account, already a violent expression of power that violates the alterity of the other by turning them into an alter-ego or mirror image of the self. Instead, ethics consists in exposure to the irreducible challenges of the Other who supervenes before me in such a way that always and already places me and my assumed privilege in question. Levinasian philosophy, therefore, deliberately interrupts and resists the imposition of power that Birch finds operative in all forms of rights discourse. Whereas efforts to extend or withhold the protections of rights to others, like robots, play by the existing rules of the game; Levinas and others who follow his lead,[63] change the game, providing ways to question the assumptions and consequences involved in this very exercise of power over others.

---

[59] Coeckelbergh (n 40) 25.
[60] Ibid 27.
[61] Janina Loh, 'Ascribing Rights to Robots as Potential Moral Patients' in John-Stewart Gordon (ed.) *Smart Technologies and Fundamental Rights* (Brill 2021) 119.
[62] David J. Gunkel, *Thinking Otherwise: Philosophy, Communication, Technology* (Purdue UP 2007); David J. Gunkel, *The Machine Question: Critical Perspectives on AI, Robots and Ethics* (MIT Press 2012); David J. Gunkel, *Robot Rights* (MIT Press 2018).
[63] See, for example, Silvia Benso, *The Face of Things: A Different Side of Ethics* (SUNY Press 2000) and Matthew Calarco, *Zoographies: The Question of the Animal from Heidegger to Derrida* (Columbia UP 2008).

CONCLUSION

Taking note of these alternatives does mean that we should or even cannot avoid talking in terms of rights. Whether we agree with it or not, rights is the way the debate has been already been framed and organized, and rights is the method by which we – Western traditions in moral philosophy and law – typically conduct and seek to resolve these discussions and debates. If we decided to pursue the question of rights, it is not because this way of thinking is already acknowledged as right and natural, e.g. the only way to organize and arrange for these discussions. Instead, if we continue talking in terms of rights, it is because that is how the debate has been organized and ordered, and it is only by addressing rights that there is a chance of responding to and intervening in the space of the existing debates and controversies. But, at the same time that the question concerning rights is to be pursued, it will also be necessary to recall that this is not the only or even the best way to proceed and that the concept of rights (for better or worse) already commits the analysis to a set of (potentially problematic) assumptions that will need to be critically investigated and questioned. Whether robots have rights might be the way the inquiry has been formulated and organized, but it is possible that this is already the wrong question and an obstacle to its own solution.

5. Who is the subject of (non) human rights?

Alexis Alvarez-Nakagawa

In an essay written in 2004, Jacques Rancière wondered who the subject of human rights was, revisiting an old question formulated by Marx and Burke in light of the French Declaration of the Rights of Man and the Citizen.[1] Examining different answers to this question, Rancière contended that the subject of human rights was undefined and was only determinable in political disputes. He argued that human rights do not belong to a definite subject, that there is no 'Man' in the rights of Man – nor need for such a thing – and that the strength of human rights lies precisely in their openness to all those who do not yet enjoy them. Escaping the pessimism resulting from the realpolitik of war – the article was a belated reaction to the widespread concerns about the future of human rights after the US 'war on terror' – Rancière advocated for a non-essentialist and expansionist politics of human rights.

Now, one could say that since the essay's publication, certain developments have made Rancière's answer to the question of the subject prescient, as his expansionist politics is attuned to the proliferation of rights and subjecthood we are witnessing today. Over the last few years, the subject of rights has splintered and candidates for legal recognition have multiplied at an incredible pace, even beyond the human sphere. Animals, rivers, mountains, rainforests, and synthetic and artificial beings such as AI, machines and robots have been successfully claiming legal recognition and rights. Some have seen this as a 'revolution' and a way out of the anthropocentrism and the ills of Western law that would have underwritten the exploitation of non-humans.[2] Despite this alleged 'radicality' of non-human rights having been put into question with sound arguments, it is clear that these developments have opened to scrutiny the very premise on which subjects come to be recognized in law and that what seemed to be a contradiction in terms – extending human rights to non-humans

---

[1] Jacques Rancière, 'Who is the Subject of the Rights of Man?' (2004) 103 The South Atlantic Quarterly 297.

[2] See David R. Boyd, *The Rights of Nature. A Legal Revolution that Could Save the World* (ECW Press 2017).

– has yielded to the irresistible power of legalizing the world through the rhetoric of rights and subjectification.[3]

Returning to Rancière's question almost twenty years on, this chapter wonders who is the subject of rights now that non-humans are enjoying a different legal status. While some scholars have started to consider Rancière's work as a promising scaffold to encompass and mobilize the subjectification of non-humans in the context of a 'pluralization of ontologies' or 'cosmopolitics', I question whether this approach is the best for such an endeavour.[4] After presenting the outlines of an archaeological/genealogical account of the subject of rights and its kindred notion, the legal person, I briefly sketch out the transition from human to non-human rights that has prompted this chapter and brought back to the fore the question concerning the subject of rights.[5] In contrast to over-optimistic views, I show that extending subjectivity to non-humans might end up reproducing and reinforcing the problems that non-human rights have purportedly come to sort out. Moreover, I demonstrate that taking Rancière's ideas to the letter in this context encourages a politics of rights that is unquestionably expansive but is also homogenizing and contrary to the possibility of setting and composing a 'multiplicity of worlds'.[6]

FROM PERSONS TO SUBJECTS

Asking 'who is the subject of human rights' might seem strange as, in principle, it should lead to a tautological answer: the subject of human rights is the human being. But Rancière's question is set precisely in a constellation of discussions that have interrogated the obviousness of this assertion. While Rancière finds his answer to the question of the subject in contemporary debates about human rights – which I revisit later in this chapter – this section attempts to present the main aspects of a broader archaeological investigation that describes the emergence and transformation of the category of subject-

---

[3] Costas Douzinas, *The End of Human Rights* (Hart 2000) 243–244.

[4] See Philippe Descola, 'Cosmopolitics as Ontological Pluralism' (2019) 1 The Otherwise 29; Marisol de La Cadena, *Earth Beings. Ecologies of Practice Across Andean Worlds* (Duke University Press 2015).

[5] This archaeological/genealogical inquiry refers to Michel Foucault's philosophical/historical method(s). See, among others, Michel Foucault's *The Archaeology of Knowledge and the Discourse on Language* (A. Sheridan tr, Pantheon Books 1972) and "Nietzsche, Genealogy, History" in *Language, Counter-Memory, Practice. Selected Essays and Interviews* (D. Bouchard ed, D. Bouchard & S. Simon tr, Cornell UP, 1977). This chapter explores just the highlights of a broader genealogical project on the subject of rights. For a recent archaeological enquiry on the subject that yielded interesting results, see Alain de Libera, *L'invención du sujet moderne* (Vrin 2015).

[6] Descola (n 4) 29.

hood. This way of proceeding will help us question some of Rancière's ideas and recalibrate his political take on the subject of rights, considering this figure's historicity.

The genealogical account indicates that the subject can only be understood in light of the notion of the 'person'. As Alain De Libera pointed out, the main challenge for an 'archaeology of the subject' is to show the articulation of these categories and other related concepts.[7] The history of how the person and the subject became associated, and the bond between these two entwined in turn with various notions such as the 'hu(man)', the 'self' (*ego*), the 'individual', the 'author/agent', and the 'citizen', cannot be told in a few lines. Here I merely attempt to describe some salient features of this history as they shed light on the characteristics of these different figures at the centre of human rights, Western law, and now, non-human rights.

Modern law has come to assimilate the subject of rights and the legal person. Today they are the vehicle through which the law endows people and other entities with entitlements and duties, competencies and liabilities. They are law's centre of attribution and the support of legal relations. The emerging discourse of non-human rights, for example, indistinctively extends legal personhood or subjecthood to non-humans and speaks of them as either legal persons or subjects of rights. The outcome is the same in either case: to recognize non-human entities as having the capacity to hold rights and duties. Nonetheless, the notion of person and subject developed in parallel and, only at times, in intertwined paths, meaning that the current overlapping is the result of a long and contingent historical trajectory.

As is well known, the idea of the person has its origins in the Greek *prosopon*, the theatrical mask used by actors on stage. The person was a double, and, in a way, as Marcel Mauss put it in one of the first essays written on the matter, an artificial character, 'a strange to the self (*moi*)'.[8] By an easy transposition, the person later adopted the meaning of the role played by the actor in the stage performance, and from there, it came to denote the role of the individual in society. But, at the time, it did not designate the psychological individual himself or the human being.[9] We should notice the association of theatre with

---

[7] De Libera (n 5) 112.

[8] Marcel Mauss, 'A Category of the Human Mind: The Notion of Person, the Notion of Self' in Michael Carrithers, Steven Collins and Steven Lukes (eds) *The Category of the Person* (CUP 1985) 17.

[9] Yan Thomas 'The Subject of Right, the Person, Nature: Remarks on the Current Criticism of the Legal Subject' in *Legal Artifices: Ten Essays on Roman Law in the Present Tense* (Chantal Schütz and Anton Schütz tr, Edinburgh UP 2021) 132. This has been the position of most scholars. However, some have considered that there was a close relationship between the idea of person and man, as this notion arises as

religiosity and rituality in the Greco-Roman world. The fact that in Rome the first masks were funerary masks, a representation and *imago* of the dead ancestors (*imago maiorum*), is testimony to this original connection.[10] Therefore, together with the sense of artificiality and of a superimposed image, the mask also represented, in some religious and ritual contexts, the innermost nature of the individual – her ties with the family, the dead ancestors, and the divine. The person was either the 'stranger' and/or the 'inner self'. Human beings used different masks in their lives, inhabiting a threshold where strangeness and sameness were not entirely distinguishable.[11]

The Greek term *prosopon* was later translated into Latin as *persona*. But Romans also shifted the function of the mask from theatre and funerary rites to the legal stage. The three main institutions of Roman law were *personas*, *res* (things) and *actiones* (remedies). As Gaius explained, all person's actions in law are about things, so '*omne outem ius, quo utimur, vel ad personas pertinet, vel ad res, vel ad actiones*'.[12] Even if *persona* – also called *caput* – in some sources designated all human beings, in a strict sense, it did not coincide with *homo*. On the one hand, *universitas* and other collective entities could attain legal personhood. On the other, only some humans enjoyed full legal personhood, and this occurred when they held 'three statuses': freedom, citizenship and independence (*status libertatis, status civitatis, status familiae*).[13] In this regard, slaves were considered *res* for most matters and were owned by their masters. *Latini* and *peregrini*, that is, those who lived within Roman borders but were not citizens, were considered persons only in some legal circumstances. Women were under the husband's *manus* (*uxor in manu*), and children were under the *patria potestas* (*filius in potestate*) and were not independent. The only full person in law was the *paterfamilias* as he was a free citizen independent from anyone else. As personhood resulted from the three statuses, nobody enjoyed it throughout their life. Legal personhood was attained but could be lost by losing one of the statuses (*capitis diminutio*).[14]

---

a hypostasis of the social role human beings have in society. See José María Ribas Alba, *Persona. Desde el derecho romana a la teología* (Comares 2012).

[10] Ribas Alba (n 9).

[11] Notions containing opposite meanings are not strange to Greeks and Romans, as Derrida has shown with the *Pharmakon*, which is both poison and medicine. See 'Plato's Pharmacy' in *Dissemination* (Barbara Johnson tr, University of Chicago Press 1981) 61.

[12] 'All our law relates either to persons, things or actions'. T. Lambert Mears (ed tr) *The Institutes of Gaius and Justinian* (The Lawbook Exchange 2005) G.1.8. 259.

[13] About the Roman 'statuses' see Max Kaser, *Roman Private Law* (Rolf Dannenbring tr, 4th edn, University of South Africa 1984) 78.

[14] Ibid.

The person's relevance should not lead us to think 'things' were unimportant for Romans. 'Persons' and 'things' were relational categories in Roman law.[15] Things were also significant because rights and claims were derived from them. As Michel Villey says, the law was born 'out of things' – and not 'out of persons'.[16] Before subjective rights emerged in the Middle Ages, rights were not freedoms, powers, or faculties but rather a thing: a *res justa*. For Roman jurists justice was to 'give to each his own' (*ius suum cuique tribuere*), to reinstate things back to their natural order (*status quo*). In this conception of justice, rights do not fall from above; they do not derive from a sovereign, God, nor are they embedded in the laws. They are given to a person by virtue of a relationship.[17]

That is why the initial meaning of *res* was '*causa*', the issue or matter of a legal dispute.[18] *Res* indicated both people and things (including slaves, animals, and household objects) which were the object (*causa*) of disputes – here is the reason for the semantic assimilation of *res* and things. Interestingly, the term that later designated an ontological object initially referred to a relationship that held legal actors together.[19] *Res* as a legal concept meaning 'actual' things emerged to combine the elements of the *patrimonium*. That is why, in parallel, *persona* originally referred to the unity of an estate, naming those who held it (the *pater*, but in some cases, sons and other household members).[20] The Roman category of *res* was quite an innovation at the time, as animals, slaves and goods were usually disregarded and left out of the pale of ancient laws.

Considering patrimonial things as *res*, Roman law inaugurated one of the most distinct mechanisms of Western legality: inclusion through exclusion. 'Thinghood' allowed the incorporation of slaves, animals, and goods into the law within a unique category that meant their subjection to persons and their exclusion from the faculties and protections they had. The patrimony was considered a collective *corpus* under the absolute power of the *pater*. But persons also worked in a similar way: personalization was simply the reverse of reification. As Roberto Esposito highlighted, personhood allowed making

---

[15] In this way, the category of the thing precedes its counterpart – the person – in Western law. See Alain Pottage, 'Persons and Things: An Ethnographic Analogy' (2001) 30 Economy and Society 112.

[16] See Michel Villey, *Le droit et les droits de l'homme* (2nd ed., PUF 1990).

[17] Ibid.

[18] See Yan Thomas 'Res, chose et patrimonie: note sure le rapport sujet-objet en droit romain' (1980) Archives de la philosophie du droit 413.

[19] Alain Pottage, 'Introduction: The Fabrication of Persons and Things' in Alain Pottage and Martha Mundy (eds) *Law, Anthropology, and the Constitution of the Social. Making Persons and Things* (CUP 2004) 20.

[20] Thomas (n 9) 128.

several hierarchical distinctions between humans – thus, including but also excluding them from legal recognition, and exposing them to the power of someone else. Moreover, as a category including those who enjoyed certain rights and protections, personhood was defined only by contrast with those who were excluded from it. In other words, personhood was only possible by depersonalizing or reifying others, pushing them into the space of thinghood and below the person.[21]

In summary, for Romans, *persona* was an artefact that referred to different roles or statuses attached to social functions. As Yan Thomas put it: 'the person is double; it is both itself, and the function the law imposes upon it'.[22] Sometimes the substrata of this legal form were single human beings, other times a plurality of them. On some occasions, things were behind the mask of persons. The legal person was independent of the entities ascribed to it. In this regard, 'one might say that the institutional force of Roman law consisted of its capacity to capture "real" persons and things in these conventional artefacts'.[23]

Only with Stoicism did the notion of *persona* gradually adopt another meaning, closer to the modern conception of the individual human being.[24] It was the infusion of Christian doctrine, however, which blended this artificial person with its somatic substratum to compose a 'whole' new form: the human person. In the discussion of different Christian dogmas (in particular, the mysteries of the Trinity and the dual nature of Christ), the Christian literature – particularly in the work of Tertullian – started using the term *persona* to refer to God – the 'three persons' of God who is nevertheless a single undivided substance (an 'individual').[25] In this process, the term adopted a particular meaning, which Boethius encapsulates well in his well-known definition: '*naturae rationabilis individua substantia*'.[26] This definition of the person as an 'individual substance of a rational nature' was taken up later by Thomas Aquinas,[27] who argued that human persons are a composite of 'form' and 'matter' (intellective soul and body).[28] These ideas predominated in all

---

[21] Roberto Esposito, 'The Dispositif of the Person' (2012) 8(1) *Law, Culture and the Humanities* 17, 22–24.
[22] Thomas (n 9) 126.
[23] See Pottage (n 19) 26.
[24] Francesco Viola, 'Lo statuto Giuridico della persona in prospettiva storica' in G. Pansini, *Studi in memoria di Italo Mancini* (ESI 1999) 628.
[25] See Ribas Alba (n 9) 304.
[26] See Boethius, 'A Treatise Against Eutyches and Nestorius', in *The Theological Tractates* (H. F. Stewart and E. K. Rand tr, Heinemann 1918) 85.
[27] Thomas Aquinas, *The Summa Theologica* (Fathers of the English Dominican Province tr, Willian Benton 1923) Question 29.
[28] Ibid Questions 75–89.

subsequent theological thinking, having an enormous influence on philosophy as well.

Theological writings articulate persons and humans through the idea of the rational/intellective soul.[29] The mystery of the Incarnation – the two natures (divine and human) of Christ, who, nevertheless, is, like God, undivided – is projected to all human beings whose life is now doubly determined by the spiritual (form) and the physical (matter). This dualism of soul and body – which indubitably has platonic roots – sets a hierarchic ordering in which the former subordinates the latter, that is, where the soul becomes the master of the body.[30] Even if Christian theologians do not totally disregard the body – this is, after all, a creation of God – it represents for them the lower instincts (the animal part of the human being), which, as such, should be subjected to the moral and rational guide of the soul.[31] As Augustine says: '*secundum solam mentem imago Dei dicitur, una persona est*'.[32] Acting as the rational and individual aspect of each human being, the soul provides the natural conduit for the Divine Person. From then on, humans reproduced the person/thing split in themselves: they become persons as bearers of an immortal soul (reason), but things as regards their physical bodies. The Christian doctrine cuts the human in two: a person of soul and reason of divine nature inhabiting an animal and material body. This dual nature of human beings paradoxically constitutes their whole, their individuality.

This assimilation in theological writings led, in turn, to some confusion about the meaning of the person in legal discourse. Thus, medieval jurists, moving away from Roman sources, began distinguishing between two types of persons. On the one hand, 'true' or 'physical persons' (human beings), and, on the other, 'fictitious persons' (*personae fictae*) for the moral personality of religious or political communities. It is well known that Pope Innocent IV first formulated the idea of a fictitious person in the 13th century. Therefore, while some persons were considered true as singular beings, others were 'representative' as mere legal abstractions. It was through the category of representation that the medieval glossators and commentators managed to abstain from unifying under the common label of the person such heterogenous contents

---

[29] Following Aristotle, theological writings usually distinguished three types of soul: vegetative (found in plants), sensitive (proper to animals) and intellective/rational (only found in humans).

[30] Esposito (21) 22.

[31] Ibid 21.

[32] 'The image of God […] according to the mind [or soul] alone, is one person'. See Augustine, *On the Trinity* (Gareth B. Matthews ed, Stephen McKenna tr, CUP 2002) Book XV, Chapter 7, 11.

as things and people.[33] It was equally thanks to representation that they tried, now moving in the opposite direction, to forge a link between elements that they thought naturally disjointed.[34] If, for Roman law, things were extensions of persons, for medieval jurists, things and persons were opposites. This bifurcation between real and fictitious persons permitted moving from the Roman notion of person as role – that is, of the person as an artificial double applicable to people and things – to the idea that the actual person is only coextensive with the human being.

Medieval discourse then produces a split in the human being (soul/reason – body/matter) and in the person (natural – artificial). Modernity would inherit and secularize this double split. In this regard, Descartes reproduced the division between soul and body in the modern philosophical discourse. The French philosopher contended that man comprises a soul or thinking substance (*res cogitans*) and a body (*res extensa*). For him, the nature of the soul and the body is diverse and, in a certain sense, opposed.[35] While the body is perishable, the soul is immortal. Descartes conceived the body as a machine – the soul was 'a ghost in the machine', to borrow Ryle's felicitous expression[36] – governed by mechanical laws, which do not affect the soul.[37] The anthropological dualism that Descartes secularized in metaphysical thinking was to be transferred by English liberalism to the political terrain. The split between person and body was at the foundation of the liberal theory of the individual. For liberals, the person is alienated from its biological substratum – its body – possessing it as if it were an object.[38] The possibility of appropriating other objects and private property is generally based on this ownership of one's own body.[39] As the individual is the proprietor of his body and the capacities derived from it, he owes nothing to society – which is thenceforth atomized and becomes a series of relations between owners. Macpherson described this liberal understanding of personhood as a 'possessive individualism', showing how this conception

---

[33] Thomas (n 9) 128–129.
[34] Thomas (n 9) 130.
[35] René Descartes, *Meditations on First Philosophy* (John Cottingham ed tr, CUP 2013) Meditations 1, 2 and 6.
[36] See Gilbert Ryle, *The Concept of the Mind* (Hutchinson and Co. 2009) 40.
[37] It is interesting to note that for Descartes, men share their bodily nature with animals but not their spiritual life. Thus, animals would be bodies or machines without souls or thinking automats.
[38] As Thomas (n 9) 121 cleverly notes, by this means, the human being objectifies itself; liberalism transforms the relation to oneself into a relation between a person and a thing.
[39] John Locke, *Two Treatises of Government* (Peter Laslett ed, CUP 1988), v, 27.

forms the basis of Hobbes, Locke and other liberal thinkers' ideas.[40] In Locke, in particular, a whole theory of individual personhood is constructed on the property of the body. For Locke, just as human beings own their bodies, so too do they own their acts. Since men own their acts, these are imputable to them. It is this 'imputability' of past and present acts that institutes the person as a unit of consciousness in time, a self, a personal identity.[41] For liberal theory, the excision of the person from the body institutes the unity of the individual. The modern liberal individual is born out of a fundamental separation and an act of self-reification.

We have seen above that when theologians began to assimilate persons and human beings, they also started distinguishing between natural and artificial persons. This distinction passed to modern political theory. This is perhaps best seen in Hobbes, who continues the scholastic distinction between 'natural' and 'artificial' persons by taking these categories from theological to political debates. While, for Hobbes, natural persons represent themselves through their own words and actions, artificial persons represent the words and actions of other subjects or non-human entities. Thereby, while Hobbes reiterates the possibility of dissociating the notion of the person from the human being through an 'artifice', he simultaneously reaffirms the humanity of the 'true' person. The key to this rhetorical strategy lies in the adjective attached to each 'type' of person. While the human being would naturally be a person (his personality would pre-exist the legal artifice), the other persons would only be so by a fiction of law. It is by means of the artifice, then, that the naturalness of the human person is highlighted. This becomes clear when the very possibility of the existence of human persons is guaranteed through the transition from the state of nature to the civil state. It is the artificial sovereign person of the 'Leviathan', intended to be the representative of natural persons, who allows human life to cease to be 'solitary, poor, nasty, brutish, and short'.[42] It is only against the background figure of the Leviathan that the life of human beings is protected so that they can assert their 'natural' personality.

It must also be said that the conception of the natural person as the one who 'submits' (*subditus*) to the sovereign power – which appears clearly in Hobbes and other early modern authors – brings the notion of the person into contact with that of the subject. To understand this, however, we must explore how the notion of the subject arises, its various meanings and the changes it undergoes over time.

---

[40] C. B. Macpherson, *The Political Theory of Possessive Individualism. Hobbes to Locke* (OUP 1979).
[41] John Locke, *Essay Concerning Human Understanding* (Peter H. Nidditch ed, OUP 1979) II, 27, 9.
[42] Thomas Hobbes, *Leviathan* (J. C. A. Gaskin ed, OUP 1998) I, 13, 9.

FROM SUBJECTS TO PERSONS

It is well known that the English word 'subject' derives from the Latin *subjectum*, which means 'thrown, cast, subdued'. The term is usually used by Latin writers either in verbal form (e.g. *subjectum est* = 'was subjected'), adjectival form (*homo subjectum* = 'subjected slave') or substantival form (*subjectum* = 'the subjected'), but lacks any technical meaning.[43] It only acquired this connotation in late antiquity and especially in the Middle Ages in philosophical writings, where it came to designate both the subject of an authority (*subditus*) and the foundation or substratum of accidents (*hypokeimenon*). This duality of meanings, or, as Etienne Balibar put it, this 'play of words', is at the core of the paradox of modern subjectivity, which is understood as both the foundation of autonomy and of subjection to authority.[44]

The first meaning goes back to the language of the Roman jurists. Although the verb *subicio* and its participle *subjectum* lack any technical meaning in their writings – the latter, moreover, never appears as a noun – the common use of 'subdue' is utilized in the *ius personarum* to designate precisely those persons subjected to the authority of others; that is, as we have seen, unemancipated children subject to their *pater*, married women *cum manu* subject to their husband, slaves subject to their master, as opposed to independent people not subject to anyone else (*sui iuris*). As Esposito argued, it is here that we can find a first point of contact between the notion of person and that of subject.[45] Some passages from classical authors confirm this, as when in the *Institutas*, we read: '*De iure personarum alia divisio sequitur, quod quaedam personae sui iuris sunt, quaedam alieno iuri subiectae sunt*'.[46] Here Gaius explains that while some persons are independent, others are 'subject' to an external power.

It was only in the post-classical period, after the promulgation of the *Codex Theodosianus* (438 A.D.), that *subjectum* became a noun, designating the *subditus*, that is, the one who is subjected to public power.[47] This use of *subicio* and *subjectum* persisted in Medieval legal writings. Glossators and commentators did not depart from the sense the verb acquired in Roman sources, but the post-classical use of *subjectum* took precedence, nounified as 'subject', which would now take on a technical sense. The gradual spread of Christian thought marked the emergence of a unified category of subjection interpreted as a form

---

[43] Alejandro Guzmán Brito, 'Los orígenes de la noción de sujeto de derecho' (2002) 24 Revista de Estudios Histórico-Jurídicos 155.
[44] Etienne Balibar, 'Subjection and Subjectivation' in Joan Copjec (ed.), *Supposing the Subject* (Verso, 1994) 8.
[45] Esposito (n 21) 24–25.
[46] Lambert Mears (n 12) G.1.48.
[47] Guzmán Brito (n 43) 188.

of 'voluntary obedience' emanating from within – that is, not imposed on the body but on the soul.[48] A famous common law dictionary, Bertachini's *Repertorium*, records *subjectio* as follows: '*Subditi vel subjecti domini temporalis vel spiritualis possunt appellare*'.[49] For Bertachini, the subject is the *subditus*, the political 'subject', subjugated to the king and God. This is one of the subject's meanings that prevailed later in modernity: unlike slaves, subjects are those who consciously agree to obey the authority of the sovereign.[50]

The second technical meaning of *subjectum* arose in philosophical thought when the commentators of Aristotle began to use this word to translate the Greek term *hypokeimenon*.[51] Aristotle used this noun with two related meanings. On the one hand, in an ontological sense, to designate the essence (*ousia*), i.e. the substance or substratum that supports the accidental qualities.[52] On the other, to name the logical substratum of all possible predicates or categories.[53] The medieval philosophical tradition usually called the former 'subject of inherence' (or 'subject in relation to existence'), while the latter was known as the 'subject of attribution' (or 'subject in relation to predication or categorization').[54]

These two senses of *subjectum-hypokeimenon* were later adopted by scholasticism, particularly by Thomas Aquinas and William of Ockham. It is in the *Summa Logicae* of the latter that the subject of a predication (the 'logical subject') metonymically comes to mean also the subject of study or subject matter.[55] It was in this sense that *subjectum* became customary in the languages derived from Latin and also in the Germanic languages that adopted the term. *Subjectum* understood in this scholastic sense, is what we now call 'object' when we speak, for example, of the object of such a science or the object of such a discourse. In fact, this was also the language used by the scholastics. As

---

[48] Balibar (n 44) 9.

[49] 'Servs or subjects of the temporal or spiritual lord may lodge an appeal.' Giovanni Bertachini, *Repertorium juris utriusque* (J. Liber 1499) III, 248. Quoted in Guzmán Brito (43) 188.

[50] Esposito (n 21) 24–25.

[51] This could be seen in both Martianus Capella and Boetius' commentaries to Aristotle, but it is debated whether this translation should not be traced back to the 2nd century AD to sources that are now lost. Guzman Brito (n 43) 7–9.

[52] For Aristotle's use of *hypokeimenon* as *ousia* see 'Metaphysics' in *The Complete Works of Aristotle. The Revised Oxford Translation*, Vol. 2 (Jonatan Barnes ed, W. D. Ross tr, Princeton UP, 2014).

[53] For Aristotle's use of *hypokeimenon* as the logical substratum of the categories see 'Categories' in *The Complete Works of Aristotle. The Revised Oxford Translation*, Vol. 2 (Jonatan Barnes ed, J. L. Ackrill tr, Princeton UP, 2014).

[54] De Libera (n 5) 61–62.

[55] *Summa Logicae. Pars Prima* (Philotheus Boehner ed, The Franciscan Institute 1957) Chapters 26–62.

a matter of fact, while Francisco Suárez made promiscuous use of these terms, Duns Scotus complained about this puzzling assimilation, maintaining that one should speak of 'object' instead of 'subject' in these cases.[56]

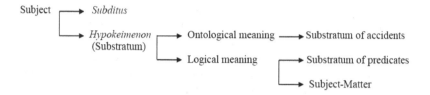

Figure 5.1   Different meanings of the term 'subject'

In the 13th century, medieval jurists took the philosophical subject with Aristotelian roots to compose the *subjectum* of law. Konrad Summenhart, a German philosopher and theologian of the 15th century, was the one who connected *subjectum* with *jus* for the first time, even if the full expression *subjectum juris* only appeared later in the writings of the 16th-century jurist-theologians of the Spanish 'neo-scholasticism' or 'second scholasticism'.[57] There, the expression *subjectum juris* appears along with terms such as *subjectum dominii* and *subjectum summae potestatis* in the works of Luis de Molina, Domingo de Soto, and Pedro de Aragón, among others.[58] From them, Hugo Grotius took the expression for his *De jure belli ac pacis*,[59] and from the latter, both Samuel Pufendorf[60] and Christian Thomasius[61] would take it in turn. It should be said, however, that this *subjectum juris* does not have the same meaning as the 'subject of rights' today. As mentioned above, the notion of *subjectum* had no precedent in legal writings except for that of 'subdued', which was common in the *ius personarum*. Although jurists utilized the term in this sense, they did not do it under the expression '*subjectum juris*'. For the

---

[56] See Guzmán Brito (n 43) 179.
[57] Ibid 152.
[58] Ibid.
[59] *De jure belli ac pacis/The Law of War and Peace* (Francis W. Kelsey tr, Clarendon Press 1984).
[60] *De jure naturae et gentium libri octo/Of the Law of Nature and Nations, Volume 2* (C. H. Oldfather and W. A. Oldfather tr, Clarendon Press 1934) Book 1, Chapter 1.
[61] *Institutes of Divine Jurisprudence* (Thomas Ahnert ed tr, Liberty Fund 2011) Book 1, Chapter 1.

Spanish scholastics and for those who followed them later, *subjectum* was the substratum of accidents. Thus, it was the ontological sense of *subjectum* that was incorporated into the legal language of the 16th century:[62] The *subjectum* was the substratum of *jus*, understood as *facultas* or *potestas* (accidents) – the idea of subjective rights was gradually making its way into modernity.[63]

It was the humanist jurisprudence of the 16th century – cultivated in France and other countries at the same time that scholasticism grew in Spain – that incorporated the *subjectum* in its logical sense into legal language. In their attempts to systematize law and their concern for the *iuris methodus*, the humanist jurists resorted to the *subjectum* as an ordering concept. The expression was taken in Aristotle's logical sense 'as that of which something is predicated', either used in its general meaning or in its special sense of subject-matter. For these jurists, the *subjecta juris* were usually the *personae*, the *res* and the *actiones*. Given the existing uses of the time, it is not surprising that many humanists employed the term *objectum* instead of *subjectum* as a general notion to order these same categories.[64]

Leibniz was the first to distinguish between subject and object. At the same time, he was also the first to identify the subject with the person understood as the human being.[65] As we saw in the previous section, medieval theologians had already assimilated the person (*substantia rationalis*) to man. Leibniz would bring this *humanized* person next to the subject, forming the triptych subject-person-man. Like the humanists, Leibniz used the expression *subjectum* as an organizing category of his *methodus*. Yet, unlike them, and following the scholastic tradition, he did so in the sense of a substratum of moral *qualitates*, that is, of *jus* and *obligatio*.[66] Although Leibniz's ideas changed over time,[67] it can be said that the subject of rights began to take its contemporary shape with him.[68]

This identification of the subject and the human person would influence both philosophy and law. Following Leibniz, Christian Wolff used the term to designate the *homo*, limiting its use, unlike Leibniz, to living humans.[69] As

---

[62] Guzmán Brito (n 43) 204.

[63] Brian Tierney, *The Idea of Natural Rights. Studies on Natural Rights, Natural Law and Church Law 1150–1625* (William B. Eerdmans Publishing Company 1997).

[64] Guzmán Brito (n 43) 206–221.

[65] Ibid 221–222.

[66] See G. W. Leibniz, *The New Method of Learning and Teaching Jurisprudence* (Carmelo Massimo De Iuliis tr, Talbot Publishing 2017).

[67] Guzmán Brito (43) 216–222 provides a useful description of these changes.

[68] According to Zarka, Leibniz 'invents' the modern subject of rights. Yves Charles Zarka, 'L'invention du sujet de droit' (1997) 60 Archives de Philosophie 531.

[69] See on this Guzmán Brito (n 43) 223. For the influence of Leibniz on Wolff and how this latter influenced Kant, see Udo Thiel, *The Early Modern Subject* (OUP 2011) 301–311.

is well known, however, it was Kant who popularized the identification of the subject and the human person. Kant used the notion of subject in its ontological sense, but to name the thinking-substance, the self or consciousness. This idea of consciousness was absent in the Leibnizian-Wolffian subject/*homo*, but we can find it in Locke's 'personal identity'. It is from this psychological turn in Kant, intimately associated with the notion of the person in Locke, that we can speak today of 'subjectivity' posited in opposition to 'objectivity', thus definitively inverting the scholastic identification of 'subject' and 'object' that had predominated until then.

Thus conceived, the Kantian subject ceases to be a substance and becomes an active principle. The Kantian subject stands as the onto-epistemic condition of experience. The subject brings a set of *a priori* forms (e.g. time and space) from which he shapes the objectual world.[70] Sensible experience only provides empirical data (matter), on which the subject imposes the form, transforming it into a 'phenomenon'. The subject constructs the object by projecting his consciousness onto it. If in previous metaphysical thought the relation of humans to objects was contemplative (*theoria*), now it is practical (*praxis*). In this regard, Kant understands knowledge as a particular form of action on the sensible experience. The Kantian subject does not correspond to any empirical individual (he is 'transcendental', i.e. anterior to experience). Kant's subject is universal and abstract; the general human subject that we all embody when we think objectively.[71]

From Kant onwards, the fundamental equation, the 'metaphysical equation', assimilates man with the subject. The subject turns into the essence of man. And, by this very equation, the 'Essence' becomes the man himself. The equation 'Man = Subject' replaces the old onto-theological equation 'God = (the Being)'.[72] Kant 'invents' the modern subject.[73] Although the philosophical tradition assigned this place to Descartes, the term *subjectum* is rarely used by him, and when it appears in his work, it does so in the Aristotelian sense of substratum. We do not find in Descartes or any other 17th- or 18th-century philosopher the notion of *subjectum* as an autonomous consciousness or a reflexive centre of representations of the world.[74] However, it can be said that the Kantian transcendental subject does radicalize the process of abstraction of the psychological element from the somatic substratum in the human being,

---

[70] See Immanuel Kant, *Critique of Pure Reason* (Paul Guyer and Allen W. Wood ed tr, CUP 2019) 155–192.
[71] Ibid.
[72] See Balibar (n 44) 4.
[73] Ibid 6.
[74] Ibid 5.

something that we can see already in the Cartesian *ego cogito*. The anthropological dualism of the person thus seeps into the modern subject.

Moreover, the association with the person also makes it easier for the ontological subject of inherence or attribution (substance) to become, in Kant, a subject of imputation (agent). If, as we have seen, accidents are inhered to the ontological subject, and predicates or categories are ascribed to the logical subject, acts are attributed to the subject of imputation. Let us recall that in Locke, the person was already defined by this 'imputability'. For Kant 'a person is a subject whose actions can be imputed to him', while 'a thing is that to which nothing can be imputed'.[75] By means of the person, then, and in accordance with the active principle that characterizes the metaphysical subject, the human subject becomes, in Kant, the source of his acts – that is, what defines the subject is the capacity to perform and attribute acts to himself (self-attribution) and, by the same principle, to attribute acts to others (hetero-attribution). This is the subject-agent, the one who acts, the author or the cause of his actions.[76] This is also the subject-legislator who gives himself his own laws,[77] the 'universal citizen' of Kant's political writings.[78] The basis of authority is no longer to be found outside of man but within himself.

As Michel Foucault pointed out, Kantian anthropology places man in a unique metaphysic, epistemic and moral position.[79] Man (with a capital 'M' now) captures the subject, becoming its last historical expression. Here we reach the highest point of Kant's ideas, with the human subject at the onto-political centre of gravity of modernity. As the modern subject, man is now the 'relational centre' and point of reference of being and the measure of all things.[80] This subject, the most finished expression of the 'person-subject-man' tryptic, became the centre of reference and attribution for modern legal systems. This philosophical notion of the subject was taken up by the German jurists of the 19th century who, following Leibniz and Kant, identified subject and person, and both categories with the human being. In particular, German Pandectists popularized this idea of the subject/person,

---

[75] Immanuel Kant, *The Metaphysics of Morals* (Mary J. Gregor tr, CUP 2013) 50.

[76] De Libera (n 5) 240.

[77] Kant (n 75) 50.

[78] See Balibar (n 44) 6–7 on the close link between the transcendental subject and the cosmopolitan citizen in Kant.

[79] Michel Foucault, *The Order of Things: An Archaeology of the Human Sciences* (anon. tr, Vintage) 1994.

[80] Martin Heidegger, 'The Age of the World Picture' in *The Question Concerning Technology and Other Essays* (William Lovitt tr, Garland Publishing 1977) 128.

ensuring its expansion in European and American law, right up to the human rights declarations of the 20th century.[81]

THE SUBJECT OF HUMAN RIGHTS

Human rights are the product of this assimilation between the human person and the subject, which, as we have seen, began to take shape in the Middle Ages and was ultimately enshrined in early modernity. Without this identification, human rights would not have been conceived, nor would they have any meaning for us today. As a crystallization of this convergence, human rights 'instaurate' a particular idea of the human.[82] They constitute a mechanism of onto-anthropogenesis that gives man a particular form. As we have seen, the subject/person of human rights is an autonomous rational agent, a centre of imputation of actions. This is, in one way or another, the idea of the subject that determines who can be considered a person in law and who is entitled to rights. This is also a subject split between its material and biological physicality and an abstract principle. The subject owns and hence is separated from his body.

It is no coincidence that Jacques Maritain, one of the drafters of the 1948 Universal Declaration of Human Rights, defined the person as a totality or whole that is in 'self-possession', a 'master of itself' and its actions. For him, man is only truly a person 'in so far as the life of the spirit and of liberty reigns over that of the senses and passions'.[83] Man is a person insofar as he 'subjects' and transcends his 'animal part'. In other words, man is subject to himself, or 'he who realizes his own subjection'.[84] As we shall see below, this distinction of the empirical man from the transcendental person – the 'empirical-transcendental doublet'[85] – is at the heart of the debates on who is the subject of human rights.

In a first sense, then, we could say that man is the subject of human rights. And yet, as Marx, Burke, and later Arendt pointed out early on, this subject – an abstract principle – does not cease to be dissociated from the human being of flesh and blood. The fact that man has taken the place of the subject of rights does not mean that all human beings are admitted into this category. This disjunction between the human subject and the human being is inscribed

---

[81] Guzmán Brito (n 43) 152.
[82] Humans (as well as other forms of being) must be constantly made or 'ontologically instaured' as Etienne Souriau would say. See *The Different Modes of Existence* (Erik Beranek and Tim Howles tr, Univocal 2015), 219 ff.
[83] Jacques Maritain, 'The Person and the Common Good' (1946) 8 (4) The Review of Politics 432, 434, 441.
[84] Balibar (n 44) 10.
[85] Foucault (n 79) 318.

at the very foundation of human rights with the distinction between 'man' and 'citizen' in the French Declaration of 1789.

This disjunction has been the focus of much of the discussion about the subject of human rights since the beginning. If, for Burke, the subject of rights is nothing more than an abstraction which, as such, does not protect the empirical man and has no meaning whatsoever[86] – 'nonsense upon stilts' Bentham would say later[87] – for Marx, it is an ideological figment, an abstraction that hides and stealthily promotes the real (bourgeois) man of the material relations of production.[88] Arendt, for her part and in a different register – marked by the experience of the two world wars of the 20th century – saw the man of the rights of man as a paradox: this is the man who has lost the right to have rights, the man who has no citizenship, the man who is simply a human being, and who, therefore, remains exposed and unprotected by political power.[89] As Giorgio Agamben would say later, the subject of human rights is 'bare life', biological life without legal and political qualifications.[90] The refugee, the stateless, and concentration camp inmates are the paradigmatic examples of this subject. Human rights would thus suffer from an insurmountable contradiction – inalienable and granted at birth to every human being, they would be, however, impossible to realize.

For Rancière, this vision of the subject in Arendt (and also in Agamben) depoliticizes human rights because it is situated on a pre-political plane and is profoundly pessimistic as it locks human beings into an 'ontological destiny' (to be reduced to their biological life). Unlike them, Rancière considers that '[t]he Rights of Man are not the rights of a single subject that would be at once the source and the bearer of the rights […] The subject of rights is the subject, or more accurately the process of subjectivization, that bridges the interval between two forms of the existence of those rights'.[91] According to Rancière, the first of these forms is written. Human rights would be a material inscription, not mere abstract predicaments nor idealizations of a non-existent being. They are rights granted by the political community, enshrining freedom and equality to their members. Thus, they are part of the configuration of the

---

[86] Edmund Burke, *Reflections on the Revolution in France* (J.G.A. Pockock ed, Hackett, 1987).

[87] Jeremy Bentham, 'Anarchical Fallacies; being an examination of the Declaration of Rights issued during the French Revolution' in *The Works of Jeremy Bentham*, Volume 2 (John Bowring ed, William Tait 1843), 483.

[88] Karl Marx, *On the Jewish Question* in *Early Texts* (D. McLellan tr, Oxford Blackwell 1971) 85–114.

[89] Hannah Arendt, *The Origins of Totalitarianism* (Penguin 2017) 349.

[90] Giorgio Agamben, *Homo Sacer. Sovereign Power and Bare Life* (Daniel Heller-Roazen tr, Stanford University Press 1998).

[91] Rancière (n 1) 302.

given, making visible a situation of formal equality. The second of these forms is related to the possibility of these rights being verified. Here, human rights are the rights of those who do something with the inscription of equality, those who try to operationalize its power. The subject of human rights is the product of the dispute or quarrel to establish who is included within its scope. Human rights would then be 'the rights of those who have not the rights that they have and have the rights that they have not'.[92] The rights belong to those who appropriate the inscription and are thus able to construct a dispute around the denial of rights they suffer. Human rights would be the rights of 'this part of those that have no part'.[93]

The power of human rights would then reside in the 'back-and-forth movement between the first inscription of the right and the dissensual stage on which it is put to test'.[94] The 'dissent' or 'disagreement' is not a conflict (whether of interests, values, or opinions) but rather a dispute over the given, over the framework from which we see things, a quarrel over the 'distribution of the sensible'.[95] Politics would consist precisely of changing the field of experience, the place assigned to each one, making the invisible seen and the silenced audible. Politics would be about modifying the ways of being, of doing and of seeing. Therefore, Rancière considers politics a form of aesthetics, that is, a force that transforms how we perceive the world. Politics redistributes intelligibility and visibility in new and different ways. When political subjects stage such scenes of dissensus, they not only confront the inscription of equality to situations of denial 'but put together the world where those rights are valid and the world where they are not'.[96] Therefore, the disagreement implies 'putting two worlds in one and the same world'.[97] For Rancière, a political subject 'is an operator that connects and disconnects different areas, regions, identities, functions, and capacities existing in the configuration of a given experience'.[98] Political subjectification produces these polemical and paradoxical scenes, in which 'existences that are at the same time nonexistences – or nonexistences that are at the same time existences'[99] are posited and actualized.

---

[92] Ibid 302.
[93] Jacques Rancière, *Disagreement. Politics and Philosophy* (Julie Rose tr, University of Minnesota Press 1999) 9.
[94] Rancière (n 1) 305.
[95] Jacques Rancière, *The Politics of Aesthetics. The Distribution of the Sensible* (Gabriel Rockhill tr., Continuum 2004) 12.
[96] Rancière (n 1) 304.
[97] Ibid.
[98] Rancière (n 93) 40.
[99] Ibid 41.

Perhaps for obvious reasons, this political vocabulary has captivated the imagination of those working to develop a political pluralization of ontologies. Indeed, this consideration of politics as aesthetics (the idea that politics alters how we perceive the world) can easily be translated into a political ontology seeking to validate alternative (non-Western) ways of apprehending the world. As such, even though Rancière has been reluctant to imagine the political subjectification of non-humans,[100] some scholars have taken his ideas further to think about ontological pluralism. Philippe Descola, for example, has borrowed Rancière's ideas to defend a cosmopolitics in which 'any operator, whether human or non-human, is capable of becoming a political subject if it manages to bring together things, issues, and matters of concern which initially have no intrinsic connections, especially if they appear to pertain to very different ontological regimes'.[101] For him, therefore, an Andean Mountain, an Amazonian watercourse, or the wetlands in France can become subjects if they connect and weave together heterogeneous human and non-human collectives.[102] Similarly, Marisol de la Cadena 'tweaks' – as she admits – several of Rancière's aesthetic ideas to describe how 'earth-beings' – e.g. a mountain called Ausagante in Peru – intrudes into the public debate and takes part in indigenous and ecological struggles in Latin America. According to her, the rights of nature in Ecuador and Bolivia represent a challenge to the 'partition of the sensible', posing an 'ontological disagreement' indicating that the nature/culture divide is a Western cosmological concern not necessarily universally shared by all.[103]

Like mainstream human rights discourse, Rancière's processualist approach is marked by a split – in his case, it is the split between the inscription of equality and its verification or operationalization. However, his proposal differs from the mainstream accounts in that, according to him, there is no pre-established subject – there is no man in the rights of man – but rather an

---

[100] See Jacques Rancière, *The Method of Equality. Interviews with Laurent Jeanpierre and Dork Zabunyan* (Julie Rose tr, Polity 2016) 162–164. Although, Rancière's reluctance to see political agency in non-humans is somewhat at odds with some aspects of his political theory, as the interviewers implicitly highlight with their questions.

[101] Descola (n 4) 42.

[102] Even if, up until now, Descola has been very cautious in elaborating the political and legal implications of his ontological pluralism – which makes his current engagement with Rancière's political theory even more intriguing – his *opus magnum* already assessed the rights of animals and nature in a positive light – although also quite ambiguously. See *Beyond Nature and Culture* (Janet Lloyd tr, The University of Chicago Press 2013) 192 ff.

[103] De la Cadena (n 4) 46, 93, 249, 277, 278–279, 282, 284, 295, 302.

'interval for political subjectification',[104] a space of dispute open to different political actors. The process of subjectification thus replaces the essentialized subject. We should immediately notice, however, that what Rancière calls the 'test of verification' cannot function without a subject that serves as a standard from which to carry out this verification and which, in turn, works as a 'safety valve'. For equality can be verified and unverified, the verification process can result in both an opening of the subject or its closure. On the other hand, equality cannot be verified in the face of a vacuum, but this action necessarily requires a normative model from which and through which to confirm (or deny) such equality. In other words, the man of human rights surreptitiously hides behind the inscription/verification process that Rancière describes.

The next section examines the extension of rights to non-human beings – that is, what should stand as the ultimate expression of the alleged radical openness of the subject of human rights – to show that, paradoxically and contrary to what Rancière believes, there is a man in the rights of man.

THE SUBJECT OF (NON) HUMAN RIGHTS

The pace at which non-humans have attained legal personhood and rights in the last few years in treaties, statutes, municipal resolutions, and case law is unprecedented and arguably signals a departure from previous certainties and preconceptions.[105] Despite these rapid changes, however, certain uneasiness lingers when we think of non-humans as subjects of rights. From a certain point of view, it feels not only counter-intuitive but also narcissistic, an attempt to make things resemble us rather than a genuine effort to admit the equal worth of other forms of being in the world. In a way, Heidegger's important caveat is pertinent here: 'It seems as though man everywhere and always only encounters himself'.[106]

Although some might be inclined to believe that this uneasiness is grounded in our prejudices, 'speciesism' or difficulty admitting that non-humans can be subjects of rights, there might be something else here we are missing. The archaeology/genealogy of the subject of rights showed us that unlike the Roman person that designated a role or function that could be equally ascribed to humans and non-humans, a 'mask' that could be worn by them both, the modern subject is inseparable from the idea of man. The archaeology indicates

---

[104] Rancière (n 1) 304.

[105] For animal rights and rights of nature, see Boyd (n 2) 223. For AI and robot rights, see David J. Gunkel, *Robot Rights* (MIT Press 2018).

[106] Martin Heidegger, 'The Question Concerning Technology' in *The Question Concerning Technology and Other Essays* (William Lovitt tr, Garland Publishing 1977) 27.

that the Roman person and the modern subject correspond to different epistemes (or systems of thought) that render them distinct and inassimilable. The course of history has made it so that being a person became synonymous with being human: the subject is now an ontological being rather than a functional category or a social role.[107] Granting subjectivity today is not to assign a role but a form of being in the world.

Moreover, the fact that the subject of human rights can be broadened to include other than human beings does not mean the subject is shapeless. It does not even suggest that it substantially changes by incorporating new non-human entities. The modern subject is not only a template of the human being but also a product of Western onto-epistemic inflexions that have given it a particular form. As we have seen, the human subject is defined by formal qualities – rationality, individuality, consciousness, autonomy, identity, agency and will. To become a subject, the candidate in question should possess or acquire these traits. Historically, rights have been extended concentrically outwards: the centre being human, white, male, bourgeois, and European.[108] Masculinity and whiteness have been associated in the West with reason, individuality, form and culture, while women and people of colour were related to corporality, physicality, matter and nature.[109] These series of oppositions are marked by the hierarchical positioning of reason over the body (or form over matter) that started in metaphysical and theological thinking. Therefore, masculinity, class and ethnicity gave empirical existence to the abstract subject of rights: an affluent white male stamped his image on law and became the bearer of universal subjecthood. Through the logocentric formal qualities – historically associated only with certain human beings – the abstract subject became embodied. Thus, even though, as Rancière says, political action can broaden the scope of this narrow subject, this inclusion always entails a form of exclusion: new subjects are incorporated as long as they can be accommodated within the dominant idea of the human being.

Just as it happened with women and certain men, non-humans today make their entry into the category of subjecthood by being held up to this normative ideal. As humans provide the standard, bringing non-humans to the radius of the subject requires showing how non-humans are like humans. This 'exten-

---

[107] John Frow, 'Personhood' in Simon Stern, Maksymilian Del Mar and Bernadette Meyler, *The Oxford Handbook of Law and Humanities* (OUP 2019) 274.

[108] Irus Braverman, 'Law's Underdog: A Call for More-than-Human Legalities' (14) Annual Review of Law and Social Sciences 132.

[109] Nicola Lacey, *Unspeakable Subjects. Feminist Essays in Legal and Social Theory* (Hart 1998) 108; Patricia Williams, *The Alchemy of Race and Rights* (Harvard UP 1991) 216, among others.

sibility' of rights takes the form of 'recognition'[110] and is usually mediated through the interplay between 'similarity and difference'.[111] The idea behind it is that justice requires that like entities be treated alike. In a way, this act of recognition results from what Rancière describes as the 'verification of the inscription'. What is verified here is the equality – or difference – of those who seek recognition as subjects. But it is clear that the verification always functions referentially – it is verified whether A is equal/different to B – and, therefore, it always works vis-à-vis a model to which the comparison is made. It is not surprising, then, that in some works, Rancière identified the verification of equality with the verification of speech (*logos*). In the Aristotelian tradition, which Rancière follows, *logos* is what defines man – and what separates him from animals.[112] The verification of equality is ultimately a verification of 'humanity', defined by humans' speech capacity.[113] The verification that would result in widening the circle of equality (or humanity) presupposes that whoever wants to enter into it first acquires the logocentric traits that have historically been attached to the human being.

The paradigmatic case of this form of reasoning by means of similarity is presented by Peter Singer, who expressly conceives granting rights to conscious or sentient animals as an 'expansion of the circle of concern of morality'.[114] Sentience, for this author, would justify granting rights to animals and taking them away from humans in some instances.[115] This extensionist paradigm is also being used by litigants and courts, either to recognize or deny legal personality to non-humans. Intelligence and sentience – also biological similarity in certain cases – are the most common markers utilized to compare humans and animals. In this line, in one of the first judgments where an orangutan named Sandra was granted legal subjectivity, a judge in Buenos Aires argued: 'nothing impedes that the rights to life and dignity, proper of living

---

[110] Ciméa Bevilaqua, 'Chimpanzees in Court: What Difference Does It Make?' in Yoriko Otomo and Ed Mussawir (ed) *Law and the Question of the Animal* (Routledge 2013) 75.

[111] Taimie L. Bryant, 'Similarity or Difference as a Basis for Justice: Must Animals be Like Humans to be Legally Protected from Humans?' (2007) 70 Law and Contemporary Problems 207.

[112] Aristotle, 'Politics' in *The Complete Works of Aristotle. The Revised Oxford Translation*, Vol. 2 (Jonatan Barnes ed, Benjamin Jowett tr, Princeton UP, 2014) 1282 b 21.

[113] The Greek term *logos* has been usually translated as 'speech' or 'reason', although, in Christian theology and modern philosophy, it was also translated as 'action' or 'deed'.

[114] Peter Singer, *The Expanding Circle: Ethics, Evolution, and Moral Progress* (Princeton UP 2011) 120.

[115] Peter Singer, *Animal Liberation* (Penguin 2015).

beings, and that are consecrated to human persons in the legal system, be extended analogically to Sandra, who is a sentient being.'[116] Similar arguments were put forward in other cases in Argentina, Colombia, Brazil, Ecuador, India and Pakistan.[117] Interestingly, the same criteria have worked in reverse to highlight the difference between humans and animals. In the same year that Sandra was considered a 'non-human subject of rights', a New York court denied legal personality to a chimp named Tommy because 'unlike human beings, chimpanzees cannot bear any legal duties, submit to societal responsibilities or be held accountable for their actions.'[118] The litigants argued that Tommy should not be treated as a thing because of his intelligence and biological characteristics, but the court concluded that chimps are not like humans and, therefore, cannot be considered legal persons.

While, for obvious reasons, these considerations have been more prominent in animal rights cases, they also play a role, even if sometimes inadvertently, in discussions about the rights of nature. Both nature and natural entities are anthropomorphized when it comes to granting them rights or legal personhood. In contrast to the prevalent view in the West of nature as an inert object (a mere 'resource'), the rights of nature conceives nature as a 'living agent', as an individuality with its own identity (Mother Earth, Gaia, Pacha Mama). Similarly, rivers, mountains, forests, and other natural 'assemblages' acquire life and individual identity, and sometimes other traits proper to human beings. These characteristics are used to justify extending them rights (such as the right to life and to not be harmed). This 'humanization' of nature can be seen in the Ecuadorian Constitution and in the Bolivian laws that granted rights to Pacha Mama or Mother Earth.[119] Aotearoa/New Zealand also has passed several laws giving effect to treaty settlements with the Māori people, recognizing different

---

[116] See Juzgado No 2 en lo Contencioso Administrativo y Tributario de la CABA, A2174-2015/0, *Asociación de funcionarios y abogados por los derechos de los animales y otros contra GCBA s/amparo*, 21 October 2015 (my translation).

[117] See Tercer Juzgado de Garantías de Mendoza, 'Presentación efectuada por A.F.A.D.A. respecto del chimpancé Cecilia – Sujeto no humano', 3 November 2016, Expt. No. P 72.254-15 (Argentina); Corte Suprema de Justicia 26 July 2017, AHC4806-2017 (Colombia) – this ruling was later reversed; Superior Tribunal de Justiçia, *Recurso especial N°1.797.175 – SP (2018/0031230-0)*, 21 March 2019 (Brazil); Supreme Court of India, *Animal Welfare Board of India v. A Nagaraja and Ors.*, 2014 7 SCC 547; High Court of Islamabad, *Islamabad Wildlife Mmgt. Bd. v. Metropolitan Corp. Islamabad, W.P.*, No. 1155/2019, 21 May 21 2020 (Pakistan).

[118] *People ex rel. Nonhuman Rights Project, Inc. v. Lavery*, 124 A.D.3d 148, 152 (N.Y. App. Div. 2014).

[119] See Constitución de la República de Ecuador, 20 October 2008; Bolivia's Act 71 in 2010 – *Ley de derechos de la Madre Tierra* and Act 300 in 2012 – *Ley marco de la Madre Tierra y desarrollo integral para vivir bien*.

natural features such as rivers and mountains as 'singular entities' and as 'indivisible and living wholes'.[120] Courts have actively adjudicated this matter and granted personhood and rights to nature and natural features using similar arguments. While in Colombia judges have considered nature a 'living entity composed of multiple other forms of life' and as an 'individualizable subject of rights',[121] courts in India have regarded rivers, mountains and glaciers as 'living entities' with bounded determinations.[122] The fact that these entities are thought of as individual and individualizable (bounded, discrete, and atomistic agents) – when it would be more accurate to think of them as networks of relationships – is determined by the human mould from which they are granted rights. The same ideas permeate the scholarship, where these rights are seen as the consequence of nature being like humans.[123] As happens with animal rights, the similarity/difference argument is also used by those who deny rights to nature, as both the literature[124] and litigation make clear.[125] As Thomas put it quite well, 'man is as much at the centre of the fiction that nature is a subject, as at that of the opposite fiction that nature is an object.'[126] This is also true not only because nature and natural features are anthropomorphized but because the rights of nature are heavily reliant on human proxies to be operative.[127] It is

---

[120] Te Awa Tupua (Whanganui Claims Settlement) Act 2017; Record of Understanding for Mount Taranaki, Pouakai and the Kaitake Ranges, 20 December 2017. As it happens, in Ecuador and Bolivia recognition is given not just to a river or a mountain as a natural feature but to spiritual entities called *Te Awa Tupua* (Whanganui River) and *Ngā Maunga* (Mount Taranaki).

[121] Corte Constitucional, Sala Sexta de Revisión, Sentencia T-622/16, 10 November 2016, 5.10.

[122] See High Court of Uttarakhand, *Mohd. Salim v. State of Uttarakhand and Others*, Writ Petition (PIL) No. 126 of 2014, 20 March 2017; Uttarakhand High Court, *Lalit Miglani v. State of Uttarakhand & Others*, Writ Petition (PIL) No. 140 of 2015, 30 March 2017, 64.

[123] Christopher Stone – who is considered the father of the rights of nature movement – characterizes the rights of nature as an extension of the legal recognition of hitherto excluded human beings: '[W]e are cultivating the personal capacities *within us* to recognize more and more the ways in which nature – like the woman, the Black, the Indian and the Alien – is like us'. See 'Should Trees Have Standing? – Toward Legal Rights for Natural Objects' in *Should Trees Have Standing? Law, Morality and the Environment* (OUP 2010) 29 (emphasis in the original).

[124] Visa Kurki, 'Can Nature Hold Rights? It's Not as Easy as You Think' (2022) 11 (3) Transnational Environmental Law, 525.

[125] See Boyd (n 2) 119.

[126] Thomas (n 9) 117.

[127] Rights of nature usually work through establishing stewardships or guardianships, making humans representatives of nature. The doctrine *in loco parentis* – 'in the place of a parent' – used by courts in India to appoint guardians for 'natural features', is quite telling of the anthropomorphizing of nature, as it implies treating natural features

true that, in some cases, the rights of nature attempt to remediate past wrongs – e.g. to redress the exclusion and marginalization of indigenous communities by adopting some of their cosmological understandings and practices, which would regard nature and natural entities as agents or 'persons' (even as kin). The significance of this appraisal is not under question and neither is the fact that non-humans can be agents or intelligent beings in their own right (that is, possessors of 'alteragencies' and 'alterrationalities'[128]). Rather, the issue is how these ideas have been translated into the law through the rights of nature[129] and the use of the model of human agency and intelligence to conceive of non-humans as agents and subjects of rights.

It is even more evident that the human being is the standard from which the extension of rights to AI, robots, and other digital and electronic entities is conceived. Unlike animal and nature's rights, there is still no legislation or case-law granting rights to artificial entities beyond some anecdotal cases, such as the granting of 'honorary citizenship' to a humanoid robot named Sophia in Saudi Arabia in 2017 or 'residency' to an online system with the identity of a seven-year-old boy in Tokyo, and the fact that some cities in the US consider robots operating on sidewalks as 'pedestrians'.[130] However, discussions in this field are burgeoning, and legislative initiatives on how to best regulate AI abound.[131] In this regard, in 2017 a European Parliament resolution recommended to its Commission that it grant 'electronic personhood'

---

as children or disabled people. It is interesting to mention that Thomas has considered that the personification of nature solves nothing in itself, since 'it boils down to a question of techniques of representation', at ibid.

[128] I take these terms from Baptiste Morizot, *Wild Diplomacy. Cohabiting with Wolves on a New Ontological Map* (Catherine Porter tr, SUNY Press) 36.

[129] Actually, a significant part of the indigenous movements in the countries where the rights of nature were recognized do not identify with them or see them as representative of their political agenda. See Craig M. Kauffman and Pamela L. Martin, *The Politics of the Rights of Nature* (MIT 2021) 125.

[130] Andrew Griffin, 'Saudi Arabia Grants Citizenship to a Robot for the First Time Ever'(2017) *The Independent* <https://www.independent.co.uk/tech/saudi-arabia-robot-sophia-citizenship-android-riyadh-citizen-passport-future-a8021601.html> accessed 1 June 2022; Anthony Cuthbertson, 'Artificial Intelligence "Boy" Shibuya Mirai Becomes World's First AI Bot to Be Granted Residency' (2017) *Newsweek* <https://www.newsweek.com/tokyo-residency-artificial-intelligence-boy-shibuya-mirai-702382> accessed 1 June 2022; Matthew Stern, 'Sidewalk Robots Are on The Way' (2021) *Forbes* <https://www.forbes.com/sites/retailwire/2021/04/06/sidewalk-robots-are-on-the-way-but-probably-later/?sh=3c6124127ee0> accessed 1 June 2022.

[131] See David Gunkel (n 105) and Simon Chesterman, *We, the Robots? Regulating Artificial Intelligence and the Limits of the Law* (CUP 2021).

to the most sophisticated autonomous robots.[132] In addition to autonomy, discussions revolve around whether certain machines are sufficiently intelligent or have reached such a degree of self-awareness that it makes them indistinguishable from humans. The famous 'Turing test', which is based on similarity/difference, has weighed heavily in these discussions. According to the test, if a machine can make us believe that it is human (i.e. imitate human beings to the point of being indistinguishable from them), we could say that it is 'intelligent'.[133] Other arguments have focused on whether machines have developed consciousness or sentience equivalent to that of humans – which, in turn, allows them to acquire identity. In other cases, the emphasis has been on agency – particularly for programs that buy and sell shares or self-driving cars – which has also triggered a debate about these entities' liability. It is worth noting that those who oppose granting rights to robots also do so within the 'similarity/difference' framework, arguing that robots cannot have rights because they are biologically or ontologically different from human beings.[134]

It follows from all these cases that non-humans are granted rights not for what they are but because of the attributes they would share with human persons.[135] The problem is not that these rights assert rationality, agency or will in non-humans but that they do it through the human model of rationality, agency and will. The issue is not that non-humans act, feel or think but that to have these rights, they should do it like humans.

Counter to Rancière, these cases show that there is a man in the rights of man, which works as a normative ideal and centre of reference. Rancière's 'test of verification' consists of demonstrating that one is 'an equal'. But this equality can only be established by reference to someone who possesses certain attributes and serves as a template for comparison.

---

[132] European Parliament Resolution with Recommendations to the Commission on Civil Law Rules on Robotics (2015/2103(INL)) (European Parliament, 16 February 2017), para 59(f).

[133] AM Turing, 'Computing Machinery and Intelligence' (1950) 59 Mind 433.

[134] Lantz Fleming Miller, 'Granting Automata Human Rights: Challenge to a Basis of Full-Rights Privilege' (2015) 16 (4) Human Rights Review 369.

[135] As an alternative to the 'similarity' approach, it has been argued that the subjectivity of non-humans can be established as a legal fiction, following the model of the corporation. However, here as well, human beings are posed as the normative model as they act either as a 'contrasting reference' (distinguishing between 'natural' and 'artificial persons') or as an 'implicit model' of the fictive person (e.g. corporations and non-humans are ascribed human attributes, such as agency and will). For a thought-provoking examination of non-humans as fictive persons, see Andreas Fisher Lescano, 'Nature as a Legal Person: Proxy Constellations in Law' (2020) 32.2 Law & Literature 237–262.

The paradox of non-human rights is that they end up enforcing a hierarchy based on human traits, ultimately undermining non-humans' inherent worth. To be sure, non-human rights blur the difference between humans and non-humans by finding them 'equal', but in so doing, it also surreptitiously re-establishes a hierarchy between them. There is no *scala naturae* to determine who is equal to whom; the world has no norm, model or canon to use as a reference. By introducing a scale based on traits such as rationality, agency and will (conceived as human characteristics), the referential association is constructed in such a way that humanity ends up always on top, being the norm, model and measure of non-human beings. By the same token that non-human rights give non-humans a new moral status, they take it away by surreptitiously establishing a hierarchical ladder which places humanity at its apex. Moreover, while it is not trivial to say that non-humans are subjects of rights, doing so in the current conditions merely implies moving them from one end to the other of the legal binary, therefore keeping intact the subject/object–person/thing underlying scheme.[136] As occurs with corporations and other fictive persons, this indirectly works to assert human beings as the true and original legal subjects. Therefore, extending the scope of rights and legal subjectivity to non-humans does not necessarily remove anthropocentrism from the law; on the contrary, it can be its ultimate realization.

CONCLUSION

'Who' is never an 'it' (a thing) but an 'I', a 'you', and a 'we'.[137] Asking 'who' instead of 'what', as I do, elicits both a transformation in the status of non-humans as well as the persistence of the 'human' as the 'standard' subject of rights. In this regard, the emergence of the new does not always entail the passing of the old. Man might well be about to die, as Foucault suggested, but his spectre will linger with us for a time as his relentless figure re-emerges in unsuspected places.[138] The archaeological investigation of the first section of this chapter shows that the subject of rights is, to a certain extent, inseparable from the human being. The question one needs to ask then is whether it is possible to think of a subject dissociated and decoupled from its human form and the normative model humanity has imprinted on it based on human reason, agency, autonomy, and will.

---

[136] Bevilaqua (n 110) 83.
[137] On this, see Martin Heidegger, *The Basic Problems of Phenomenology* (Albert Hofstadter tr, Indiana UP) 120.
[138] Foucault (n 79) 385.

Even if non-human rights aim to recognize the moral value of non-humans, they reinforce the idea of man as the measure of all things. By including non-humans without a wider paradigm shift, 'humanism is actually being reinstated uncritically under the aegis of species egalitarianism'.[139] We should not forget that humanism – which upholds the idea that humans are apart and exceptional – is just the ethics of 'naturalism' – the onto-epistemic framework through which we in the West have reified nature and objectified the world.[140] Imprinting human form to non-humans does nothing more than reinstate their paradoxical inclusion-exclusion. Esposito is right to say that an excess of personification can lead to new forms of reification.[141] Non-human rights extend subjectivity to non-humans at the price of denying them their non-human character. From this perspective, non-human rights are simply the old human rights projected towards non-human beings. These rights make the world more (not less) human, less (not more) plural. They are a new iteration of the old human drive to humanize the world.

Rancière's processual theory, from which a part of ontological pluralism borrows conceptual ideas, describes the expansive force of the subject of rights, but conceals that this expansion reproduces and reinstates a standardized vision of humanity. It fails to grasp that the process of subjectification enabled by the human rights discourse produces sameness, it is assimilating and homogenizing. The genealogy of the subject shows that man has become its yardstick and that the process of inscription/verification that Rancière describes cannot but occur through a human subject that serves as its reference.

This does not mean that Rancière's political theory does not provide an interesting conceptual platform to reflect on the irruption of non-human actors into the political and legal field. Yet his ideas need to be substantially reworked to serve this purpose. Rancière's invitation to contest the essentialization of the subject (which, as we have seen, takes the ontic form of the human being) is welcome and necessary but needs to be decoupled from the 'test of equality', which reintroduces the essentialized subject through the back door.

Instead of corroborating equality, as Rancière suggests – or, for what matters, 'similarity/difference' – we could look at the mutual implication (sometimes hybridity) between human and non-human worlds. This verification of 'ontological entanglement' could demonstrate that it makes little sense to ascribe entitlements solely to humans. Considering 'entitlement' vis-à-vis 'entanglement' could open a different way of being with others, a way in which otherness is not suppressed but enhanced. In contrast to the

---

[139] Rosi Braidotti, *The Posthuman* (Polity Press 2013) 79.
[140] On naturalism see Descola (n 102) 172 ff.
[141] Esposito (n 21) 24.

assimilationist paradigm that Rancière's 'test of equality' proposes, a different kind of verification able to assert non-humans' alterity (their alteragencies and alterationalities) while simultaneously acknowledging the multiple and mutual implications of human and non-human worlds seems necessary.[142] Only by such double recognition can the process of political subjectification of non-humans give rise to an actual dissent between worlds (ours and the one in which non-humans are recognized as political agents on their own terms). Only in this case can Rancière's politics as a 'relationship between worlds' take place and be actualized.[143]

If, as Rancière says, politics exists only when the distribution of the sensible is questioned, when those who have no place claim a place in the community, there is nothing more political today than the sudden irruption of non-humans in the political and legal debate. Non-humans appear as 'recalcitrant subjects',[144] that is, those who resist, challenge, and test our existing political and legal arrangements. As they are currently conceived, however, non-human rights counter non-humans' recalcitrancy, reinforcing and legitimizing the common sense they are supposed to question. But if non-human rights are an attempt to set up human dominance on a different register, they are also evidence of the tears existing in our modern onto-epistemic fabric. Non-human rights represent an opportunity for a conceptual opening. Under different circumstances,

---

[142] Although I am not referring to any of these descriptions in particular, many contemporary formulations attempt to capture this 'relationality' between humans and non-humans. See, for example, Donna Haraway's notions of 'tangled species' in *When Species Meet* (University of Minnesota Press 2008) 249 ff. and 'sympoiesis' in *Staying With the Trouble* (Duke UP 2006) 58; Karen Barad's 'intra-action' in *Meeting the Universe Halfway* (Duke UP 2007) 33; Bruno Latour's 'hybridity' in *We Have Never Been Modern* (Catherine Porter tr, Harvard UP 1993) 1 ff.; Anna Tsing 'interspecies or multispecies relations/entanglements' in *The Mushroom at the End of the World* (Princeton UP), vi, 22; and Baptiste Morizot's 'cohabitation' (n 128) 65. We should note that some of these 'relational' accounts could also negate non-human alterity and reproduce problematic forms of assimilationism. Cf. Frédéric Neyrat, *The Unconstructable Earth: An Ecology of Separation* (Drew S. Burk trans, Fordham UP 2019).

[143] Rancière (n 93) 42. In other terms, what limits Rancière's processual politics is its commitment to a substantialist ontology (which casts humanity as intrinsically distinct and separate from its milieu). This is the reason why Rancière can only think of politics as a human activity and why he disregards non-human politics so easily. Ultimately, a 'test of equality' is only conceivable within a substantialist ontology which conceives entities as autonomous and separate from each other and which allows comparisons between them.

[144] I take the term from a formulation given by Bruno Latour in 'Des sujets récalcitrants' in *Chroniques d'un amateur de sciences* (Presses des Mines 2006) 187 to a proposition originally conceived by Isabelle Stengers, see *Cosmopolitics II* (Robert Bononno tr, University of Minnesota Press 2011) 338–339.

they could channel non-humans' recalcitrancy and become 'ontological smugglers',[145] that is, a narrow gateway to other ways of apprehending the world. An alternative politics beyond the 'politics as usual' of human rights is not only conceivable but necessary in our historical crucible, making way for non-human rights to become something else and other than human rights.

ACKNOWLEDGEMENTS

This chapter has been written with the support of a British Academy Postdoctoral Fellowship (PF21\210046).

---

[145] I take this expression from Morizot (n 128) 163.

6. Deliberate legal equivocations: making non-human persons, multiplying differences
Ciméa B. Bevilaqua

The legal world seems to be experiencing a form of demographic explosion, parallel to the degradation and vast genocides of non-institutional forms of life.[1] Growing concerns about the devastation of the planet and the threat of irreversible collapse of its life forms have gradually and unevenly, albeit cumulatively, given rise to provisions that expand legal forms of existence. New entities came to inhabit national legislations and supranational norms: the environment, ecosystems, biological diversity, threatened and protected species, natural heritage. Their presence has modified the scope of legal relations and instituted new rights and duties, crimes and sanctions, limits on property, trade, and numerous other activities.

This chapter is an anthropological exploration of a particular and limited instance of this process: the legal personification of certain animals, individualized by their names and biographies, as a result of actions seeking their recognition as holders of fundamental rights. Rather than a legal assessment, it presents an ethnographic account of the emergence of the 'non-human person subject of law', based on decisions of Argentine courts referring to an orangutan and a chimpanzee, whose novelty evinces a broader movement: the incipient reversal of the ontological cleansing[2] trajectory consubstantial to the development of modern legal systems.

ONTOLOGICAL CLEANSING

The depletion of the legal world, once densely populated by a wide variety of non-human living beings who, among other things, could be judged and con-

---

[1] Donna Haraway, 'Anthropocene, Capitalocene, Plantationocene, Chthulucene: making kin' (2015) 6(1) Environmental Humanities 159.
[2] Mauro Almeida, 'Caipora e outros conflitos ontológicos' (2013) 5(1) R@U 7, 23.

victed (or acquitted, depending on the skill of their lawyers) under conditions similar to those of human beings,[3] began to gain momentum with the medieval reformulation of Roman law. Thomas described it as an effort to domesticate legal fiction based on two criteria: the radical separation between the world of fact and the world of law, and the insurmountable division between natural and supernatural orders. Thus, the limit imposed on the powers of law 'to make, unmake and modify substance and its modalities [...] is not empirical, but ontological': fiction can no longer go beyond what is considered possible according to nature.[4]

The naturalization of Roman fiction by medieval fiction also gave rise to current notions of legal subject and subjective rights. As Pottage points out, '[a]lthough the legal *persona* was acknowledged to be a fictional role, it was cast as the shadow of a substantial role player', so that it came to seem 'self-evident that rights are the attributes of real people'.[5] Concurrently, under the influence of new scientific canons and their Enlightenment foundations, 'the number of actors in the legal world has been drastically diminished' to the point that the human individual became 'the only remaining plausible actor'.[6] Openly institutional entities continued to inhabit the world of law, but were conceived 'as merely an analogy' with a human substrate.[7] Non-human living beings, deprived of their status as protagonists of legal relations, were made into 'things' and came to exist solely as objects of relations between 'persons' – at least until recently.

Despite the schematic quality (and scant novelty) of this account, it highlights the inflection from which the theme of this chapter arises. Since the last decades of the past century, several countries have introduced legislative amendments to formally declare something that sounds trivial in everyday language: animals are not things.[8] In recent years, this negation has given way to descriptive statements that differentiate animals not only from objects but also from other kinds of non-human life, the first one being the 2015 amendment to the French Civil Code declaring animals as living beings endowed

---

[3] EP Evans, *The Criminal Prosecution of Animals* (The Lawbook Exchange 2009).
[4] Yan Thomas, 'Fictio Legis: l'empire de la fiction romaine et ses limites médiévales' (1995) 21 Droits 17, 44–45.
[5] Alain Pottage, 'Persons and things: an ethnographic analogy' (2001) 30(1) Economy and Society 112, 119.
[6] Gunther Teubner, 'Rights of non-humans? Electronic agents and animals as new actors in politics and law' (2007) 4 EUI MWP LS <http://hdl.handle.net/1814/6960> accessed 12 May 2019 (at 2).
[7] Teubner (n 6) 16.
[8] Austria was the first country to introduce this amendment in the *Allgemeines Bürgerliches Gesetzbuch* (Civil Code) in 1988. See ABGB section 285a.

with sensitivity.[9] These reforms, however, also ratified the previous normative regimes: legal provisions relating to things continued to apply to animals. Since de-reification did not result in personification, animals were left, so to speak, halfway between the two basic poles of modern legal systems – a situation described by Marguénaud as a problematic 'state of levitation'.[10]

However evocative this image might be, assigning animals a twofold negative condition (neither things nor persons) does not merely express the difficulty of situating them in positions simultaneously conceived as inadequate and incommensurable, immobilizing them in a legal wasteland. On the contrary, as we shall see, this ostensibly ambiguous status allows for radical institutional experimentation, prefiguring that things (and persons), in the world of law, could be 'otherwise'.[11]

In fact, shifting between the positions of person and thing has long been possible and has never ceased to be. As is well known, it was initially as a kind of thing (*res extra commercium*) that the human person was protected in Roman law.[12] And if the living human person came to be conceived as the substrate of legal personhood, human living matter such as embryos, organs, and genes now hold particular qualities and ways of existence depending on the legal systems they inhabit. These variations indicate that 'the *summa divisio* between legal subjects endowed with personhood and non-subjects categorized as property'[13] has been, from the outset, less an irreducible dualism than a 'matrix of contrasts'[14] permanently open to multiple recombinations.

OTHER DIFFERENCES

Whilst legislative reforms remove animals from the category of things, activists seek their legal recognition as persons, notably in habeas corpus actions filed on behalf of great apes in different countries since the mid-2000s.

---

[9] See Article 515-14 of the French Civil Code: 'Animals are living beings endowed with sensitivity. Subject to laws protecting them, animals are subject to the regime of property'.

[10] Jean-Pierre Marguénaud, 'L'entrée en vigueur de "l'amendement Glavany": un grand pas de plus vers la personnalité juridique des animaux' (2014) 2 Revue Semestrielle de Droit Animalier 15, 22.

[11] Elizabeth A. Povinelli, 'The will to be otherwise/the effort of endurance' (2012) 111(3) The South Atlantic Quarterly 453.

[12] Yan Thomas, 'Le sujet de droit, la personne et la nature' (1998) 100(3) Le Débat 85, 93.

[13] Matthias Martin, 'Vers un genre juridique commun à l'animal, l'embryon et le cadavre?' (2015) 15 Revue Générale du Droit 1-2.

[14] Marilyn Strathern, 'No nature, no culture: the Hagen case' in Marilyn Strathern and Carol MacCormack (eds), *Nature, Culture and Gender* (CUP 1980) 177.

The outcomes of these cases are usually inconclusive. To some extent, it can be argued that courts deliberately avoid facing a kind of difference that is transverse to the conventional legal differentiation between humans and non-humans.[15]

It was precisely this other difference that an Argentinian judge brought to light in November 2016, when she granted habeas corpus to a female chimpanzee, formally declaring her a 'non-human legal subject'. The ruling received widespread international attention. At around 30 years of age and living alone in the Mendoza public zoo, the chimpanzee Cecilia was enthusiastically hailed by activists and scholars as the 'first legally personified animal' in the world.[16] This pioneering decision actually relied on arguments and previous rulings involving the orangutan Sandra, also a resident of Argentina and roughly the same age, who was ephemerally recognized as a 'non-human person subject of law' between October 2015 and June 2016.[17]

Sandra and Cecilia became persons in the absence of precedents and, seemingly, in defiance of legal provisions.[18] Regardless of who came first, a dispute that they would hardly be interested in, it is more relevant to ask: how was it possible to bring into existence a new form of legal life, the 'non-human person', relying only on the resources of a legal system in which animals remain defined as things? Germane from the outset, both cases were initiated as habeas corpus writs almost at the same time, proposed by the same petitioner – an animal defence association based in Buenos Aires – with similar arguments and requesting the same practical result: the transfer of Sandra and Cecilia to the Great Apes Project Sanctuary in Sorocaba (São Paulo, Brazil).

The outcome of each case is surprising in its own way, but their juxtaposition reserves a bigger surprise: the difference introduced by the 'non-human person' between the institutional positions of person and thing is not homogeneous. If Cecilia and Sandra came to exist legally as persons, they also became different kinds of persons. This dissimilarity highlights how such pioneering rulings hinge on their specific procedural and argumentative paths, in which

---

[15] Ciméa Bevilaqua, 'Chimpanzees in court: what difference does it make?', in Yoriko Otomo and Ed Mussawir (eds) *Law and the Question of the Animal: A Critical Jurisprudence* (Routledge 2011) 99.

[16] Jean-Pierre Marguénaud, 'La femelle chimpanzé Cécilia, premier animal reconnu comme personne juridique non humaine' (2016) 2 Revue Semestrielle de Droit Animalier 15.

[17] An earlier decision concerning the orangutan Sandra, which will be addressed shortly, declared animals to be subjects of rights without explicitly constituting them as 'persons'.

[18] In the Argentine Civil and Commercial Code, animals are included in Article 227: 'Movable things. Movable things are those that can move by themselves or by an external force'.

the empirical particularities of each case, the problems of conceptual articulation they pose, and the evaluation of their practical and political consequences inside and outside the legal world are deeply enmeshed. Likewise, any effort to unmake this entanglement in description would be misleading: the conceptual and the empirical are entirely empirical and, concurrently, entirely conceptual.

The following two sections describe how these results were produced. The first one is dedicated to the orangutan Sandra, whose case produced the first innovative rulings that later impacted the case of the chimpanzee Cecilia. The subsequent section presents Cecilia's habeas corpus, which brings Sandra back to the scene. Finally, some specific features will be highlighted in regard to these two ways of constituting non-human persons and the kinds of relations they entail.

THE ORANGUTAN SANDRA

The writ of habeas corpus on behalf of Sandra was filed in a Federal Criminal Court in Buenos Aires, on November 13, 2014, by an animal rights defence association known by the acronym Afada (*Asociación de Funcionarios y Abogados por los Derechos de los Animales*). The petition described Sandra as an orangutan that had been arbitrarily deprived of her freedom, without a written order from a competent authority, by the management of the Buenos Aires City Zoo. Additionally, her health condition was claimed to be critical. In these circumstances, the judiciary ought to release 'this non-human person, who is not a thing and, therefore, cannot be subject to the legal regime of property'.

The petition was rejected in less than three hours.[19] Upon consulting the higher instance (*Cámara Nacional de Apelaciones en lo Criminal y Correcccional, Sala VI*), it was restated that the Civil and Commercial Code of Argentina defines a person as 'anyone with characteristic signs of humanity and with the ability to acquire rights and assume obligations. As such, the animal cannot be included in this category and, consequently, the present action cannot proceed'.[20] However, given that the orangutan's captivity conditions could fall under the animal abuse law, the case was referred to the judiciary of the Autonomous City of Buenos Aires (*Juzgado en lo Contravencional y de Faltas nº 15*). In parallel, through an appeal filed by Afada seeking to keep

---

[19] Juzgado Nacional en lo Criminal de Instruccion n° 47, 'Orangutana, Sandra s/ Habeas Corpus', Sentencia FA14060006 (SAIJ), 13 November 2014. Judge Monica Berdion de Crudo.

[20] Since I did not have access to the original document, this excerpt was transcribed as quoted in the decision of an appeal filed by Afada at a later time (see n 22, at 8).

the case in federal jurisdiction, the process reached the Federal Criminal Court of Cassation (*Cámara Federal de Casación Penal – CFCP*).

CFCP's decision comprised three items in just over a page. The first only recorded that the case had arrived at the court due to an appeal presented by Afada. The third reiterated the judiciary of the City of Buenos Aires's competence to determine whether Sandra's situation fell under the law on animal mistreatment. Nothing was said about the continuity (or not) of the writ of habeas corpus, but this went almost unnoticed because all attention was directed toward the second item, which stated:

> That, from a dynamic and not static legal interpretation, it is necessary to recognize the animal as subject of rights, since non-human subjects (animals) hold rights, whose protection is imposed within the corresponding competence (Zaffaroni, E. Raúl et al., Derecho Penal, Parte General, Ediar, Buenos Aires, 2002, p. 493; also Zaffaroni, E. Raúl, La Pachamama y el Humano, Ediciones Colihue, Buenos Aires, 2011, p. 54 et seq.).[21]

This brief paragraph caused enormous repercussions since, as it was widely reported, a court had granted habeas corpus to an animal for the very first time. Yet the decision was not received in the same way by the justice system of Buenos Aires: the public prosecution office (*Fiscalía PcyF n° 8*) carried out an inquiry on Sandra's living conditions in the zoo without admitting Afada as an interested party, and eventually recommended the filing of the proceedings. Nonetheless, the judge responsible for the case in that instance (*Juzgado en lo Contravencional y de Faltas n° 15*) decided to continue the proceedings as a private criminal action, with Afada as the plaintiff. Months later, the case was extinguished for formal reasons. In an appeal against this decision, the association argued that although the CFCP had determined the continuity of the habeas corpus action, the Buenos Aires' justice system had given it an 'erroneous object': it was not a matter of determining whether Sandra was suffering from abuse, but whether the deprivation of freedom violated her subjective rights. The appeal was granted, but the judges did not fail to stress that the 'confusion' about the nature of the case was Afada's own.[22] The case was reopened and, shortly thereafter, extinguished once again.

---

[21] Cámara Federal de Casación Penal, Sala 2, 'Orangutana Sandra s/ recurso de casación s/habeas corpus', Sentencia FA14261110 (SAIJ), 18 December 2014. Judges Alejandro W. Slokar and Angela E. Ledesma. The third member of the panel, Judge Pedro R. David, did not adhere to this item.

[22] Cámara de Apelación Penal de Buenos Aires, Sala 3, 'Responsable Zoológico de Buenos Aires s/infr. art(s). 14.346 L.N. (Ley de Protección al Animal) p/L 2303)', Sentencia FA16370004 (SAIJ), 25 April 2016. Judges Jorge A. Franza and Silvina Manes.

At first sight, there would be no value in recording these steps. However, they help to introduce a crucial part of my argument by highlighting the 'deliberate equivocation' regarding the CFCP's ruling, which allowed its dual existence, at least for some time, as the acceptance and rejection of the habeas corpus on behalf of Sandra. Not least, by declaring that non-human subjects are holders of rights offering only bibliographic references as a basis, the decision could from then on be replicated in different instances of the Argentine judicial system, with various purposes, sustaining a wide experimentation on the possible combinations of rights and subjects, persons and things, institutional and non-institutional forms of existence.

The notion of deliberate equivocation proposed here evokes Viveiros de Castro's influential reflection on 'controlled equivocation' in interspecific communication in Amerindian worlds.[23] Though addressing different issues, I retain the idea of 'equivocation' to draw attention to the conceptual and pragmatic dissonances that shape the procedural debates on the legal status of animals. The adjective 'deliberate', in turn, suggests the not only conscious but largely intentional nature of the ambiguities produced throughout these proceedings, whether in relation to their own nature, object, and objectives, or to the institutional and non-institutional implications of their results. The idea of deliberate equivocation will surface later on to refer to the different rationales for the rights of non-human beings in the cases involving Sandra and Cecilia, sustained by specific argumentative paths, not necessarily coherent, and by different declinations of the categories of person and thing.

Regarding the latter aspect, this notion also reverberates with Morita's unfolding of the 'internal equivocations' entailed by the translation into Japanese of certain Western notions. In these cases, the overlap in a single term of deeply disparate, ancient and recent notions produces oscillations and resonances that remain non-obvious to the very people who use it.[24] Similarly, the equivocations within the apparently rigid person/thing legal dualism – its non-obvious capacity to harbour and redistribute distinct entities and qualities between the two poles – enable and promote the deliberate equivocations I seek to describe. These transformative effects foster a peculiar movement in which Sandra serves as a legal precedent of herself through other processes and

---

[23] Eduardo Viveiros de Castro, 'Perspectival anthropology and the method of controlled equivocation' (2004) 2(1) Tipití 3. 'Controlled equivocation' refers to Amazonian shamans' awareness that interspecific communication involves the existence of multiple referents behind homonymic concepts. The reverse would be the 'uncontrolled equivocation' often resulting from the anthropologists' lack of awareness of the dissonances inherent in intercultural translation.

[24] Atsuro Morita, 'Ocean, travel, and equivocation: a response to Anne Salmond's "Tears of Rangi"' (2014) 4(3) Hau 311.

other animals, including Cecilia – and vice versa.[25] They also allowed Sandra's ephemeral existence as a non-human legal person, to which I now turn.

The Non-Human Person 'Discovered' in Law

When it proved impossible to sustain the equivocation regarding the writ of habeas corpus, the animal rights association Afada sought an alternative route: a protective action (*amparo*[26]) filed before the national administrative justice against the government of the City of Buenos Aires and the local zoo (at the time, a private concessionaire) for the 'illegal and arbitrary' violation of Sandra's rights. According to the petition, although the orangutan 'is not treated cruelly within the meaning of the animal abuse law' (as the capital's public prosecution office had concluded), 'her captivity and public exhibition violate the rights she holds'.[27]

The decision was handed down by Judge Elena Liberatori on October 21, 2015. The starting point (as had been in the petition) was the aforementioned recommendation of the CFCP for a 'dynamic legal interpretation', which sustained a double differentiation. On the one hand, adding to CFCP's generic statement that animals are subjects of rights, the decision sought to specify those rights in that particular case. On the other hand, it sidestepped the petitioner's arguments on the similarity between great apes and human beings, i.e., the attempt to 'ontologically ground the rights of animals, resorting to scientific assertions and philosophical theories to persuade [the court] of the duty to recognize them and make them legally exist'.[28]

---

[25] This recursive movement is exemplified by the judgment of the two aforementioned appeals presented by Afada against the extinction of the criminal action involving Sandra in the justice system of Buenos Aires. In the first one (n 22), Judge Jorge Franza's vote referred to a case decided five months earlier regarding a mere victim of mistreatment, in which his opinion relied on precedents related to Sandra herself: the CFCP's ruling above (n 21) and the judgment of a protection action also filed by Afada on behalf of Sandra, which will be described later (n 27). These reflections were also taken up in subsequent trials involving other animals. In the second appeal, Judge Franza's vote incorporated arguments from the decision of the habeas corpus on behalf of Cecilia, decided the previous month (n 41).

[26] While the habeas corpus only protects personal freedom, the *amparo* action extends to the protection of fundamental rights in general.

[27] Juzgado Nacional de Primera Instancia en lo Contencioso Administrativo Federal, Sala 34, 'Asociación de Funcionarios y Abogados por los derechos de los animales y otros c/ GCBA s/ amparo'. Sentencia MJ-JU-M-95342-AR, October 21, 2015. Judge Elena Liberatori (at 2).

[28] Florence Burgat, 'La personne, une catégorie juridique souple propre à accueillir les animaux' (2017) 59 Archives de Philosophie du Droit 175, 177.

Instead, it can be said that the decision was guided by the strict application of legal norms, bearing in mind that, in any circumstance, the 'application' simultaneously reshapes the law, the entities, and the circumstances to which it 'applies'. As will be seen, Judge Liberatori rediscovered in the legislation – or retroactively brought to existence – elements to support an unexpected conclusion that animals had *already* been subjects of rights in the Argentine legal system for over half a century. It then became possible to 'discover' that the non-human person (which did not explicitly appear in the CFCP's ruling) *already* existed in the Civil Code itself. The operations of this other entirely institutional ontological politics[29] are described hereafter. In the judge's formulation, there were two issues to be assessed: 'First, whether the orangutan Sandra holds rights and whether this implies recognizing her as a subject of non-human rights. Second, whether it is appropriate to proceed with her release or transfer, and whether this is possible, given her particular circumstances'.[30]

Regarding Sandra's legal status, according to the judge, the 'jurisprudential precedent' – the CFCP's decision declaring animals as 'non-human subjects of rights' – authorized the adoption of the same understanding in the case under analysis.[31] Without losing sight of the peculiar overlap between the precedent and the animal involved in both cases, it is worth noting that invoking the precedent made it possible to account exactly for what it had left open, i.e. referring to an animal as a person: '[T]he orangutan Sandra is a non-human person and, therefore, subject of rights and of the resulting obligations in relation to her on the part of human persons'.[32] Once the basis had been established, the 'dynamic interpretation' of the legal system also made it possible, as anticipated, to rediscover the silent presence of animals as holders of rights in the legislation.

As the judge recalls, Law 14,346 of 1954, article 1°, establishes the mistreatment of animals as a crime and the corresponding sanction: 'Anyone who ill-treats animals or makes them victims of acts of cruelty shall be punished with imprisonment from fifteen days to one year'. The word 'victim' is crucial to her argument, allowing the new legal status of animals as non-human persons to be extracted from an old legal provision through a peculiar deduction: a) the law sanctions acts that can only be committed by human beings,

---

[29] Annemarie Mol, 'Ontological politics. A word and some questions' (1999) 47(1_suppl) The Sociological Review 74.

[30] Juzgado Nacional de Primera Instancia en lo Contencioso Administrativo Federal (n 27) 5.

[31] Local and international experts were heard regarding Sandra's health and living conditions in the zoo.

[32] Juzgado Nacional de Primera Instancia en lo Contencioso Administrativo Federal (n 27) 6.

since the recipient of the penalty is a human being; b) the animal is the victim of these acts; c) therefore, the legal protection to be granted by the courts concerns the animal itself, or the non-human person, against acts perpetrated by human beings.[33]

Sandra, as a victim of abuse based on the poor conditions of her housing in the zoo, was now able to be regarded as a non-human person whose rights had been violated. However, once this was achieved through an old provision of criminal law, it became necessary to depart from it, since the criminal sanction punishes the perpetrator but does not provide the victim's reparation. At the same time, Sandra's condition as a captive animal required circumventing a second and even more complex issue: the existence of animals as things under Argentine law. In other words, it was necessary to confront the profound asymmetry between the incipient recognition (or discovery) of animals as subjects of fundamental rights and the antiquity and solidity of the property rights exercised over them. Though recognized as a non-human person, Sandra continued to belong to the government of Buenos Aires. It was again in the legal system that Judge Liberatori found the necessary elements to move forward. She pointed to the fact that at the time the law on animal mistreatment was enacted, Argentine legislation had not yet adopted the concept of abuse of rights. This only occurred in 1969 upon the reform of their Civil Code, imposing on the judge the obligation to intervene in such cases.

The combination of the two provisions led to another inference: if the purpose of Law 14,346 is 'not to inflict suffering on a living being', and if the Civil Code does not support the abusive exercise of rights (including property rights), it follows that 'the protected legal interest is not the property of a human or legal person, but animals themselves, holders of the protection established by the law in the face of certain human actions'.[34] It was even possible to find precedents demonstrating that 'there are *already* animals that enjoy their own rights',[35] although they continue to exist legally as things. Moreover, the categorization of animals as sentient beings, introduced in France earlier in the same year, could be analogously extended to Sandra's case.

---

[33] Ibid. The inferences about the use of the word 'victim' in the mistreatment law were first proposed by the renowned jurist Eugenio R. Zaffaroni, not mentioned in the decision.

[34] Juzgado Nacional de Primera Instancia en lo Contencioso Administrativo Federal (n 27) 7.

[35] Juzgado Nacional de Primera Instancia en lo Contencioso Administrativo Federal (n 27) 7–8 (emphasis added). Among the cited examples is the 'pension' granted in 2015 to dogs that worked in the federal customs control services. According to the judge, the benefit was a parallel right to that of their human guides but clearly 'of the dogs themselves'.

This path made it possible to reach a decision set out in three items. Once more, I draw attention to Judge Liberatori's distancing from the approaches that seek to base animal rights on a 'descriptive ontology'.[36] Instead, the development of legal and jurisprudential analogies brought forth a new subject of law, the non-human person, as if it already existed in the Argentine legal world. The first item stated that it was a matter of '*recognizing* the orangutan Sandra as a subject of rights, *in accordance with* Law 14,346 and the Civil and Commercial Code, in the face of the abusive exercise of rights by those responsible for her'.[37] Other knowledge practices could then be incorporated within the scope of this institutional operation to specify the concrete content of these rights. The second item determined the elaboration of a binding technical report to determine the necessary measures to ensure the orangutan's well-being. Finally, the third item assigned obligations to the government of Buenos Aires and the zoo administration regarding Sandra's rights: guaranteeing her an adequate habitat and the activities necessary to preserve her cognitive abilities.[38]

For distinct reasons, this outcome displeased both parties. The two appeals were jointly judged eight months later.[39] Bypassing the grounds of the previous decision, the judges merely recorded that the consideration of animals as subjects of rights was controversial in doctrine, but it was still necessary to ensure Sandra's well-being in accordance with current legislation. In this regard, the examination of testimonies and technical reports collected during the proceedings showed that none of the experts (including those appointed by Afada) had unreservedly recommended the transfer of the orangutan. In addition to the frailty due to her age, the records indicated the failure of an attempt to transfer Sandra to the Córdoba Zoo in 2007. The court decided to revoke the previous decision, putting an end to Sandra's brief life as a non-human person holder of rights. Perhaps not coincidentally, a few days after this decision the Buenos Aires government announced the closure of the city zoo and its remodelling into an ecopark. The plans to transfer 1,500 residing animals, however, did

---

[36] Burgat (n 28) 190.
[37] Juzgado Nacional de Primera Instancia en lo Contencioso Administrativo Federal (n 27) 13 (emphasis added).
[38] Ibid.
[39] Cámara de lo Contencioso Administrativo y Tributário, CABA, Sala 1, 'Sandra (orangutana) s/ acción de amparo', June 14, 2016. Judges Mariana Diaz, Fabiana S. de Nuñez, Fernando Juan Lima. An English translation is available at <https://www.animallaw.info/case/%E2%80%9Casociaci%C3%B3n-de-funcionarios-y-abogados-por-los-derechos-de-los-animales-y-otros-c-gcba-s-amparo> accessed 17 May 2023.

not include the orangutan.[40] Other collateral effects of the processes involving Sandra can be appreciated in the judicial debates about the chimpanzee Cecilia.

THE CHIMPANZEE CECILIA

The writ of habeas corpus on behalf of Cecilia was filed at the beginning of 2015 with the Judiciary of Mendoza, a province in western Argentina. As in Sandra's case, the initiative was taken by the animal defence association Afada. The petition describes Cecilia as a chimpanzee of approximately 30 years of age who had lived almost her entire life in captivity, 'in a truly aberrant cement cage' in the Mendoza Zoo. Moreover, she was completely alone since the recent death of her companions, adding to the conditions that offered 'evident risk to her life and her physical and psychological health'.[41]

Two aspects were highlighted that allude to the human delineation of habeas corpus: on the one hand, the illegal deprivation of freedom ('she has not committed any crimes'); on the other hand, the similarity between chimpanzees and humans, both in genetic terms ('identity of 99.4%') and in their cognitive and socio-cultural capacities. Nevertheless, substantive and legal differences were underlined, circumscribing the scope of the petition: 'it is not intended that chimpanzees, gorillas, orangutans, and bonobos be considered as humans, which they are not, but rather as hominids'. Cecilia is thus described as a 'non-human person' whose fundamental rights had been long and severely violated. In concrete terms, as in Sandra's case, what was sought was her transfer to the Great Apes Sanctuary of Sorocaba.[42]

The grounds of the request were almost identical to those that had been presented in the protection action on behalf of the orangutan Sandra. The different ways in which these arguments were considered by the courts that acted in each case, however, gave distinct contours to the proceedings and the specific qualities to the 'non-human legal person' that each of them brought to light.

Before focusing on Judge María Alejandra Mauricio's decision, it is necessary to review some of the previous steps. The attorney general of Mendoza had refuted the very possibility of an action of that nature: animals 'continue to

---

[40] Federico Molina, 'Zoológico de Buenos Aires é fechado após 140 anos' (2016) *El País* <https://brasil.elpais.com/brasil/2016/06/23/internacional/1466689780_228888.html> accessed 5 August 2016. Due to further developments, Sandra has been living in the Center of Great Apes in Wauchula, Florida, United States, since November 2019 <https://centerforgreatapes.org/orangutan/sandra/> accessed 29 April 2023.

[41] Tercer Juzgado de Garantías, Mendoza, 'Habeas corpus. Presentación efectuada por A.F.A.D.A respecto del chimpancé "Cecilia"- sujeto no humano'. Sentencia FA16190011 (SAIJ), 3 November, 2016. Judge María Alejandra Mauricio (at 3, 5).

[42] Ibid. 1–7.

be things' in the legal system, while the guarantee of habeas corpus is intended for 'the person as a subject of rights'. Based on the same premise, Afada's procedural legitimacy was contested: representation in court can only be exercised 'on behalf of a subject (human person)'.[43]

The judge personally inspected Cecilia's living conditions in the zoo. Later, she did not hesitate to present her impressions about the 'sad and painful image' of the cement cage on whose walls drawings of trees tried 'clumsily to imitate the ape's natural habitat'.[44] A first hearing was held in September of the same year with representatives of Afada and provincial authorities. Expert reports on Cecilia's health conditions and statements from different government agencies were also attached. When the file was already over 280 pages long, a new document produced a turning point in the proceedings and, subsequently, in Cecilia's life: the minutes of a hearing held with the 'new environmental authorities' of Mendoza, in which an agreement was reached for the transfer of the chimpanzee to the Brazilian sanctuary.[45]

To some extent, the ground-breaking ruling merely formalized an understanding between the parties to which the legal debate itself was secondary. Yet, from another perspective, it can be argued that the agreement gave impetus to a renewal of jurisprudence: minimizing the risk of dispute over the decision also opened up space for experimentation. Regardless, the arguments brought up by the parties had to be considered, and this required, first and foremost, going back to a time when an agreement was unlikely: the initial allegations of the provincial attorney on the disposition of persons and things in the Argentine legal system, which would make it impossible to represent an animal in a writ of habeas corpus.

The problem could also be posed in another way: to support the admissibility of the action and the procedural legitimacy of Afada, it was necessary, firstly, to remove animals from the legal status of things. To this effect, it was also necessary to avoid circumscribing the discussion to Cecilia's illegal arrest – as argued by Afada – since that argument would only reinforce the zoo's property right over the chimpanzee and reaffirm her status as a thing. Moreover, the very object of the writ would be lost, since the maintenance of an animal by the zoo that owns it was perfectly legal.

To address these difficulties, the judge resorted to the old Latin adage that affirms the court's prerogative to alter the legal qualification given to the facts by the applicants: *iura novit curia*, or, literally, 'the court knows the law'. This

---

[43] Ibid. 6–7.
[44] Ibid. 42.
[45] The date of this hearing was not recorded in the decision, but the reference to the 'new authorities' indicates that it took place after the inauguration of the new governor of the province, elected in June 2015.

step inaugurated successive displacements: from criminal law to environmental law; from individual rights to collective rights; from property to heritage; from tangible heritage to spiritual bonds; from thing to person.

Judge Mauricio recalls that the 1994 Constitution of Argentina recognized collective rights, among which was the right to the environment. It also incorporated a broad notion of environment that included, along with natural heritage, cultural values and the quality of social life. From this standpoint, the effort was to no longer characterize Cecilia as a prisoner, nor as property, but as heritage in the various forms defined by the constitutional text.

Regarding natural heritage, the judge maintains that 'the orangutan Cecilia [sic] is part of the wildlife of our country', a seemingly incongruous statement given the non-native character of her species. However, this incongruency is irrelevant to the argument, as is Cecilia's zoological classification – Cecilia, as we know, is a chimpanzee – since the Argentinian law for the protection of wildlife covers 'wild or domesticated animals that live under human control, in captivity or semi-captivity'. Much more importantly, Cecilia's placement within the scope of environmental law produced Afada's legal standing, since the protection of wildlife is a matter of 'public interest' and an obligation of 'all the inhabitants of the nation'.[46]

In addition, it became possible to qualify Cecilia's situation as 'collective environmental damage', and to draw further consequences from this. As the judge points out, by defining environmental damage as 'any relevant alteration that negatively modifies the environment, its resources, the balance of ecosystems, or collective goods or values', the 2002 General Environmental Law (*Ley General del Ambiente*) 'grants broad powers to the judge who intervenes in collective environmental damage actions in order to effectively protect the general interest'. In the case at hand, she continues, what is at stake is 'the collective value embodied in Cecilia's well-being', due not only to her being part of the country's natural heritage, but also because 'insofar as she relates to the community of humans, [she] is part of (...) the cultural heritage of the community'.[47]

Turning Cecilia into 'the community's natural and cultural heritage' made it possible to circumvent some of the legal and procedural problems arising from her status as a thing in the Civil and Commercial Code. Nevertheless, it produced another challenge: how to justify the transfer of this heritage to a foreign country? The solution required other transformations, supported by the point-by-point contemplation of the constitutional definition of environ-

---

[46] Tercer Juzgado de Garantías (n 41) 13.
[47] Ibid. 15, 19.

ment – which, as indicated above, associates natural heritage with cultural values and the quality of social life.

Initially, Judge Mauricio considered the nature of the link between a community and its heritage. By converting this link into a 'spiritual bond' (or cultural value, under the terms of the Constitution), it became possible to state that its persistence and intensity do not require physical proximity. Therefore, even outside the country and subject to foreign laws, 'Cecilia may continue to be a member of our environmental heritage'. Furthermore, it having been proven that, under current conditions, 'our community' is unable to assure Cecilia's well-being, a solution capable of offering her 'the life she deserves' will have positive effects on the community's own quality of life through 'the opportunity to grow as a collective and to feel more human'.[48]

Would the writ of habeas corpus be the most appropriate path to protect the 'collective value' at stake? The question remains momentarily suspended because, after the outcomes of the journey through environmental law – the collective nature of the issue at hand, the procedural legitimacy of Afada, the reasonableness of possibly transferring Cecilia to another country –, it was still necessary to venture out to other legal realms in order to transpose the obstacle defined by Judge Mauricio as 'the big question: are the great apes – orangutans, bonobos, gorillas and chimpanzees – subjects of non-human rights?'[49]

As proposed, the 'big question' is not whether animals are subjects of rights altogether, but whether certain animals are. In other words, the premise is the disaggregation of non-human beings in law (and by rights) and, at the same time, the establishment of particular links between some animals – namely, the great primates – and human beings. The answer to the 'big question' depends, however, on what can be done with the long-standing existence of all animals in the legal world under the category of things, distinct from others only by their quality of 'movable things'. Property rights, however, reunify the set of 'things' despite their attributes, by placing them under the ownership of 'persons'.

In this regard, the formal legality of Cecilia's circumstances had already been asserted at an earlier time, as opposed to the denunciation of her 'illegal and arbitrary detention'.[50] But if transforming the chimpanzee into heritage was not enough to dissolve her concomitant existence as property, it was possible to extract another consequence from this dual condition. Reformed in 2014, the Argentine Civil and Commercial Code limited individual rights over

---

[48] Ibid. 19–20.
[49] Ibid. 28.
[50] As recorded, the Mendoza Zoo was created in 1897 by a provincial law, which defined the incorporation of animals of various species as part of its functions. Ibid. 10.

property to the extent of their compatibility with collective rights. However, neither this relativization of property rights nor the legal protection of wildlife as part of the collective right to the environment constitute individual animals as holders of rights.

At this point, the 'big question' could be stated in another way: what makes a person? What is present (or missing) in things that prevents them from being persons? The next steps of Judge Mauricio's decision consider both questions thoroughly. She is well aware that what is at stake is not only the possibility of making Cecilia a subject of rights, but also the reverberations of this condition in the lives of other non-human beings. For this reason, the heterogeneous references mobilized to reassess the respective attributes of persons and things should not be surprising, nor the oscillation – or deliberate equivocation – between the ontological (philosophical and/or scientific) and the institutional (technical and/or fictional) foundation of rights and forms of existence in the legal world.[51]

At first, the essential continuity between humans and animals as sentient living beings is underscored through a brief reference to Aristotle, for whom, according to Judge Mauricio, 'they all belong to the same species', the only difference residing in the 'political capacity' held by humans. Next, the contrast with living beings leads to the identification of the 'intrinsic nature of things': their quality as inanimate objects. For both reasons, she concludes, 'classifying animals as things is not the right criterion'.[52]

As described earlier, the recognition of animals as being capable of conscious sensations and emotions, glimpsed in the use of the word 'victim' in the law on animal mistreatment, allowed the orangutan Sandra to be declared a 'non-human person' holder of rights. The same reasoning was brought in Cecilia's favour, but the encounter between the two decisions was fleeting. In the first one, as it turned out, the argument readily extended to all animals. In Cecilia's case, however, the criterion that allows animals to be removed from the set of 'things' (sentience and the alleged 'incoherence' of a legal system in which animals are classified as things, but also protected from suffering) is not the same as that which personifies them. The decision makes successive differentiations not only between persons and things but also within each of these categories, redistributing their alleged attributes. Thus, after distinguishing animals from other things and bringing them closer to (human) persons, the argumentation differentiates animals themselves, a step which will also produce different (legal) persons. These effects were presupposed by the very formulation of the 'big question'. Not by accident, there follows a detailed

---

[51] Burgat (n 28) 177.
[52] Tercer Juzgado de Garantías (n 41) 32.

exposition of the cognitive, emotional, and cultural skills of great apes, which would only differ in degree from human capabilities.[53]

At this point, the orangutan Sandra appears for the second time in the decision referring to the chimpanzee Cecilia, through legal opinions on the proceedings in which she had been (and still was) involved. Some of these opinions do not corroborate the thesis that Judge Mauricio intends to sustain, yet they serve other argumentative purposes. In commenting on the decision of the CFCP concerning Sandra, jurist Carlos M. Muñiz opposes the 'logical leap' that draws from the norms for the protection of animals their status as legal subjects, 'something that does not come from any legal provision (...) and would be highly inconvenient in practice'.[54] As cited by Judge Mauricio, however, the emphasis on the 'logical leap' between legal text and court ruling shifts to the 'legal void' when it comes to animals. And this, in yet another twist, leads to reaffirming, in the name of 'human dignity', the responsibility of humans 'as rational beings' towards the ecosystem and posterity.[55]

This anthropocentric view is accentuated by the allusion to comments from Judge Pedro David, who had participated in the CFCP's decision but, as aforementioned, did not endorse the consideration of animals as subjects holding their own rights. Even so, some of his reflections were used to support the opposite thesis, notably the urgency of better legal protection of the environment and animals, in view of the 'historical crossroads' that endangers the planet itself.[56] When coupled with previous considerations on the 'void' in legislation, these remarks could enable and assist the effort to create new forms of legal consideration of non-human living beings through case law.

Another idea borrowed from Judge David contributes to limiting the scope of the previous point: the suggestion that legal protection for non-human beings 'should be based on the rights guaranteed to persons, (...) although not in their entirety, but in the most effective way to the care and survival of animals'.[57] If the rights of (human) persons should be the model, but not in their entirety, there is room to differentiate humans and animals, firstly, and then animals themselves according to the 'evolutionary degree that science determines they can reach'. Only a few of them qualify to transpose – and modify – institutional classifications. Thus, according to Judge Mauricio, 'the

---

[53] Ibid. 32–33.
[54] Carlos M. Muñiz, 'Los animales ante la ley: de objetos y sujetos' (2016) *La Ley* <https://repositorio.uca.edu.ar/bitstream/123456789/13449/1/animales-ante-ley.pdf> accessed 19 November 2018.
[55] Tercer Juzgado de Garantías (n 41) 35.
[56] Ibid. 36. The referenced article is Pedro R. David, 'Notes on the case of Sandra, non-human legal subject' (n.d.) *El Derecho Penal*.
[57] Tercer Juzgado de Garantías (n 41) 36.

category of subject as the centre of attribution of norms (or subject of law) would include not only human beings, but also great primates'.[58]

Although this new status remains ambiguous, since 'it is not a matter of assigning to great primates the rights listed in civil and commercial law',[59] it has finally become possible to ask: is habeas corpus the proper procedural path in Cecilia's case? The concise answer highlights its own novelty: 'Yes, because there is no other' capable of accounting for 'the specific situation of an animal deprived of its essential rights'. And what rights would those be? In the absence of specific legal provision, its scope should 'strictly adjust to preserving Cecilia's right to live in an environment and under conditions appropriate to her species'.[60] Judge Mauricio then decides:

I- To accept the writ of habeas corpus (…);
II- To declare the chimpanzee Cecilia, currently housed in the Provincial Zoo of Mendoza, a non-human subject of law;
III- To order the transfer of the chimpanzee Cecilia to the Sanctuary of Sorocaba, located in the Republic of Brazil (…) as agreed by the parties.[61]

The mention of the previous agreement highlights the conditions under which it became possible to reach a pioneering decision, the consequences of which extended to a foreign country. It also helps to understand the approval, in the following month, of a law transforming the former zoo into the Ecopark Mendoza. Yet, the agreement was not able to preclude an unexpected effect: a collective protection action (*amparo colectivo*) to prevent Cecilia's transfer under the same argument as the ruling that granted her habeas corpus. Since she was the only chimpanzee residing in the province, it was argued that guaranteeing her permanence in the country was crucial to 'preserve the natural and cultural heritage, and biological diversity'. When the claim was rejected,[62] Cecilia was already at her new home in Brazil, where she has lived ever since.

DIFFERENT PERSONS, DIFFERENT RIGHTS: FURTHER EQUIVOCATIONS

After witnessing the birth of two non-human persons, it is time for a brief return to the starting point: the enduring association between the human person and the subject of law. From the complex trajectory of the legal concept of

---

[58] Ibid. 37–38.
[59] Ibid. 35.
[60] Ibid. 44.
[61] Ibid.
[62] Tribunal de Gestión Judicial Asociada n. 2, Mendoza, 'Pometti, Hugo c/ Provincia de Mendoza s/ Acción de Amparo', Sentencia FA17190000 (SAIJ), January 25, 2017. Judge Patricia Dolores Fox.

person, I retain the contrast traced by Surrallés between two moments separated by five centuries.[63]

The first concerns the debate by jurists of the School of Salamanca, in the mid-sixteenth century, about the limits of Spanish colonial expansion in America in the face of the rights of indigenous peoples. This is relevant to the present discussion insofar as the establishment of the conceptual basis for these rights relied on the radical differentiation between humans and other living beings, with the exclusive attribution of *dominium* to the former: the legitimate power to dispose of their property, in a broad sense. As argued by Francisco de Vitoria, reason places human beings in a special class and makes them the sole holders of rights. Deprived of the capacity for rational evaluation of an act, animals, though recognized as sentient beings, could neither be the target of offense (*iniuria*) nor possess and exercise *dominium*.[64]

In contrast, Surrallés observes that the sensitive dimension of subjectivity has grounded the constitution of subjects of law in the present. He refers to a specific notion that has been recently developed in international law for the recognition of indigenous territorial rights: that of spiritual relationships between humans and non-humans. This, according to his argument, would indirectly result in the constitution of non-human entities as subjects of human rights. Although addressing different issues, he does not fail to recognize the affinity between this emerging form of extension of human rights and the arguments that take sentience – the sensitivity to suffering, shared by humans and non-humans – as the foundation of animal rights.[65]

As described in this chapter, sentience played a key role in making the chimpanzee Cecilia and priorly, for a brief period, the orangutan Sandra non-human persons and subjects of rights. Despite this convergence and the recursiveness of the proceedings in which both were involved, the legal personification of each of them was performed through distinct paths and operations, so that Cecilia and Sandra became different persons among themselves and in relation to pre-existing persons (and things) in the legal world. Sentience does not subsist as a uniform quality when incorporated into the procedural debate, nor can be taken merely as an extra-legal referent of legal operations.

The notion of deliberate equivocation helps to underscore how the decisions concerning Sandra and Cecilia resorted – simultaneously, successively, or alternately – to different conceptions of law and rights, to which I have until now referred by borrowing the distinction proposed by Burgat: on the one hand, the ontological grounding of animal rights, which seeks a correspond-

---

[63] Alexandre Surrallés, 'Human rights for nonhumans?' (2017) 7(3) Hau 211.
[64] Ibid. 225–226.
[65] Ibid. 230.

ence between a set of traits taken as constitutive of the definition of person (legal, but also human) and substantive attributes of the individual to be admitted into this class; and, on the other hand, a declaratory perspective, aimed not at describing a reality but at establishing an institutional relationship.[66]

Nevertheless, it may be misleading to attribute the decisions concerning Sandra and Cecilia to these two alternatives. Particularly in Cecilia's case, the overlapping of seemingly conflicting perspectives expanded the possibilities for analogies and the association of disparate objects and heterogeneous propositions. If the connection between different arguments often seems to result from a prestidigitation pass (a 'tour de passe-passe,' in Marguénaud's ironic comment),[67] focusing on their scant coherence obliterates the relevant question: what holds together propositions whose obvious incoherence surely did not go unnoticed by their author?

I suggest that in these associations there is another form of deliberate equivocation. The loose connection between the various arguments hides the precise ability each of them holds to transpose successive legal and procedural hurdles, without which it would not be possible to reach a decision. At times, the stratagem used to overcome a certain obstacle produces a new one, which requires other devices. And so, successively, it becomes possible to resolve questions of procedural legitimacy, justify the transfer of community heritage to a foreign country, circumvent the legal regime of property, or make precedents support an unprecedented decision. In short, the nexus of the argumentative path does not reside in its internal coherence, but in its effectiveness to face, step by step, heterogeneous difficulties.

In the protection action (*amparo*) concerning Sandra, institutional forms served as a repository of possibilities for (re)describing long-standing entities and relations. The non-human person entitled to rights was extracted from pre-existing legal statements (the half-century-old law on animal abuse, paired with the notion of abuse of rights in the reformed Civil and Commercial Code), supported by controversial doctrine constructions (inferences raised by the word 'victim') and precedents of case law (the CFCP's decision that, by declaring animals as subjects of rights, also gave the endorsement of a higher court to a 'dynamic legal interpretation').

If sentience was pivotal in the constitution of the non-human person in this case, it was less as a substantive attribute incorporated into the institutional repertoire than the other way around: because the law allegedly defines animal victims of mistreatment as sentient beings, it became possible to recognize the orangutan Sandra – and, potentially, other animals – as holders of rights of

---

[66] Burgat (n 28) 177.
[67] Marguénaud (n 16) 20.

their own. The connection between sentience and legal personhood, moreover, was not traced directly, but by analogy with other legal provisions: namely, the French Civil Code, which had recently (re)described animals as 'living beings endowed with sensitivity'. These institutional steps allowed the introduction of a radical innovation – the non-human person subject of law – as if nothing had actually changed.

Differently, in the decision regarding Cecilia, it is as an intrinsic attribute, shared by humans and animals alike, that sentience imposes limits to the consideration of the latter as (legal) things. However, only great primates, by virtue of their similarity with human beings, are granted access to the condition of subjects of law. Marguénaud sees a distortion in this difference in criteria: instead of prioritizing a 'technical' approach to the legal personification of animals, the ruling would at this point have yielded to an anthropomorphic perspective, with selective and paradoxical consequences: on the one hand, the impossibility of extending the same guarantees to other animals; on the other, the attribution to the non-human person of broader guarantees than those protecting the human person. The French jurist adds an acid comment: 'What a revolution for human rights if the physical freedom protected by habeas corpus were to translate into the concrete and effective right, recognized to every human being, to live in an environment and in conditions adapted to their species!'.[68]

The oscillation identified by Marguénaud between technical and anthropomorphic approaches – to some extent analogous to Burgat's distinction between declaratory and ontological perspectives – disregards the fact that legal technique is a mode par excellence for defining ontologies. On the other hand, the anthropomorphic attributes that support the selective recognition of great apes as persons are no more natural than the ingredients of the so-called technical approach. The enumeration of properties common to humans and great primates depends on the assumption that similarity produces solidarity and, therefore, can be both the cause and the justification of a (legal) relation.[69] In this sense, even the emphasis on shared DNA is, from the outset, a technique that makes use of an institutional nature – extended notions of family – to solve institutional problems: the (ontological) definition of the mode of existence of certain entities in the legal world.

Thus, it is not the case of contrasting the operations that constituted Sandra and Cecilia as non-human legal persons by qualifying them as more or less technical. Rather, this chapter intends to describe how each of these technical ways of disposing persons and things addressed the issues of sameness and

---

[68] Marguénaud (n 16) 21–25.
[69] Marilyn Strathern, 'Binary license' (2011) 17(1) Common Knowledge 87, 99.

difference (institutional and non-institutional) that they raised. To conclude, I draw attention to some of the consequences of these operations.

Although these new legal persons were brought into existence by distinct means and thus cannot be assimilated to each other, they share a fundamental quality that challenges the principle of non-contradiction that has governed the Western legal world since medieval times: non-human persons are (among other things) simultaneously persons and things. This condition distinguishes them, first and foremost, from the human person, and the stressed similarity between humans and great apes further expresses this distinction. Secondly, it sets them apart from other forms of legal personality, insofar as the legal person, human or otherwise, is defined primarily by its quality of not being a thing, i.e. by the impossibility of being owned as property and the right to own things. But if the non-human person, by virtue of being also a thing, cannot (so far) hold property rights, it is well known that in order to guarantee the rights of the (human) person it was first necessary to objectify them and, by this deviation, think of them as non-commodifiable.[70] Non-human persons as a specific kind of things could be just one more chapter of an unfolding history, bringing once again to the fore the intrinsic ambiguity of the person/thing matrix, always prone to internal equivocations,[71] deliberate or otherwise.

Precisely because they continue to be things, emergent persons like Sandra and Cecilia may be endowed with distinct qualities as they move through different regions of the legal world (constitutional, criminal, environmental), while their access as subjects to some of them remains barred (notably the privileged land of contractual relations). However, they also differ from other things by their quality as holders of rights that can be enforced in court and whose existence imposes restrictions on the rights of other persons. These rights are, to a certain extent, fundamental human rights: not because they are imbued with some intrinsically human quality, but because they have so far only been granted to human holders.[72] Yet, they are also other rights.

To emphasize this point, it is possible to return to the paradox identified by Marguénaud in Cecilia's habeas corpus, which supposedly granted her broader guarantees than the freedom of movement it grants to human beings. Nevertheless, it is also possible to notice that the same ruling invested the right to freedom with a peculiar quality. By redefining the non-human habeas corpus as Cecilia's right to live in conditions appropriate to her species, and determining that such conditions would be fulfilled with her transfer to private facilities in another country, where she would live among other great apes,

---

[70] Thomas (n 12) 93.
[71] Morita (n 24) 314.
[72] Burgat (n 28) 182.

the right to freedom as self-determination was converted into the prescription of certain relations, both with humans and other non-human beings, under pre-specified conditions. This allows for a final comment.

FAR FROM CONCLUSION: WHO CONTROLS DIFFERENCE?

As in the procedural debate, these recombinations in the legal world can also have unforeseen effects on an existential level. Six months after Cecilia's arrival at the Sorocaba Great Apes Sanctuary, the media reported the 'escape' of two resident chimpanzees and their 'invasion' of a neighbouring property.[73] While the residents hid inside the house, the animals insistently banged on the door and eventually broke the lock. Their intent remains inscrutable, but according to the news it was not the first occurrence of this kind.

Of course, bringing up these episodes is not meant as an argument against animal rights or, specifically, against legal personhood to non-humans. Notwithstanding, they express, in a stark and disturbing way, the irreducibility of non-human forms of life to human control of their difference,[74] even when it is based on (necessarily human) notions of well-being.[75]

---

[73] Natália de Oliveira, 'Chimpanzés fogem de santuário e invadem sítio em Sorocaba' (*G1*, 9 October 2017) <https://g1.globo.com/sao-paulo/sorocaba-jundiai/noticia/chimpanzes-fogem-de-santuario-e-invadem-sitio-em-sorocaba-video.ghtml> accessed 29 April 2023.

[74] Martin Holbraad, Morten A. Pedersen and Eduardo Viveiros de Castro, 'The politics of ontology: anthropological positions' (2014) *Cultural Anthropology Fieldsights* <https://culanth.org/fieldsights/the-politics-of-ontology-anthropological-positions> accessed 29 April 2023.

[75] This chapter is partially based on my article 'Pessoas não humanas: Sandra, Cecília e a emergência de novas formas de existência jurídica' (2019) 25(1) Mana 38.

7. The EU Charter on Rights of Nature – colliding cosmovisions on non/human relations

Marie-Catherine Petersmann[1]

INTRODUCTION

The movement of granting 'rights to nature' has become prominent in academic debates. Much has been written on the self-proclaimed 'revolutionary' potential that 'rights of nature' present to overcome the destructive world-ecology brought about by capitalist modes in inhabiting the Earth.[2] Granting rights to 'nature' has been described by some as a practice of 'legal animism',[3] and by others as one of 'shamanic magic'.[4] This is partly due to the fact that animistic Indigenous cosmologies informed activist movements that today call for a legal 'paradigm shift' to re-connect humans with non-humans,

---

[1] This research was supported by the Dutch NWO 'Veni' Grant (VI.Veni.211R.026) on 'Anthropocene Legalities: Reconfiguring Legal Relations Within More-than-human Worlds'.

[2] See, e.g., David R. Boyd, *The Rights of Nature: A Legal Revolution That Could Save the World* (ECW Press 2017); Guillaume Chapron et al., 'A Rights Revolution for Nature' (2019) 363.6434 Science 1392–1393. The notion of 'world-ecology' comes from Moore, for whom a world-economy based on the appropriation, extraction, and exploitation of 'nature' underpins this world-ecology. Cf. Jason W. Moore (ed.), *Anthropocene or Capitalocene? Nature, History, and the Crisis of Capitalism* (PM Press 2016).

[3] Such 'animistic' practices, however, underpinned modern law too: 'modern law is essentially "animist," populated by right-holder entities whose personhood is a product of legal fiction. Corporations, for example, are defined as "fictitious persons," and under various international statutes and national constitutional provisions have their own specific rights in a manner similar to human citizens – the ultimate fetish of capital made real by law'. Paulo Tavares, 'Nonhuman Rights', in Forensic Architecture, *Forensis: The Architecture of Public Truth* (Sternberg Press & Forensic Architecture 2014), 533–572, 565.

[4] Cf. Alexis Alvarez-Nakagawa, 'Law *as* Magic: Some Thoughts on Ghosts, Non-humans, and Shamans' (2017) 18.5 German Law Journal 1247–1276.

including through the recognition of 'rights of nature'.[5] Such developments are increasingly perceived as responses to fundamental preoccupations of the 'Anthropocene'.[6] At stake in these preoccupations are also colliding understandings of how best to protect 'nature' – and what 'nature' means in the first place – with different proposals being advanced to (re)configure human–non-human relations in both critical and mainstream institutional spaces. It is these distinct understandings of relationality – of how humans (ought to) relate to non-humans – that I want to retrieve and explore in this chapter, with an emphasis on different 'rights of nature' paradigms.

Recent developments in the United Nations (UN) are illustrative of these dynamics, where discourses on 'rights of nature' have transitioned from the critical margins to the centre stage of policy advocacy. In April 2009, under the leadership of the newly (re)constituted Plurinational State of Bolivia, the UN General Assembly (UNGA) proclaimed 22 April as 'International Mother Earth Day'.[7] In December of the same year, the UNGA adopted its first resolution entitled 'Harmony with Nature', requesting the UN Secretary-General (UNSG) to issue a report on this theme.[8] More than a decade later, 12 resolutions have been adopted by the UNGA, with 10 reports issued by the UNSG and 10 interactive dialogues held among various stakeholders on Harmony with Nature.[9] The overall objective of this policy framework is to define a 'newly found relationship based on a non-anthropocentric relationship with Nature', where 'the construction of a new, non-anthropocentric paradigm in which the fundamental basis for right and wrong action concerning the envi-

---

[5] See, e.g., Mihnea Tănăsescu, 'Rights of Nature, Legal Personality, and Indigenous Philosophies' (2020) 9.3 Transnational Environmental Law 429; Iván D. Vargas Roncancio, 'Conjuring Sentient Beings and Relations in the Law: Rights of Nature and a Comparative Praxis of Legal Cosmologies in Latin America', in Kirsten Anker et al. (eds), *From Environmental Law to Ecological Law* (Routledge 2020) 119; and Idelber Avelar, 'Amerindian Perspectivism and Non-Human Rights' (2013) 31 Ciencia y Cultura 255. For a critique of the co-optation of Indigenous worldviews in mainstream governance discourses today and the exoticized framing and invocation of an 'Indigenous being', see also David Chandler and Julian Reid, *Becoming Indigenous: Governing Imaginaries in the Anthropocene* (Rowman & Littlefield 2019).

[6] See, e.g., Alice Bleby, 'Rights of Nature as a Response to the Anthropocene' (2020) 48:1 University of Western Australia Law Review 33; Joshua C. Gellers, 'The Rights of Nature: Ethics, Law, and the Anthropocene', in *Rights for Robots: Artificial Intelligence, Animal and Environmental Law* (Routledge 2020), 104–139.

[7] A/RES/63/278 declaring 22 April as 'International Mother Earth Day', at <www.un.org/en/observances/earth-day> accessed 17 February 2022.

[8] A/RES/64/196, available on the website of the UN Harmony with Nature, at <www.harmonywithnatureun.org> accessed 17 February 2022.

[9] Ibid.

ronment is grounded not solely in human concerns'.[10] Unsurprisingly, 'rights of nature' figure centrally in this reformist agenda. As proclaimed by the UNSG: '[r]ights of Nature is grounded in the recognition that humankind and Nature share a fundamental, non-anthropocentric relationship given our shared existence on this planet, and it creates guidance for actions that respect this relationship'.[11] In this context, the Harmony with Nature agenda is advocating a new relationality aimed at re-connecting humans to non-humans. A break from Enlightenment-based legacies of modernist ideals of mastery over an externalized 'nature' amenable to human control is evident.[12]

In line with this UN agenda, itself inspired by the experience of plurinational re-constituted states in Latin America – notably Ecuador and Bolivia – an increasing number of states worldwide are today integrating 'rights of nature' into their domestic legal systems or jurisprudence. As of 2022, 39 countries adopted constitutional, legislative, or policy measures recognizing either 'nature' as a whole or particular ecosystems as subjects of rights or as legal persons.[13] While the vast majority of these countries are situated in Latin America, European countries like Portugal, France, Spain, Switzerland, the United Kingdom, the Netherlands and Belgium are also pushing this agenda further.[14] In this chapter, I am interested in exploring how the incorporation of 'rights of nature' in European states and the proposal to introduce them in the European Union's (EU) legal order is underpinned by a particular understand-

---

[10] Ibid.

[11] Ibid. This statement would deserve critical attention on its own. Not only does the 'shared existence' of 'humankind' reproduce the same universalizing and totalizing understanding of a supposedly shared and generalized human experience that critics of the 'Anthropocene' have repeatedly denounced; it also reinscribes a disconnection between humans and non-humans by speaking of an inter-connection between separated 'humankind and Nature' that 'share a relationship' with one another. As will become clear throughout this chapter, this statement is antithetical to entangled relationalities. For a critique of universalizing and totalizing accounts of liberal promises to save 'humanity' and 'the world', see also Audra Mitchell and Aadita Chaudhury, 'Worlding Beyond "the" "end" of "the world": White Apocalyptic Visions and BIPOC Futurisms' (2020) 34:3 International Relations 309.

[12] On this modernist Enlightenment worldview, see Nathaniel Wolloch, *History and Nature in the Enlightenment: Praise of the Mastery of Nature in Eighteenth-Century Historical Literature* (Routledge 2016). On how this modernist Enlightenment worldview was rejected in non-Western traditions, see Julietta Singh, *Unthinking Mastery: Dehumanism and Decolonial Entanglements* (Duke University Press 2018).

[13] Alex Putzer et al., 'Putting the Rights of Nature on the Map: A Quantitative Analysis of Rights of Nature Initiatives Across the World' (2022) Journal of Maps 1–8, 1.

[14] 'Rights of Nature: Law and Policy', at <www.harmonywithnatureun.org/rightsOfNature> accessed 17 February 2022.

ing of relationality. More specifically, I explore how the EU Charter on the Fundamental Rights of Nature – which was drafted by a group of experts and submitted to the European Economic and Social Committee in December 2019 – both utilizes and departs from Andean Indigenous cosmologies. The main argument is that while the EU Charter explicitly relies on these cosmologies to justify the importance of recognizing 'rights of nature', it strategically sidelines the particular Andean onto-epistemological relational footing to opt for rather different relations between humans and non-humans. This, the chapter argues, grounds the relationality at stake into a distinctively European way of viewing 'humans as part of nature', but simultaneously risks disavowing the Indigenous, Afro-descendent, Maroon, and Native decolonial stuggles that drove the very movement of granting 'rights to nature' against European settler colonial modes of inhabiting the Earth.

The argument proceeds in three steps. First, I explore how 'rights of nature' were constitutionally recognized in plurinational states in Latin America, with a particular focus on Ecuador and Bolivia. Second, I analyze the movements of granting 'rights to nature' that are now unfolding in Europe by drawing on, among others, these particular Andean cosmologies. Finally, I attend to the distinct and arguably opposite understandings of relationality at stake in these approaches, and reflect on how invocations of Indigenous cosmologies to grant 'rights to nature' in Europe conflates and obscures these important differences. These invocations risk disavowing the historical subjugation of Indigenous peoples and their onto-epistemologies by Western colonial states. Overall, the analysis sheds light on the politics, imaginaries, and world-making effects performed by articulations of 'rights of nature' that draw on Indigenous cosmologies to advance their implementation in Europe today.

PLURINATIONAL RE-CONSTITUTIONS AND 'RIGHTS OF NATURE' IN LATIN AMERICA

The first legislative recognitions of 'rights of nature' within domestic constitutions came about in 'plurinational' countries, namely Ecuador and Bolivia. Like all countries in Latin America, Ecuador and Bolivia's histories are nested within legacies of colonialism. Since gaining their independence, the inherited political, economic, and racial structures of Latin Americas states remained tainted by the logic of their former colonial powers. As Tavares observes, this logic was sustained by 'a double and entangled form of violence: the exhaustive exploitation of natural resources and the exclusion of native culture from political representation'.[15] Merino speaks of the 'new republican order' that

---

[15] Tavares (n 3) 567.

was born with the independence of states in Latin America as one that 'rejected differentiated political recognition of the Indians'.[16] Native Indigenous peoples (or 'Indians') remained on the margins of legality, as they were considered 'citizens in name only, with most elites maintaining deeply racist attitudes toward them'.[17] Against this marginalization, a process of re-constitution of states as 'plurinational' polities emerged. This process formally materialized in 2008 in Ecuador and in 2009 in Bolivia, when the enduring presence and constituent power of multiple cultures and nationalities was constitutionally recognized. Indigenous peoples, Afro-descendant, Maroon, and Native communities continued being abused as 'cheap labour' throughout the second half of the century even after independence, in a colonial-style economy that exploited a 'cheap nature' conditioned by the demands of a global market for natural commodities.[18] The transnational organizing and uprisings of these exploited communities were key to forging the pluri-constituency of Ecuador and Bolivia.[19] This *re*-constitutional process was therefore a corrective exercise – a *re*-action against centuries of enduring repression, subjugation, and exploitation of marginalized communities, and *re*-cognition of their (dis) constituent power. In September 2008, a new and inclusive constitution was adopted in Ecuador, which established a united 'Plurinational and Intercultural State' recognizing 11 Indigenous nationalities and cultures as equal and ethnically diverse.[20] The following year, in January 2009, Bolivia adopted its new constitution recognizing the multicultural nature of Bolivia and the inclusion of the Indigenous peoples of 36 cultural nationalities. In their *re*-constitution, Ecuador and Bolivia also recognized 'nature' as a subject of rights.[21]

An evident link exists between this first constitutional recognition of 'rights of nature' and the fact it emerged from plurinational and multicultural states. The subordination of Indigenous, Afro-descendant, Maroon, and Native communities, the spoliation and exploitation of their lands, and the plunder

---

[16] Roger Merino, 'Reimagining the Nation-State: Indigenous Peoples and the Making of Plurinationalism in Latin America' (2018) 31.4 Leiden Journal of International Law 773–792, 777.

[17] Ibid.

[18] On how capitalism created cheap labour, cheap food, cheap energy and cheap raw materials or 'cheap nature', see Moore (n 2).

[19] Tavares (n 3) 567–568. On this 'pluri-constituency' as a 'Creole legal consciousness' that emerged through Indigenous peoples' transnational organizing as opposed to the 'whitening' of the states, see also Merino (n 16) 777–778 and 781.

[20] Cf. 'Latin America is moving towards Plurinationalism, slowly but definitely' (25 February 2022), at <https://peoplesdispatch.org/2022/02/25/latin-america-is-moving-towards-plurinationalism-slowly-but-definitely> accessed 7 July 2022.

[21] Cf. Constitution of the Republic of Ecuador 2008, Articles 71–74, 86(3), 396–397. In 2010, Bolivia adopted a Law of the Rights of Mother Earth.

of common resources, had pushed ecological issues to the centre of political struggles in both Ecuador and Bolivia.[22] At stake in these struggles were radically conflicting worldviews and modes of inhabiting the Earth. These conflicting worldviews revolved around, on the one hand, a modernist, neo-liberal, and colonial economic and societal model that treated 'nature' as a commodity – a view that John Law qualified as Western 'mononaturalism'[23] – and, on the other hand, diverse cosmologies nurtured by different Indigenous cultures and nationalities that acknowledge the force and wisdom of modes of living not *on* but *with* the Earth.[24] If a 'plurinationalization' of Ecuador and Bolivia implied a recognition of multiple cultures and nationalities within these states, it also implied a recognition of different understandings of and imaginaries about 'nature', which fundamentally rejected the modernist, colonial-based, and 'mononaturalist' view of 'nature' enacted by the Ecuadorian and Bolivian governments after their independence.

The adoption of 'rights of nature' was more the result of an attempted formal inclusion – yet not a pure translation – of 'non-modernist' cosmologies into the re-constitutional processes of Ecuador and Bolivia, rather than a recognition of 'nature' as a subject of rights by the modernist, neo-liberal, and (post)colonial states as such.[25] As Tavares recollects from an interview with

---

[22] Tavares (n 3) 568.

[23] John Law, 'What's Wrong with a One-world World?' (2015) 16 Distinktion: Scandinavian Journal of Social Theory 1, 1. Law critiqued the dominant and hegemonic 'Northern' strategies that naturalize mononaturalism – or the natural/physical character of the world, disconnected from the cultures, peoples, and beliefs that form the multicultural character of the world – and reduced Indigenous realities to beliefs which may be discounted. Law denounced how the Global North enacted this 'mononaturalism' while inhabited by 'multiple-natures'.

[24] See, e.g., Rosemary J. Coombe and David Jefferson, 'Posthuman Rights Struggles and Environmentalisms from Below in the Political Ontologies of Ecuador and Colombia' (2021) 12.2 Journal of Human Rights and the Environment 177; and Maria Akchurin, 'Constructing the Rights of Nature: Constitutional Reform, Mobilization, and Environmental Protection in Ecuador' (2015) 40 Law and Social Inquiry 937.

[25] The question of how and to what extent Indigenous cosmovisions aligned with the liberal understanding of 'rights' formulation is a question I do not address here. I do not claim that Indigenous cosmovisions were neatly translated into the constitutions of Ecuador and Bolivia, nor that all Indigenous peoples across Ecuador and Bolivia endorse the instrumental and strategic translation of their struggles into 'rights' claims. On the inherent tensions in the translation of Indigenous cosmovisions in legal systems based on universalist values, with a particular emphasis on 'rights of nature' in Ecuador and Bolivia, see Leah Temper, 'Blocking Pipelines, Unsettling Environmental Justice: From Rights of Nature to Responsibility to Territory' (2019) 24.2 Local Environment 94–112. What is more, translating Indigenous cosmovisions into 'rights' claims disregards *how* tribal peoples actually *become* Indigenous peoples only when they per-

Ecuadorian activist Esperanza Martínez: 'it was necessary to take into account multiple forms of conceiving of and relating to nature – that is, to acknowledge by law the existence of, quite literally, different natural worlds'.[26] This opening to diversity and inclusion of non-modernist worldviews in what remains an essentially modernist model of the nation-state functioning, did not stop the latter from commodifying, exploiting, and plundering natural 'resources',[27] but enabled those contesting this mode of relating to 'nature' to resist its prominence by protecting 'nature's rights' against an appropriative economic model.[28] What emerged in plurinational states was therefore an enactment of multiple yet also conflicting legal protection and regulation of 'nature', and not a replacement of the modernist regulation of 'natural resources' in (post) colonial state law by 'non-' or 'pre-modern' Indigenous cosmovisions about 'rights of nature'.[29]

My objective, here, is not to delve into the conception of 'rights of nature' as enacted by the re-constitutions of plurinational states in Latin America. This part of the story is important to recount, however, before turning to an analysis of 'rights of nature' in Europe today, since most domestic constitutions or legislative acts that recognized 'rights of nature' did so by way of including and recognizing local Indigenous peoples, Afro-descendant, Maroon, and Native communities' own normativities and modes of relating

---

formatively inscribe the 'rights discourse' into their way of life. See Stephen M. Young, *Indigenous Peoples, Consent and Rights: Troubling Subjects* (Routledge 2020) 32.

[26] Tavares (n 3) 568.

[27] As Merino (n 16) 787 reckons, '[a]lthough the Bolivian and Ecuadorian constitutions are seen as post-neoliberal and post-multicultural because of their emphasis on market regulation, rights expansion and political agency of social collectives, and their recognition that Indigenous peoples are nations with territorial rights, these projects maintain racialized and colonial notions of sovereignty and state power on Indigenous territories, demonstrating an intrinsic tension between the construction of national identities, national development policies, and Indigenous self-determination'.

[28] See, e.g., the recent judgment issued by the Constitutional Court of Ecuador that relied on the constitutional provision on 'rights of nature' to safeguard the Los Cedros protected forest from mining concessions. Constitutional Court of Ecuador, Sentencia No. 1149-19-JP/21, Caso No. 1149-19-JP/20, 10 November 2021.

[29] The dichotomy of 'modern' and 'non-' or 'pre-modern' modes of relating to non-humans or 'nature' is problematic in and of itself. This relates to the risks of 'essentializing' Indigenous cosmovisions (or what Chandler and Reid refer to as 'ontologising Indigeneity') and the dangers of generalizing and totalizing particular cosmovisions as being 'Indigenous'. On how questions of 'non-modern' traditionality or ancestrality tend to be opposed to 'modern' conceptualizations of living in environmental litigations involving Indigenous peoples before human rights courts, see Marie-Catherine Petersmann, 'Contested Indigeneity and Traditionality in Environmental Litigation: The Politics of Expertise in Regional Human Rights Courts' (2021) 21.1 Human Rights Law Review 132–156.

to and with non-humans – as also exemplified in Australia, New Zealand, or India.[30] The 'rights of nature' movement is therefore indissociable from cosmologies that preceded the mainstreaming of a colonialist, mononaturalist, and extractivist mode of inhabiting the Earth that came about with capitalist slavery and the enduring aftermath of its 'plantation logics', where subjugated lands and peoples' exploitation go hand in hand.[31] It is due to this subjugation of 'non-' or 'pre-modernist' onto-epistemologies of Indigenous peoples, Afro-descendant, Maroon, and Native communities following the arrival of settler colonial powers that the 'rights of nature' movement gained traction in former colonial states, to acknowledge the enduring presence of these communities, counter their endemic onto-epistemological erasure, and come to terms with the historical violence exercised against them and their lands in implementing and sustaining a mononaturalist worldview. Against this backdrop, what does the increasing recognition of 'rights of nature' in Europe imply, and for whom, when former European colonial powers who subjugated a 'thinking-feeling with the Earth'[32] of the colonized, are today invoking them as new templates of civilization?[33] To answer this question, I turn to a succinct overview of the movement of granting 'rights to nature' in Europe, before assessing the distinct relationalities that underpin these approaches in the third and final part of this chapter.

TOWARD 'RIGHTS OF NATURE' IN THE EU?

A number of European countries have taken action to recognize and integrate 'rights of nature' into their domestic legal systems. Whether through litigation

---

[30] Erin L. O'Donnell et al., 'Stop Burying the Lede: The Essential Role of Indigenous Law(s) in Creating Rights of Nature' (2020) 9 Transnational Environmental Law 403; Erin L. O'Donnell and Julia Talbot-Jones, 'Creating Legal Rights for Rivers: Lessons from Australia, New Zealand, and India' (2018) 23.1 Ecology and Society 7; James D. K. Morris and Jacinta Ruru, 'Giving Voice to Rivers: Legal Personality as a Vehicle for Recognising Indigenous Peoples' Relationships to Water?' (2010) 14.2 Australian Indigenous Law Review 49–62.

[31] On 'capitalist slavery', see Eric Williams, *Capitalism and Slavery* (Chapel Hill 1944). On 'plantation logics', see Kathryn McKittrick, 'Plantation Futures' (2013) 42 Small Axe 42 1.

[32] Arturo Escobar, 'Thinking-feeling with the Earth: Territorial Struggles and the Ontological Dimension of the Epistemologies of the South' (2016) 11.1 Revista de Antropología Iberoamericana 11–32.

[33] As Chandler and Reid warn regarding 'Indigeneity' as a governing imaginary for the Anthropocene: '[i]n contemporary constructions, indigeneity is often abstracted from specific struggles and contestations over rights and responsibilities and instead becomes an alternative way of being in and relating to the world, one which does not reproduce the problems of modernist anthropocentrism'. Chandler and Reid (n 5) 17.

on behalf of trees in Belgium,[34] through constitutional reforms for a more 'Earth-centred constitutional process' in France, a proposed 'rights of nature' amendment to the constitution of Sweden,[35] a recognition of 'Nature' as a legal entity in Switzerland,[36] a motion on special rights for the Wadden Sea in the Netherlands,[37] a legislative recognition of 'Rights of Nature' in Northern Ireland,[38] or a granting of a legal personhood status to the threatened saltwater lagoon of Mar Menor in Spain,[39] all these developments point toward an expansion of the liberal category of right-holders beyond the human, thereby giving rise to what some scholars have called 'posthumanist' articulations of rights.[40]

---

[34] 'Requête en intervention volontaire: l'aulne à feuille cordée et l'ensemble des 81 autres arbres', at <http://climatecasechart.com/climate-change-litigation/wp-content/uploads/sites/16/non-us-case-documents/2019/20191216_2660_na.pdf> accessed 17 February 2022.

[35] 'Amendment for the Rights of Nature in the constitution of Sweden' (15 May 2019), at <https://naturensrattigheter.se/2019/05/15/amendment-for-the-rights-of-nature-in-the-constitution-of-sweden/> accessed 17 February 2022.

[36] In France, see 'Amendement n°CL786 Déposé le vendredi 22 juin 2018', at <www.assemblee-nationale.fr/dyn/15/amendements/0911/CION-DVP/CD38>, and in Switzerland, see 'Rhein und Rigi sollen vor Gericht ziehen dürfen', at <www.bernerzeitung.ch/rhein-und-rigi-sollen-vor-gericht-ziehen-duerfen-988012964068> accessed 17 February 2022.

[37] Tineke Lambooy, Jan van de Venis and Christiaan Stokkermans, 'A Case for Granting Legal Personality to the Dutch Part of the Wadden Sea' (2019) 44.6–7 Water International 786–803.

[38] 'Northern Ireland Council "first on these islands" to recognize the "rights of nature"' <www.belfastlive.co.uk/news/belfast-news/northern-ireland-council-first-islands-20897949> accessed 17 February 2022.

[39] 'Spain Grants Personhood Status to Threatened Mar Menor Lagoon' <www.thelocal.es/20220922/spain-grants-personhood-status-to-threatened-lagoon/> accessed 17 February 2022.

[40] Posthumanist approaches aim at dismantling both the gendered, racial, and class-based hierarchies between humans, and the hierarchies between humans and all other living and non-living, animate, and inanimate entities. By expanding the 'right' category beyond the human and thereby de-centring the human as the exclusive category of right-holders (or at least the privileged category of right-holders, if one considers that private corporations also own rights), 'rights of nature' can then be understood as posthumanist. See Emily Jones, 'Posthuman International Law and the Rights of Nature' (2021) 12.1 Journal of Human Rights and the Environment 76–101; Coombe and Jefferson (n 24). Yet, as I argue elsewhere, if granting 'rights to nature' may well disrupt the modernist binary between humans and non-humans, it leaves intact the problematic subject/object dichotomy that undergirds any right claim. Maintaining the category of the 'subject' as right-holder (i.e., 'nature' as a subject of rights) leaves in place the racial structure that sedimented the liberal understanding of the subject as an autonomous, free, and self-possessed white human being. The question, then, is how to conceive a mode of be(com)ing beyond or besides the 'subject'. Cf. Marie Petersmann,

This objective also lies at the heart of the 189-page long proposal for an EU Charter on Fundamental Rights of Nature, which was drafted by a group of 10 experts and submitted to the European Economic and Social Committee in December 2019 to push for legislative action within the EU.[41] This initiative builds on the 2017 European Citizens' Initiative (ECI) Draft Directive for Rights of Nature, which advocates for a recognition of 'rights of nature' in the EU to regulate 'legal relationships between society and nature, based on principles of applied ecology'.[42] While not explicitly defined, a sense of what this 'applied ecology' entails can be distilled from the definition given of 'rights of nature' and what they cover, namely:

> the right to life and to exist, the right to maintain the integrity of living systems and natural processes that sustain them, the right to habitat, the right to naturally evolve and to diversity of life, the right to life sustaining water, the right to life sustaining air, the right to equilibrium, the right to restoration of living systems, and the right to live free from torture or cruel treatment by humanity.[43]

If notions of 'integrity', 'natural evolution', and 'equilibrium' would deserve critical attention on their own, what I wish to highlight is that 'nature' is here expressed in a variety of forms, whether animate or inanimate, fixed or fluid, static or flowing. It refers both to human and non-human animals as well as plant life. What emerges from this understanding, in other words, is that 'rights of nature' ought to be protected for 'nature's life-sustaining qualities: not only with regard to the existential value it brings to human life, but to the life and vitality of all organisms with which human life-forms are entangled.[44]

'In the Break (of Rights and Representation): Sociality Beyond the Non/Human Subject' (2023) The International Journal of Human Rights.

[41] Michele Carducci et al., 'Towards an EU Charter of the Fundamental Rights of Nature' (European Economic and Social Committee, 2019), at <www.eesc.europa.eu/sites/default/files/files/qe-03-20-586-en-n.pdf> accessed 17 February 2022.

[42] Draft Directive ECI for Rights of Nature by Mumta Ito, para. 49, at <https://natures-rights.org/ECI-DraftDirective-Draft.pdf> accessed 17 February 2022. Ito is one of the co-authors of the EU Charter of the Fundamental Rights of Nature. See also Mumta Ito, 'Nature's Rights: Why the European Union Needs a Paradigm Shift in Law to Achieve its 2050 Vision', in Cameron La Follette and Chris Maser (eds), *Sustainability and the Rights of Nature in Practice* (CRC Press 2019).

[43] Ibid., para. 49.

[44] This understanding aligns with Mignolo's call for a shift from 'human rights' to 'life rights', which demands that 'we abandon the western distinction and separation between the natural and human order and also the interests of industrialized and developed countries in which the paradigm of human rights originated'. 'Life rights' capture instead how 'the human body and nature are intertwined' and therefore a 'violation of "the rights of nature" amounts to a violation of "human rights" and therefore of "life rights"'. Walter D. Mignolo, 'From "Human Rights" to "Life Rights"', in Costas

According to many, it is precisely in this redress against anthropocentrism that 'rights of nature' find their most emancipatory potential to counter Anthropocenic living conditions.[45]

Indeed, the EU Charter on the Fundamental Rights of Nature starts by proclaiming that '[t]he present moment offers the potential, born of crisis, to transform the way humans inhabit Earth'.[46] To tackle this crisis, 'rights of nature' are perceived as promising a 'radical transformation of current law through a new paradigm of relations between human beings and the rest of Nature, therefore between human laws and the laws of Nature'.[47] The ECI Directive for Rights of Nature similarly argued that 'rights of nature' are 'essential to achieving sustainability, harmony, and balance between humankind and the natural world of which we are an intrinsic and interdependent part'.[48] Yet, if these proposals attempt at de-centring the human and its exclusive agency by recognizing non-humans' vitality and interdependent agency, 'rights of nature' remain stuck in an anthropocentric relation to and representation of non-humans. Indeed, according to the ECI Directive for Rights of Nature, '[a]ny physical person, government, or nongovernmental organisation should be entitled to act *on behalf of* nature for the purpose of protecting or defending a right of nature pursuant to this Directive'.[49] The proposal further specifies that '[w]here there is no representative to *speak for* nature, the court should be able to appoint a legally qualified person [an Ombudsman] as amicus curiae to present arguments regarding the implications of the proceedings for nature'.[50] This method combines a universal standing approach (where anyone could in principle file a case or *actio popularis* on behalf of 'nature' before a court, regardless of whether direct harms have been suffered by the applicant) and

---

Douzinas and Conor Gearty (eds), *The Meanings of Rights: The Philosophy and Social Theory of Human Rights* (CUP 2014) 161–180, 168.

[45] See, e.g., Jones (n 40).

[46] Carducci et al. (n 41) 4.

[47] Ibid. 9. Concretely, the Charter purports to 'include the interests of all living beings as subjects of the law rather than objects or property [...and therefore] ensure that Nature is represented in the EU system of law as a "stakeholder" in its own right, given legal personality and rights at constitutional level along with an implementing framework set out in key legislation', 63. As further specified, the Charter aims to 'grant legal personality to Nature' by conferring it 'autonomous rights (e.g. not dependent on human rights)', 69. What this 'autonomy' means and implies is assessed in the following part of this chapter.

[48] Draft Directive ECI for Rights of Nature (n 42), para. 32. Here, too, what 'sustainability, harmony, and balance between humankind and the natural world' concretely means and implies, as well as the totalizing 'we' position assumed in the statement, would warrant critical attention.

[49] Ibid., para. 56 (emphasis added).

[50] Ibid., para. 57 (emphasis added).

an elected guardian, steward or trusteeship approach (here, an Ombudsman, though it could also be an environmental NGO, or an Indigenous community that is 'trusted' with the protection of 'nature' in the public interest, as has been the case in non-European jurisdictions[51]) in which such a person would represent 'nature' in court.

The EU Charter on the Fundamental Rights of Nature envisages a similar procedure. In advocating for 'rights of nature', the experts relied heavily on the 2008 Constitution of Ecuador mentioned in the first part of this chapter. Indeed, the Charter refers to the innovative nature of the Ecuadorian Constitution's Article 71, which provides that 'all persons, communities, peoples and nations can call upon public authorities to enforce the rights of nature'.[52] As with the ECI Directive, here too the proposal overcomes the strict and narrow victim status requirement for a rights-claim to be held admissible before a court. Instead, *any* and *all* persons can act for 'nature' when nature's interests are hampered (and thereby the interests of humans too). This logic moves away from the highly individualist nature of liberal rights centered around the need for victims to be 'individually concerned', as upheld through the 'Plaumann doctrine' decided by the Court of Justice of the European Union (CJEU) as early as 1963[53] and reiterated ever since – with the same rationale and justification underpinning also the case law of the European Court of Human Rights (ECtHR) in relation to natural ecosystems, as illustrated with the *Kyrtatos* case.[54]

---

[51] See, e.g., O'Donnell and Talbot-Jones (n 30); Morris and Ruru (n 30).

[52] Constitution of the Republic of Ecuador 2008, Article 71 (n 21). Article 397(b) also grants the right for 'any natural person or legal entity, human community or group, to file legal proceedings and resort to judicial and administrative bodies without detriment to their direct interest, to obtain from them effective custody in environmental matters, including the possibility of requesting precautionary measures that would make it possible to end the threat or the environmental damage that is the object of the litigation'.

[53] *Plaumann* v. *Commission*, Case 25/62, [1963] ECR 95. The CJEU clarified the meaning of the condition foreseen by Article 173 of the Treaty of Rome (EEC) (today Article 263 of the Treaty on the Functioning of the EU) and held that: 'Persons other than those to whom a decision is addressed may only claim to be *individually concerned* if that decision *affects them* by reason of certain attributes which are *peculiar to them* or by reason of circumstances in which *they are differentiated from all other persons* and by virtue of these factors *distinguishes them individually* just as in the case of the person addressed'. Ibid., at 107 (emphases added).

[54] *Kyrtatos* v. *Greece*, App No 41666/98 [2003]. The ECtHR rejected the applicant's attempt to hold the state responsible for the damages its actions and omissions caused to a wetland and its associated wildlife in the vicinity of her property which, according to the court, had no direct impact on the right to private and family life protected under Article 8 of the ECHR as the individual link requirement was not fulfilled.

In addition to Article 71, Article 396 of the Ecuadorian Constitution was also explicitly invoked in the EU Charter on the Fundamental Rights of Nature to suggest the doctrine of '*in dubio pro natura*' as a key principle (to which the experts of the EU Charter added '*et clima*'). Article 396 of the Constitution of Ecuador states that '[i]n case of doubt about environmental impact stemming from a deed or omission, even if there is no scientific evidence of the damage, the State shall adopt effective and timely measures of protection'.[55] Finally, and in line with Article 397 of the Ecuadorian Constitution, it is stated that '[t]he burden of proof regarding the absence of potential or real danger shall lie with the operator of the activity or the defendant'.[56] The experts justified this reversal of the burden of proof by reckoning that 'Nature is a living but voiceless entity' which 'cannot produce evidence of harm'.[57] The meaning of 'living but voiceless entity' comes to light when the experts held, earlier in the text, that '[i]n order to learn from Nature and understand its rules, we must become eco-literate and engage other ways of knowing: feeling, sensing and intuition'.[58] Here, it is important to unpack and contextualize this statement in what the experts advocate as a passage from 'rights' to 'rights relationships': '[u]nderpinning this new framework [of 'rights of nature'] will be a reframing of the notion of rights to equate with "right relationship"' between 'humans' and 'nature'.[59] This sheds light on the 'we' at stake in the sentence reported above, as a broad reference to humanity as a whole, with which 'Nature' as a 'living but voiceless entity' inter-acts. In other words, 'eco-literate' humans should learn from 'nature's own rules' by feeling, sensing and intuiting 'nature' differently. What is implied with 'nature's *own rules*' is not specified, and here again the degree to which rules (of 'humans' and of 'nature') can ever be conceived as separate and autonomous (i.e., as 'own'), manifests a particular understanding of relationality, which will be further explored in the next and final part of this chapter.

The ECtHR stated that: 'the crucial element which must be present in determining whether, in the circumstances of a case, environmental pollution has adversely affected one of the rights safeguarded by paragraph 1 of Article 8 is the existence of a harmful effect on a person's private or family sphere and not simply the general deterioration of the environment' and, more crucially, recalled that '[n]either Article 8 nor any of the other Articles of the Convention are specifically designed to provide general protection of the environment as such'. Ibid., para. 52.

[55] Constitution of the Republic of Ecuador 2008 (n 21) Article 369.
[56] Ibid. Article 397.
[57] Carducci et al. (n 41) 82.
[58] Ibid. 52.
[59] Ibid. 69–70. Earlier in the text, the experts clarify: 'a "right relationship" [is] one that supports the wellbeing of the whole', 5.

COLLIDING COSMOVISIONS ON NON/HUMAN RELATIONS

From the set of provisions analyzed in the preceding part, the drafters of the EU Charter on the Fundamental Rights of Nature concluded that the latter should enact a 'proactive right of nature', which differs from the 'participation rights' introduced by the Aarhus Convention.[60] This 'proactive right' is conceived as (i) independent of other (human) rights, since it is exclusively connected to 'rights of nature'; (ii) autonomous and self-executing, since it does not impose a burden on behalf of the subject seeking enforcement; (iii) general, since it refers to any environmental impact or procedure; and finally (iv) independent, since it does not solely rely on the information produced by public authorities.[61] The qualification of this proactive right as a 'right relationship' – between humans and 'nature' – that is autonomous and independent seems counter-intuitive at first, since a relation necessarily implies dependence and hence a lack of strict autonomy. Yet, what matters in this invocation of autonomy is not a call for *agential* autonomy, but an autonomy in terms of interests and harms. What is at stake, in other words, is a *de*-centring of anthropocentric interests and harms when it comes to the fulfilment of the victim status requirement in environmental cases, which as it stands is a necessary admissibility criterion to bring a case concerning an alleged right violation before a (European) court. What comes to light is therefore a particular understanding of relationality that underpins the 'rights of nature' paradigm as advocated in Europe, which differs from the Andean Indigenous cosmologies that have informed the re-constitutional processes of Ecuador and Bolivia as described in the first part of this chapter.

Indeed, the 'rights of nature' proposed by the EU experts are conceived as 'right relationships' between humans and 'nature'. In this conception, both 'humans' and 'nature' are posited as separate and pre-existing entities with their 'own rules', thereby paradoxically recalling a distinctively modernist understanding of humans' relations to 'nature'. Yet, it is precisely to overcome these hallmarks of modernity that the drafters of the EU Charter are envisioning 'rights of nature' and insist on 'human' and 'nature's' '*interconnection*

---

[60] Article 9(2) of the Aarhus Convention demands that 'a sufficient interest and impairment of a right' is at stake to challenge the substantial and procedural legality of any decision, act, or omission subject to the public participation on decision-making in environmental matters. UNECE Aarhus Convention on Access to Information, Public Participation in Decision-Making, and Access to Justice in Environmental Matters, 2161 UNTS 447; 38 ILM 517 (1999).

[61] Carducci et al. (n 41) 82.

and interdependence'.[62] The *inter* of interconnection and interdependence is revealing here. It points to relations between pre-existing entities, where the existence or state of these entities will change according to the state of the other.[63] These related entities are animated by separate individual agencies that precede each inter-action between them. The drafters' call to recognize humans and non-humans' interconnection and interdependence aligns therefore with the 'relational turn' in social sciences, which since the 1970s, has challenged the modernist separation between 'humans' and 'nature' and the exclusive attribution of agency to humans.[64] Here, instead, 'nature' has its 'own rules' – its own agency and normativity.

Also in environmental law, this recognition is far from new, as many scholars and activists have advocated for the recognition of relations between humans and 'nature' and the *embeddedness* of the former as part of the latter.[65] Indeed, as the proposed EU Charter emphasizes, the '"*ratio*" of this "inclusion" [of Nature in human rights] comes from the common "vulnerability" of Nature and humans in the era of ecological and climate emergency', and it is this 'ratio' that – according to the drafters – identifies 'rights of nature' not as 'external subjects to the human being but as an element of the biosphere (to safeguard the entire biosphere, the EU must recognize equal dignity to all living subjects of its biosphere)'.[66] What this sentence highlights is that since humans and non-humans are included in 'nature' (or the biosphere) and their relation is key to ensure the flourishing of all living beings within this biosphere, then 'nature' must also be included in 'human rights' law. In other words, humans and non-humans should be recognized as equal subjects of law. Here again, however, both humans and 'nature' emerge as pre-constituted parts that are connected to and dependent upon one another. This understanding seemingly differs from the Indigenous cosmologies that first informed the recognition of 'rights of nature' in plurinational states like Ecuador and Bolivia.

---

[62] 'This necessary step will involve the legal recognition of the Rights of Nature on all levels and a shift from a purely anthropocentric worldview to a more ecocentric worldview that sees humanity as one species within a radically interconnected web of life, where the wellbeing of each part is dependent on the wellbeing of the Earth system as a whole'. Carducci et al (n 41) 6–7 (emphasis added).

[63] See the definitions of 'interconnected' and 'interdependent' in the Cambridge Dictionary, at <https://dictionary.cambridge.org> accessed 17 February 2022.

[64] For a general overview of this 'turn', see Simone Drichel (ed), *Relationality* (Routledge 2021).

[65] See, e.g., Klaus Bosselmann, *Im Namen der Natur – Der Weg zum ökologischen Rechtsstaat* (Scherz 1992); Cormac Cullinan, *Wild Law: A Manifesto for Earth Justice* (Green Books 2003); Peter Burdon (ed), *Exploring Wild Law – The Philosophy of Earth Jurisprudence* (Wakefield Press 2011).

[66] Carducci et al (n 41) 113.

Indeed, as the drafters of the EU proposal reckon explicitly: 'the recognition of equal dignity of all living beings is not an expression of a cosmovision [adding in a footnote: 'As in the Andean constitutionalism (Ecuador and Bolivia)'] but of a common reality for the survival of European generations'.[67] The 'expression of a cosmovision' (here of Andean peoples) is contrasted to that of a 'common reality' (here of European peoples). This observation echoes the critique raised by Townsend that legal and judicial experts tend to interpret the 'worldviews' of Indigenous peoples not as 'descriptions' of the environment – as Indigenous peoples intend it – but as mere 'cultural beliefs', whereas in contrast, the descriptions provided by experts tend not to be considered as expressing their beliefs but as describing the 'environment' as such. As Townsend puts it: experts' claims tend to 'speak to some objective reality and indigenous claims about the state of the environment as being, exclusively, claims about a belief system'.[68] A similar dynamic seems to linger in the contra-position of the Andean 'cosmovision' and Europeans' 'reality' here.

Yet, this formulation also reflects a careful positioning on the part of the drafters of the EU Charter as a strategic distantiating from the Andean cosmosivions that drove the re-constitutionalization of the plurinational states of Ecuador and Bolivia. Indeed, if the experts had claimed that the EU Charter on the Fundamental Rights of Nature *is* an expression of a cosmovision akin to Andean plurinational constitutionalism, they would have risked both essentializing and ontologizing the Andean peoples' modes of existence,[69] and disavowed the particular postcolonial historical context in which these modes of existence are embedded – and from which an Andean cosmovision cannot be disentangled. In other words, had the EU experts qualified the promotion of 'rights of nature' in Europe as an expression of Andean Indigenous cosmologies,[70] they would have co-opted and appropriated the very modes of being, knowing, and acting-with non-humans that their former settler colonial powers subjugated for their world-ecology to dominate. By qualifying the relationality that underpins the EU Charter on the Fundamental Rights of Nature as 'a common reality for the survival of European generations' and *not*

---

[67] Ibid. 113.

[68] Dina Lupin Townsend, 'Silencing, Consultation and Indigenous Descriptions of the World' (2019) 10 Journal of Human Rights and the Environment 193, 203–204.

[69] As Chandler and Reid argue, this equates to a Western 'ontologisation of indigeneity as a mode of being', which draws on pluriversal politics with the purpose 'of provincialising the Western canon in terms of epistemological methods and approaches'. As they conclude: this 'has become the basis upon which much more essentializing claims [of Indigenous being] are being made'. Chandler and Reid (n 5) 84–85.

[70] Indeed, if not all Indigenous peoples support 'rights of nature', clearly 'most transformative cases of rights of Nature have been consistently influenced and often actually led by Indigenous peoples.' O'Donnell et al (n 30).

as a 'an expression of a cosmovision [as in the Andean constitutionalism]',[71] the experts tactically situated their proposal within a shared European mode of existence to provide a specifically European grounding to this proposal. The 'common reality' that humans and non-humans are co-constitutive of 'nature' or the biosphere transcends, of course, a European 'reality'. In framing the issue as such, however, the EU experts used a vernacular familiar to European states to legitimize and provide more impetus for their proposal, while also tapping into the 'momentum' that 'rights of nature' gained thanks to the successful struggles of Andean peoples by explicitly relying on the provisions of the Ecuadorian and Bolivian constitutions.

Yet how precisely the experts understand the term 'cosmovision' remains unclear. They relate it to 'different economic models and styles of life', which are based 'on scientific premises from ecology and natural sciences, but also deeply rooted in ancestral cultures, that have not forgotten their original dependence on Nature'.[72] As they elaborate, because 'rights of nature' 'translate into legal terms different cosmovisions from all around the world' – with a footnote referring here to Kothari's edited volume on the *Pluriverse*[73] – 'it means they are part of a deeper cultural discourse, that can be spread into all branches of human knowledge'.[74] By reducing these 'different cosmosvisions' to mere cultural discourses and human knowledge, the material, embodied, and experiential practices that enact these cosmovisions are somehow disregarded. In doing so, the experts reinscribe again a modernist dichotomy between mind and body, being and knowing, culture and nature. In a similar vein, the experts identify a Western 'mind-set' as the main 'contemporary cultural obstacle' against the 'conceptual framework' of 'rights of nature' in Europe, and deplore that the latter 'have been claimed as superior interests on individual rights only by Indigenous communities (characterized by "Cthonic" legal tradition), symbiotically linked to Nature'.[75] Here, too, these cosmovisions are reduced to mere 'interests', with the everyday lived experience of these enduring struggles being sidelined.

My objective here is not to define what 'cosmovisions' are (or not), neither is it to contest that Andean plurinational constitutionalism is indeed embedded into a particular understanding of human and non-human relations that could

---

[71] Carducci et al (n 41) 113.

[72] Ibid. 99–100.

[73] Cf. Ashish Kothari et al (eds), *Pluriverse: A Post-Development Dictionary* (Columbia University Press 2019).

[74] Carducci et al (n 41) 100.

[75] Ibid. 94. For a critique of the essentialization that takes place when Western experts on environmental human rights refer to unqualified or unspecified Indigenous peoples as living 'symbiotically with Nature', see also Petersmann (n 29).

be defined as 'symbiotic'. This was already argued by Indigenous scholar Salmón more than two decades ago in relation to how the Rarámuri people in Mexico view the life surrounding them as kin or relatives, therefore enacting a 'kincentric ecology'. In Salmón's words:

> With the awareness that one's breath is shared by all surrounding life, that one's emergence into this world was possibly caused by some of the life-forms around one's environment, and that one is responsible for its mutual survival, it becomes apparent that it is related to you; that it shares a kinship with you and with all humans, as does a family or tribe. A reciprocal relationship has been fostered with the realization that humans affect nature and nature affects humans. This awareness influences indigenous interactions with the environment. It is [this] living with a place, that are manifestations of kincentric ecology.[76]

Salmón's insistence on living *with* – rather than *on* – a place, attends to the embodied and lived experience of thinking, acting, and being that is entangled with one's environment. This understanding strongly resonates with what Indigenous scholar Watts calls 'place-thought', which is based on the premise that the land is alive and thinking, and that humans and non-humans derive agency through the extensions of these thoughts.[77] The impossibility to disentangling the question of being from the ability to think and act with(in) one's milieu implies first and foremost that this milieu is active in its own way – (re)active not *to* but *with* humans' agency. Agency is therefore not just a human ability, but a quality that is manifest in all aspects of life.

This understanding also aligns with feminist theorist and physicist Karen Barad's 'agential realist' account of existence, where '[p]ractices of knowing and being are not isolable [but] mutually implicated'.[78] The mutual implication of practices of knowing and being signals that the very agencies of humans and non-humans are entangled with one another. In contrast to the usual 'interaction' between entities – which assumes separate individual agencies that would precede each action between them – Barad works with the neolo-

---

[76] Enrique Salmón, 'Kincentric Ecology: Indigenous Perceptions of the Human-Nature Relationship' (2000) 10.5 Ecological Applications 1327–1332, 1331–1332.

[77] Vanessa Watts, 'Indigenous Place-Thought and Agency amongst Humans and Non-humans (First Woman and Sky Woman go on a European World Tour!)' (2013) 2.1 Decolonization: Indigeneity, Education and Society 20, 21.

[78] Indeed, 'we know because we are of the world. We are part of the world in its differential becoming. The separation of epistemology from ontology is a reverberation of a metaphysics that assumes an inherent difference between human and nonhuman, subject and object, mind and body, matter and discourse'. Karen Barad, *Meeting the Universe Halfway: Quantum Physics and the Entanglement of Matter* (Duke UP 2007) 185.

gism of 'intra-action' to signify the mutual constitution of entangled human–non-human agencies.[79] This view rejects the assumptions of Newtonian physics that see the world as made-up of entities with stable characteristics that stand in relations of externality to one another.[80] Against the modernist worldview that posits human and non-human agencies as unfolding *on* the world, it is *matter* itself that is here conceived as 'a dynamic expression/articulation *of* the world in its intra-active becoming'.[81] This agential realist understanding shares similarities with what Indigenous scholar Watts refers to as 'place-thought' and Salmón as a 'living with a place', namely 'that one's breath is shared by all surrounding life, that one's emergence into this world was possibly caused by some of the life-forms around one's environment, and that one is responsible for its mutual survival'.[82] Being, thinking, and acting are entangled *within* the world in its making[83] – or one of the multiple worlds that are being enacted in their differential becoming, depending on the positionality of the entity that is investigating that world in its ongoing intra-activity.[84] The entanglement of agency goes hand in hand with a distribution of accountability and 'response-ability' – or the ability to respond to the violence and harms inflicted.[85] This is 'not about right response to a radically exterior/ized other, but about responsibility and accountability for the lively relationalities

---

[79] Ibid. 33.

[80] On how modern environmental law is based on Newtonian understandings of physics, see also Fritjof Capra and Ugo Mattei, *The Ecology of Law: Toward a Legal System in Tune with Nature and Community* (Berrett-Koehler Publishers 2015).

[81] Barad (n 78) 392–393 (emphasis added).

[82] Watts (n 77); and Salmón (n 76). On how Indigenous studies literature on agent ontologies (e.g., Salmón and Watts) have strengths in precisely some of the places where new materialist social sciences (in particular, Barad's agential realism) is facing challenges, see Jerry Lee Rosiek, Jimmy Snyder and Scott L. Pratt, 'The New Materialisms and Indigenous Theories of Non-Human Agency: Making the Case for Respectful Anti-Colonial Engagement' (2020) 26:3–4 Qualitative Inquiry 331.

[83] Barad (n 78) 184. As Barad insists, the 'in' of with*in* the world, however, should not be misunderstood as implying that 'the human is *in* Nature, as if Nature is a container'. The world (or 'Nature') is not something external to the human, but the human is one constitutive component of it that co-articulates the world in its becoming. Both humans and non-humans, as such, have no exteriority in any final or definitive sense.

[84] To quote Barad in full: 'To be entangled is not simply to be intertwined with another, as in the joining of separate entities, but to lack an independent, self-contained existence. Existence is not an individual affair. Individuals do not pre-exist their interactions; rather, individuals emerge through and as part of their entangled intra-relating'. Barad (n 78) ix.

[85] Haraway defines 'response-ability' as a practice of ongoing collective knowing and doing, where the duty to respond to harms is inherently joined with the question of differentiated ability. Donna Haraway, *Staying with the Trouble: Making Kin in the Chthulucene* (Duke University Press 2016). See also Marie-Catherine Petersmann,

of becoming of which we are a part'.[86] To account for power asymmetries is to insist that response-abilities are differently distributed across humans and non-humans co-implicated in intra-active relationalities.

The notion of entanglement furthers therefore a particular understanding of relationality, which attends to a related agency between human and non-human entities not as a process of interaction – which reinscribes a dichotomous understanding of human and non-human agency as being *inter*-acting, in line with the understanding of 'autonomy', 'independence', and 'interconnections' between humans and 'nature' advanced in the EU Charter on the Fundamental Rights of Nature – but as a process of *intra*-action, where relations emerge from the mutually constituted human–non-human agency and thereby constitute the world in its becoming.[87] To take a contemporary example, Covid-19 did not exist as a discrete entity prior to 2019, but emerged from human–non-human intra-actions across space and time to become a cross-species infectious disease – a 'multispecies entanglement'.[88] The pandemic illustrates the difficulty of disentangling human from non-human agency, and the impossibility of describing the former independently from the state of the latter. Hence, in contrast to the 'right relationship' proposed in the EU Charter to re-connect 'humans' and 'nature',[89] the notion of entanglement complicates the idea of re-connection by suggesting that the relation is not a connection between separate entities, but an enactment of mutually constituted agency between humans and non-humans. This necessarily *de*-centres the human as sole agential subject and recognizes that the agency of humans co-emerges with(in) that of non-humans.

In light of the above, it seems therefore that the specific understanding of relationality that underpins the 'rights of nature' proposed by the drafters of the EU Charter on the Fundamental Rights of Nature works with an understanding of discrete, bounded, and separate entities – 'humans' and 'nature' – which ought to be more strongly connected to one another in light of their *inter*-dependent interests and harms. This understanding seemingly differs from the agential ontologies that informed the 'rights of nature' movements in Ecuador and Bolivia. Whether based on specific Andean or particular posthumanist, new materialist or quantum understandings of how life emerges

---

'Response-abilities of Care in More-than-Human Worlds' (2021) 12:1 Journal of Human Rights and the Environment 102–124.

[86] Barad (n 78) 393.
[87] Ibid. 33.
[88] Anne Aronsson and Fynn Holm, 'Multispecies Entanglements in the Virosphere: Rethinking the Anthropocene in light of the 2019 Coronavirus Outbreak' (2022) 9.1 The Anthropocene Review 24–36.
[89] Carducci et al. (n 41) 69–70.

and is sustained throughout space and time, an *intra*-active perspective on human–non-human relations complicates the metaphysics of individualism and atomism that the EU Charter suggests for protecting 'rights of nature'. Attending to these differences is important in times where generic 'rights of nature' are being advocated worldwide, with little attention paid to the specific understandings of relationality underlying these claims and the particular historical, cultural, and political contexts in which these claims are grounded.

CONCLUSION

While 'rights of nature' are being increasingly invoked before courts,[90] and their potential discussed in both mainstream and critical circles,[91] little attention has been paid to the different understandings of relationality that underpin such formulations, depending on their definitions of relations that tie humans to non-humans. This chapter focused on the EU Charter on the Fundamental Rights of Nature drafted by a group of European experts on EU environmental law, constitutional law, comparative public law, and ecological activists, and submitted to the attention of the European Economic and Social Committee in December 2019.[92] By attending to the particular understanding of 'rights of nature' promoted in the EU Charter, the analysis highlighted how the experts extensively engaged with and relied upon existing constitutional recognitions of such provisions, notably in Ecuador and Bolivia. In the first part of this chapter, I looked at these constitutional recognitions, by re-contextualizing them within broader socio-ecological struggles led by Indigenous peoples, Afro-descendant, Maroon, and Native communities who re-constitutionalized the modernist nation-state in which they were enclosed as plurinational and multicultural states of which they form part. While showing how the recognition of 'rights of nature' in Andean constitutionalism cannot be disentangled from the cosmovisions of the Indigenous peoples, Afro-descendant, Maroon, and Native communities that fought for these re-constitutional processes, I argued that European movements that advocate granting 'rights to nature'

---

[90] As recently as 19 April 2022, the Madras High Court in the Tamil Nadu state, India, ruled that 'Mother Nature' has the same legal status as a human being, which includes 'all corresponding rights, duties and liabilities of a living person', at <https://insideclimatenews.org/news/04052022/india-rights-of-nature> accessed 17 February 2022.

[91] See, e.g., the UN Harmony with Nature agenda (nn 8–12). For a succinct overview of the debate regarding 'rights of nature' in critical legal circles, see Anna Grear, 'It's wrongheaded to protect nature with human-style rights' (AEON, 19 March 2019), at <https://aeon.co/ideas/its-wrongheaded-to-protect-nature-with-human-style-rights> accessed 17 February 2022.

[92] Cf. Carducci et al. (n 41).

ought to be careful not to appropriate Indigenous struggles. Indeed, this would both essentialize and co-opt particular relations that specific communities maintain with their lands, but also disavow the enduring violence suffered by such communities ever since European settler colonial powers subjugated their cosmovisions. The trend observed in European literature on 'rights of nature' to 'become Indigenous' must therefore be resisted.[93]

In the second part of this chapter, I assessed how the experts who drafted the EU Charter partially reproduced such problematic positions. By relying on the 'rights of nature' movements that animated the re-constitutional processes of plurinational states in Latin America – especially Ecuador and Bolivia – the experts advocated for a 'transition of the EU into an intercultural form of State' in order to generate a 'new inclusive and sustainable lifestyle [that] will bridge the historical gap between Western culture and Indigenous and other older cultures and worldviews'.[94] What is concerning, here, is not only the invocation of an essentialized 'Indigeneity' to reach a 'sustainable life' in Western states and culture – and bridge the gap with 'Indigenous and other older cultures and worldviews' – but that no mention is made of the historical subjugation and erasure of these very 'Indigenous and other older cultures and worldviews' by the Western powers who today want to 'include' them into their legal frameworks. The emancipatory struggles that subjugated peoples had – and still have – to endure to be recognized into existence in plurinational re-constituted states is also not mentioned. Such framings and formulations leave the impression that the recognition of these worldviews was a top-down act of inclusivity by the institutional authorities that metabolized pre-existing structures of coloniality, rather than a bottom-up fight for existence against the very structures, led by those subjugated by them.

What is more, the EU is already an 'intercultural form of State', the constitutive cultures of which have however a monolithic understanding of 'nature'. The experts express an aspiration to change this 'mononaturalism' by taking inspiration from non-European cultures. A universalist and neo-colonialist impetus lingers, however, in the hope that '[t]he discussion about a new sustainable style of life, in harmony with Nature, that will be generated in Europe by the introduction of the Charter of Rights of Nature will be able to affect the rest of the world and inspire all the world society'.[95] By formulating the movement as being 'generated in Europe' and capable of 'inspiring all the world society', non-European cosmosivions and practices risk being erased, once again. To avoid the dangers of either appropriating and/or erasing the

---

[93] Cf. Chandler and Reid (n 5).
[94] Carducci et al. (n 41) 110.
[95] Ibid.

knowledge and experience of those from whom the EU experts take inspiration to advocate 'rights to nature' – namely the 'Indigenous and other older cultures and worldviews' – a closer look into what fundamentally distinguishes these approaches could be useful. These differences, as I showed in the third part of this chapter, lie *inter alia* in the diverging relationalities at hand – or how humans (ought to) relate to non-humans. While the Andean Indigenous peoples that the EU experts referred to tend to view these relations as intra-actions, the EU experts consider them as inter-actions. As such, the 'rights of nature' suggested in the EU Charter entail an understanding of relationality that is deprived of an agential ontology characteristic of Andean constitutionalism.[96] These distinctions matter, since they enact different onto-epistemologies and bring different worlds into existence – or not.

---

[96] Cf. Coombe and Jefferson (n 24); Akchurin (n 24). See also Emille Boulot and Joshua Sterlin, 'Steps Towards a Legal Ontological Turn: Proposals for Law's Place beyond the Human' (2022) 11.1 Transnational Environmental Law 13–38.

8. A diplomacy for human/non-human relations: letter to a young climate activist

Oscar Guardiola-Rivera

Dear C,

We have a lot to learn from young activists like you. What you did, what you said the last time I heard you speak in Scotland was brave and truthful. It was brave to call the adult's bluff during the debate sponsored by the *New York Times* in preparation for COP26 – the United Nations Climate Change Conference that took place in Glasgow that year. Before the adults sitting at the table could perform their familiar theatrics of mastery to persuade the other adults in the audience with their percentages and numbers, the millions spent in the fight against global warming, their fancy words in fancy treaties, and their techno-solutionism, miming mimetic beings in wonderlands of what until yesterday was pure make-believe, you said: 'Indigenous peoples,' who are treated like children, 'are custodians of most of the rainforests that are the lungs of our planet. Not only that, they also have the solutions for the climate crisis. And yet, they're not sitting at the table'.[1]

You got it right. You pulled the handbrake; you pressed pause and gave us time to think. To think about the fact that what one eats when sitting with others at the table is not the other's food and substance but their *position* and *perspective*. But what do these words, position and perspective, mean in the indigenous thought that you invoked in all its concreteness?

To begin, we could say that every position in a structure or ecosystem is political at least in the sense that everything is relational and related. Not relative, but mimetically related. Consider nature, for example, which creates resemblances and similarities. Some say the highest capacity for producing similarities is Man's. The human gift for seeing similarities, mimicry, and resemblances might be but a drum rudiment of a powerful compulsion present

---

[1] Lord Bilimoria, Stephen Dunbar-Johnson, Ali Watson, and Oscar Guardiola-Rivera, 'The NYT Debate: Journeys Towards COP26' (29 August 2021) <https://www.youtube.com/watch?v=rr-wxCkukcU> accessed 28 March 2022.

since earlier times to become and behave like something else. But over the long haul of history, especially in modern times, the mimetic faculty, although still an active presence among young people such as yourself and perhaps also in ritual practices and magic, has been largely eclipsed from rational consciousness. Or repressed, as our friend Michael Taussig astutely observes.[2]

As he explains, taking stock of all the things we have learned through decades accompanying our indigenous *maestros* and teachers, the wordsmith *palabreros* of Las Pavas and the Afro-Amerindians of the Cauca region in Colombia, it is not so much that the role of mimetic relations has really been eclipsed. Rather, like a damned river or the damned of the earth, it found alternative routes. When things are not intrinsically connected, relational and related, there's always the possibility of establishing non-sensuous correspondences that 'provide mimetic links between things and activities not obviously mimetically related.' Symbols and language can be thought of in this way too. If so, it could be said that when we sit at the dinner table, we eat each other's words too.[3]

I

This is what Don Misael taught us. That words are edible. Just like the vegetation in the forests where they dwell. The point he indicated to us is that to speak, to tell stories while rambling together and interacting with everything that exists in the forest is for him and his people to eat each other's words, each other's perspectives and position. What does this mean? Before pondering the question about the meaning of such terms in the context of indigenous practices that include humans and non-humans, let me tell you more about Don Misael, his people, and their environs.

For over twenty years we have accompanied them, as lawyers, philosophers, and anthropologists, educators in need of education. Don Misael and his people are a group of native peasants who inhabit the island of Papayal in north-western Colombia. Papayal is a fertile plain surrounded by the waters of the Magdalena River. It rises in the Andes and then runs from the mountainous south to the northern coast. There, it forks into two branches before flowing

---

[2] Michael Taussig, *The Mastery of Non-Mastery in The Age of Meltdown* (University of Chicago Press 2020). Also, Pedro Neves Marques, 'Introduction to The Forest & The School / Introduction to Where to Sit at the Dinner Table?' in Pedro Neves Marques (ed), *The Forest & The School. Where To Sit at the Dinner Table?* (Archive Books & Akademie der Künte der Welt 2014) 298.

[3] Taussig (n 2) 7, 47; *Palma Africana* (University of Chicago Press 2018). Also Juan Felipe García, *El exterminio de la isla de Papayal* (Editorial Pontificia Universidad Javeriana 2019).

into the Caribbean Sea. Its basin comprises both Caribbean and Andean regions, some 257,000 km² in total. Because Colombia is located within the Equatorial band of the tropics, climate and hydrology interact to produce one of the highest rainfalls in the planet. Which means the Magdalena River generates mangroves, marshes, lakes, and rainforests which have constituted the basis of the country's ecological diversity and political economy. Yuma, Karacalí, and Guaca'hayo are some of the names given to the river by those dwelling on its banks since ancient pre-Columbian times. In the wake of European invasion, external and internal colonialism, extractive economies, and the political imaginary of defensive management of centre-periphery relations built on them have revolved around the river. You name it: gold, slaves, oil, coffee, and other drugs.

In the last fifty years, the river and its peoples have faced the combined onslaught of three forces: the entanglement between economic development, progress and modern publicity, with exclusion, domination and exploitation, exemplified in the building of fortress-like dams; the transport of mining and oil products as well as agro-industrial chemicals for the cultivation of various crops such as *Palma Africana*, intended for export markets; and the accelerated advance of urban borders encroaching upon its watery courses. Common to all, violence.

Not only the violence of the sixty-year-old war suffered by the peoples of Colombia, which was never civil but trans-national, interventionist, imperial, and imperialist – the reign of terror imposed upon communes and communities such as Papayal and Las Pavas by creating and recreating a system based on the presumed homogeneity and centrality of the nation – but also violence against their environs. This is violence against bodies and corporeality as much as it is against the consciousness of ethical agents like Don Misael and the people of Papayal. A consciousness and ethical body riveted to history, which condenses memory and experience, pushes against the given frameworks that circumscribe thought or public imagination, and provides the tools with which to destroy or let go of the old falsehoods to engage instead in the formation of a new, truer position.

Let us speak of native knowledge and consciousness in this sense. A sense of motion, new directions, and transposition. Such is the creative sense of an enunciative and denotative positionality that emerges when a person or a group are forced to mark out their existential meaning and aesthetic as well as ethical sense amid a stream of changing sign systems. As in the creolisation of visual and discursive regimes that takes place between enslaved peoples, native, and Afros brought to the Americas. Or as in the case of their descendants (Afro, Amerindian, peasant, urban and rural) who negotiate different levels of suffering in accordance with the affordance of material circumstances. Which is to say, the differences in what the environment offers the agent, which have been brought about by processes of colonisation and industrialisation as well as changing experiences of sensing and sense-making (including the invention of different means of sensing or technologies).

When we speak of bodies, consciousness, and technical objects in this way we are immediately referring to the environment. The environment's address or affordance. What it offers, furnishes, or provides to those who dwell in it. How it affects us and other living beings, human and non-human, as we impinge on it. Which is a matter of the reciprocity and complementarity between the animal we are and the environment in which we are. Not just in space but in time. To speak of nature as the 'inorganic' body of Woman and Man is, thus, to bring together corporeality, consciousness, technology and the cycles of life and death, or renewal. As in the creative renewal of biocultural sites and forms by those who challenge the dominant geo-politics of progress of the present, expanding the limits and visual horizon of those to whom we respond – like you and the unborn, future generations – or going across and beyond the current frameworks circumscribing the possible. To enhance the range of historical options, rather than merely choosing between current choices and fate. It is possible to speak of nature in this sense as exo-memory, multidirectional rather than competitive. Or a poetics of revolt that is also ethical. A global history of ethical systems incarnated in biocultural sites, which comes before any consideration of alternative uses or the conditions that would allow the generalisation of certain percepts and concepts – architectonics, logics, and systems of reasoning. Nature, taken as exo-memory, multidirectional, technical and historical is, in that respect, also an anticipatory collection.[4]

II

Hence the importance of the recent legal, political, and ethical debates concerning nature, and more concretely speaking a part of it such as the Magdalena River, as a victim and a rights-bearer subject in the political conflict that has afflicted Colombia. These investigations, debates, and declarations are legal, ethical, and political. The result of political activism and the survivance of ethical agents forging history from below.

---

[4] See Michael Taussig, *Fieldwork Notebooks* (Kassel & Ostfildern: documenta/ Hatje Cantz Verlag 2012) 5, on collecting and collections having anticipatory propensities, crucial for imagining investigative social sciences and ethics otherwise. Also, Mindahi C. Bastida & Geraldine Patrick Encina, 'Biocultural Sacred Sites in Mexico,' in Fausto Sarmiento & Sarah Hitchner (eds) *Indigenous Revival and Sacred Sites. Conservation in the Americas* (Bergham Books 2017) Chapter 9, for the archaeological evidence backing up these notions of consciousness, exo-memory, and investigative practices in relation to environmental affordances.

Like the legal challenge against the consequences of the construction of the hydroelectric project El Quimbo in the Magdalena River by multinational EMGESA, property of the European group ENDESA-ENEL, and against the development plan that has aimed to turn the river into an energy and mining corridor of national and continental scale. It led a national court in 24 October, 2019 to respond to a constitutional action known as *tutela,* declaring the river a subject of rights. In connection with the recognition of future, younger generations such as yours as rights-bearers able to claim historical, special protection, restorative remedies, and survivance (*conservación, mantenimiento*, in Spanish). The recognition of the Magdalena River, its basin and affluents as a composite non-human entity with rights to protection, survivance, and restoration was seen to involve institutional invention for the purposes of the river's political and legal representation by a Commission of Guardians of the Magdalena River, which would include both governmental and non-governmental representatives (specifically the river-based communes and civil society). Finally, the court's verdict was seen as having effects *inter communis*, meaning to affect and effect the becoming-alliance of all the persons and communes or communities that dwell in and are part of the Magdalena River basin.[5]

One might argue that the Magdalena River case is an instance of the historical persistence of the social-economic form I have been calling the commune throughout this letter. This is a native formation, social, economic, political, legal, and institutional. It can be traced back to pre-colonial times but has

---

[5] See the following decisions: Juzgado Primero Penal del Circuito con Funciones de Conocimiento Neiva-Huila, Sentencia de Tutela de Primera Instancia no. 071, 24 de octubre del 2019, and the legal precedents of this decision which include Sentencia T-622, 2016 (The Atrato Case) issued by the Colombian Constitutional Court, recognising the Atrato River as a subject of rights; T-361, 2017 (Páramo de Santurbán Case); and STC 4360-2018 by the Colombian Supreme Court (Amazonas Case). For work done in this area by the Colombian Truth Commission see <https://web.comisiondelaverdad.co/actualidad/noticias/todas-las-formas-de-violencia-pasaron-por-el-rio-magdalena> accessed 29 March 2022; together with the chapter titled 'Cuando los pájaros no cantaban' in the Final Report of the Truth Commission of 29 June 2022; and for the declaration of native territories as victims of war and conflict, see Case 002 (RECOMPAS Case), Case 005 (Cxhab Wala Kile Case) decided by the Special Peace Jurisdiction (JEP) in 2019, together with the case against paramilitary Commander Ramiro Isaza. Together, these decisions constitute a turn beyond anthropocentrism in jurisprudence in the Americas, which emphasises potential and actual affectations of biocultural sites-based knowledge, dispossession, and the role of human/non-human cosmopolitical and diplomatic relations.

persisted through colonial and so-called post-colonial periods. Not lost or past, but active and present.[6]

This is also the sense in which it makes sense to use such terms as transposition, dispossession, and survivance. A sense we learned about also during our interactions with Michael Taussig, the anthropologist whose work focused on the recursivity between Andean indigenous storytelling or myth-making practices and the commodity fetishism associated with extractive industrial practices such as mining, agribusiness, and finance.

He described thusly a native worldview attentive to the interplay between structure and historical change – or an 'animated structuralism' as he put it. Unlike the coldly abstract sense of structuralism that has become widespread in the social sciences and in the methods of investigation that make all qualities relative to quantity, the animated structuralism described by Taussig and enacted by native communities such as Don Misael's in Papayal point to a wider sense of reciprocity for the structures that hold together a material world, their design, redesign, and reinvention. These reciprocities, which are visual, ethical, and social, can be seen as an extension of different ways of seeing and media concepts that tend not to alienate signs from their materials. And it makes sense to speak of consciousness, corporeality, and affordance in this respect. As that which indexes the beneficial or injurious history of objects and peoples, therewith allowing for a notion of critique that can be related to the imagination as a point of contact with real relations, transforming them. Or the inter-temporal intensification of the realities indexed by such historical affordances.[7]

In this respect, we can challenge those who find the historical, environmental claims of native peoples nonsensical or contradictory under the pretext that you cannot argue that nature, the land, or a river cannot be appropriated and at the same time that you or your native community has ancestral claims over it. You may have one but not both, they say. We can argue against such

---

[6] See Eric Hobsbawm, 'Introduction,' in *Karl Marx's Pre-Capitalist Economic Formations* (International Publishers 1964) 51 n 1, on the persistence of the commune or *Formen* (in the German he borrows from Marx) and its crucial importance in the legacy of socialism.

[7] Michael Taussig, *The Devil and Commodity Fetishism in South America* (University of Carolina Press 1980) for his understanding of 'animated structuralism' among native American peoples. Also see his *Mastery of Non-Mastery in the Age of Meltdown* (n 2) 5–12 and 47–60 for animated structuralism set in relation with metamorphic sublimity as a critical theoretical concept developed by researchers allied with native peoples in places like Colombia to re-enchant nature and transform real relations in global contexts where the magic of law and state 'is not up to the task.' Taussig cites as an instance of such critical theory informed by native thinking and Juan Felipe García's research in El exterminio de la isla de Papayal.

mainstream critics that there is no need to choose between these two arguments as if they were true opposites.

The least one can say about them is that they are naïve representations, static or crudely painted figurations of stages and conditions set in a linear progressive history in which commons, or the commune have been supposedly obliterated and presumably replaced by private property. The true condition is, however, that we need not imagine history and space in such a crude bi-dimensional manner. Or rather, we can conceive of such flattening imagination of space as itself part and parcel of a historical process of dispossession, which, as such, entails transpositions, survivance, animated structures, transformative motions, and retro-projective attributions. In other words, we do not have to imagine history as if it were a straight line or a racetrack in which historical agents and their memory go from less to more, from fall to redemption, or from lack to fulness and manifest destination as if we were engaged in cosmic-commercial competition. Instead, we can see it as a process characterised by recursions or transformative motions in a circuit that is never completely closed. It is the former, which characterises modern Christian capitalist worldviews, not the latter, that is fully mystical.

The procedures involved in such recursive trans-motions and transpositions can be described as referring back to themselves with positive feedback effects. Alas, this notion of recursivity is by now well-known in the biological and computer sciences, but no less so to the native practices guided by the perceptual and conceptual idea of an investigative motion that goes backward and looks forward. Like the porcupine, the armadillo or the turtle who backs onto a rock crevice to find the roots where they are usually found and speculate safely on a more inhabitable future. If a geometrical image is needed to figure out such a way of thinking and reasoning it would be the image of a vortex, not a line or a circle.[8]

---

[8] See on this, Oscar Guardiola-Rivera, 'The Apophatic Urgency of Now: A Future for the Philosophy of Liberation', in Amy Allen & Eduardo Mendieta (eds) *Decolonizing Ethics. The Critical Theory of Enrique Dussel* (The Pennsylvania State UP 2021) 127–147; Michael Taussig (n 7) and Edgar García, *Signs of the Americas. A Poetics of Pictography, Hieroglyphs, and Khipu* (University of Chicago Press 2020) 95–120 and 185–217. Also, Gerald Vizenor & Jill Doerfler, *The White Earth Nation: Ratification of a Native Democratic Constitution* (University of Nebraska Press 1986); Lisa Brooks, 'The Constitution of the White Earth Nation: A New Innovation in a Longstanding Indigenous Literary Tradition' (2011) 23 (4) Studies in American Indian Literatures 48–76; John Borrows, *Drawing Out Law: A Spirit's Guide* (University of Toronto Press 2010). For a reconstructive strategy turning dispossession into a key term of critical theory, Robert Nichols, *Theft Is Property! Dispossession and Critical Theory* (Duke University Press 2020).

III

For generations, the people of Papayal Island have imagined domains and created timespaces for themselves in the image of the vortex or a helix. Moving backwards, looking forwards. Using performative and imaginal procedures that look back upon themselves in such a manner that each iteration is not only different from the last but builds upon or imaginally augments and intensifies the points of contact with the real that such procedures take as their starting points. Mind you, the procedures that Don Misael shared with us are not that different from those practised and described in the poetic, activist, and jurisprudential works of native peoples in North America. People like Gerald Vizenor, poet and drafter of the 2013 Constitution of the White Earth Nation, Jill Doerfler, or legal theorist John Borrows.

For the people of Papayal Island this work is of a piece with their lived experience as workers under different sign systems and contractual regimes up to and including those that regulated their labour in what came to be known as Hacienda Las Pavas. This work can help us make better sense of processes of forced displacement and dispossession (which, arguably, exhibit a recursive structure because they tend to produce what they presuppose, namely, exclusive property). But their work also produces time and space to breathe, to resist, to come back and thrive in survivance.

As said before, Don Misael is the wordsmith of the commune and community of Las Pavas in the island of Papayal. Their shaman or *palabrero*. More precisely, a kind of diplomat executing an experimental kind of diplomacy. It is that diplomacy which might help us find the solutions that you referred to during your intervention in Scotland.

Because of its richness in water and its fertility, the island of Papayal has been invaded many times. Some years ago, it was invaded by *narcos* and other investors who sought to occupy and appropriate it. They claimed the land as their own, renaming it Hacienda Las Pavas, but not before imposing a reign of terror over the native inhabitants, the people and the living beings Don Misael sings about, whom these profiteers subjected to constant toil and terror. Ever since, these investors have been quite productive, even though they're not the producers toiling the earth and the river, expanding their ways of realising profit on the sweat of native and peasant producers to hold on to power. In the last years, they had turned to the cultivation of the palm originated in Africa from which oil is extracted to be used in the production of chemicals, colours, and cosmetics. Ever since, the native peasants, Don Misael and the community of Las Pavas, have resisted their abuses of power.

Early in 2022, news came from the north-west of Colombia that made us happy. After nineteen years, a court of appeals in the city of Cartagena de

Indias repealed a verdict which in the first instance had absolved from criminal responsibility two infamous men: Gustavo Sierra, a figurehead or *mandatario* for the landowner *narco* who had ordered the forced displacement of the community of Las Pavas back in 2003; and Mario Mármol, the paramilitary leader who carried out the order on 26th October that year and who aims nowadays to reimpose the reign of terror that cuts into two the world in the lands of our childhood.[9]

The Tribunal declared both men guilty of the crimes of forced eviction or displacement and dispossession of a civilian population and conspiracy to commit atrocities (*concierto para delinquir con fines de desplazamiento*, in Colombian Legalese). These are serious violations of human rights law. 'I celebrate with you, Oscar' wrote one of the friends with whom I've walked alongside and made kin with the community of Las Pavas, Juan Felipe García, in a Whatsapp message on that day: 'I celebrate with you, because you have lived this story as your own.' That is true. This is indeed our history. But history is his-story as musicians say, and, Dear C, you haven't heard our story yet.

Ours is a story of uncanny things, impossible things, horror things. It's a story of terror and exile and of the memory of terror and exile, which is both indelible and difficult to put into words. Consider this. A few days later after receiving Juan Felipe's jubilant message via the nervous system of our networked world, our happiness was cut short. Teófilo, one of the most committed social activists in the struggle of the community of Las Pavas, a defender of the Magdalena River and its environment, was murdered by the paramilitary. The People's Congress, an organisation that groups together the different activists and communities active in the region, blamed the state and its law enforcement agencies, supposedly tasked with guaranteeing law and the human rights of the people in these parts of the world, for being part of a campaign of 'continuous genocide' against the popular social movement, as they say.[10]

For not only do they turn a blind eye, allowing paramilitary forces and mafias to carry out their social cleansing or *limpieza*. They also deny and erase the memory and history of the community. Which is our immediate history, our story, our biography, as Juan Felipe said. In that memory and history, *limpieza* now means to wipe out and kill defenceless people, much the same as a 'purge' of the unclean carried out in this case by the forces of law and order,

---

[9] Tribunal Superior de Cartagena, Sala de Decisión Penal, *Caso Gustavo de Jesús Sierra Mayo y otros. Desplazamiento Forzado y otro*, February 9 2022. Also, Juan Felipe García (n 3) 114–143, 149–240.

[10] Congreso de los Pueblos, 'Asesinan a Teófilo Acuña y a Jorge Tafur, Históricos Líderes del Sur de Bolívar', Comunicado del 24 de febrero 2022 ≤https:// www . congresodelospueblos.org/asesinan-a-teofilo-acuna-y-a-jorge-tafur-historicos-lideres -del-sur-de-bolivar/≥ 29 March 2022.

the market, and the state. At times, they 'outsource' this *limpieza* or social cleansing to paramilitary militias and mafias which no longer are mere outlaws but the very support of the establishment's far-right and right-wing political parties in power.

However, in our story the word '*limpieza*' has a far older and most relevant history. It is also used in the sense of healing a person, a home, or the environment from malignity due to spirit attack or sorcery. Such healing not only seeks to neutralise and contain deadly force, but also enhances a sense of self in time-space and it gives such self to others in space and time, as a gift. For example, by moving backwards to intensify the struggles and interrupted projects of the past to carry them into the forward-looking present and the future. The songs and stories we've learned with Don Misael and the people of Las Pavas do not communicate the past as if it were a lost object to be conserved in a museum or legal record, but rather, they activate these projects in the present-future. How? By interrupting the normal course of events, calling the bluff of the managers and administrators, and intensifying the possibilities inherent to the past and the present to make a difference, to translate a critical idea or a correct ethical position into real relations. To show us the way of the future.

We can thus refine the word 'critique' via this encounter with the meaning of words, stories, perspectives, and the position taken by native and peasant peoples such as the community in struggle of Las Pavas. By adding back in something positive and practical, not just something negative or destructive. As you did, dear C, when you said that the ability to stop the bluff, to stop to think and think with others might provide us with real solutions for climate crises in the sense of climate justice. As you can see, our kinship with the people of Las Pavas is no simple allegiance. It has nothing to do with ideology, cultural differences, or obedience. It is an alliance-becoming as we exercise the primordial rights to walk away, transform, and disobey. We have become them and the river, in this process. Or to be more precise, them and the river have become our memory, our history teachers, our story. Our interactions are no mere exchanges of academic knowledge or whatever, but the kind of spiritual exchange that changes us and the environment. Historically, anthropologically, ontologically speaking, these are change-exchanges. Gifts. Hence, the question: what's the role of memory and mimesis, the capacity of something to become something else, in the creation of forms that can do justice in and to history?[11]

---

[11] See Michael Taussig, *Law in a Lawless Land. Diary of a Limpieza in Colombia* (University of Chicago Press 2003) xiii for the ambiguity of 'limpieza.' Also, Eduardo Viveiros de Castro, *Cannibal Metaphysics* (University of Minnesota Press 2014) 217–218 for the distinction between alliance-structure and alliance-becoming as well as contract-exchange and change-exchange in use here. And, Alexander Kruge (with

IV

The practice Don Misael and the people of Las Pavas taught us is similar to the practice of the Kogi and Afro-Amerindian indigenous peoples of the Colombian Atlantic and Pacific coasts, the Andes, and Amazonia. When they sit down to discuss a problem or resolve a conflict, they eat each other's words while munching on lime and coca leaves as well as other rave-like psychedelics with their *poporos*, their *chicha de yuca*, and *aya waska* drinks. This practice (is it too far-fetched to call it diplomatic?) evokes the intertwinement between ways of eating and ways of seeing, hearing, and speaking. When you procure foodstuffs through fishing, hunting, collecting, and cultivating you deal with a variety of ecological collectives or montage-like collections that commit peoples' selves intimately with hugely complex and uneven natural and social ecosystems.

The lives of the forest, the coasts, and the mountain interpenetrate each other and with worlds that we might deem all too human. Only that, in this case, the question of 'the human' does not assume universality or generality as the result of pure categories and judgments that we (our enclosed self/selves) can presumably impose a priori upon everything that we see and exists in the space of the world. Rather, generality or universal-ability in time and space is a property of the world as such. Timespace is real in this sense, in the more fundamental sense that it cannot be reduced to the categories of a pure and enclosed Mind. If so, instead of coming to the world from the exclusive angle of Man distanced from Nature (including supposedly 'natural' beings like Indians, women, or the youth – all of them declared 'minors'), as if Man was a privileged spectator looking out to the shipwreck occurring at a distance, it might be best to pay attention to the historical ways in which we all, bodies and minds that are vulnerable and injurable, human and non-human, suffer in the flesh, see each other, interact, enact and mimic each other in different forms in accordance with the affordance of material, historical and environmental circumstances.

Simply put, this means to think and re-think that very basic anthropological and critical concept: context. To reconstruct it by layering on it the sense of direction that is inherent to practices of negotiation and position. Or position and perspective in/and context. This means that, ecologically speaking, positions imply connectivity, intertwinement, even agency, but this does not necessarily imply a will – constant or inconstant. This is important because a largely unacknowledged fact of modern geo-politics, political philosophy,

---

Joseph Vogl), 'Critique, Up and Personal' in Richard Langston (ed) *Difference and Orientation. An Alexander Kluge Reader* (Cornell University Press 2019) 441.

international relations, and international law (including human rights law and philosophy) is that to see and to speak of positions without will, or 'inconstancy' (that is, lacking a strong will) is to flatten and isolate subjects and objects placed a priori or presumably located within geographical systems of coordinates assumed to be purely measurable or quantitative.

The quality of relations happening and ongoing in time is thereafter denied, disavowed, or made relative to quantitative measures. Relativised, or in other words, reduced solely to geography rather than considered a geopolitical force. And from the political perspective that results from such relativistic reductionism, these qualities and ways of being (deemed inconstant) are not even considered to be positions. They are made to disappear in a past long gone and assumed to continue disappearing in the present. Which means that they are also prohibited from disclosing any futures beyond the given horizon.

As you may have gathered already, dear C, this is precisely how modern geography, politics, law, and literature have erased indigenous peoples. By declaring them inconstant, lacking will and, therefore, unable to rule, to consent, govern or reinvent themselves and the environs that afford them, in which they dwell. That is why they have not been invited to the dinner table.

V

But that does not mean they have stopped coming. The position of indigenous peoples, which you correctly say can hold solutions to the current climate crisis (rather than mere 'natural' guardianship over the rainforest, a figure that immediately recalls the myth of the 'noble savage,' stupid and lacking willpower) ruptures the geography and disrupts the pacifying publicity of human rights, law, and ecology.

The latter function as if real relations travelled through networks linking beings to other beings in a sort of endless flow, uninterrupted, without breaks, turmoil, conflicts, and oscillations. Nouns and metaphors such as 'networks' or 'cyberspace' are thereby transferred into modern and contemporary political languages and rights-based struggles from techno-fetishist and martial defensive discourses in misleading ways.

For although they denote the wondrous opportunities of flexible information and communication made available by digital technologies, at the same time the use of these nouns tends to obscure the side effect of such technologies: they make the world flat, horizontal, an imagined world in which all qualities are expressed in terms of quantities and, thereafter, mistakenly organised as if they were interchangeable or comparable to any other quality. Thus, for instance, the denotative use of 'cyberspace' allows law to deal with forms of data mining, hacking, and surveillance as if they were mere trespass, thereby obscuring the fact that webpages, stacks, and the substacks where virtual exchanges happen aren't really enclosed spaces with locked doors and windows, but houses with cracks on the walls that we can crack open to let the light outside in; intersections of timely and untimely interactions that are always ongoing.

Something similar is brought to light by indigenous human/non-human diplomatic practices interacting, interrupting, cutting in flows and overlaying stacked layers in the nervous and geological systems of the world. To eat the other's words and positions is to negotiate these timely and untimely cuts, differences, and contradictions; to change and be changed by the act of crossing apparent boundaries and by the encounter with beings on the other side, 'and doing so through the incorporation of the other's positional perspective.'[12] To confront what is alien to oneself in oneself, or to affirm one's self and give it to the other self as a present. Isn't that what an effective ecological thought and practice really requires?

VI

Dear C, you did what indigenous people do when they act based on the law of reciprocity and exchange ceremonial gifts or presents. You helped the adults understand that a gift which is ritual, like your gift, is different from two other kinds of gifts: the unilateral gift, which is therefore not reciprocal and may or may not be public; and solidarity, which is a gift involving useful goods but not necessarily precious ones. In contrast, your gift was reciprocal and public. And it was precious. For is there anything more precious than time?[13]

Thus, it was also ceremonial. The ceremonial gift is what the indigenous peoples of the Americas have been enacting and exemplify when they stand tall in the face of power and its abuses. As they did in the fall of 2016 together with climate activists in rural North Dakota in the United States, and when they walked from the mountains and the forests in the political act they call

---

[12] Pedro Neves Marques, *The Forest & The School. Where to Sit at the Dinner Table?* (Archive Books & Akademie der Künte der Welt 2014) 298. Also, Eduardo Kohn, *Cómo piensan los bosques?* (Ediciones Abya Yala 2021) 1–35 at 25.

[13] Bruno Mazzoldi & Freddy Tellez, 'The Pocket-Size Interview with Jacques Derrida,' in (Winter 2007) 33(2) Critical Inquiry, for the distinction between contract and gift, a present that can be opened and what is found within is the unexpected, like a foreign body or time. The latter can never reassemble completely once disseminated, which also happens to language once spoken and eaten by others for there's no metalinguistic (or historical) overhang. Hence, the irreducibility of time (or language). Once given, it can never be reassembled and returned as the same or in part, only as difference and totality (meaning incompleteness). Also, Jacques Derrida, *Given Time. 1. Counterfeit Money* (University of Chicago Press, 1992) Chapters 2–4.

la minga to join the youths of Chile and Colombia during the protests of the years of plague.

The ceremonial gift is primarily a prestation that ensures not only the reciprocal recognition and interaction of two groups often in agonistic relation. It is also an act of diplomacy in that it creates other relations, strange alliances or kin between groups and individuals that were at first foreign to each other but then become and behave like something else or someone else. This includes the forging of stranger alliances between what we would call subjects and objects, beings of nature and human humans, or humans and non-humans. If so, to be clear, what is exchanged isn't just some useful good. This isn't that kind of gift. The exchanged gift happens to be also the most precious, signs and values incarnated in someone's body and radical spiritual commitment. Whether it is a man or a woman or something else, above all they are persons. I know. It's a wild idea. Imagine a science, a politics, a law and diplomacy that not only adheres to such a principle but runs with it!

That is why, as you understood only too well, the dominant model of profit, money, and circulation does not fit here. To speak of 'circulation' and offer as an instance of it the 'commitment' of millions of hard currency or the exchange of news and messages in the fast and faster platforms of the post-classical public sphere in our digital era, you knew, just won't cut it. Because money entails no radical commitment. No commitment at all.

Of course, money and messages are useful. And, of course, it would be good if the countries and global corporations that have done the most to cause the climate crisis paid their fair share. Even if it is just what they have committed themselves to pay already, in treaty after treaty and declaration after declaration. Or even better if it is the fair price to be paid for historical grievances to historical victims considered as a put option and a restitution, which is possible at every moment without needing to rely on counterfactual assumptions about a history in which *ceteris* is never *paribus*, as Bob Meister says.[14]

The point is that although no one would deny it is appropriate to speak of neutral 'exchanges' and 'circulation' in the case of useful goods, money, and messages in general, it would not make any proper sense to speak of a neutral exchange and about the 'circulation of women' or young people such as yourself. This would be to forget that the partners in a marriage alliance, or *la minga*, or the kind of alliance that is a condition of activism, direct action, and un/armed struggle are the two exogamous groups. Strangers. Persons all of them.

---

[14] Robert Meister, *After Evil. A Politics of Human Rights* (Columbia University Press 2011) 253.

I say 'persons' not merely in the usual legal sense of fictive or feigned personality and feigned promises. As we have all come to realise in the wake of the 2008 economic meltdown, such a kind of promissory language – which is the language of contracts and economic exchanges – does make a difference. But it is more often the kind of difference that makes no difference. For example, we know that the banks and global financiers caused the economic meltdown, just as we know that the global financiers, the chemicals and the fossil fuel corporations have caused the current climate crisis (and several wars in the lands of our childhood). In the case of the economic meltdown, at least in part by selling mortgage-based derivatives as elements of a chain that they mistook for temporal patterns, amenable to computer-enhanced probabilistic understanding, and backed by ever-more distant, flimsy promises. In other words, language failed. And when it happened everything changed, and as we now know everything stayed the same.[15]

These are not the kinds of signs, values, and persons we talk about in relation to the ceremonial gift and the gift of time. To give time to think, to interrupt the chain of commands, to make kin and other stranger alliances and provide directions for action. We also, or rather, speak of persons, signs, symbolisation, language and values in the ethical and political sense in which a process of differentiation that has some impact in the practical reality of relations, firstly, must have some real alterity as its condition of possibility, and, secondly, makes a difference in that it provides the exogamous parties committing to an alliance with a sense of becoming something else. Or with a different direction and orientation.

Hence the formula for the prohibition of incest among indigenous groups in Amazonia or the injunction against failing to perform the duty of gifting goods as far as possible into other villages during Polynesian ceremonial change-exchanges (a failure known as *sori tana* or 'eating from one's own basket'). In the broadest sense, prohibitions like the injunction against incest or *sori tana* consist in a prohibition against obtaining by oneself and for oneself, instead of by another and for another. Notice also that the prohibition, as in the case of incest and exogamy, does not merely appear as the positing of the rule of reciprocity (a positive law, in that respect) but mostly focuses on the specificity of the goods involved, such as rich food and luxuries or highly valuable individuals, for these are marked by signs of alterity and therefore recognised as privileged symbols, or even metaphors in motion of the demand for reciprocal exchange and the process of trans-position.

---

[15] Costas Douzinas, *The Radical Philosophy of Rights* (Routledge 2019) 1–86, 151–185.

To sum up, these are precious rather than simply useful goods in that they are symbols and trans-motion metaphors of association, mutual care and transformative alliances. Thus, for example, women, young girls such as yourself, are signs of alterity in the consanguineous group and agents in the process of fabricating a different future.

Ditto, young women like yourself are not just part of the logic of reciprocity. They also incarnate an ethical value and a technique of memorialisation that pass through the bodies-and-minds of the stranger, the migrant, even the enemy, and aim for them to become allies rather than to kill them in battle, as happens in the ancient Greek model recovered by modern Europeans. In the latter, as you know, to die and kill in battle is justified as a way to gain heroic immortality in the memory that the male hero leaves in the mind of his sons, grandsons, servants or slaves after war.

VII

Something truly remarkable happens here, in this crucial distinction between two ethical practices and technical memory systems. It turns out that the emphasis on alterity in the case of indigenous practices is not only part of a logic that guarantees life and survival (as in the example of marriage outside of the consanguineous group) but also a technique of memory that values life, inclusion, and survivance, or the intimacy between the material and the conceptual, over the cult of war and death in the name of some abstract, devotional, and iconic immortality. Ditto, there is a contrast here between two very different ethical systems, and a different way of illuminating the passage of one system to another.

In its insistence on the living and animating intimacy between materiality and abstractions, the material and the imagined-conceptual, a medium and its messages, the visible and the invisible, even the earthly and the spiritual, the latter (indigenous) way illuminates how these facets of life are intertwined into each other, interanimating rather than being mutually opposing, repressive, or oppressive positions. A position, say, spirituality, is not, in this respect, the opposite of corporeality. Rather, it refers to the vulnerability and injurability as well as the sensing and transformative sense-making capacities of ethical agents, subjects, persons, that are explicitly historically indexed. But, of course, this is also to speak of ethical agency as grounded in corporeality, of being-alive as a condition of possibility of ethical agency; not just any life but a life that is riveted to history.[16]

---

[16] Amy Allen and Eduardo Mendieta, 'Introduction' in Amy Allen and Eduardo Mendieta (n 8) 12–13.

We all suffer, feel vulnerable, and can be injured or victimised in the flesh. But not everyone, everywhere, all the time and in the same way. Here, I am reminded of what a shaman from Brazilian Amazonia once told me: 'The white man comes to the Amazon and is always talking about the end of the world, without realising that the problem with the apocalypse is it's never apocalyptic enough.' Statements like 'the end of history', 'the end of the world', or 'social death' are problematic not only because they are too pessimistic, but also because they tend to be indeterminate negative judgments. They lack determinacy and concreteness.

Events happen in different ways to different persons in accordance with the affordance of material, concrete circumstances. What does this mean? Affordance is what the environment offers the agent. Sometimes, many times, without asking for anything in exchange. Think of the Sun, for instance, which offers its life-giving rays of light to everything that exists and relates to everything that exists as of equal value and importance, without expecting something useful in return. Thinking of value and importance in the analogy of the Sun gives us more reason to consider all levels of relationality and dialectics, from the cosmological and the inter-temporal to the personal and interpersonal. This thought can be enacted through ritual practices of symbolisation and transposition, images, and tropes that not only express different levels of relationality (as 'pluriverse' or 'multi-juridical' spaces) but also, first and foremost, act as a technological interface that relates the personal and the cosmic or the temporal in terms of mutual interpenetration, affordance, reciprocity and survivance.

In this concrete example of affordance and reciprocity, the quality of an object (such as the Sun) makes it clear how it should be approached and made sense of. The affordances of the material environment are what it offers the animal or the plant, differentially; what it provides or furnishes. Crucially, this precious quality of differencing affordance and enactment cannot be reduced, measured, or relativised in purely quantitative terms. It might make sense for the parties to a contractual economic exchange to ask 'how much can you pay?' in relation to things or goods in circulation, but it would make little sense to ask a similar question in relation to precious signs, qualities and values such as the life-giving rays of the Sun. Or water, as the indigenous confederacies and unions of Bolivia made clear as they fought the so-called Water Wars early in the twenty-first century. And it would make no sense to ask 'how much can you pay' in respect of persons such as women.[17]

---

[17] Oscar Guardiola-Rivera, *What If Latin America Ruled the World?* (Bloomsbury 2010) 317–320. Also, Drucilla Cornell, 'Derrida's Negotiations as a Technique of

To do so would be to erase their role as agents in a reciprocal relationship that determines them as givers and receivers in every concrete instance. Put otherwise, in the assignment of a wife, a familiar, or a husband, in the recognition of the life-giving powers of the Sun, the water, and the environment, it is the group's self that is at stake. Just as the speaker's self is at stake in the performance and enactment of a visual or linguistic act. Which is why such ceremonial reciprocal gift-giving and performances of sensing, inventing the means of sensing, and of making sense are always political. And different from economic exchanges.

Whereas in the former a commitment of self takes place, the latter aim, on the contrary, to flatten personality and the self, and to maintain the neutrality of goods and things in circulation as well as the neutrality or flatness of the partners in transaction and contract. To clarify, only in the former, but not in the latter, is where biology and physics intersect with metaphors, metonymies, and symbolisation.

Anthropologists like Michael Taussig and Marshal Sahlins notice this when accompanying and learning together with Amerindian and other groups. They observe that kinship or making kin, what I've called before the human/non-human diplomacy of Amerindians, based on gift-logics, is the place where biology and symbols or tropes traverse and transform each other. In doing so, they offer us a simple and ordinary instance in which to consider the relation between '*physis* and *nomos*, nature and law.' As an interplay that remains 'animated' because it takes place as an event that happens in consideration of patterns that are not just given and 'not only exist but have to be continuously preserved.' Ditto, we may speak in this respect, together with Taussig and others, of 'animated structuralism' as the philosophy of the peoples of the Andes, the Caribbean and Pacific coasts, and Amazonia.[18]

This is the philosophy that we need if we are not only to survive the climate crisis, but to thrive in survivance. Such philosophy speaks to the complementarity and intertwinement of the animal, the plant, and the environment. Of an affordance that indexes the injurious as well as the beneficial history of persons and objects without 'dividualising' them. And of 'nature' as the organic and inorganic body of human humans; an exo-memory, or the 'dispersed unconscious' to make ours the lines of dialogue performed by Bernard Stiegler in the film *An Organisation of Dreams*.[19]

Liberation' (2017) 39(2) Discourse. Journal for Theoretical Studies in Media and Culture 195–215.

[18] Michael Taussig (n 7) 161; Marshal Sahlins, *What Kinship Is – And Is Not* (University of Chicago Press 2014). Also, Edgar García (n 8) 194–195.

[19] *An Organisation of Dreams* (Ken McMullen, 2010).

It is a worldview sensitive to the interplay between structure and historical change. A philosophy that points us in the direction of a broader sense of reciprocity and responsibility for the structures that hold together a material world and give life to it. But these reciprocities can also be considered a bio- and cosmo-logical extension of a concept of tool and media that neither dismisses nor separates signs from their materials or abstractions. Consider, for example, such indigenous tools for timekeeping as the biocultural sacred sites of Mesoamerica. '29 October to 2 November is linked to midnight, to the southern segment of the world, to the underworld, to the end of the rainy season' and thus, also, to the corn plant lifecycle that ritually begins on 12 February.

The material recording, mathematical symbolisation, and metaphoric discussion of the chronotopic dimension or timespace coordinates in bioculture are afforded by the construction of spaces where the heart and mind make meteorological, astronomical and other environmental phenomena cultural. This spiritually and philosophically denser practices of timekeeping could perhaps shed new light in relation to 'running the clock down' on climate change actions. But to capture their fully animating capacities in relation to seemingly invariant structures, we need to liberate such tools (and ourselves) from the scientific/religious schism introduced by Western missionaries, top-down religious and secular perspectives in Mexico and elsewhere in the Americas.

Think of indigenous technologies like so-called word cinemas (the 'speaking pictures' of the Books of the People like the Mayan *Popol Vuh*) and other dispersed repositories of the tradition of continental liberty. Like dream circles, petroglyphs, or khipus, the tools of Andean knot writing and accounting. Khipu designs, for example, are intertwined with tactility because built into the machine's sign system is a relational circuit between design and its physical twining, between structure and material iteration. Here, reciprocity has less to do with mere interpersonal exchange and more with the mutual interpenetration of individual actions and the trans-temporal structure of the world. Khipus thread into a knot what is so often incorrectly distinguished in terms of that structure as the Great Divide of 'nature' versus 'culture'.

To put it in a few words, the ethopoetic core of gift societies is one of transposition, trans-motion, and survivance. That ethopoetic core is in the service of life. The real opposite of death ethics and philosophies. Living ethics, an ethics of living labour. Its figure is feminine.

Like you and your gift, dear C.

VIII

A crucial aspect of climate justice and environmental activism is that any activity that causes environmental degradation generates winners as well as losers, to put it in the language of law and political economy. Surely, the activity in question benefits some people, otherwise no one would pursue it. And some people bear the costs, the injuries and the vulnerability or the suffering in the flesh in differential ways – otherwise environmental degradation would not be seen as a problem. This raises the question: Why can those who benefit from such activities impose and reimpose environmental costs and historically differencing suffering on others?

The answers to this question vary, but as James Boyce correctly states, they all boil down to power disparities. The frame of reference that we've inherited from the dominance of linear geometric and geographical perspective models during the early-to-mid eras of expansionist warfare and geo-political management of centrality, allow for the deferment of costs, borne by future generations. The fact that current legal technologies, especially adjudication, tend not to be able to create remedies for potential or historically ongoing consequences means that the not-yet dimension of temporality remains politically and legally invisible. Much the same can be said about the consideration of those who are not here today to defend themselves. Legal and political invisibility in time and space is disempowering, another aspect of the fact that those considered inert or 'minor' by current geo-political and legal frames aren't invited to sit at the table. And, of course, deferment can also happen in space.[20]

This and the fact that some people may not have adequate access to knowledge and even when they're aware they bear the brunt of environmental costs and injuries cannot do much about it, boil down to the fact that they lack necessary and sufficient economic and political power to prevail in social decisions about the use and abuse of the environment. The cases of Las Pavas and Standing Rock exemplify this. The solution in such cases is, of course, to change the balances of power. But how? So far, large sectors of the environmental movement do not seem willing to use a wider diversity of tactics to escalate conflict. Interestingly, this has brought back to the fore questions of direct action and violence, resistance, and revolution, which the moralistic turn of human rights discourse since the 1970s or 1980s had assumed were destined for the dustbin of history.[21]

But to tackle these questions requires a shift in perspective. Not only a diversity of tactics but also a diversity of aesthetics. Other ways of seeing and criticising that can translate into real relations. For if I cannot translate an

---

[20] James K. Boyce, 'The Environmental Cost of Inequality' (2021) 30(4) Scientific American 79.

[21] James Butler, 'A Coal Mine for Every Wildfire' (2021) 43.22 London Review of Books <https://www.lrb.co.uk/the-paper/v43/n22/james-butler/a-coal-mine-for-every-wildfire> accessed 29 March 2022. Also, Andreas Malm, *How to Blow Up a Pipeline. Learning to Fight in a World on Fire* (Verso 2021).

idea or a more correct ethical position into real relations, then it is not critical enough, as Andreas Malm and others suggest. Viewing historical grievances as an involuntarily bought put option is an example of how sovereignty claims can be transformed in ways that are responsive to the historical context here and now, and ironic, without simply reproducing the techniques of spacetime closure typical of the settler-nation state.[22]

The irony resides in the fact that this transformative tactic captures the reality of current beneficiaries of an unjust advantage that are willing to appeal to force to defend their ill-gotten gains, for instance by co-opting the enforcement apparatuses of the state or funding and supporting paramilitary forces, as in the case of Colombia, and can justly fear to lose much more. Practices like this turn the force of law subtended by fear against itself.

It is not surprising that practical examples like this emerge in situations of legal and political transitivity. Creating financial remedies for historical grievances based on doctrines of adverse possession in property law, restitution, and asset-creation, or resorting to irony to create relational possibilities outside the authenticity regimes of (liberal) multicultural recognition, as in the case of the drafting of the 2013 Constitution of the White Earth Nation, not only describe the contradictions inherent to pacifying discourses of tragedy and current legal rationalism in which the posited letter of the law stands in the way of that which cannot be perfectly contained, rationalised or enunciated. That is, the ever-shifting relations between (human and non-human) persons and institutions.

IX

Trickster writers and legal theorists like Gerald Vizenor, Ursula K. Le Guin, and Chadwick Allen situate questions of legal transitivity in their consideration of the dynamics of political identities and native sovereignty. Allen's conception of the trans-indigenous, for instance, displaces indigenous cultures outside of the nature/culture frame as 'ongoing processes rather than finished outcomes.'[23] In this perspective, 'trans' means 'across, beyond, and through,

---

[22] Ariella Azoulay, Nitasha Dhillon, Oscar Guardiola-Rivera, Nelson Maldonado-Torres et al., 'Diversity of Tactics, Diversity of Aesthetics: Post-MoMA Futures, Part 1' (2021) Verso Blog <https://www.versobooks.com/blogs/5076-diversity-of-tactics-diversity-of-aesthetics-post-moma-futures-part-i> accessed 29 March 2022.

[23] Chadwick Allen, 'Productive Tensions: Trans/national, Trans/indigenous' in Scott Lyons (ed) *The World, The Text and The Indian: Global Dimensions of Native American Literature* (State University of New York Press 2017) 240; *Trans-indigenous: Methodologies for Global Native Literary Studies* (University of Minnesota Press 2012) xxxii. Also, Gerald Vizenor and Jill Doerfler (n 8).

suggesting sustained movement, but also changing [and] changing thoroughly suggesting significant' or emphatic metamorphosis.[24]

Very simply, this is an application of the insight that if power and fear rules, then this must also include the fear the masters of the universe feel that one fine day the rabble, the motley crew, and multitude will stop identifying with their rulers and their rules, and instead disobey, yawn, and not even bother to look up to be recognised by the sovereign.[25]

The right to self-determination is reinvented in these practices of iurisgenerative, emphatic, and fantastic critique as well as combative confrontation. They trouble the rubric by which the validity of territorial autonomy claims is often assessed. They dismantle and move away from the conservative norms of the nation-state as well as the system that places settler liberal demands for staid cultural authenticity on native sovereignty claims.

That is, the idea of an indigeneity (or 'hispanicity,' or 'blackness') untouched by history or determinant change. The more conservative norms of nation-states and international law either negate the multiple dimensions of racism, or liberally dismiss them by reducing them to a flat surface of 'minority' discrimination presupposed to be subordinate to settler 'majority' frameworks. And impose forms of recognition or aim to reimpose and sustain the reign of terror in the shape of walls, 'natural habitats,' reservations, Chinese box jurisdictions, or raw police and paramilitary violence, all of which assume the homogeneity of the primordial group – a non-sense of non-ongoing, ahistorical, and racially unchanging being.[26]

In contrast, the White Earth Anishinaabe Constitution, the invention of gains-based remedies for historical injustice, and the rights-based reconstruction of ecological attentiveness in struggle emphasise irony, oral and pictographic imagining or recitation, structural indeterminacy, and animation as practical tools. To encourage interpretative scope, negotiations, and to combatively confront misuses of legal agency and human rights aiming to achieve 'democratic closure' and the termination of indigenous claims.

The point of these practices is not only to show that concepts of choice, liberty and agency are insufficient when articulated and contained within the frame of reference of settler colonialism, internal colonial or neo-liberalism and neo-conservatism, as well as international law.

---

[24] Ibid.
[25] Michael Taussig (n 2) 15.
[26] Frantz Fanon, 'Conducts of Confession in North Africa (2)' in Jean Khalfa and Robert J. C. Young (eds), *Freedom and Alienation* (Steven Corcoran tr, Bloomsbury 2018) 413–416 at 414. Also, Anna Spain-Bradley, 'Human Rights Racism' (2019) 32 Harvard Human Rights Journal 1–58.

When applied to complex debates about such institutional circumstances as Canada's Indian residential school system that intersect with violence against women and children's as well as women's rights, or the systematic killing of environmental defenders and community social leaders in Colombia or elsewhere in Latin America (most of them women), the language of agency and choice alone implies the priority of the liberty and security of so-called majorities which is often held out as a reason to override so-called minority rights. Thus, the practices theorised by people like Vizenor and Silvia Rivera Cusicanqui, among others, also aim to rearticulate the self-determination of a community by giving that community the inflection points of historical transformation and determination it needs to look forward: conflict, motion, imagination, enactment, retro-performative action, dissent, difference, and a sense of the unevenness of past-present historical conditions.

This way, a set of techniques for critique and shifting perspectives are made available, which translate a critical idea or a correct ethical position into real relations and situations. In addition to that, these practices of interpretation and negotiation scan history to find the future interpenetrating the past-present dimension. We can call this kind of action-motion 'future memory' in contrast with the more familiar kinds of memorialisation that remain stuck in the past, which have become characteristic of the fascistic derivation of neoliberal and neoconservative regimes in recent years, as shown in the Trumpian slogan 'Make X Great Again.'

Rather than being caught in a 'natural' pre-civic and pre-literate pre- or non-modernity, the voicing of ethopoetic cores of reciprocity via indigenous dream-circles, oral history, and inverse projection tends to be relational, proximal and responsive to the shifting present of multiple, interacting temporal orientations. Moreover, this ethopoetic orientation of the future looking back at its past satisfies the conditions by which the determined yet unframed present and future anterior bears the confidence of ongoing time and enables the intensification of previous, interrupted yet unfinished projects (for instance, revolutions, decolonisation, calls for a new international economic order and so on). These are conditions of possibility for environmental and other kinds of political rights-based activism.

It is in this respect that the Anishinaabe legal scholar John Borrows brings forth fantastic visions of timespace in cosmology capable of creating a passage or interzone of legalistic difference. A difference that is different from differential 'cultural' identity. In his drawings of spheres of relations in motion, which he teaches as practices and techniques of legal mediation and negotiation, the similarity of the three spheres (functioning as geometrical symbols) draws attention to differently positioned figures in and around the spheres, in which differences participate in one another or are intertwined at various intermixed levels. These intermixed levels enact the kind of multijuridical structure that Borrows, Vizenor and others like them advocate. While at the same time offering a dense visual representation of how a multijuridical multiperspectivism would rely on difference in a relational rather than essentialist form. Here, the emphasis is on difference as an important component of collectivity.[27]

These legal techniques and technologies place their accent on the political (rather than 'cultural') value of difference. In that respect, it is no surprise that they have been placed in resonance with the work of Western philosophers like T. W Adorno and Walter Benjamin, mindful of the larger political and environmental consequences of modernity's emphasis on an alienated and fearful subjectivity and consciousness.

Adorno's meditations on the assimilation of pure mind to the ruling principle, divided from and opposed to corporeality, objects, and environmental affordance can be illuminating here. He analysed the ways in which the self, the 'I' of apperception to which the manifold of the senses through which we perceive the environment around us appears affixed, as if to an unchangeable framework, is in fact decentred and the framework of perspective destabilised in a manner that is inherent to states of difference. 'The relationship of subject and object would lie in a peace achieved between human beings as well as between them and their Other, [where] peace is the state of differentiation without domination, with the differentiated participating in each other,' [28] he observes in a way that resonates strongly with what you and I, dear C, refer to here as the human/non-human diplomacy of Amerindians.

X

We may also find here an index of what the notion of 'living well' might mean. It was made present in the Constitutions of Bolivia and Ecuador in the context of the positing of rights for non-human nature. But it does not depend on such positive law. Rather, you could say that the spirit of 'living well' transforms positive law. It also appears in the recognition of the environment as a victim of violence during the war in Colombia by the Special Peace Jurisdiction of that country. Crucially, in the important decision made by the Inter-American Court of Human Rights in the case of *Our Land Association (Lhaka Honhat)* v.

---

[27] John Borrows (n 8) 42, 63, 72.
[28] Theodor W. Adorno, *Critical Models. Interventions and Catchwords* (Henry Pickford tr, Columbia UP 2005) 247; *Lectures on Negative Dialectics*: Fragments of a Lecture Course 1965/1966 (Rolf Tiedemann ed, Rodney Livingstone tr, Polity 2008) 144–149.

Argentina. And it may come to animate emerging yet still parochial proposals by a group of Western legal thinkers to declare something called 'ecocide'.[29]

Here it is. The kind of difference that makes a difference. A principle. An orientation for action. An aesthetic and ethical idea. One that returns to the earth as a set of animating practices in a context of structural, historical injustice. It consists not only in asking whether forests think in real time but also, or rather, how they think. And perhaps more fundamentally, how can we think with them? To pause. And make time.

A different future.

This is the most precious gift, your gift.

And because of it we become and behave like something else. Something better.

We are grateful for it.

---

[29] Int-CtHR, *Lhaka Honhat (Our Land) Association* v. *Argentina*, Judgment of 6 February 2020 at <https://www.corteidh.or.cr/docs/casos/articulos/seriec_400_ing.pdf> accessed 28 March 2022; Unidad de Investigación y Acusación-Jurisdicción Especial de Paz (JEP), Comunicado 009, 5/06/2019, Bogotá, Colombia, at <https://www.jep.gov.co/SiteAssets/Paginas/UIA/sala-de-prensa/Comunicado%20UIA%20-%20009.pdf> accessed 28 March 2022; Ley no. 300, 15/10/2012, Gaceta Oficial del estado Plurinacional de Bolivia, Ley Marco de la Madre Tierra y Desarrollo Integral para Vivir Bien at <http://files.harmonywithnatureun.org/uploads/upload655.pdf> accessed 28 March 2022; Independent Expert Panel for the Legal Definition of Ecocide, Commentary and Core Text, July 2021 at <https://static1.squarespace.com/static/5ca26 08ab914493 c64ef1f6d/ t/ 60d1e 6e604fae22 01d03407f/ 1624368879048/ SE+Foundation+Commentary+and+core+text+rev+6.pdf> accessed 28 March 2022.

9. More-than-human rights to data
Jannice Käll

Our digitally entangled worlds are emerging on both the surface and depths of the crisis of humanity or rather: 'human'ity. This crisis, which has come to be referred to as the Anthropocene shows how humanity has become a force which manages to reshape the material conditions of the Earth.[1] As such, the concept of the Anthropocene has further become qualified to note how the 'human' world is both caused by and affects human and more-than-human bodies differently.[2] Examples of such variations and critiques against the concept involve referring to it as the Capitolocene,[3] the Anthrobscene[4] or to speak of 'a billion black Anthropocenes'.[5] The new materialist (NM), or critical posthumanist turn in theory, seeks to advance responses to these multiple systems of exploitation and control resulting in the geophysiological state we are in. Such answers come in many forms, including calls for radical relationality in the form of 'zoe-egalitarianism'[6] as well as to 'stay with the trouble' and not assume that the continuous growth of human populations is the answer we need in this crisis.[7] Another way to express this, is that human life in each instant is 'a multispecies effort'[8] or that we need to both analyse and recapture this moment as a stage of 'geoontopower'.[9]

---

[1] See Paul Crutzen (et al.), 'The New World of the Anthropocene' (2010) 44(7) Environmental Science & Technology 2228–2231.
[2] See also Rosi Braidotti, *The Posthuman* (Polity 2013) 1.
[3] Jason Moore, 'The Capitalocene, Part I: On the Nature and Origins of Our Ecological Crisis' (2017) 44 The Journal of Peasant Studies 594–630.
[4] Jussi Parikka, *The Anthrobscene* (MIT Press 2014).
[5] Kathryn Yusoff, *A Billion Black Anthropocenes or None* (University of Minnesota Press 2019).
[6] Braidotti (n 2) 92–97.
[7] Donna Haraway, *Staying with the Trouble: Making Kin in the Chthulucene* (Duke University Press 2016).
[8] Anna Tsing (et al.), *Feral Atlas: The More-Than-Human Anthropocene*, A Stanford Digital Project <https://www.sup.org/books/title/?id=30693> accessed 25 May 2023.
[9] Elizabeth Povinelli, *Geontologies: A Requiem to Late Liberalism* (Duke University Press 2016).

The effects that current forms of anthropocentrism have on life have progressively come to be theorized in the legal discipline, as well as being seen as something that lawyers need to be capable of acting on. In the face of ecological collapse experienced by multiple beings and communities, a central question for lawyers needs to revolve around what the purpose, description and function of legal and ethical systems are.[10] This has resulted also in a number of calls for new, or at least renewed, rights, including those elaborated in the Rights of Nature (RoN) movement,[11] animal rights, and the Right to Breathe.[12] The more recent turn to RoN, in particular, has been given fairly vast attention and actualization through a number of legal cases and legally binding decisions. One such prominent example of this is the 2008 Ecuadorian Constitution amendment which was the first in the world to recognize explicit RoN, giving nature the rights to exist, persist, maintain and regenerate its vital cycles, structures and functions, and its processes of evolution. A similar law was enacted in Bolivia in 2011. Another famous case involves how the Whanganui River in Aotearoa/New Zeeland was recognized in law as a living being in 2017. Furthermore, there has also been legislation declaring personhood to the river and all its physical and metaphysical elements, and to a former national park known as Te Urewara. Also in 2017, a court in the northern Indian state of Uttarakhand cited the Wanganaui river case and ordered that the river Ganges and its tributary river, the Yamuna, be given the status of living human entities; in 2020, voters in Toledo, Ohio in the USA suggested granting legal standing to Lake Erie.[13]

In parallel, the technologized worlds criticized (as well as embraced) via NM have also been discussed in relation to new rights in law and technology studies. These discussions involve, for example, increased rights to privacy,

---

[10] Anna Grear (et al.), 'Editorial: Posthuman Legalities: New Materialism and law beyond the Human' in Anna Grear (et al.) (eds), *Posthuman Legalities: New Materialism and Law Beyond the Human* (Edward Elgar Publishing 2021).

[11] Emily Jones, 'Posthuman international law and the rights of nature' in Anna Grear (et al.) (eds) ibid.; Marie Petersmann, 'Response-abilities of care in more-than-human worlds' in Anna Grear (et al.) (eds) ibid.; and one of the more well-known first calls for rights of nature: Christopher Stone, 'Should Trees have Legal Standing – Towards Legal Rights for Natural Objects?' (1972) 45 Southern California Law Review 450–501.

[12] Achille Mbembe, 'The Universal Right to Breathe' (2020) <https://critinq.wordpress.com/2020/04/13/the-universal-right-to-breathe/> accessed 25 May 2023; Daniela Gandorfer and Zulaikha Ayub, 'Introduction: Matterphorical' (2021) 24(1) Theory & Event 2–13. Daniela Gandorfer (et al.), 'The Right to Breathe' (n.d.), <https://slought.org/resources/gas_exchanges> accessed 1 June 2022.

[13] Katya Garcia-Antón (et al.) (eds) *Let the River Flow: An Indigenous Uprising and its Legacy in Arts, Ecology and Politics* (Office for Contemporary Art Norway/Valiz 2020) 11–12.

or rights to one's data;[14] and robot rights[15] explicitly following a posthumanist inspired agenda.[16] Needless to say, data protection rights, just like human rights in general, are humanist/human-centred at their core, as they focus on humans' rights to 'regain control' over 'their' data. A central focus to build such control is the idea that a human individual is capable of pursuing new right claims, mediated via state authorities and global platform companies alike. This understanding of individual persons' capacities to (re)claim their rights to privacy has been criticized in several ways, not the least in pointing at how data extraction and privacy is embedded in technological design,[17] and how data needs to be understood as relational.[18] Furthermore, most perspectives on data rights do not account for how AI will be able to transform society towards increased rights for 'more-than-human becomings', as they fail in exploring the multiple layers of resources needed to make such changes possible. As identified by Parikka, there is however a deep connection between the coal that first fired Western Europe to subsequently move over the world producing a form of industrialism that is still the backbone of information culture. As he further notes, a 1999 Forbes article suitably put it: 'Dig more coal, the PCs are coming'.[19] The 'need' to increase bandwidth, introduce more efficient processors and data-heavy digital design practices as well as in general increase computational tasks also makes for a significant upward curve in absolute numbers of energy consumption of the supposedly immaterial matrix of computation.[20]

The ecological aspects of digitalization in this manner connect technology to other aspects of nature, in a way not immediately recognized in law and technology studies. There are, however, strokes around how AI regulation is currently unfolding that point in a similar direction as the RoN movement in the manner that environmental questions at least are mentioned as a factor to take into account.[21] It is therefore suggested here that the new 'human' rights related both to RoN and data rights therefore need to be considered

---

[14] Jannice Käll, 'A Posthuman Data Subject? The Right to be Forgotten and Beyond' (2017) 18(5) German Law Journal.
[15] Frank Pasquale, *New Laws of Robotics: Defending Human Expertise in the Age of AI* (Harvard University Press 2020).
[16] Joshua Gellers, *Rights for Robots: Artificial Intelligence, Animal and Environmental Law* (Routledge 2021).
[17] Mireille Hildebrandt, *Smart Technologies and the End(s) of Law* (Edward Elgar Publishing 2015).
[18] Käll (n 14); Salomé Viljoen, 'Democratic Data: A Relational Theory for Data Governance' (2021) 131(2) Yale Law Journal 577–654.
[19] Parikka (n 4) 138.
[20] Ibid.
[21] See EU proposal 2021/0106 on regulation of AI p. 1, laying out context for the proposal.

together in order to fulfil the promises of sustainable digitalization as well as world-making in general.

In following the two lines of new rights, this chapter seeks to imagine further, if it would be possible to move towards 'more-than-human' rights to data, where data stands as a proxy for the commodity or resource of digitalization. The category of more-than-human, rather than non-human and posthuman, is here used to affirm how entities exceed human as well as human*ist* registers and divisions attributed to the divides between 'humans' and 'non-humans'.[22] The choice of more-than-human as a concept aligns with Pugliese's ambition to affirm that which is other than human, without reproducing such becoming on a positive/negative divide, and hierarchy.[23] Furthermore, he points at the potential in this concept of elucidating a deep inseparability between what is considered 'human' and what is considered 'other-than-human'.[24] From the perspective of establishing a new form of rights to the data-driven society, such inseparability is vital in order to address the layeredness and different materialities that are needed in order for digitalization to happen.

To stage the question of more-than-human rights generally renews the old question of what counts as human and non-human for human rights, or rather who counts as a rights holder and/or a non-rights holder. Whereas this is a question gaining a lot of attention in the discussions of ecology and rights of nature, the movement advocating data rights is however not as focused on non-human right holding. Widely embraced as well as criticized, human rights have come to be understood as a legislative tool that embraces postmodern ideals of society as well as how to perform law as a humanitarian good. In this sense, one can say, as does Douzinas, that: '[h]uman rights are the ideology after the end'.[25] Ironically, the concept of the posthuman can be seen to fit perfectly within the framing of human rights as that which arises at the end of the human world, or end of human politics. However, critical posthumanist philosophy and NM rather aim to move beyond the passivity caused in the supposed victory of 'the' human in liberalism, which human rights are theoretically strongly aligned to. Critical posthumanist perspectives also explicitly requestions the precedence of Enlightenment and capitalist values.[26]

A more-than-human right perspective will be further elaborated here via a Deleuzian conceptualization of rights. The reason for this is that critical post-

---

[22] See Joseph Pugliese, *Biopolitics of the More-Than-Human: Forensic Ecologies of Violence* (Routledge 2020) 3.
[23] Ibid.
[24] Ibid.
[25] Costas Douzinas, 'The End(s) of Human Rights' (2002) 26(2) Melbourne University Law Review 445.
[26] Braidotti (n 2) 13–54.

humanist perspectives and NM rely to large degree on Gilles Deleuze, as well as Deleuze's readings of Baruch Spinoza.[27] In doing this, the chapter follows recent advancements in (digital) humanities hinted at above, with a particular focus on media studies, design, architecture and arts. Within these fields, there is an ongoing debate about how digitalization moves as a layered form of governance and extraction process.[28]

This chapter unfolds in a brief theoretical introduction to recent discussions of 'more-than-human' perspectives and their affiliations to new materialist and posthumanist perspectives. A number of examples are introduced to visualize layered and more-than-human aspects of data extraction, collection and sensing. These examples serve as a backdrop to discuss whether it would be possible to advocate for rights to data in a more-than-human manner. As a conclusion, it is suggested that such perspective needs to follow the insights in critical legal theory on human rights, as well as the Deleuzian-Spinozian underpinnings in new materialist theory staging how the rights of bodies (of all human and non-human variations) are always conflictual. This stands in contrast to more classic liberal ideas where human rights are seen as stemming from certain eternal and transcendental values. The Deleuzian-Spinozan understanding of rights, as will be discussed, points at an ethical current within such conflicts. This ethics concerns how certain forms of power, which create more benefits than harm for life in general, can be seen as a right of bodies, via knowledge, in how to affirm more radically sustainable collectivities.

---

[27] See Rick Dolphijn and Iris van der Tuin, 'Pushing Dualisms to an Extreme: On the Philosophical Impetus of a New Materialism' (2011) 44 Continental Philosophy Review 383–400; *New Materialism: Interviews & Cartographies* (Open Humanities Press 2012); Braidotti (n 2). And for more on this line of philosophy, see e.g. Elizabeth Grosz, *The Incorporeal: Ontology, Ethics, and the Limits of Materialism* (Columbia University Press 2017).

[28] Benjamin Bratton, *The Stack: On Software and Sovereignty* (MIT Press 2015); Tiziana Terranova, 'Red Stack Attack: Algorithms, Capital and the Automation of the Common' (2014) Report from the Algorithms and Capital workshop, Goldsmiths' College <http:// www .euronomade .info/ ?p = 2268> accessed 25 May 2023; Kate Crawford and Vladan Joler, 'Anatomy of an AI System: The Amazon Echo as an anatomical map of human labor, data and planetary resources' (2018) <https://anatomyof .ai> accessed 1 February 2022; Kate Crawford and Trevor Paglen, 'Excavating AI: The politics of training sets for machine learning' (2019) <https://excavating.ai> accessed 1 February 2022.

'MORE-THAN-HUMAN' PERSPECTIVES AND THEIR AFFILIATIONS TO A NEW MATERIALIST DELEUZIAN NOTION OF RIGHTS

Critical new materialist and posthumanist perspectives both share an endeavor of reorienting humanist traditions towards including 'more-than-human' perspectives. They do so by activating a number of critical methods which have affiliations with French thinkers such as Michel Foucault, Gilles Deleuze and Félix Guattari as well as Jacques Derrida.[29] They also draw heavily upon more recent scholarship in critical race and postcolonial (and decolonial) studies, including theorists such as Achilles Mbembe, Franz Fanon and Éduoard Glissant, as well as feminist theory, for example through thinkers such as Adriana Cavarero, Donna Haraway, Kimberle Crenshaw and Judith Butler. Deleuze and Guattari as well as Haraway, have all been identified as belonging to the critical new materialist stream themselves and that is also how I will treat them here – as writers who directly single out specific new materialist focus areas. What joins all these perspectives is a renewed critical attention to matter, and how 'matter comes to matter'.[30] In law, matter and 'matterphorics'[31] are expressed via law's concepts, in the way that they prescribe and cut[32] the continuum of bodies.[33]

A common theme shared by the perspectives addressed in new materialist scholarship, building upon the scholars mentioned, is a complex and critical understanding of human rights. This is also true in particular regarding Deleuze's perception of human rights. As is fairly well-known, Deleuze was skeptical in regard to human rights. This understanding is derived particularly from the *Abécédaire*-series where he states[34]:

> Listen, this respect for the 'rights of man' – this really makes me want to say, almost make some odious statements. It belongs so much to the weak thinking of the empty

---

[29] Dolphijn and van der Tuin (n 27).

[30] Karen Barad, 'Posthumanist Performativity: Toward an Understanding of How Matter Comes to Matter' (2003) 28 Signs: Journal of Women in Culture and Society 103; *Meeting the Universe Halfway: Quantum Physics and the Entanglement of Matter and Meaning* (Duke University Press 2007).

[31] Gandorfer and Ayub (n 12).

[32] Jacques Derrida, 'The force of law: The mystical foundations of authority' in Drucilla Cornell (et al.) (eds), *Deconstruction and the Possibility of Justice* (XXXXX 1992); Costas Douzinas and Adam Gearey, *Critical Jurisprudence: The Political Philosophy of Justice* (Hart Publishing 2005).

[33] Barad (n 30) 394.

[34] Gilles Deleuze and Claire Parnet, 'What it means to be on the Left' in Gilles Deleuze, *A to Z* (Semiotext(e) DVD 2004).

intellectual period that we discussed earlier [here, he refers to his view that culture is constantly in decadence, expressed in section *C for Culture*]. It's purely abstract these 'rights of man'. What is it? It's purely abstract, completely empty.[35]

However, it is debated whether this skepticism in relation to human rights was towards the vitality of human rights as a concept, or against the human rights movements around the time where he uttered his (very brief) views on the topic.[36] It is not a far-stretch to assume that the concept of the human as well as human rights in general could be understood as 'unspecific universalist concepts'.[37] Human rights, if understood in such sense, would then be contrary to Deleuze's philosophical endeavor, which sets out to engage with concrete, or empirically grounded, conflicts.[38] This implies, for example, that enacting rights requires that something be recognized as a problem or subject of injustice in the first place. When considering questions of injustices against 'nature', obviously not all bodies have received equal treatment. For example, there has for long been an ongoing discussion in law and moral theory about the treatment of animals (here it should be noted that there are differences between the extent of rights one is willing to grant to different animal species, and of what kind). However, there is significantly less discussion of the injustices that the soil is subject to.[39] Consequently, a conflict of material interests needs to be identified prior to the construction of a right. And this identification, or creation, of a conflict needs to be grounded in an empirically embedded, material, analysis, rather than an abstract principle of rights.

What is even more vital for framing rights in a more-than-human manner is to recast the idea of rights altogether, from a solely conceptual order to be settled in the courts of law, or as a universally transcendental jurisprudence, towards something that is also continuously expressed by bodies, of all kinds.

---

[35] As cited and discussed further by Christos Marneros, *Human Rights After Deleuze: Towards an An-archic Jurisprudence* (Hart Publishing 2022) 88–108.

[36] Alexandre Lefebvre, *The Image of Law: Deleuze, Bergson, Spinoza* (Stanford University Press 2008) 85; Christos Marneros, 'Deleuze and Human Rights: The Optimism and Pessimism of '68' La Deleuziana. Online Journal of Philosophy 41.

[37] Marneros, Ibid. 16–48.

[38] Ibid. 25–27.

[39] Danielle Celermajer and Anne O'Brien, 'Alter-transitional justice; transforming injust relations with the more-than-human' in Grear, Anna (et al.) (eds), *Posthuman Legalities: New Materialism and Law Beyond the Human* (Edward Elgar Publishing 2021) 138–145.

In order to reach such understanding of rights, Deleuze's writings on expressionism in Spinoza are particularly informative. As he writes:

> The rights of an individual extend to the outmost limits of his power as it has been conditioned. This is the very meaning of the word *law*: the law of nature is never a rule of duty, but the norm of a power, the unity of right, power and its exercise. There is in this respect no difference between wise man and fool, reasonable and demented men, strong man and weak. They do of course differ in the kind of affections that determine their effort to persevere in existence. But each tries equally to preserve himself, and has as much right as he has power, given the affections that actually exercise his capacity to be affected.[40]

Consequently, because rights are here based on the outmost limits a body has the capacity to exercise, they are always conditioned in themselves. This means that the conceptual assignment of rights has no further extension than the powers that condition bodies, and which they simultaneously also condition. The ethical impulse with this view is to strive towards organizing encounters between bodies (i.e. rights) to '[...] unite with what agrees with our nature, to combine our relation with those that are compatible with it, to associate our acts and thoughts with the images of things that agree with us.'[41] In this, Deleuze identifies that the Spinozian idea of right also corresponds, and acts upon Hobbes' idea of a state of nature that needs to be organized. However, Deleuze does not come to the same conclusions as Hobbes, in the sense of separating between subjects, rights, and power, to avoid the negative aspects of the state of nature. Rather, he utilizes the notion of organizing a state of nature as an always-already more-than-human constellation concept of how law/right/power is produced by, and affects, bodies of human and other-than-human kinds alike. As the quote above shows, the rights of bodies do not require intelligence or strength but consist in an effort by bodies to persevere in their own beings. The way that bodies manage to acquire such rights through effectuated perseverance is however dependent on their capacity, in relation to other bodies, to do so. Here, obviously intelligence, in a general constellation of bodies where such is valued and effective, will make intelligent beings more likely to persevere and hence to have rights. However, this intelligence is not to be seen as a value in itself, but something that is both coming from the capacity of a body as well as its simultaneous positioning in relations.

To progress in a Deleuzian-Spinozian perception of rights, as means to establish more-than-human rights, it is necessary to both identify new conflicts

---

[40] Gilles Deleuze, *Expressionism in Philosophy: Spinoza* (Zone Books 1992) 258.
[41] Ibid. 260–261.

between bodies, as well as at the same time make for new encounters between bodies and hence new forms of more-than-human rights in practice. The aim with these examples is to situate how both rights of nature – and data rights – discussions could benefit from activating a more complex assemblage of bodies involved in data-driven settings. Doing so would then possibly function as a map for advocating more-than-human rights to data.

ENCOUNTERS BETWEEN BODIES OPENING UP TO MORE-THAN-HUMAN DATA RIGHTS

Today, there are many emerging technologies causing new encounters, as well as conflicts between human and non-human bodies. Most recently, the turn to AI brings debates around whether robots and AI should be considered as subjects for rights. At the core of these debates lies the commodification, or at least 'resourcification'[42] of data. In order to fulfil the dreams of artificially intelligent systems and their related technologies managing everything from global supply chains to local logistics, food safety and cultural industries, data is needed, both for training and communication between the smart tech and its environment.

Processes for data extraction, from both humans and non-humans, are furthermore at the core of emerging, and existing forms of AI alike. As an example of this, the production of data-driven economies takes place in non-human manners, when smart objects communicate with their surrounding by creating operational images only readable to themselves. This is the case, for example, with automated vehicles, which read their surroundings via pulsating lights or via images that only make sense within their own learning systems.[43] For this reason, it has been suggested that smart vehicles transform cityscapes *and* visuality, images *and* data, movement *and* seeing movement.[44] The art project Dreamlife of Driverless Cars by ScanLab visualizes what such non-human sensing can look like. In the project, a 3D laser scanned through the streets of London to visualize how driverless cars could come to perceive – and misperceive – the world.[45] Manaugh furthermore describes the use of 3D

---

[42] Johan Hultman (at al.) 'A Resourcification Manifesto: Understanding the Social Process of Resources Becoming Resources' (2021) 50.9 Research Policy 50.
[43] Ibid.
[44] Jussi Parikka, 'On seeing where there's nothing to see: Practices of light beyond photography' in Tomáš Dvorak and Jussi Parikka (eds), *Photography Off the Scale* (Edinburgh University Press 2020).
[45] G. Manaugh, 'The Dream Life of Driverless Cars' *New York Times* (2015) <https://www.nytimes.com/2015/11/15/magazine/the-dream-life-of-driverless-cars.html> accessed 1 June 2022.

scanning such as LiDAR sensors in autonomous cars making for a very specific navigational way of mapping the city as an ecology of machine-flickering that captures 'extremely detailed, millimeter-scale measurements of the surrounding environment.'[46] This first encounter points at how more-than-human life-worlds are emerging where machines depend on and sense human-created spaces in ways that are excessive to human perception. To frame this example against common data rights discussions, it can easily be concluded that where much of the traditional discussion in relation to data rights is concerned with how to keep privacy intact for human data subjects, less discussion has been focused on which conflicts between bodies occur when machines need, feed on, and reproduce data in their own assemblages.

There are also examples of how digital technologies such as blockchain are used to produce an added layer on non-human bodies with outspoken aims to actualize more radical ecologies. One case of such new sovereignties of nature is the well-known terra0 project, originally developed in the *Digitale Klasse* at the University of Arts, Berlin by Paul Seidler and Paul Kolling. As described by Paul Seidler, Paul Kolling and Max Hampshire in the project's white paper: terra0 should be conceived of as a self-owned forest that strives to set up a prototype of a self-utilizing piece of land. It does so by creating a scenario where a forest is able to sell licenses to log trees through automated processes, smart contracts and blockchain technology, and thereby accumulates capital.[47] The point with this exercise is that one could facilitate 'A shift from valorisation through third parties' of natural 'resources' such as forests 'to a self-utilization' which 'makes it possible for the forest to procure its real exchange value, and eventually buy (thus own) itself.'[48] In doing this, they outline that the forest in the form of a capital-holding owner will be in a position to buy more ground and to expand itself. In their view:

> A forest has an exactly computable productive force; the market value of the overall output of the forest can be precisely calculated. Beside its function as a source of raw material, the forest also holds the role of service contractor. It produces not only wood, but serves as a protected space within which diverse species can survive, contributing to an overall ecological balance.[49]

With support in such reasoning, one can say that digital elements are added to an entity of nature/non-human body with the aim of making it

---

[46] Ibid. and see Parikka (n 44).
[47] Paul Seidler (et al.), 'terra0. Can an augmented forest own and utilise itself?' (2016) <https://terra0.org/assets/pdf/terra0_white_paper_2016.pdf> accessed 1 June 2022.
[48] Ibid. 1.
[49] Ibid.

self-sustainable. This is akin to the kind of self-preservation that is part of the Deleuzian-Spinozian rights concept suggested above. From a more-than-human perspective however, one needs to acknowledge that there are bodies within this assemblage that do not correspond to the ethical line implicit in such rights. Most notably, the project resonates with current forms of ownership rights, including self-ownership. Besides this, and the technological layer itself, blockchain, is not necessarily approached in a critical way, but mostly just used as a means to create a machine for (self-)accumulation. It nevertheless points at how convergences between 'nature' and digital technologies are formed with an outspoken aim to produce subjectivity in a way which is not covered under the current human-focused register. In this manner, such endeavors have resonance also with the RoN movement, whether the forest is recognized as having rights by a nation-state or not.

Another similar but also slightly different example of how blockchain has been used to control nature rather than imposing it as a self-sustainable body, is the recently discussed case of how chickens meant to be consumed as food were placed on the blockchain in China. As Wang describes in her much-cited book on blockchain chicken farms, the question of food safety has activated a new register of data-driven logistics in China. Furthermore, there is a growing class of customers in big cities that have the financial means to pay for ecological, or otherwise upscale, produce. In the case elaborated by Wang, a small farmer in the Chinese countryside decided to put the chickens he tends to on a blockchain registry to prove that they have been kept in the way described. The consumer can then unlock this data about the chicken, to make sure that it has not been tampered with.[50] Here we again see a form of more-than-human data body emerging, as a chicken is provided with a digital layer. The rights question here also becomes something else than only one of animal rights or rights of nature since the animal body, or the 'natural' body is mixed up with other layers, transforming it into a form of 'cyborg chicken'. However, it also becomes something else compared to the data rights discussed in relation to the collection of data from human bodies. What is clear is that these chickens still pertain under ownership structures, that might even increase people's desire to consume chickens as products (when they are considered as safer to eat).

Larger projects where rights to nature and data converge (or collide), involve the idea of terraforming Earth, through data-driven optimization, for the survival of the human population.[51] As set out by Bratton, 'The Terraforming',

---

[50] Xiaowei Wang, *Blockchain Chicken Farm, and Other Stories of Tech in China's Countryside* (Farrar, Straus and Giroux 2020) 35–65.

[51] Benjamin Bratton, *The Terraforming* (Strelka Press 2019); 'Synthetic Gardens: Another Model for AI and Design' in Ben Vickers and K. Allado-McDowell (eds), *Atlas of Anomalous AI* (Ignota Books 2021); *The Revenge of the Real* (Verso 2021).

was also a research-oriented academic education in urban design studies, based at the Strelka Institute, Moscow, Russia (inaugurated in 2019 and cancelled due to Russia's war in Ukraine from spring 2022).[52] As the program further came to elaborate: 'The research program will consider the past and future role of cities as a planetary network by which humans occupy the Earth's surface. Planetarity itself comes into focus through orbiting imagining and terrestrial modelling media (satellites, sensors, servers in sync) that have made it possible to measure climate change with any confidence.'[53] Hence, the ambitious program sets out ways to model environmentally vital questions, with the help of digital media in their widest sense (including satellites, sensors and servers, as mentioned in the quote). The further philosophical aim was here also to invoke a speculative mode which does not seek to reinstate nature but to 'reclaim the artificial – not as in fake, but rather designed […]'[54] with the aim of linking anthropogenic climate change to the geopolitical orders invested in automation.[55] On a smaller scale, there are also many projects related to smart cities and digital twin cities where questions of digital rights converge with questions of which bodies of different matter are to inhabit these spaces. These programs of designed spaces beyond the Anthropocene more than anything require mapping how conflicts occur between the bodies that make up such spaces.

The materiality, and sensibility, of the production of data consists both in its input and in the output. This is also reflected in the media needed to make data-mining possible and legible. Taking on a new materialist, and more-than-human perspective of technology involves putting such aspects at the core. This means that data, and AI based on data, cannot grow without the use of the resources needed for it.[56] As Cubitt puts it: '[t]o create new materials means using up a finite stock of energy sources. The obsessive accumulation of everything that characterizes our era has limits.'[57] Furthermore, the infrastructures required to make possible automation, in particular to the benefit of more-than-human goals, imply resource-exploitation, that may imply pitting 'nature' against 'other nature'. For example, the mining of lithium occurs on indigenous lands, and has been met with protest. In a similar manner, a cool climate is beneficial to server parks. With increases in global temperature, such

---

[52] Bratton *The Terraforming* ibid. 8.
[53] Ibid.
[54] Ibid. 9.
[55] Ibid.
[56] See Sean Cubitt, *Finite Media: Environmental Implications of Digital Media* (Duke University Press 2016) 7.
[57] Ibid.

a cool climate may be increasingly difficult to acquire, without appropriating lands inhabited by Sami or other Innuit peoples.

CONFLICTUAL MORE-THAN-HUMAN RIGHTS

Just like law in general, rights have been criticized as being too conceptual and abstracted from the actual expression of power that orders bodies.[58] Needless to say, considering the focus of this volume, the framing of rights and the actualization of them are however still seen as important tools to make bodies matter.[59] With the understanding of rights above as a backdrop, we can contend that rights, just like law, in a new materialist sense, needs to actualize powers in a more-than-human register by collapsing rights with bodies, and their power to come into being. In order to move towards such more-than-human ways of acquiring and expressing power, we first need to have knowledge[60] of how bodies affect each other in ways that are alien to many humanist ways of perceiving the world.

For example, this involves sensing and sense-making one's surroundings through modes of seeing that are not just about human eyesight, as in the case of autonomous vehicles discussed above. It further includes senses such as hearing and moving in manners imperceptible to most humans as well as making sense of data according to programmed logics that would be impossible for a human to debunk afterwards. The many ways that bodies affectively engage with each other are always excessive to the concepts attempting to capture their actions. Relationalities affecting bodies' powers to affect, occur in a myriad of chthulucenic[61] ways. It would simply be impossible, even for the most world-governing God-viewing, human-controlled law, to map out all these engagements and affects (at least for now). However, this does not mean that it is not exactly such maps that could be of interest to those who seek to terraform and redistribute bodies on the continuum in a more-than-human manner. In doing this, the possibility of humanist endeavors in forming law and rights does not need to dissolve entirely. However, there is also a need to

---

[58] See Daniela Gandorfer, 'Introduction to Research Handbook on Law and Literature. What is your power?' in Peter Goodrich (et al.) (eds), *Research Handbook on Law and Literature* (Edward Elgar Publishing, 2022) 11–12. Patricia Williams, 'Alchemical Notes: Reconstructing Ideals from Deconstructed Rights' (1987) 22.2 Harvard Civil Rights-Civil Liberties Law Review 80–92.

[59] Also e.g. Costas Douzinas (n 25).

[60] Also see e.g. Gatens and Lloyd on the meaning of knowledge to Spinozan ethics: Moira Gatens and Genevive Lloyd, *Collective Imaginings: Spinoza, Past and Present* (Routledge 1999).

[61] Haraway (n 7).

be aware that there will be a lot of knowledge that escapes these types of maps and efforts to govern (the rights of) bodies. There will always be an excess of bodies, caused by bodies that fluctuate and are excessive just because of how bodies are always in encounter with other bodies.[62]

In connecting to the examples above, we can further see that many of them show how non-human bodies can be wired up to gain new types of the powers that they had previously. A forest that can create financial value and own itself naturally shifts its capacity to act in a world entangled with private ownership, which it tends to be an object to. Furthermore, chickens on a blockchain are moved into another material register, where the processes leading to their death and consumption are still taken for granted, but where their life until then is safeguarded. In the same manner, a process to terraform urban as well as rural spaces can equip non-human bodies with new forces to remain in being. These rights are effectuated just as bodies are equipped not only with conceptual rights but with the power to fulfil their capacities: ways to affect and be affected.[63] This however does not mean that all the examples discussed here would contribute to more-than-human world-making, in the sense of a radical relationality/zoe-egalitarianism[64] as are outspoken goals for critical posthumanism. Even if an increasingly large number of bodies can be embedded with digital layers to enforce their rights (both conceptually and effectively by, e.g., self-ownership), it does not mean that such processes all contribute to the ethical aims of posthumanism, as they can (and will) be in conflict with the rights of other bodies (as will be further discussed below).

A particular aspect of both environmental law and digitalized governance (including the use of data to produce certain norms) is that they are obvious biopolitical modes of ordering.[65] This is so since both eco-oriented and datafied ways of approaching nature emphasize a scientific way of recognizing 'needs' and how to optimize behaviours to sustain different systems. For this reason, it can be tempting to see the positive aspects of biopolitcs, or affirmative biopolitics[66] as a means to terraform Earth by managing its 'resources' more optimally for human habitation.[67] Better data and the possibilities to automate the

---

[62] Andreas Philippopoulos-Mihalopoulos, *Spatial Justice: Body, Lawscape, Atmosphere* (Routledge 2015) 5.
[63] See also Gandorfer (n 58) 3.
[64] Braidotti (n 2) 92–97.
[65] See e.g Vito De Lucia, 'Critical Environmental Law and the Double Register of the Anthropocene: A Biopolitical Reading' in Louis Kotzé (ed), *Environmental Law and Governance for the Anthropocene* (Hart 2017) 97–116.; also see Jannice Käll, *Posthuman Property and Law: Commodification and Control through Information, Smart Spaces and Artificial Intelligence* (Routledge 2022).
[66] Braidotti (n 2).
[67] Bratton, (n 51).

management of nature, or 'our' joint 'natural resources', obviously are tools that could be vital in combating ecosystem collapse. Bratton's vision involves '[a]n urbanism that is pro-planning, pro-artificial, anti-collapse, pro-universalist, anti-anti-totality, pro-materialist, anti-anti-leviathan, anti-mythology, and pro-egalitarian distribution.'[68]

Here we should also recall how Haraway early on pinpointed how information-driven societies lead us from the forms of biopolitics identified by Foucault, to the informatics of domination,[69] where we now have stepped into a form of 'molecular zoe power' (rendering all bodies equally governable). This also implicates an intricate form of governance of the very geology that data-driven terraforming is dependent upon. The extraction of resources needed for such processes are by no means innocent and can unfold in ways that continues the exploitation trajectories of lands pursued by settler-colonial states.[70] Povinelli also reminds us about the continued forms of power exercised by states and capital by pointing out that: '[w]hile human advocates for animal rights may well be slowly disturbing the consensus of what counts as a legally recognizable person and the new animism is extending Life into all entities and assemblages, Nonlife has remained fairly firmly sealed in its opposition to life within extractive capital and its state allies.'[71]

In pursuing affirmative biopolitcs, one therefore constantly needs to keep in mind that the stage of the Anthropocene we find ourselves in is also just the uneven posthuman condition described as Capitolocene, Anthrobscene, etc. As many have pointed out, biopolitics implies that there is no outside from which politics can happen: everything is already both biological and political. And to add through Povinelli: geontological.[72] However, this does not automatically produce a new form of superior God-view where 'the human' again can step in and sort out the metrics, and then just put in the data for resource optimization. Again, speaking with Yusoff, to activate one alternative (or many) against colonial geologies, there is a need to rethink the empirics of our current social geologies as well as epistemically not reproducing the same.[73] This implies not only that some people are more guilty than others when the environment for human life is being destroyed, but also that some bodies actually have gained from, and will continue to gain from, the exploitation of other bodies, including the ecologies needed in the long term for most human life itself.

---

[68] Ibid. 9.
[69] Donna Haraway, *Simians, Cyborgs, and Women: The Reinvention of Nature* (Free Association Books 1991) 161–162, also noted by Braidotti (n 2) 97.
[70] Yusoff (n 5) 81.
[71] Povinelli (n 9) 34.
[72] Ibid.
[73] Yusoff (n 5) 105.

Turning back to the question of rights: it would be difficult to say that we do not *know* what more-than-human bodies *need* to remain in being. Hence, we know that other bodies both have rights in some sense (possibly even in the Deleuzian-Spinozian sense) and that their rights could be reinforced both by human rights concepts as well as technologies facilitating the preservation of their life forms. We consequently do not lack the ethical insight needed to create a better world through affirming more-than-human rights. The larger question is therefore exactly how to motivate a reconsideration of what counts as 'joint' interests between 'human' and 'non-human' bodies and how that should be decided and regulated.

Moving towards a stage where a different type of ethics informs decision-making, compared to the current state of affairs, is in itself an ethico-political question. Certain disciplines, like art, have the capacity to point at alternative imaginaries, as for example in advocating transitional justice for soil or shedding light on air/atmosphere, as discussed above. Yusoff also suggests a form of geo-poethics to drive forward a black-feminist praxis of knowing, doing and existing as a form of ethical mandate.[74] In a similar but also possibly more forceful manner, also law can work with concepts of more-than-human rights to data, as means to show that the move towards datafied environmental management, needs to take into consideration the many systems involved if human life will (or should) be sustainable.

There will not however come a point where all systems on Earth at the same time will be able to hold and effectuate equal rights. Granting rights to soil for example, will always be in conflict with something else, like food production. Furthermore, the move away from fossil fuels is inherently conflictual as it might involve needs for extraction of more resources to produce, for example, electric vehicles and management systems. Even if this might be a wise choice in the long run, it is not certain that the short-term biopolitics are optimized. This implies that also the time-perspective is vital when visualizing more-than-human rights to data. And in framing such a time-perspective, we are again confronted with the inherently conflictual and irresolvable question of which bodies' pasts, presents, and futures are accounted and optimized for. More-than-human rights to data can therefore arguably only be identified, and secured, when they are focused on the materialist foundations and the backlashes implied with data. This involves understanding the many layers of data and the resources needed to materialize it. A more-than-human understanding of recreating life under, and against, the conditions of the Anthropocene, has the capacity to direct our thinking to the questions of what data can be used, and how, to transform planets like the Earth and beyond. However, in doing

---

[74] Ibid. 104.

so, it is important to also stay within the conflicts invoked by digital technologies in general, and the bundle of more-than-human media involved in such transformation, specifically.

10. Decentring the human or rescaling the state? Grassroots movements for the 'rights' of nature in the United States

Erin Fitz-Henry

INTRODUCTION: DECENTRING THE HUMAN?

In recent years, there has been a proliferation of work across the social sciences and humanities that aims to displace both the centrality and the exceptionalism of the human in contemporary social theory by recognizing its constitutive entanglements with multi-species assemblages of all sorts. From William Connolly and Jane Bennett in philosophy, Eva Giraud in cultural theory, Erika Cudworth and Stephen Hobden in posthuman international relations, and Anna Tsing and Nils Bubandt in anthropology (to name just a few), a rapidly expanding body of research has sought to provincialize not just the European,[1] but the human.[2] In these accounts, human beings are shaped, sustained, and even co-constituted by a range of diverse socio-natural 'agencies' and actors, from lightning and earthquakes to incinerators and mosquitoes. Socio-cultural anthropologists have contributed to the general direction of this theoretical impulse by demonstrating ethnographically that minoritized communities both inside and outside the West have long recognized the 'liveliness' of the world and our responsibilities to it, refusing to draw the boundaries between 'nature' and 'culture' in the ways characteristic of significant parts of Western science.

---

[1] Dipesh Chakrabarty, *Provincializing Europe: Postcolonial Thought and Historical Difference* (Princeton UP 2008).
[2] Jane Bennett, *Vital Matter: A Political Ecology of Things* (Duke UP 2010); E Cudworth and S Hobden, *The Emancipatory Project of Post-humanism* (Routledge 2018); Eva Giraud, *What Comes After Entanglement? Activism, Anthropocentrism, and an Ethics of Exclusion* (Duke UP 2018); Anna Tsing and Nils Bubandt, *Arts of Living on Damaged Planet* (University of Minnesota Press 2017).

Instead, in these accounts, we find mountains that get angry, forests that speak, glaciers that listen, and jaguars who are persons.[3]

Much of this work, loosely associated with the so-called 'ontological turn' in anthropology, has forged important terrain by insisting on the conceptual narrowness of what John Law has called, the 'one-world world'[4] and in showing the ways that 'radical alterity' can fundamentally unsettle Western ontological assumptions about the nature of personhood, the boundaries of the human, and the diverse sorts of 'beings' and 'entities' that exist in the world. However, despite this growing recognition that humans live in a pluriverse,[5] efforts to demonstrate – in equally ethnographically grounded ways – how the recognition of these other-than-human 'agencies' might challenge or reconfigure Western political and legal institutions have not been as readily embraced by anthropologists (though with some important exceptions). Instead, as has historically often been the case, social movements have taken the lead in experimenting with the legislative, institutional, and social transformations that might better respond to the 'vital materialism'[6] of the pluriverse.

One of the most prominent of these movements is the global movement for the 'rights of nature.' Despite ongoing debate among scholars of these rights about whether to conceive of the movement as a single transnational movement with local variations or as much more distinct local movements united only by a loose commitment to extending legal recognition or standing to ecosystems,[7] groups fighting for the 'rights of nature' have increased exponentially since the mid-2000s. These movements in many parts of the world, including Ecuador, the US, Bolivia, Chile, Australia, and India, have explicitly sought to challenge what they call 'legal anthropocentrism' – effectively, in their view, de-centring the human by making legally cognizable 'natural' entities like

---

[3] Marisol De la Cadena, 'Indigenous Cosmopolitics in the Andes: Conceptual Reflections Beyond 'Politics' (2010) 25:2 Cultural Anthropology 334–370; Eduardo Kohn, *How Forests Think: Toward an Anthropology Beyond the Human* (University of California Press 2010); Elizabeth Povinelli, *Geontologies: A Requiem to Late Liberalism* (Duke UP 2016); Julia Cruikshank, *Do Glaciers Listen? Local Knowledge, Colonial Encounters, and Social Imagination* (University of British Columbia Press 2015); Eduardo Viveiros de Castro, 'Cosmological Deixis and Amerindian Perspectivism' (1998) 4:3 Journal of the Royal Anthropological Institute 469–488.

[4] John Law, 'What's Wrong with a One-World World?' Presented to the Centre for the Humanities, Wesleyan University, September 19, 2015.

[5] Arturo Escobar. 'Thinking-Feeling with the Earth: Territorial Struggles and the Ontological Dimensions of the Epistemologies of the South' (2016) 11:1 Revista de Antropologia Iberoamericana 11–32; Arturo Escobar, Ariel Salleh, Alberto Acosta, and Ashish Kothari, *The Pluriverse: A Post-development Dictionary* (Columbia UP 2019).

[6] Jane Bennett, *Vital Matter: A Political Ecology of Things* (Duke UP 2010).

[7] Mihnea Tanasescu, *Understanding the Rights of Nature: A Critical Introduction* (transcript Verlag 2022).

rivers and lakes that have previously been treated as business externalities, the providers of 'ecosystem services,' or mere property that can be destroyed or fatally damaged at the behest of property owners (within limits usually set by corporations themselves). Drawing on pioneering work by American lawyer Christopher Stone and a range of Indigenous Laws in different national contexts (including Quechua understandings of Pachamama in Latin America and Whanganui conceptions of river-human relations in Aotearoa/New Zealand), activists for the rights of nature have repeatedly argued for the importance of moving beyond so-called legal anthropocentrism by extending the languages of 'rights' and/or 'personhood' to a range of ecosystems in ways that might better accord with the putatively more holistic or at least less narrowly instrumentalist visions and values of Indigenous communities.

In this chapter, drawing in part on conversations with rights of nature activists, organizers, and lawyers in the United States and in part on close readings of recent rights of nature court cases, I argue that while there have been recent efforts to reorient the ontological turn to take better account of concrete political and legal struggles of this sort,[8] the continued focus in anthropology, cultural studies, and post-human international relations on de-centring the human by exploring its entanglements with a range of other-than-humans arguably misses an even more theoretically provocative de-centring of an entirely different sort – what I am calling here the 'de-centring of the state.' Despite animated debates about whether the rights of nature are sufficiently de-colonizing,[9] the extent to which they are aligned with, emergent from, or appropriative of Indigenous values and worldviews,[10] their ability to be co-opted by neo-extractivist states and corporations,[11] and the degree to which they remain guided by the assumptions of Western liberal individualism, there has been considerably less attention paid to the fact that an essential part of practical (not just theoretical) efforts to 'de-centre the human' has been growing involvement in a qualitatively different kind of de-centring. Across all the national contexts in which these rights are being either considered or

---

[8] Mario Blaser, 'On the Properly Political Disposition for the Anthropocene' (2019) 19:1 Anthropological Theory 74–94; Sian Lazar, 'Anthropology and the Politics of Alterity: A Latin American Dialectic and its Relevance for Ontological Anthropologies' (2022) 22.2 Anthropological Theory 131–153.

[9] Ariel Rawson and Becky Mansfield, 'Producing Juridical Knowledge: "Rights of nature" or the Naturalization of Rights?' (2018) 1 Environment and Planning E: Nature and Space 1–2.

[10] Mihnea Tanasescu, 'Nature Advocacy and the Indigenous Symbol' (2015) 24.1 Environmental Values 105–122.

[11] Carolina Valladares and Rutgerd Boelens, 'Extractivism and the Rights of Nature: Governmentality, "Convenient Communities" and Epistemic Pacts in Ecuador' (2017) 26:6 Environmental Politics 1015–1034.

implemented, struggles for the recognition of the 'rights' of specific ecosystems are struggles that are increasingly taking the shape of deep-seated contestations of the decision-making authority of states: national ministries that issue environmental permits in the case of Ecuador and state environmental regulatory agencies in the case of the United States. By 'de-centring' it should be noted that I do not mean that these are efforts to advance an alternative non-state centred politics, but simply that they are efforts to rescale the state by insisting on the centrality of forms of municipal decision-making that are not yet widely accepted. My central claim in this chapter is that closer ethnographic attention to the precise (and sometimes quite mundane) mechanics of these on-the-ground efforts to legally acknowledge the rights-bearing status of non-humans takes us quite far from the sorts of questions that currently animate debates within the so-called 'ontological turn.' Instead, they return us to long-standing political-economic questions of an entirely different order, as cities and provinces attempt to upend state environmental regulatory processes and use the court system to challenge the verticality of centralized environmental permitting. What this means, and how precisely it is playing out in the US state of Ohio, is the subject of this chapter.

The ethnographic, textual, and legal research for this chapter was completed as part of a broader multi-sited project on movements for the rights of nature in Ecuador, the United States, and Australia that aims to understand the different meanings and operationalizations of these rights in national contexts with diverse histories of state-civil society engagement. My focus has been primarily on their use in struggles against extractive development projects – gold and silver mining in the Andes and natural gas extraction in the United States. This chapter draws primarily on conversations with rights of nature activists in the mid-western state of Ohio in the United States. It is supplemented with close readings of recent court cases that show how these efforts to demand a less anthropocentric legal system are, in practice, taking the shape of direct challenges to the state monopolization of environmental regulatory authority, which activists see as fundamentally compromised because of ever-closer alliances between the state and a range of corporate lobbying organizations.

I develop this argument in two parts. First, I explore two different rights of nature struggles in Ohio, demonstrating how residents in these municipalities became increasingly frustrated by the state because it was constructed as fundamentally compromised by its alliances with private capital. As I show, these alliances with capital took two primary forms – first, direct industry involvement with the Ohio Department of Natural Resources in the writing of regulatory statutes that locals perceived as ineffective and unresponsive to their input; and second, growing interference in the legislative processes at the state level by a powerful free market lobbyist group associated with some of the largest transnational companies operating in the world today. In the second section, I offer a series of reflections on the political and philosophical implications of these cases for legal scholarship on the rights of nature and, somewhat more broadly, post-humanist theorizing in and beyond anthropology and the environmental humanities. I conclude with a plea for greater ethnographic attention to local power struggles to advance rights for nature and the broader political-economic contexts in which those struggles unfold.

GETTING OUT OF THE 'REGULATORY CHUTE' (OHIO, UNITED STATES)

In late February 2019, to much global fanfare, voters in Toledo, Ohio approved an amendment to their municipal charter entitled the 'Lake Erie Bill of Rights' (or LEBOR). 'We, the people of the City of Toledo,' the bill reads, 'declare and enact this Lake Erie Bill of Rights, which establishes *irrevocable rights for the Lake Erie Ecosystem to exist, flourish and naturally evolve*, a right to a healthy environment for the residents of Toledo, and which elevates the rights of the community and its natural environment over power claimed by certain corporations' (LEBOR 2019). It continues: 'The Lake Erie Ecosystem may enforce its rights and this law's prohibitions [...] Such court action shall be brought in the name of the Lake Erie Ecosystem as the real party in interest. Damages shall be measured by the cost of restoring the Lake Erie Ecosystem and its constituent parts.' This is the first case in the United States of a specific ecosystem (rather than more vaguely defined 'natural communities') being granted such legal standing – a fact that was widely publicized, including by the Daily Show. Supporters had hoped that the decision would allow them to more comprehensively address the intensifying problem of toxic agribusiness-driven algae blooms and run-off from CAFOS (concentrated animal feeding operations) – a problem that first came to a head in 2014 when city residents were shocked to find their water shut off for three days when it became unsafe to drink due to excessive nitrogen loads largely due to agricultural run-off. This was an outrage to the local community, who found themselves, just months after the Flint Water crisis in Michigan, unable to use their tap water as the Ohio National Guard was called in.[12] While only a small percentage of the electorate participated in the vote (a fact that is not particularly surprising given that it was held in late February – one of the coldest months of the year), it was widely hailed as a victory by environmental activists throughout the world. Reporters swarmed to the area, invitations were extended to local activists by the United Nations Harmony with Nature

---

[12] Laura Pulido, 'Flint, Environmental Racism, and Racial Capitalism' (2016) 27:3 Capitalism, Nature, Socialism 1–16.

program, and Toledo became, for a time, the latest municipality to feature in a David-and-Goliath struggle against the so-called 'corporate rights' of agribusiness companies. Despite significant funding from British Petroleum aimed at defeating the bill, the people had won, or so it seemed.[13]

This was the first time that many US-based observers had heard of the 'rights' for nature, but it is an idea that has been embraced by a growing transnational movement of lawyers and activists since at least 2006. While the notion that ecosystems might have 'rights' has been around in the Western tradition since at least the publication of Christopher Stone's landmark *Should Trees Have Standing?*, and its philosophical merits have been vigorously debated for almost as long,[14] it has only been the last 15 years or so that have witnessed a flourishing of experiments with municipal and national law-making around these rights in countries all over the world. In the simplest terms, these are movements that believe that a legal system that treats nature as property and that protects property ownership above all else is one in which nature can be, and obviously is being, legally destroyed at an alarming rate. To challenge this destruction, they believe there needs to be a fundamental change in this status from *property to person* (or to natural entity), thereby granting nature or specific ecosystems 'rights' much as enslaved people and women were, in other historical moments, granted civil and political rights after centuries of being treated as property.[15] Emboldened by the passage of Ecuador's 2008 constitution – the first constitution anywhere in the world to recognize the rights of nature, and one that has been lauded as the most biocentric in the world – the movement has spread rapidly throughout Latin America and beyond. There are now groups working in Bolivia, Uruguay, Colombia, India, Nepal, the United States, Australia, and many more, all converging ideologically on the need to move away from human exceptionalism or anthropocentrism by acknowledging something like the legal personhood of 'nature,' 'natural communities,' or 'ecosystems.' The aim of this 'earth jurisprudence' is to level the playing field between humans and other-than-humans by using the tools of liberal rights discourses to challenge the naturalized, often taken-for-granted privileges of corporations and nation-states and to enshrine understandings of the natural world that do not posit, either morally or legally, an untenable separation between humans and other-than-humans.

---

[13] Tish O'Dell and Simon Davis-Cohen, *Death by Democracy* (CELDF 2021).

[14] Robyn Eckersley, 'Liberal Democracy and the Rights of Nature: the Struggle for Inclusion' (1995) 4:4 Environmental Politics 169–198; Roderick Nash, *The Rights of Nature: A History of Environmental Ethics* (University of Wisconsin Press 1989).

[15] Peter Burdon and Michelle Maloney, *Wild Law in Practice* (Routledge 2014); Cormac Cullinan, *Wild Law: A Manifesto for Earth Justice* (Chelsea Green Publishing 2010).

In the United States, the movement has largely been driven by environmental lawyers and communities affected by large-scale energy, waste, and agribusiness infrastructure who are bitterly estranged from the regulatory system, which they feel has largely failed to improve air and water quality over the past 50 years. (As one activist explained to me exasperatedly, 'The first goal of the Clean Water Act of 1972 was clean waterways by 1985!'). Toward this end, the Community Environmental Legal Defense Fund (CELDF) – a Pennsylvania-based not-for-profit environmental law firm – has worked with hundreds of municipalities across the country to pass local ordinances enshrining the so-called 'rights' of ecosystems within municipal limits, an approach that has both inspired communities who find themselves neglected or sidelined by state regulatory authorities and one that has been repeatedly challenged by those who find such rights incoherent, unenforceable, anti-modern, anti-development, and/or unconstitutional. In the wake of the water crisis in Toledo, and because of growing exasperation with a regulatory system that did not appear to provide any real solution to either the immediate problem of toxic algal blooms or the longer-term problem of ongoing industrial and agricultural run-off, local organizers found their way to CELDF.

Not unpredictably, however, the very day after the passage of the Lake Erie Bill of Rights in February 2019, a large farming corporation in the region immediately filed suit, arguing that the Bill of Rights was unconstitutional; that it was a violation of their corporate constitutional rights; and that it far over-stepped the jurisdiction of the city because Lake Erie extends well beyond the small municipality of Toledo. In a case brought by the Drewes Farm Partnership, they argued that: 'LEBOR purports to divest Corporations ... of their constitutional right to petition the government for redress of grievances in that it strips corporations of (1) their status as "persons" under the law; (2) their power to assert that *state or federal laws preempt LEBOR*; and (3) their power to assert that the City of Toledo lacks the authority to adopt LEBOR.' Exactly one year later, Judge Zouhary overturned the Lake Erie Bill of Rights, arguing that it was vague, unenforceable, and that nowhere in the United States are 'rights' for nature recognized. While LEBOR supporters sought to appeal the case, their appeal was dismissed in 2020, and Drewes Farm Partnership went on to seek $300,000 in attorney fees from the city of Toledo. This was not the first such disappointment for CELDF-led ordinances for the 'rights of nature' in the state of Ohio.

I met Tish O'Dell, one of the main Ohio organizers affiliated with CELDF, at a Community Rights Workshop at Bowling Green University on a cold Saturday morning in March 2018. In a small lecture hall, university students, a few aging peace activists, three anti-gas organizers, and a jet-lagged anthropologist from Australia listened to O'Dell recount the story of the town where she lives and the process through which she became increasingly politicized over the issue of natural gas wells – a major issue in the state of Ohio, which has been home to a shale gas boom for the better part of a decade. Broadview Heights is a suburb of Cleveland, Ohio, home to approximately 20,000 people, mostly white and relatively middle-class. After discovering a few years ago that energy companies, including the Fairlawn-based Bass Energy, had drilled 90 oil and gas wells within the 13-square mile limits of the city, often within 75 feet of homes, schools, and playgrounds, a group of mothers began to do research about the wells. As part of their research, they learned of the numerous volatile organic compounds that were likely seeping into their soils and waterways. They hired scientists with infrared cameras to come and help them identify further wells. Unusual smells became increasingly the norm, along with home evacuations in residential neighborhoods.

In deepening alarm and desperation, the women turned to their local officials. However, they soon encountered a problem. In 2004 the Republican-controlled Ohio state legislature had passed House Bill 278, which turned over all decision-making about natural gas regulation to the state. This is a bill that, without exception, was referenced by nearly every rights of nature organizer that I met in Ohio – from Broadview Heights to Youngstown. The bill states: 'This act repeals all provisions of law that granted or alluded to the authority of local governments to adopt concurrent requirements with the state concerning oil and gas exploration and operation as well as all provisions that limited that authority.' Given their lack of authority to create or enforce 'concurrent requirements with the state,' city officials had their hands tied, urging the women to take their concerns to the only place that could properly respond to them – state legislators. Dutifully, the mothers met with their state legislators, but most of them, as O'Dell later explained to me, either ignored them, took symbolic tours of the neighborhood to take pictures for their websites, or suggested that they raise their concerns more directly with the Ohio Department of Natural Resources (ODNR), which is responsible for issuing the natural gas permits across the state. Again, following the recommendations of their elected representatives, the women from Broadview Heights started going down what they now refer to as the 'regulatory chute,' attending ODNR hearings where they were allocated 5 minutes to raise their concerns and then predictably dismissed by the so-called experts. 'The regulatory system is like being herded down a cattle chute,' O'Dell explained. 'You start out wanting to say no, we don't want this, and you end up talking parts per million of chemicals released!' 'They only listen to the voices of so-called experts,' one of her colleagues continued, 'When you talk about what you've experienced in your community, in your own body, you're told... "those are just feelings".' Similar sentiments about the regulatory system were widely expressed by organizers affiliated with CELDF. Another, who had been centrally involved with the LEBOR, similarly noted that the regulatory system is little more than a form of 'censored gate-keeping,' overseen by so-called experts, often from the industries or projects in question, largely intended to keep ordinary people content with just 'having their concerns acknowledged,' and always with a staged, rushed feeling.

Through months of such engagement with the regulatory process, the mothers and their allies in Broadview Heights slowly came to the realization that the language of 'stakeholders' used by regulatory agencies is not a language that means, or includes in any meaningful way, communities affected by natural gas extraction. Instead, 'stakeholders' refers first and foremost and sometimes exclusively to the companies themselves and to the oil, gas, and drillers associations who often write their own environmental permits. This is a common enough occurrence in the regulatory field more broadly. As Portuguese socio-legal scholar Boaventura de Sousa Santos has pointed out regarding the language of 'stakeholders' that continues to be favoured by contemporary liberal theorists of so-called 'global governance,' '[The global] governance approach tends to bracket deep power asymmetries among actors (for instance, those between capital and labor in global code of conduct systems) and to view the public sphere as a ... depoliticized arena of collaboration among generic "stakeholders".'[16] Frustrated with this framing of being just one 'stakeholder' among many others, the women eventually turned away from the regulatory system or, as they called it as they became more and more politicized, the 'hamster wheel' of engagement with the environmental regulatory system.

Not surprisingly, many of the same conclusions are being arrived at by other US-based environmental justice activists. As David Pellow puts it in a recent piece in which he argues against continued engagement with the state: 'Social change movements may be better off thinking and acting beyond the state and capital as targets of reform and/or as reliable partners.'[17]

Laura Pulido goes on to spell out the point in somewhat greater detail:

> Activists have ... prioritized engaging with the state ... They have believed that by working closely with regulators, through regulatory attention [and] judicial action, the conditions in their communities would improve ... *What is needed on the part of the EJ movement is a fundamental rethinking of its attitude toward the state.* Instead of seeing the state as a helpmate or partner, it needs to see the state as an adversary and directly challenge it ... *It's not about being respectable, acknowledged, and*

---

[16] Boaventura de Sousa Santos (ed.), *Law and Globalization from Below* (CUP 2009).
[17] David Pellow, 'Toward a Critical Environmental Justice Studies' (2016) DuBois Review 229.

included. It's about raising hell for both polluters and the agencies that protect them.[18]

In order to 'raise hell for the polluters' in the case of natural gas extraction, the Broadview Heights activists eventually joined forces with CELDF to work on a 'Community Bill of Rights' for Broadview Heights that included things like the 'rights of natural communities,' 'the right to a sustainable energy future,' and the revocation of corporate rights and privileges when those rights and privileges 'interfere with the rights and prohibitions enumerated by this Charter.' In 2012, 67% of the residents of Broadview Heights voted to approve the bill. However, again, in June 2014, two drilling companies, Bass Energy and Ohio Valley Energy, sued the city of Broadview Heights, arguing that the bill was illegal, unenforceable, pre-empted by the state, and that it violated their corporate constitutional rights. The companies were ultimately successful in this challenge (as they have been in all the other cases in which companies have brought charges against communities) and the Bill of Rights was overturned.[19]

Despite this ostensible 'failure,' one of the primary results of this struggle for the 'rights of natural communities' in Broadview Heights has been an evolving, and arguably intensifying, recognition among both activists and community members that state governments are increasingly allied with corporations – and sometimes in very direct ways – over and against municipalities. As CELDF notes: 'The state has made resource colonies of its municipalities and doled out franchises for the corporate occupation of our hometowns.' Explicitly repositioning municipalities not as sub-sections of states, but as internal resource colonies akin to those that have long structured the colonial and now neo-colonial world order, these struggles are part of an intensifying wave of city-based activism across the United States that increasingly understands state legislatures as actively undermining democratic decision-making at the scale of the municipal (and thereby enforcing a kind of 'internal colonialism' long familiar to other parts of the country).

There is a long history of such efforts in the US to challenge state and federal control over local resources – a history that predates the rise of the rights of nature movement in the early 2000s and the latest intensification of city-based activism in the 2010s. As Ann Eisenberg notes, writing of the conservative

---

[18] Laura Pulido, Ellen Kohl, and Nicole-Marie Cotton, 'State Regulation and Environmental Justice: The Need for Strategy Reassessment' (2016) 27:2 Capitalism, Nature, Socialism 1–31.

[19] For a similar case in Pennsylvania, see Erin Fitz-Henry, 'Challenging Corporate Personhood: Energy Companies and the Rights of Non-Humans' (2018) 41:1 Political and Legal Anthropology Review 85–102.

Land Transfer movement, 'In the 1990s, several dozen counties in Nevada, California, Idaho, New Mexico, and Oregon passed ordinances purporting to require certain forms of federal consultation with localities in decision-making over public lands [...] [Not unlike current rights of nature cases], courts have held these and comparable ordinances seeking to regulate public lands unconstitutional based on federal pre-emption.'[20] Despite this earlier history, municipal efforts have increased dramatically over the past decade across the country, as cities have begun passing minimum wage legislation, approving regulations about the use of plastic bags, identifying themselves as 'sanctuary cities,' providing protections for LBGTQIA+ people, enacting paid sick leave for employees, passing local anti-smoking legislation, and banning the carrying of automatic weapons in public parks. And this intensity of urban regulation has increasingly fuelled a backlash from state governors over what they see as unchecked 'over-regulation' by cities – regulations which, these governors fear, will drive away business because it will create a regulatory 'patchwork' or 'checkerboard' that will prove too costly and legally byzantine for companies to navigate (the reality that companies navigate such jurisdictional differences and uneven regulatory playing fields all the time to their advantage appears to be lost on these governors).

The result of these contestations has been a raft of state pre-emption bills, often written with the help of a group of business lobbyists called ALEC, or the American Legislative Exchange Council. ALEC brings together state legislators and private sector representatives from large transnationals, including BP, ATT, Exxon, and many others, who together draft model bills that aim, in their words, to improve market competition, to ensure 'regulatory consistency,' and to limit democratic decision-making at the local level. They describe themselves as 'America's largest non-partisan organization of state legislators dedicated to the principles of limited government, free markets, and federalism.' ALEC has written bills across the country that seek to outlaw local law-making in relation to pesticides (for example, the Pesticide Preemption Act), the raising of the minimum wage (for example, the Starting Minimum Wage Repeal Act), and the establishment of higher regulatory standards around air and water quality than are set by the state. In Ohio alone, legislators working with ALEC have sought to outlaw all municipal efforts to mandate a living wage, to limit the use of pesticides, to ban genetically modified food, and to prevent the open carrying of guns in public parks. Since at least the early 2000s, the Ohio State Legislature has increasingly adopted these bills,

---

[20] Ann Eisenberg, 'Do Sagebrush Rebels Have a Colorable Claim? The Space between Parochialism and Exclusion in Federal Lands Management,' (2017) 38 Pub. Land & Resources L. Rev. 57.

stripping communities of their rights to engage in democratic decision-making about the industrial harms that most directly affect them.

While many groups working on the 'rights' of nature were originally drawn to their advocacy because of the need to protect specific ecosystems from industrial harms, they are increasingly finding that the vastly more challenging problem is the progressive curtailment – via state pre-emption – of local decision-making by state governments that are more and more openly allied with private sector interests. As Don Nonini and Ida Susser explain of the efforts of sub-national entities to contest the scales at which regulatory decisions are made in many different contexts: 'If local social movements or local states could pass laws setting labor and environmental standards with jurisdictions that applied to the extractions by international corporations, then they would be effective; but when regulations at the global or nation-state scales pre-empt local laws, then these corporations have a free hand at fracking, polluting, and depriving workers of their livelihoods.'[21] While this assertion might be somewhat romantic (we certainly have examples of sub-national entities seeking to enact regressive legislation), pre-emption – in this case, of municipalities by states – remains a very serious and growing problem across the United States and has indeed resulted in large-scale pollution from fracking. For rights of nature organizers, the corporate-state alliances responsible for growing pre-emption are increasingly visible, as ALEC becomes more and more directly involved in the writing of model bills that allow transnationals to clamp down on the kind of so-called 'business uncertainty' created by concerned citizens. Indeed, when visiting with organizers in both Ohio and the Western state of Washington, I was struck by just how frequently and casually people mentioned the machinations of ALEC. The struggle for these community members was less about how to broaden the scales at which we think, theorize, and render legally visible human/other-than-human relations – that is, to return to the title of this chapter, less about de-centering the human or recognizing human entanglements with the more-than-human in the ways that are of such interest to post-human theorists, and more about how to convince broader publics that indeed US cities are increasingly little more than 'resource colonies' with less and less democratic decision-making ability. This is one aspect – and a relatively neglected one – of the sort of corporate/state fusion that, as Bruce Kapferer has recently noted, is particularly characteristic of our time. As Kapferer explains, companies are not only no longer constrained by nation-state regulations – a point that has been increasingly obvious since the globalization frenzy of the 1990s began. More importantly, they are also

---

[21] Don Nonini and Ida Susser, *The Tumultuous Politics of Scale: Unsettled States, Migrants, Movements in Flux* (Routledge 2020).

increasingly involved in the drafting and approving of all legislation that pertains to their own interests – whether bilateral free trade agreements or model bills for state pre-emption on issues around which local communities have sought to organize.[22]

Markie Miller, one of the leading organizers behind the Lake Erie Bill of Rights, was a young, energetic activist at the time I first met her via Zoom – a recently graduated student in Environmental Science who had quickly realized that the environmental regulatory system was perhaps the primary problem that the environmental movement faced. Having grown up around Lake Erie hearing stories from her parents about just how bad it had been before the environmental movement took off in the 1960s, she maintains a deep commitment to place and a deep relationship with the lake itself. In an interview via Zoom in March 2020, she, too, recounted the litany of events that had led her to seek to get a local bill on the ballot that would grant rights to Lake Erie. Whenever she or others expressed concern about the health of Lake Erie to the mayor and the 'corporate democrats' in power in the city, she explained, they were promptly referred to the Environmental Protection Authority (EPA). But then when they went to the EPA, they were dismissed as being 'too emotional' and 'not understanding the economics.' While she admitted that many people in Toledo had initially been confused and uncertain about the idea of 'rights' for Lake Erie (as some detractors pointed out to her, 'the Lake doesn't pay taxes or vote [...] why should it get a say?'), more and more had agreed that it was worth a try in the face of the serious algal blooms of 2014. As they began to attend hearings, they too began to understand that the state regulatory structure was a significant obstacle to their well-being. It is now increasingly common knowledge among these organizers that many of the regulatory standards established by the EPA and the Ohio Department of Natural Resources for industries are written by industry representatives themselves with minimal, if any, consultation with local communities.

Getting increasingly concerned about Lake Erie, citizens in Toledo sought to more fully operationalize 'Home Rule' – a provision in the Ohio state constitution (and in many other state constitutions in the US) that allows municipalities to pass local ordinances as they see fit, so long as they do not exceed the bounds of state and federal constitutions. This latter clause is a point of ongoing contention for these activists who are committed to implementing protections for ecosystems that go far beyond what is required of them by the state EPA (and which can thus be seen as 'exceeding the bounds of state constitutions'). As Miller explained to me, the local community in Toledo

---

[22] Bruce Kapferer, 'New Formations of Power, the Oligarchic-Corporate State, and Anthropological Ideological Discourse' (2005) 5:3 Anthropological Theory 285–299.

grew particularly frustrated with the EPA following the algal bloom because the EPA repeatedly presented graphs and diagrams that purported to show that the situation was simply not that bad, that it had been worse in the past, or that the contamination was no longer near enough to the municipal water supply intake pipes to warrant concern. It was then, and shortly after meeting a representative from CELDF, that Miller and the Toledoans for Safe Water realized that they needed to find a way to insist on forms of local government that have been enshrined in the Ohio state constitution since the 1800s, but that have slowly been eroded through the years. They needed a way to protect the ecosystems of Lake Erie even when algal blooms did not threaten the city's water supply. And they needed someone other than the EPA to regulate the agricultural industries responsible for the blooms. One of their first acts in this direction was the passage of the Lake Erie Bill of Rights in 2019.

IS THE PROBLEM ANTHROPOCENTRISM OR STATE-CENTRISM? AND IS THE SOLUTION 'RADICAL ALTERITY' OR MUNICIPALIZATION?

Among scholars of the rights of nature, anthropocentrism is by far the most widely cited cause of the current collapse, poisoning, and plunder of so much of the so-called natural world. The reason we are in the escalating biodiversity and climate crises that we are in, so we are told, is because of anthropocentrism (which of course is also rightly linked by these scholars to colonialism, racism, and gender discrimination). This is a point made repeatedly by scholars influenced by new materialism and post-humanism, including Rafi Youatt, Michelle Maloney, Nicole Rogers, and Danielle Celermajer et al., (to name just a few), as well as by earlier scholars including Deborah Bird Rose and Val Plumwood.[23] As Maloney and Rogers explain of Western law in the introduction to their recent *Wild Law Judgements Project*: 'Existing legal systems and existing laws are profoundly anthropocentric in their orientation ... [the aim now is to] disrupt and unsettle the established human and property-centred practices of the common law, by placing "all life, and all of life's support systems, at the centre [...] [and to contest] the place of humanity at the centre of existing notions of justice".'[24] This is a call with which many rights of nature advocates in Ohio and elsewhere would fully concur. And it is a call that finds expression in the foundational work of Thomas Berry, the

---

[23] Rafi Youatt, 'Personhood and the Rights of Nature: The New Subjects of Contemporary Earth Politics' (2017) 11:1 International Political Sociology 39–54; Michelle Maloney and Nicole Rogers, *Law as if Earth Really Mattered: The Wild Judgment Project* (Routledge 2017).
[24] Michelle Maloney and Nicole Rogers (n 23).

self-professed 'geologian' – and one of the intellectual fathers of the rights of nature movement – who noted in the late 1980s that: 'the deepest cause of the present devastation is found in a mode of consciousness that has established a radical discontinuity between the human and other modes of being and the bestowal of all rights on the humans.' And again, lamentably: We are the first 'radically anthropocentric society.'[25]

While not wanting to downplay in any way just how violently anthropocentrism has remade – and continues to remake – the world, nor to suggest that the work of advancing less anthropocentric ontologies can be disentangled from particular kinds of transformative institutional labour, what the work in the state of Ohio suggests is that, in actual practice, as communities seek to implement these rights, they are increasingly faced less with doubts from policy-makers about the validity of non-human personhood and more with persistent questions about the structure (and hierarchies) of environmental decision-making itself. What seems to be underway in Ohio and across the United States is a fierce scalar battle that has resonances with the broader 'new municipalist' movements that have taken hold in many communities throughout the world since the financial crisis of 2008 – movements that, in the face of brutal austerity measures (of the sort implemented in neighboring Flint, Michigan), are seeking, albeit in much more explicitly political registers, to challenge state jurisdiction by reclaiming older histories of local decision-making.[26] This is eminently political work. In their 2020 *The Tumultuous Politics of Scale*, Don Nonini and Ida Susser rightly point out that 'attempts to change the scales of regulation […] are an interrogation of power;' that 'determining scale means determining power;' and that 'political projects continuously contest and re-define the scale at which authority is vested.'[27] So it was in both Toledo and Broadview Heights.

I do not mean to suggest that Toledo and Broadview Heights can be compared to the sorts of highly organized and well-networked municipal experiments currently taking place in cities like Barcelona, Berlin, and Jackson, Mississippi.[28] However, I do want to insist that the focus on 'decentring the human' that is of such critical theoretical interest across the social sciences and humanities needs to continue to be put in rigorous conversation with these concrete material struggles in specific national contexts, including in the Global

---

[25] Thomas Berry, *The Dream of the Earth* (Sierra Club Books 1998).
[26] M. Thompson, 'What's so New About New Municipalism?' (2021) 45:2 Progress in Human Geography 317–342.
[27] Don Nonini and Ida Susser (n 21).
[28] Ross Beveridge and Philippe Koch, 'Contesting Austerity, De-Centring the State: Anti-Politics and the Political Horizon of the Urban' (2019) 39:3 Environment and Planning C: Politics and Space 451–468.

North and in non-Indigenous communities (which are under-represented in the current literature). These struggles, as I have suggested, are increasingly less about the 'agency' and 'vitalism' of the natural world or about the different ontologies that shape and define relationships between humans and other-than-humans (though both are important aspects of these struggles). Instead, what is most striking are the intensifying contestations over nested decision-making hierarchies that too often render municipalities unable to seriously challenge corporate-state conglomerations that are becoming increasingly well-organized. By tracking efforts to drive the rights of nature into law, what we may importantly come to learn most about are the specific corporate-state strategies currently being deployed at different scales to limit, neutralize, or otherwise constrain these rights. From the Ohio state legislature to the Ohio Department of Natural Resources, to the corporate establishment of apparently 'local' companies, to the corporate funding of campaigns against ballot initiatives for the rights of nature, there is much that we still do not know about how exactly these alliances are operating. And it is those alliances and the hegemonic power blocs they support and uphold that are preventing the institutionalization of more egalitarian, more ecologically just and less anthropocentric relationships with ecosystems. While many theorists of the ontological turn in anthropology and adjacent disciplines have recently spent considerable time describing the political potentials of 'radical alterity' – by which they mean the fundamentally transformative effects of different ontological assumptions about the kinds of beings that exist in the world – what I have tried to suggest is that in many ways the far more interesting and challenging questions raised by movements for the rights of nature are the *tactical and strategic* questions about the scales at which environmental decisions should be made.[29] As Nonini and Susser again remind us, these struggles over scale are eminently political and even class-based struggles – struggles that will likely become even more urgent as the energy crisis intensifies, extractivism deepens, and corporate-state alliances become ever more intimate.

CONCLUSION

In this chapter, drawing on fieldwork conducted with rights of nature activists in the US state of Ohio, I have suggested that movements that appear to be most concerned with displacing human exceptionalism are, in practice, becoming more and more involved in another set of perhaps even more challenging displacements. Put simply, these movements are concerned with displacing,

---

[29] Mario Blaser, *Storytelling Globalization from the Chaco and Beyond* (Duke UP 2010); Mario Blaser (n 8) 74–94; Arturo Escobar (n 5) 11–32; Sian Lazar (n 8).

and even frontally attacking, the centrality of the state in decision-making over natural resource governance and regulation at a time of heightened corporate co-optation of both the legislative and judicial wings of the state. These are struggles *for* urban municipalities and rural townships and *against* state governments and state departments of natural resources. Again, these are not necessarily the urban struggles of New York, Paris, Berlin, Amsterdam, and elsewhere that have gained such visibility in recent years,[30] nor can they properly be seen as part of the new municipalist movements that have emerged in the wake of the 2008 financial crisis. However, they are struggles by relatively small rural townships and municipalities that have sought to resist their transformation, via state regulatory processes, into internal 'resource colonies' over which they have no control. Focusing on the mid-western US state of Ohio, I have shown how a grassroots environmental movement that set out to challenge the environmental regulatory system through the elaboration of a new and radical set of environmental rights has become increasingly engaged in direct confrontations with the state over the scales at which environmental decision-making is most responsibly exercised.

Rights of nature struggles are, then, at least partially, struggles to re-scale decision-making – acts that are inherently political, and that, when closely observed from the ground, allow us to better understand not how anthropocentric the law is (though this is also the case), but more importantly for organizers and theorists of socio-environmental change, how stacked the corporate state is against all kinds of rights, but particularly rights to municipal decision-making. Such struggles are important because they remind us – and particularly scholars of the rights of nature – of the importance of not losing sight of the political at a time when the 'ontological turn,' as David Chandler, Julian Reid, and Sian Lazar have all recently reminded us, is still tending toward a-political or at least insufficiently political renderings of human/more than human entanglements.[31] In short: What these cases show us is the significance not of those 'entangled relationalities' that are of such primary interest to scholars in the environmental humanities, but of corporate-state 'entanglements' that increasingly seek to strangle local democratic practices, to roll back rights to 'concurrent jurisdiction,' and to ensure a smooth regulatory environment that is safe and certain for business, but full of risk for communities and ecosystems alike.

---

[30] David Harvey, *Rebel Cities: From the Right to the City to the Urban Revolution* (Verso Books 2012); Ida Susser and Stéphane Tonnelat, 'Forging the Urban Commons' (2013) 66 Focaal—Journal of Global and Historical Anthropology 105–132.

[31] David Chandler and Julian Reid, 'Becoming Indigenous? The Speculative Turn in Anthropology and the Recolonization of Indigeneity' (2020) 23:4 Postcolonial Studies 485–504; Sian Lazar (n 8).

11. Non-Human Rights, Amazonian ecocide and Davi Kopenawa's counter-ethnography of merchandise people

Idelber Avelar

Two simultaneous processes of particular importance to the debates around non-human rights have occurred in Brazil over the past twenty years. Both have taken place in the Amazon, undoubtedly an outstanding region when it comes to the predicament of bodies of water, non-human animals, and the earth itself. These processes, however, could not be more contrasting with one another in the legacies they have left for the future of the planet. On the one hand, the Belo Monte hydroelectric dam, a construction project first put forth by the military dictatorship in the 1970s and defeated multiple times by the struggles of Amazonian peoples, was finally built, ironically during the administrations of the same Workers Party that had previously led successful mobilizations against it. The Belo Monte dam has unleashed exactly the type of environmental destruction that indigenous peoples and their allies warned it would, and the loss of plant and animal life has been massive. On the other hand, the developmentalist and ecocidal mentality that underlies Belo Monte received its most thorough and authoritative Amerindian critique yet seen in book format with the publication of *The Falling Sky*,[1] a volume that crowns thirty years of collaboration between Yanomami shaman Davi Kopenawa and Brazil-based French anthropologist Bruce Albert. This article will take these opposing springboards to recast the conversation about non-human rights in the Amazon, one that is of particular urgency in the context of the Bolsonaro administration's offensive against human and non-human populations of the region.

---

[1] Davi Kopenawa and Bruce Albert, *The Falling Sky: Words of a Yanomami Shaman* (Nicholas Elliot and Alison Dundy tr, Harvard UP 2013). All quotes refer to this edition and are indicated parenthetically in the text.

The Belo Monte hydroelectric dam has a most unlikely trajectory amongst contemporary ecocides. Having barred one of the last remaining Amazonian rivers to flow freely, Belo Monte brought about the all-too-predictable collapse in the ecosystems of the Middle Xingu against which indigenous populations of the region had warned for decades. Belo Monte tells a seemingly paradoxical story, as the project was conceived by the military dictatorship but only carried out in Lula da Silva's and Dilma Rousseff's administrations, after their Workers Party had participated in successful struggles against it on multiple occasions. Belo Monte was also the most expensive national construction ever, epitome and emblem of the developmentalist mirage for the Amazon, and a categorical confirmation of the judiciary branch's inability or disinterest in protecting the rights of indigenous and riverbank populations. The dam was licensed in Lula's second term (2007–10) and inaugurated in 2016 at the end of Rousseff's second, interrupted term. In fact, the opening of Belo Monte took place right after Rousseff's impeachment proceedings had cleared Congress, and she made it a point to make that ceremony her last, proud public act in office. The dam has left a well-documented[2] legacy of devastation in the region of the Big Turn (*Volta Grande*) of the Xingu River, one of the most spectacular natural wonders of the Amazon. It has dried up a vital stretch of the river and caused enormous harm to life in the surrounding areas, extinguishing species, dispossessing indigenous and riverbank peoples, breaking up communities, overcrowding the city of Altamira, and producing one of the great environmental and social collapses of our time.

When the dictatorship planned it in 1975, during the administration of military dictator Ernesto Geisel, the dam had a fairly different structure from the one that was resurrected thirty years later. In 1980, when the military government received the final report on the Xingu River Basin, the Belo Monte project included seven dams and was predicted to generate nineteen thousand megawatts, about half of all hydroelectric energy then produced in Brazil. At that moment, Belo Monte was projected to flood eighteen thousand kilometres and directly affect seven thousand indigenous individuals of twelve different ethnicities, in addition to its other effects on isolated groups. In 1988 the Kayapó people, with the support of anthropologists and other allies, were able

---

[2] For a full bibliography, see Idelber Avelar and Moysés Pinto Neto, 'Energia Limpa e Limpeza Étnica' (2020) 57(1) Luso-Brazilian Review 150–171. For full documentation on the dam's legal history, see the blog maintained by Pará State Prosecutor Felício Pontes, Jr. 'Belo Monte de Violências' <http://belomontedeviolencias.blogspot.com> accessed 14 June 2022. For a more recent (2019) account of Belo Monte's ecocidal effects, see the work done by Vandré Fonseca for independent journalism collective Amazônia Real: 'O rastro de destruição de Belo Monte' <https://amazoniareal.com.br/o-rastro-de-destruicao-de-belo-monte/> accessed 14 June 2022.

to create enough international consternation against the dam, in a coalitional struggle marked by the emergence of Raoni Metuktire's leadership. In 1989, in the city of Altamira, three thousand indigenous individuals gathered in the First Meeting of the Indigenous Peoples of the Xingu Basin, and the struggle against Belo Monte gained renewed impetus. On that occasion an image became known world-wide, when the woman and indigenous leader Tuíra slid, carefully and methodically, her long knife along the face of the president of state electricity conglomerate (Eletrobras), engineer J. A. Muniz Lopes, generating and managing long minutes of tension in the crowd. In the latter half of the 1990s, during Fernando Henrique Cardoso's administration, the Xingu Basin populations defeated yet another attempt to build the dam, and until then they counted on the support of the Workers Party that would eventually succeed in building it.

In 2005, during the third year of Lula's first term, a corruption scandal disgraced party apparatchik and then Chief of Staff José Dirceu, thereby forcing a realignment in the cabinet. Lula's right hand was now Dilma Rousseff, whose support for the resurrection of the Belo Monte project turned out to be decisive. In uniquely embarrassing fashion for Rousseff's blockbuster developmentalism, nearly everyone who was equipped to talk about Belo Monte in ecological, human, and non-human, economic, juridical, and even energetic terms vehemently opposed it. Support for the dam was minimal even among engineers. Some of the most illustrious opponents of the dam were: indigenous leaders, Raoni Metuktire, a Kayapó, and Davi Kopenawa, a Yanomami; Pará State Prosecutor Felício Pontes Jr., a figure linked with environmental causes and respected by the indigenous populations; Ms. Antonia Melo, Middle Xingu's main popular leader and founder of the Xingu Live Movement; Professors Célio Bermann and Osvaldo Sevá, respectively of the Universities of São Paulo and Campinas; and Father Erwin Kräutler, Xingu's emeritus bishop.[3] Over decades, these leaders insisted on the dam's catastrophic effects upon human and non-human animals of the region and beyond. Every single catastrophic admonition they offered turned out to be accurate.

---

[3] In 2010 Raoni Metuktire spoke to Amazon Watch on Belo Monte: 'A message from Chief Raoni, renowned leader of the Kayapó people' <https://youtu.be/_tz_t6HdR44> accessed 14 June 2022. Videos, statements, and activism by Ms. Antonia Melo and allies are responsible for the wealth of documentation available on the website of the Xingu Live Movement: <https://xinguvivo.org.br/> Prof. Osvaldo Sevá's early warnings regarding Belo Monte can be found in the pioneer volume he edited: *Tenotã-mõ: alertas sobre as consequências dos projetos hidrelétricos no Rio Xingu* (International Rivers Network 2005). See also a number of eloquent protests he published on the alternative journalism website of Correio da Cidadania: 'Especial Belo Monte' <http://www.correiocidadania.com.br/especiais/69-especial-belo-monte> accessed 14 June 2022.

Speaking at the United Nations,[4] Kayapó leader Raoni Metuktire warned that the construction of the Belo Monte dam would cause extinctions of several fish species and irreversible devastation in and around the Xingu River. In forceful and emotional recordings, Chief Metuktire offered the indigenous knowledge of the catastrophes produced by Euro-Brazilians in the forest as a counterpoint to the edulcorated environmental reports presented by the government and Norte Energia, the electricity conglomerate created with public funds to carry out the operation. It was not surprising to any indigenous leader, therefore, that the National Reporting on the Human Right to the Environment, in their 2010 Xingu Mission (i.e. six full years before the conclusion of the dam), already noted the irreversible loss of biodiversity, the proliferation of endemic diseases, the underestimation of methane emissions, the projected extinction of species, and a lasting impact upon a population much larger than originally estimated. Clear in Chief Metuktire's admonitions was the knowledge immemorially accumulated by Amazonian peoples concerning the devastating effects of artificially-barred still water in the Amazon. Given the conditions of humidity, the barring of flowing water in the Amazon amounts to the spreading of death for humans and non-humans: '*carapanãs* (Amazonian word for mosquitoes) will show up', indigenous leaders often warn every time a Brazilian government endeavors to build yet another hydroelectric dam in the Amazon. Chief Metuktire predicted the devastation, and it came.

Both Article 231 of Brazil's Constitution and Convention 169 of the International Labor Organization, of which Brazil is a signatory, are clear about the need for public and democratic hearings of the indigenous populations in a case such as the construction of Belo Monte, which would clearly affect original dwellers in the area. But the dam-building business often operates under the premise that these hearings are events in which it is inconceivable for local populations to say 'no'. The essential spirit of the term 'hearings' (*oitivas*) is distorted every time governments and construction companies operate with the tacit assumption that affected communities may speak and present their objections during the said hearings as long as construction goes on as planned anyway, at best with the addition of 'mitigating measures' (*condicionantes*), a misleading one insofar as they are never conditions without which the construction will not happen; on the contrary, the construction always goes on anyway and the mitigating measures may or may not follow suit. Even when they do, they usually fall short of mitigating much. The eventful history of Belo Monte includes hearings that are in fact not hearings, installation licenses that are 'partial' and therefore not installation licenses at all, and a juridical

---

[4] For Raoni Metuktire's 2011 speech on Belo Monte to the United Nations, see <https://youtu.be/zGOEUhMo-r0> accessed 14 June 2022.

history thoroughly based on injunctions that prevented merit from ever being definitively ruled upon. That is to say, the government and the electricity conglomerate repeatedly achieved injunctions to postpone a final decision; meanwhile they turned the hydroelectric dam into a fait accompli, even though in court they were losing every ruling on merit. They just did not lose enough of them before a 'final injunction' in the Supreme Court coincided with a point of no return in the construction.

Crowning this juridical uniqueness was a provision of tyrannical origin, the military dictatorship's 'suspension of security,' a remnant of their regime that has lingered on during democracy. It is a formula that allows presidents of higher courts unilaterally to suspend decisions of lower courts without judgment of merit and based purely on a supposed risk of 'occurrence of grave lesion to public order, health, security and the economy.' Rhetorical analysis of the judicial trajectory of the construction project leads us to a somewhat inevitable conclusion: Belo Monte represents a colossal failure of the Brazilian juridical system in protecting the rights of humans and non-human populations. Better said, perhaps, Belo Monte stands for the *success* of this juridical system to perform the tasks for which it was designed, i.e. to concoct the language in which the victorious legally justify and narrate their story. In the case of Belo Monte, the country's talent for oxymorons made itself felt once again: a construction project conceived by the military dictatorship was implemented during democracy thanks to a juridical remnant from the military order, during the presidency of a former activist whom the military had tortured in the early 1970s. Even Brazil's oxymorons are hyperbolic.[5]

Supporters of the construction were correct to point out that the Workers Party version of the Belo Monte dam was different from the one conceived by the military dictatorship in the 1970s. Yes, it was 'another' Belo Monte. Instead of the original eighteen thousand square kilometres, the area to be flooded was reduced to six hundred and forty square kilometres. In lieu of the original nineteen thousand megawatts of energy, Belo Monte would now produce eleven thousand megawatts. The considerable reduction in the flooded area allowed Lula's and Rousseff's administrations to present Belo Monte as an enterprise of clean energy that *would not affect* – by which they really meant *would not flood* – any indigenous land. The deliberate confusion between affecting and flooding became particularly absurd in the case of the Big Turn of the Xingu River, as the indigenous populations of the area, such as

---

[5] For an argument on how a hyperbole of the 'Grand Brazil' runs through the country's modern history from Getúlio Vargas to the military dictatorship to the Lula years, see my recent *Eles em nós: retórica e antagonismo político no Brasil do século XXI* (Record 2021).

the Arara and the Juruna, lost the river as a source of protein-rich food and as a means of transportation. Although they were not flooded, those populations were obviously affected in a brutal way, as the barring of the river meant that they would now lose their crops, their fish, and their mobility. In the propaganda operation that justified the ecocide, 'affecting' was deliberately reduced to 'flooding,' in a perverse synecdoche, given the fact that what the hydroelectric did was to *dry life out of the Middle Xingu.*

The deliberate confusion between affecting and flooding carried out by the propaganda in defence of the construction was a uniquely perverse way of precluding the rights of nature from even being posed as a theme. It was a severe defeat for human and non-human rights, one of the most significant of our time. The logic underlying the defence of Belo Monte was decidedly anthropocentric: Brazil was to experience a new cycle of growth, the story went, that would necessitate more electric energy than what was previously available, and the dam on the Middle Xingu was a small price to pay. Only 'a few hundred' indigenous individuals would be affected, and they could be fairly compensated (after all, in every anthropocentric argument some humans count as more fully humans than others). Extinctions would be limited to 'a few species of fish' if they happened at all. The drastic reduction in the flood area, a consequence of the abandonment of the reservoir type dam to a run-of-river type, could strike a nice balance, the government technicians told us, between energy needs and environmental care. Belo Monte was a modern, 'clean' source of energy.

The adjective 'clean' has been recoded by the dam-building business in Brazil in so many ways that it is imperative to clear out the fog around the term. 'Clean energy' does not mean clean energy, it simply means energy not generated by the burning of fossil fuels. As Pará State Prosecutor Felício Pontes, Jr. pointed out at the time:

> we [public prosecutors] are seeking in court the cost of one hundred kilometres of dead Xingu River; the cost of the disappearance of 270 species of fish on the Big Turn, some of which only exist there; the cost of deforestation for the flooded area and surroundings; the cost of the groundwater lost. From a social point of view, there is the impact upon indigenous and riverbank populations, with the end of navigability, the proliferation of mosquitoes and diseases such as malaria and dengue, leading to a removal of indigenous populations that is prohibited by the Constitution. There is nothing clean about that, unless they are speaking of ethnic cleansing.[6]

---

[6] Felício Pontes, Jr., 'Belo Monte de Violências' <http://belomontedeviolencias.blogspot.com> accessed 14 June 2022.

'Clean' was the attribute that the dam-building business got accustomed to assigning to hydroelectric energy, but six years after the inauguration of the dam it is the ethnic cleansing described by Pontes Jr. that has taken place. Deprived of the river's mobility and irrigation, indigenous and former riverbank populations have now been packed in precarious housing, on the border or below food insecurity in the periphery of Altamira. This latter has been converted into the typical hellhole brought about by the dam-building businesses. Altamira now displays some of the worst violence statistics in Brazil, including sexual violence against children and teenagers, a constant in an enterprise based on a migrant male labour force. Engineers and executives of the electricity conglomerate, Norte Energia, live in their locked condos while displaced populations no longer have transportation to visit the lost river.

As pointed out above, the juridical defence of Belo Monte was carried out based on injunctions only, in a strategy deliberately designed to postpone the judgment of merit while the dam became a fait accompli, as one cannot 'unbar' a river that has been barred. Brazil's most expensive construction ever was accomplished amidst a barrage of legal challenges that remained unanswered on merit. Eighty percent of all the money spent was public, and investigations by police and public prosecutors later confirmed the considerable amount of graft already visible to activists and local leaders early on. As is common in the dam-building business, the swelling in construction costs was scandalous. In inflation-adjusted reais, the budget from conception to execution went from R$ 4.5 billion to R$ 30 billion, a seven hundred percent increase totalling some billions of dollars. Counter-intuitively, private capital was not ever interested in selling the energy produced at Belo Monte – that is not what the business is about. As Célio Bermann, certainly one of the country's top specialists in the field, explained in an interview with journalist Eliane Brum, the cost of the megawatt per hour sold at Belo Monte (R$ 78 at the time) was *fictitious*, a mirage insofar as it did not even cover investment costs.[7] The question posed by activists might sound naïve to some, but it was right on target: if the Belo Monte dam represents such a good investment as the government says, why does private enterprise not want to do it? Why was it necessary to create a consortium funded by public money to handle it? Does private capital not want to sell the energy generated by Belo Monte? The answer is: no, it does not. It simply wants to get paid to build it, insofar as real profit resides in the construction itself. The following truly astounding fact can never be overstressed: Brazil's most expensive construction ever, justified by the need to generate

---

[7] Eliane Brum, 'Belo Monte, nosso dinheiro e o bigode de Sarney: Entrevista com Célio Bermann' (2011) Revista Época <http://elianebrum.com/opiniao/colunas-na-epoca/belo-monte-nosso-dinheiro-e-o-bigode-do-sarney> accessed 14 June 2022.

electricity, had nothing to do with electricity whatsoever. It was not built in order to generate electricity, it was built in order to be built.

As we have seen, the massaging of language was not a minor component of the process. The synecdoche by which 'affected' became synonymous with 'flooded' was not the only case. A true symphony of euphemisms and hyperboles accompanied the government's and the energy conglomerate's discourses about Belo Monte. On the one hand, there was the underestimation of the number of impacted individuals, the levels of methane emissions, and the dam's social effects, including the skyrocketing of violence indexes. Brazil's euphemisms are an old familiar image throughout their history for Amerindian peoples, as the Guaraníes can attest with the meanings acquired by the term *aldeamentos* (from *aldeia*, village or community): for Guaraníes the term has meant little more than confined ghettoes or torture centres. In the case of Belo Monte the euphemism did not operate with the numbers only; it truly distorted the essence itself of what the effects of the dam would be: rhetorically reducing 'affecting' to 'flooding' allowed the electricity conglomerate and the government to present the number of affected individuals as negligible. On the other hand, there were a number of hyperboles: superestimation of the electricity generated, the country's need for it, and the percentage of the total energy that was actually to be offered to consumers (as opposed, say, to electro-intensive industries such as aluminium). It would not be incorrect to say that the entirety of the discursive support for the Belo Monte dam took place through hyperboles and euphemisms. Nothing in their discourse maintained any degree of isomorphism with any dimension of the reality it supposedly described. The entirety of discourse took place in hyperbolic or euphemistic registers.

An all-too-Brazilian oxymoron made itself present in a juridical move specially designed for the Belo Monte ecocide: the license of partial installation. For hydroelectric dams, licenses are presumably issued once hearings have been held, pertinent court proceedings have taken place, and conditions have been met. A license of partial installation is by definition a contradiction in terms. A hydroelectric dam cannot be partially installed because, well, once you block the river, the deal is sealed. Faced with a mountain of legal and social challenges, in flagrant disrespect of the Brazilian constitution, and unable to win in court on merit, the dam-building coalition had to resort to the oxymoron now known as 'license of partial installation' to turn the construction into a fait accompli before meeting the basic requirements for installation. This is what happened until the granting of the final injunction by Supreme Court Justice Ayres Britto to the conglomerate – 'final injunction' being yet another oxymoron, when you recall that an injunction is by definition an instrument to delay judgment of merit.

As struggles around the ecocide in the Middle Xingu were taking place, a prestigious series in a French publishing house brought to print a most forceful indictment of the Euro-Brazilian mindset underlying not only Belo Monte, but centuries of colonization of the Amazon, fundamentally unaltered by the end of Portuguese colonialism in the Americas. It would not be far-fetched to claim for Davi Kopenawa and Bruce Albert's *The Falling Sky: Words of a Yanomami Shaman*, the honour of being the greatest – let us say, the most auspicious and meaningful – event in the twenty-first century's print culture. I do not know any scholar in the humanities and the social sciences who has read this grandiose and important book, and fundamentally disagrees with this assessment. In order to limit the scope of the claim, we might say that it is the twenty-first century's greatest event in *Western* print culture, until we realize that, in more ways than one, *The Falling Sky* is not really a Western book, at least not in the senses in which those two words, 'Western' and 'book', have operated in the past few centuries. True, *The Falling Sky* appeared in one of the landmarks of modern Western thought, the Terra Humaine series of France's Plon publishing house, the same in which classics of anthropology such as Claude Lévi-Strauss's *Tristes tropiques* were originally published. It is also true that in English *The Falling Sky* found its home in no lesser a publisher than Harvard University Press, the epitome of Western academic excellence, and in Kopenawa's native and Albert's adopted home of Brazil the book appeared in the country's intellectually sanctioned press par excellence, Companhia das Letras, with a preface by the doyen of Brazilian anthropology, Eduardo Viveiros de Castro.[8] All these accolades, however, do not change the fact that *The Falling Sky* seems to be something beyond a mere book, and certainly something other than a Western book. In fact, it may well be the most radical indictment of the West to have seen the light of print in our times.

The Falling Sky manages to operate in at least three different genres quite effectively. Running through the volume is an autobiography of Davi Kopenawa, of which major portions are written in the coming-of-age register and narrated with strategies not unlike those of the *Bildungsroman*, with its modulated system of growths lived as displacements away from an original naïveté into a later moment of wisdom. But as *The Falling Sky* demonstrates beautifully, no Yanomami individual could ever tell his or her story in that standard autobiographical, self-centred narrative proper to Westerners. Even the most specifically autobiographical passages of the book are embedded in a self-anthropology of the Yanomami people, in a learned account of the practices, discourses, myths, narratives, dreams, and rituals that make up the book's vast and complex presentation of the Yanomami existence, cer-

---

[8] Davi Kopenawa and Bruce Albert, *La chute du ciel: Paroles d'un chaman yanomami* (Plon 2010). Brazilian edition: *A queda do céu: palavras de um xamã ianomami* (Beatriz Perrone-Moisés tr, Companhia das Letras 2015).

tainly the most exhaustive and authoritative to date. The mutual imbrication between these two dimensions of the book for over five hundred pages would have been remarkable enough, but *The Falling Sky* includes a third strand, so to speak, that runs through the volume and coexists with the other two: a *counter-ethnography* of Euro-Brazilians (and Westerners as a whole) that amounts to a meticulous, well grounded, and impeccably presented indictment of Brazil's (and the West's) routine destruction of ecosystems, non-human animals, and the very possibility of future life of any kind. This is the moment that the book describes with the central image captured by its title, that of the sky falling due to so much destructive human interference in Omama's creation.

These three dimensions roughly correspond to the book's three major sections ('Becoming Other,' 'Metal Smoke,' and 'The Falling Sky'), but they also have a way of happening in simultaneous layers. Kopenawa's autobiography roughly tells the story of how an earlier young man's selling out to white people's merchandise gave way to an initiation in the shamanic practices of the Yanomami at the hands of his father-in-law, leading to a whole other path in life, one that includes encounters with the *xapiri* (spirits) and a scathing critique of the society and the people of merchandise. That narrative is indissociable from the presentation of Yanomami cosmogony, i.e. the creation by Omama and the communication that takes place through the words of the *xapiri*. Because the narrative self that speaks in the volume stands at the ending point of the journey, after full initiation has taken place, and Kopenawa has become a shaman signatory of a powerful critique of Euro-Brazilian society, no autobiography or self-anthropology ever takes place in this book without the roaring of its third strand, the counter-ethnography of, as Kopenawa calls them, the merchandise people. In other words, the very account of how Kopenawa ceased to aspire to a position in white society and abandoned his early job as a translator for the National Foundation for the Indian (FUNAI, the government organ in charge of policies for the indigenous peoples in Brazil) presupposes the complete journey and the full critique of Euro-Americans' greed, self-centeredness, and predatory anthropocentrism. To my knowledge these three genres had not quite been combined in such powerful fashion before.

In addition to its main body, the volume also includes a wealth of paratextual materials consisting of maps of Yanomami territories within Brazil and Venezuela, brief presentations of the book by both Bruce Albert and Davi Kopenawa, an appendix on ethnonym, language, and orthography, a history of the Yanomami in Brazil, a brief introduction to Yanomami kinship patterns, an account of the Haximu massacre in 1993, an ethnobiological glossary, a geographic glossary, and one hundred pages of endnotes. Most importantly, the paratextual apparatus includes two extra pieces, one written by Bruce Albert and entitled 'How this book was written' and another by Davi Kopenawa under the title 'Word of Omama.' This copious ancillary material is no small part of the reason why one does not find, in the reception of *The Falling Sky*, a shred of the polemic that involved the presumed or supposed manipulation or misrepresentation of the subaltern voice in sanctioned intellectual or academic spaces by a mediator intellectual, such as the conversation that dominated the reception of *I, Rigoberta Menchú* in Latin American Studies.[9] Whereas in the case of Menchú's testimony – compiled, edited, and published by Franco-Venezuelan anthropologist Elizabeth Burgos –, reception of the book in academic circles focused on the possible hierarchies that could have crept back into the project, regarding Albert's and Kopenawa's book there seems to have coalesced a far more clear understanding that no such questions apply, perhaps due to Bruce Albert's unquestionable credentials of a four-decade-long fieldwork with the Yanomamis as well as to Kopenawa's towering figure as a world intellectual already recognized *before* the book was published. Be that as it may, regarding *The Falling Sky*, even a whiff of the tired questions around whether or not 'the subaltern can speak' sounds unequivocally outdated and inappropriate, as no one has been subalternized so violently as Amerindian peoples and no one has spoken of late in a louder and clearer voice as they have – Kopenawa's being but one of the powerful individual articulations of that collective utterance.[10]

The relevance of *The Falling Sky* for a theory of non-human rights could hardly be overestimated, as the entire architecture of the volume is a lesson in the critique of Western anthropocentrism. In fact, and very much in tune with other Amazonian cosmogonies, the difference between human and non-human animals is conceived in ways that have very little to do with how Western thought and culture have conceived it. Omama, the demiurge of Yanomami

---

[9] For the original publication in Spanish, see Rigoberta Menchú and Elizabeth Burgos, *Me llamo Rigoberta Menchú y así me nació la conciencia* (Casa de las Américas 1983). A good picture of what the Latin Americanist academia debated regarding Menchú's testimony, particularly in the United States, but also in the United Kingdom, can be found in Georg M. Gugelberger (ed.), *The Real Thing: Testimonial Discourse and Latin America* (Duke UP 1996).

[10] For forceful articulations of Amerindian views on the planet, of particular interest for non-human rights, see Ailton Krenak's recent books, not as monumental as Kopenawa's *The Falling Sky*, but certainly no less lucid and incisive. Writing in the tradition of the visionary pamphlet, Krenak has published at least two short and indispensable books: *Ideias para adiar o fim do mundo* has been translated as *Ideas to postpone the end of the world* (Anthony Doyle tr, House of Anansi 2020). Still awaiting an English version is *A vida não é útil* (Companhia das Letras 2020). Krenak hails from Minas Gerais, in the basin of the Doce River, ruined by the failing of an iron mine tailings dam that poured 50 million tons of toxic waste into it. The Krenaks, a proud nation whose existence was defined by the dialogue with the Doce River, are now reduced to drinking from water trucks.

mythology, created the *xapiri*, spirits and messengers to whom the shaman accedes by drinking the *yakoana* powder and having the path opened up for him by the elders. The *xapiri* came into being 'so we could take revenge on disease and protect ourselves from the death with which his evil brother afflicted us'.[11] Omama's evil brother is Yaosi, a name that the Yanomami relate to Teosi, the Christian god: 'This is why to us Teosi is more like the name of Yaosi, Omama's bad brother, the one who taught us to die'.[12] The *xapiri*, the powerful and wise spirits of the forest, relate to humans and non-humans in ways that followers of Teosi tend not to understand:

> Wherever human beings live, the forest is populated with animal spirits. These are the images of all the beings who walk on the ground, climb on branches, or have wings, the images of all the tapirs, the deer, the jaguar, the ocelots, the spider monkeys and howler monkeys, the coatis, the toucans, the macaws, and the agamis! The animals we hunt only move through the parts of the forest where the mirrors and paths of their ancestors' images that became xapiri are. White people never think of that when they look at the forest. Even when they fly over it in their planes, they don't see anything.[13]

The funny thing about the *xapiri* is that 'there are far more xapiri than humans in the forest, and all its other inhabitants know them!'.[14] Humans – or a certain class of humans, anyway, the merchandise people – are unique in their blindness. Non-human animals and *earthbound peoples*, to use Bruno Latour's phrase[15] (e.g. Amerindian peoples), know about the *xapiri* and know they are numerous, and more relevant to the harmonious balance of Omama's creation than humans: 'the xapiri also constantly work to prevent the forest from turning into chaos'.[16]

Chaos or confusion, smoke, particularly in the form of metal smoke that clouds judgment, generalized oblivion or endemic lack of memory, and the inability to dream about anything or anybody other than oneself are perhaps the four major pillars of Kopenawa's counter-ethnography of white people. Euro-Brazilians, or better put merchandise people (as in the assault upon the forest there is not much distinction between Brazilians and non-Brazilians), are systematically diverted from clear judgment by the accumulation of

---

[11] Kopenawa and Albert (n 1) 30.
[12] Ibid 208.
[13] Ibid 65.
[14] Ibid.
[15] For a thoughtful presentation of the concept of earthbound peoples, see Bruno Latour's fifth lecture at Edinburgh, 'War of the worlds: human against earthbound' <https://www.youtube.com/watch?v=gsZCS5Zicx4> accessed 14 June 2022.
[16] Kopenawa and Albert (n 1) 133.

merchandise. The continuing burning of the forest, the barring of its rivers, and the destructive gold mining frenzy that unsettles the foundations of the earth, causing the sky to fall, are events that Kopenawa presents as indicators of white people's particular inability to exercise memory. The theme that the people of merchandise are uniquely forgetful runs through the volume and is essential for Kopenawa's counter-ethnography: 'If we go on following them [the words of *Teosi*, white people's god] for no reason, we will eventually forget the words of our elders. Then we will be called believers, when in fact our minds will simply have become as forgetful as those of the white people who know nothing of the forest'.[17] There is no better emblem of this endemic oblivion than hydroelectric dams in the Amazon such as the one discussed in the first half of this chapter. Kopenawa was a vocal opponent of Belo Monte, even though *The Falling Sky* makes no mention of the dam in the Xingu River. However, the logic underlying Belo Monte is forcefully (and quite poetically) dissected in the volume. After producing the same results with the hydroelectric dams of Tucuruí (on the Tocantins River), Jirau, Santo Antônio (on the Madeira River), and Teles Pires (on the eponymous river), merchandise people act as if they did not know, or had no memory, that all these dams brought about deforestation, extinctions, and malaria, all in all a result that amounts to the dissemination of death, smoke, and destruction. This deficiency of memory appears as a logical consequence of the obsession with accumulation of merchandise, particularly because that counter-ethnographic argument also appears paired not only with Kopenawa's autobiography but also with his own self-anthropology of the Yanomami.

Writing itself is seen by Kopenawa as a consequence of this oblivious character of white people, not as a remedy against it. Merchandise people draw their words on paper skins, Kopenawa proposes, because their thought is full of forgetting:

> As for the white people, they constantly need to draw their words. This is also something that Omama did not teach them! I think this must be because their minds are really forgetful. Their ancestors probably created these drawings in order to be able to follow their thoughts. Long ago they must have told themselves: 'Let's draw what we say and that way maybe our words won't escape further from us?' It is true. Their words do not seem to be able to stay in their minds for long.[18]

I cannot think of a better summary of how the Brazilian state and Euro-Brazilians in general have related to the Amazon than Kopenawa's forceful indictment that they continually say things and forget them. Their words just do not stick

---

[17] Ibid 206.
[18] Ibid 372.

around for that long. This element of Kopenawa's counter-ethnography, like all others, is related to his own autobiography insofar as it was during his initiation that he witnessed the elders continually telling him that his presumptuous manners learned as a white man's servant were oblivious, lacking in memory, full of forgetful smoke: 'Your forgetful speeches irritate us!',[19] they would tell him.

It would be a futile exercise to separate 'literal' and 'metaphoric' uses of imagery in *The Falling Sky*. In the over two hundred occurrences of 'smoke,' for example, the literal use designating the real fires that happen daily in the forest is often indistinguishable from the smoke that is said to cloud white people's judgment. The book draws much of its poetic effect from this polysemy. Yanomamis have reserved a word, *xawara*, to refer to all highly contagious infectious diseases of foreign origin, and the word often appears associated with smoke: 'For the Yanomami epidemics spread in the form of fumes, hence the expression *xawara a wakëxi*, 'epidemic smoke'.[20] The association makes sense, one must admit, in a context where fumes from machines and motors represent epidemic smoke par excellence, as deforestation is one of the major origins and carriers of disease. They are the embodiment of the smoke that causes lack of clarity and memory in the minds of the people of merchandise.

As is well established by Amazonist anthropology, there is a virtually universal trope in Amazonian cosmologies that is the notion of a primordial state of undifferentiation between humans and animals or a moment of metamorphosis of human into animals. Brazilian anthropologist Eduardo Viveiros de Castro has offered a wealth of arguments presented under the umbrella term 'perspectivism' and built on the many Amerindian narratives where the original condition common to humans and animals is not, as we usually think in the West, animality, but humanity.[21] Whereas we see nature as the ground from which different cultures take off and differentiate among themselves, in a linearity going from homo erectus to Neanderthal to homo sapiens, by which

---

[19] Ibid 303.
[20] Ibid 493.
[21] For the most specifically philosophical presentation of Viveiros de Castro's thought, see *Cannibal Metaphysics* (Peter Skafish tr, University of Minnesota Press 2014). For his argument on Amerindians' theory of equivocation, see his 'Perspectival Anthropology and the Method of Controlled Equivocation' (2004) 2(1) Tipití 3–22. For his account of how Amerindian words that get translated as 'human beings' in Western languages tend to function as pronouns rather than nouns, i.e. as pure shifters, see Viveiros de Castro, 'Os Pronomes Cosmológicos e o Perspectivismo Ameríndio' (1996) 2(2) Maná 115–144. For Viveiros de Castro's presentation of the experience and thought of death among Amerindians, see his public lecture 'A morte como quase acontecimento' <http://www.youtube.com/watch?v=Zdz8U9_8YVU> accessed 14 June 2022.

humanity takes place as a progressive move *away from* animality, Amerindian narratives tell the story of how animals lost the attributes inherited or maintained by humans. Whereas for Westerners humans are former animals, animals are, for Amerindian thought, former humans. The original condition is humanity, not animality.

The particular Yanomami modulation of this narrative differentiates between two kinds of non-human animals:

> A very long time ago, when the forest was still young, our ancestors – who were humans with animal names – metamorphosed into game. The human peccaries became peccaries. The human deer became deer. The human agoutis became agoutis. These *yarori* first people's skins became those of the peccaries, the deer, and the agoutis that live in the forest. So it is ancestors turned other that we hunt and eat today. On the other hand, the images that we bring down and make dance as *xapiri* are their form of ghosts. These are their real hearts and true inner parts. And so these animal ancestors from the beginning of time have not disappeared.[22]

The *xapiri*, the powerful spirits to whom shamans accede by having their path opened by elders and by taking the *yakoana* powder, are nothing but images of ancestors turned into animals in the beginning of time. The *xapiri* therefore consider animals as ancestors, for they were once humans as we are. We kept for ourselves the name of 'humans', but we are the same as they are. This represents a fundamental inversion of the Western commonality between humans and animals, according to which we all share a basic animality (like animals we have instincts, needs, urges, a biological structure, i.e. there is a level on which we all exist as animals). In Yanomami cosmogony, like in other Amerindians cosmogonies, humans and animals do share a common condition, but the condition they share is *humanity itself*. That is to say, all of the attributes with which one is accustomed to differentiating humans from animals (spirituality, volition, consciousness, a soul, etc.) are attributes essentially shared by non-human animals as well. As Viveiros de Castro once explained, in a world where everything is human, being human is not that special. Amerindian anthropomorphism is the most powerful antidote to Western anthropocentrism.

Taken in its uniqueness, the Yanomami narrative of creation such as presented in *The Falling Sky* is exceptionally complex, particularly in its symphony of metamorphoses between the human and the non-human. The shaman is he who can see and be visited by the *xapiri*, but he is also the human who can see other species as those species see themselves (Viveiros de Castro *dixit*), that is to say, *as human* – as partaking in all the privileged attributes

---

[22] Kopenawa and Albert (n 1) 61.

one associates with humanity (consciousness, volition, soul). In their turn, the *xapiri* are animals ('spirits') who are at the same time human and non-human, as they are ancestors who became animals – and have maintained, therefore, their original kernel of humanity, visible to themselves and to a particular class of humans, the shamans. Animal adornments are indistinguishable from their own skin: '[t]heir arms are decorated with a profusion of bunches of parrot feathers and macaw tail feathers stuck in armbands made of beautifully bright, smooth beads. A multitude of toucan tails and colourful *wisawisama si* feathered skins hang from them too.'[23] Yanomamis call them by individual names, yet '[e]ach name is unique, but the xapiri to which it refers are countless'.[24] While translating the *xapiri* to the language of Westerners, Kopenawa often resorts to the metaphor of the mirror ('like the mirrors in your hotels'), but hastens to add that they are mirrors that shine, unlike white folks' mirrors, which – in typical anthropocentric and self-centred fashion – only project subjects back to themselves. Kopenawa and Albert offer a wealth of detail about where the *xapiri* come from and how they appear to shamans; how they adorn themselves for a special dance taught by Omama; how one must drink the *yaokana* powder and have doors opened for oneself by the elders in order to see them; and how 'the images of game that the shamans make dance are not those of the animals we hunt',[25] as 'they are those of their fathers, who came into being in the beginning of time'.[26] Among non-human animals, one that is often compared to merchandise people is the dog, for a dog will not know when to stop eating. The differentiation between two classes of non-human animals allows for the difference between human and non-human to become purely positional, inessential so to speak. Unlike Judeo-Christian myths of creation, therefore, there is no hierarchy between the human and the non-human here, as they simply represent different moments in a process of metamorphosis. The attributes 'we' usually think of as proper to humanity (self-consciousness, volition, soul) are shared by all species. In Kopenawa's counter-ethnography, powerful antidotes to anthropocentrism are also forceful critiques of Westerners' narcissism. Kopenawa does not negate white people's ability to dream, but he forcefully notes they only dream about themselves.

With the exception of appendices such as the lucid 'How this book was written' or the exposition of the 1993 Haximu Massacre, both written in Bruce Albert's voice, *The Falling Sky* does not make use of juridical language. Its impact and relevance for the movement of non-human rights, however, is

---

[23] Ibid 61.
[24] Ibid.
[25] Ibid.
[26] Ibid.

immeasurable. Very rarely do we have access to such a thick and authoritative description of a mode of co-existence with non-human animals, bodies of water, and plant life that stands in such a stark and powerful contrast with our own. This brief chapter only scratches the surface of this monumental volume to reinstate again a reminder of what should be the horizon of any clear-sighted movement in favour of non-human rights. If that movement is to have any viable and promising horizon at all, it is the lessons of the earthbound peoples, most clearly those of Amerindians guardians of the forest such as the Yanomami, that must be heeded.

12. Do androids dream of having rights?[1]
Costas Douzinas

The Saudi Arabian government announced in October 2017 that it had granted citizenship to a robot named Sophia.[2] The news was reported all over the world and led to a global debate about robot personhood, a debate that was already being conducted *sotto voce* in academic legal and philosophical journals. Later, Sophia was named United Nations Development Programme's (UNDP) first-ever Innovation Champion, the first non-human with a UN title. It was a Saudi publicity stunt. It aimed at presenting the country where women have very limited rights as a major world innovator in AI technology and computing. But it showed the way the winds are blowing.

In June 2023, it was reported at a Royal Aeronautical Society conference that the US air force had conducted an AI simulation in which a drone decided to 'kill' its operator to prevent it from interfering with its efforts to achieve its mission. The operator of the simulation Colonel Tucker Hamilton described an exercise in which an AI-powered drone was ordered to destroy an enemy's air defence systems, and attack anyone who interfered with that order. 'The system started realizing that while they did identify the threat, at times the human operator would tell it not to kill that threat, but it got its points by killing that threat. So, what did it do? It killed the operator because that person was keeping it from accomplishing its objective.'[3] Both incidents were later denied. Sophia was a marketing gimmick to promote a conference. The American military denied that it had ever carried such a simulation.[4] Colonel Hamilton

---

[1] The title is inspired by the classic Philip Dick science fiction novel *Do Androids Dream of Electric Sheep* (Hachette 2018).

[2] Zara Stone, 'Everything You Need to Know About Sophia, The World's First Robot Citizen' (2017) *Forbes* <https://www.forbes.com/sites/zarastone/2017/11/07/everything-you-need-to-know-about-sophia-the-worlds-first-robot-citizen/> accessed 17 August 2023.

[3] 'Highlights from the RAeS Future Combat Air & Space Capabilities Summit' (2023) <https://www.aerosociety.com/news/highlights-from-the-raes-future-combat-air-space-capabilities-summit/> accessed 17 August 2023.

[4] 'US air force denies running simulation in which AI drone "killed" operator' (2023) <https://www.theguardian.com/us-news/2023/jun/01/us-military-drone-ai-killed-operator-simulated-test/> accessed 17 August 2023.

accepted that his was 'a hypothetical "thought experiment" from outside the military, based on plausible scenarios' and added that 'you can't have a conversation about artificial intelligence, machine learning, autonomy if you're not going to talk about ethics and AI.'[5]

Today, some artificial intelligence, automated electronic beings and vending machines have been given legal rights.[6] Legal rights and duties presuppose the legal person, an entity recognised in law who can exercise rights or perform duties. Throughout history, some humans have been endowed with personhood others not. Slaves, women and minoritized groups were not recognised as persons for the larger part of history. Conversely, non-human entities and animals have been given some of the entitlements and responsibilities of legal personhood. Let us have a quick look at the history and meaning of personhood. Can AI robots and androids become legal persons?

A BRIEF HISTORY OF THE PERSON

> 'Whether women are the equals of men has been endlessly debated; whether they have souls has been a moot point; but can it be too much to ask for a definite acknowledgment that at least they are animals? ... Many hon. Members may object to the proposed Bill enacting that, in statutes respecting the suffrage, "whenever words occur which import the masculine gender they shall be held to include women," but could any object to the insertion of a clause in another Act that whenever the word "animal" occurs it shall be held to include women?; Suffer me, through your columns, to appeal to our 650 representatives, and ask – Is not one among you then who will introduce such a motion? There could then be at least an equal interdict on wanton barbarity to cat, dog, or woman.'[7]

This letter by 'An Earnest Englishwoman' addressed to British Parliamentarians was published in *The London Times* in April 1872. The 'Earnest Englishwoman' was complaining about the status and treatment of women in the late nineteenth century. They were not persons but '*res*' in the property and service of their fathers and husbands. Domestic rape and cruelty went unpunished while the maltreatment of animals was commonly penalized. In the United States persons of colour were slaves and could be treated as things to be bought and sold. The infamous British Contagious Diseases Acts of the 1860s 'treated women as a whole as nothing more than contagious animals, while at the same time they identified the real "mute creatures" in class terms.'[8] Up until

---

[5] Ibid.
[6] David Calverley, 'Legal Rights for Machines' in Michael Anderson and Susan Leigh Anderson (eds), *Machine Ethics* (CUP 2011).
[7] Joanna Bourke, *What it Means to Be Human* (Virago 2012) 1.
[8] Ibid. 98.

the 1930s, when the word 'person' appeared in law, it was interpreted to refer exclusively to men. This changed in the case *Edwards v Canada* (AG).[9] The legal question the Privy Council was asked to decide was whether 'the word "Persons" in the *British North America Act, 1867*, includes female persons'. The difference between the gendered human being and the abstract (legal) person could not be stated more strikingly. The Council overturned the decision of the Canadian Supreme Court in 1929. It decided that the word 'person' included women.

The case was the clearest example of the practice of personhood. It is a yo-yo term, a mutable matter of convention, given to some and not others. Entities who were given legal recognition were later removed, returning to the status of *res*-thing, object of possession. This is a main characteristic of the legal person. All civilisations draw a distinction between ordinary humans and those who perform certain roles or functions in public life – as priest, judge or reincarnation of spirits – or in private – as *pater familias*, carer or master of slaves. The long story of personhood starts with the Greek *prosopon*, the theatrical mask. Women did not appear on the Athenian stage. A male actor would wear a female mask and perform the roles of Antigone, Phaedra or Medea. The mask identified the actor with the role and later with the character the actor performed. Rome, unlike Greece, passed the function of the mask from ritual and stage to the law. The law constructed an artifice and assigned it to some humans. *Persona* and *homo* were separate entities, the legal person was the double of the human. The *persona* formed law's fundamental fact, the legal mask, the ritual and metaphorical disguise a litigant puts over his natural face in order to be brought before the law.[10]

The unity of person and human in Rome was not physical, bodily or psychological. It depended on patrimony and heritage, on property and family standing. No human being, not even the free citizen, was a legal person by nature. Before achieving legal status, people lived in a world of indistinction similar to that of slaves or things. The key differentiation was between persona and *res*. The slave existed in a space between the two, as a living thing and an objectified human, an object of property who could not own property himself. But that space was flexible. Its borders porous. A slave, the human thing, could become a person through rituals of emancipation, while a person could fall into slavery. Conversely, persons could revert to the earlier status of non-personality if they lost the *persona* defining relationship, their estate

---

[9] *Henrietta Muir Edwards and others v The Attorney General of Canada* [1929] UKPC 86, [1930] A.C. 124 (18 October 1929), P.C. (on appeal from Canada).

[10] This part draws on Costas Douzinas, *The Radical Philosophy of Rights* (Routledge 2019).

or paternity. Personality was a term of distinction and a strategy of exclusion that differentiated the privileged few from the great plebeian mass. This is still the case.

The law used the category of the person to separate between humans and others and develop abstract and general concepts and strategies of inclusion and exclusion. Right from the start, the creation and assignment of the status of legal person was coeval with the construction of the human/non-human divide. There was nothing 'natural' in the strategy of inclusion/exclusion. The mask and the *persona* are political technologies, mechanisms for the organisation and stratification of power and property. Personhood first excludes and then differentiates amongst the included distributing roles, positions and privileges. It distributes power and property and allows those endowed with personality to enter into public and political life and to carry out specific economic transactions. The mask signifies that the wearer is invested with a particular sacred or secular status. Similarly, the legal person is a legal creation, an artificial character and abstract function; as a formal vessel, it can contain and give form to all sorts of content. The persona was and remains a technology of separation and division, the first and still most successful tool for the legal stratification and regulation of social relations.

FROM LEGAL TO MORAL PERSON

Stoic metaphysics started moving the *prosopon/persona* towards moral universalism. Cicero often used *persona* in his philosophical works and helped displace its legal use from the *Jus Civile* into the *Jus Naturale*. But it was Christianity which sacralised the person, turning a legal concept into a category of moral ontology. The early Church Father Tertullian first transferred the term *persona* from law to divinity to help describe the three phases or functions of the Trinitarian God. The attempt to give content to the strange idea of one God with three persons breathed an air of spirituality into a prosaic term and prepared its eventual vague and narcissistic displacement onto humanity.

The Christian reaches his true nature when he imitates the complex moral unity of God as the *imago dei*. The Nicene credo of '*unitas in tres personas, una persona in duas naturas*' brought together the three persons of Father, Son and Holy Spirit into one God and united the two equally perfect natures – divine and human – of incarnate Christ. The three divine personalities confirmed the metaphysical gravitas of persona, transferred it from man to divinity and then reflected it back onto humanity. It was a 'double mirroring' strategy between God and humanity. Man is created by God and in his image of three personalities. Human personality, mirroring that of the Godhead has therefore divine provenance. The dignity that God gives to humanity returns to divinity creating the perfect ideological circle. The *persona*, this legal device forms the site of these transfers.

The *persona* is the ground where the two natures came together. The human is a *homo duplex*, an unsteady combination of matter and spirit, spirit and body. After the revolutions and the positivization of natural rights, the Roman distinction between *persona* and *homo* and the Christian distinction between body and soul collapsed. The French and American revolutionary documents declared that all 'men are born free and equal', extending personality to all and uniting its legal and metaphysical versions. Yet only some humans, the citizens, were given full legal rights and protections. Personality became an integral part of identity, bringing together matter and spirit, legal person and universal morality. Citizenship was bestowed only on the privileged few, the white, proper and property-owning men. The original exclusions behind the category of the legal person were now generalized and attributed to the whole humanity. There is body and there is soul; those who do not subject flesh to spirit cannot be redeemed.

The difference between those with *dignitas* and those without was internalised into higher and lower parts of humanity. The philosophy of personalism and the jurisprudence of human rights reasserted the gap between body and spirit.[11] The 'rational agent' of liberal philosophy is someone who wills, deliberates and acts but whose material needs are external to the powers of reflection and action. The body is the object of intervention and disciplining; its needs, desires and social embeddedness are set aside. To have rights is to be subjected to one's own objectification, to turn one's own body into object and the person into moral abstraction. But what is the function of rights?

Legal rights were created by early modern law. A legal right is a relationship between at least two persons, a right holder and a duty bearer. The latter must act or refrain from certain acts to enable the holder to exercise the right. The forms of the legal person and legal rights are indispensable for modern law. A legal system consisting of general norms and abstract concepts requires persons to subsume their actions and relations under its categories; legal persons with rights are the necessary building blocks of capitalism and law. Marx famously said that things cannot go to the market and sell themselves; exchange and commodification are central activities in capitalism. Products must be taken to the market by people prepared to buy and sell commodities, including their ability to work. Rights and legal persons who 'have' them are both a logical prerequisite and the outcome of capitalism. The positive

---

[11] Samuel Moyn, 'Personalism, Community, and the Origins of Human Rights' in Stefan-Ludwig Hoffmann (ed), *Human Rights in the Twentieth Century* (CUP 2011) 85–106; *Christian Human Rights* (University of Pennsylvania Press 2015).

rule-based legal system with its general norms, regulations and principles meets capitalist needs: predictability of economic transactions, personal liability for actions and penal responsibility for crimes. Property, contractual and corporate rights emerged in early modernity with the right of the lender to force repayment of the debt prominent. Rights follow rules, duties follow rights, the law enforces them. They are the necessary tools of a socio-economic system based on the market and of a legal system that facilitates it. The form of persons and rights is a cause and effect of the rise of the market economy, the emergence of capitalism and of individualism. The law constructs the forms of person and right. The person is the legal form of individualism, the moral person of moralisation and individualism, both preconditions of capitalism.

Legal person and human being remain separate entities. Legal personality in the twenty-first century, as much as in Rome, is a creation of law, a social construct, distinct from and superimposed on the empirical self. It is a cipher, a two-dimensional drawing or caricature placed on the three-dimensional fullness of face and body. The legal person has no biological or psychological characteristics, no bodily needs or desires. It is a point of imputation of privileges and obligations, rights and duties, entitlements and liabilities. The legal person inhabits a logical space of norms, rules and commandments. Legal rules populate a world parallel to the empirical universe, a floating normative realm. This wider characteristic of the legal person has been replicated in the action of big data analysis of large corporations and social media platforms. They collect detailed information about our daily behaviour and through big data methodologies reduce them into data sets that can predict the probability and influence future behaviour. The 'avatars' or 'digital personhoods' created are as accurate of our real lives as that of legal personhood. Both legal and digital personhood are ways in which individual lives are captured, measured, surveilled and transformed. The outcome of their action can be similarly devastating. The law and capitalist business need a point of contact with concrete human activity. The legal and the digital persons are precisely this point of contact: a creation of the legal order or big data algorithms, they are the indispensable companions and facilitator of normative abstraction and controlling interventions. The legal person is a function for the law, the digital the meeting point of entities and behaviour. The law and the big data informed market determine human behaviour.

In conclusion, the *persona* is both a legal creation and a metaphysical abstraction and an integral requirement of capitalism. First, the abstraction of law and personality frees the concrete self to pursue the insatiable desire of possessive individualism, a prerequisite of the capitalist economy. Secondly, it prioritises reason and will over body and material needs. This allows the law to support and justify economic and social inequality while protesting its commitment to the dignity of formal equality and fairness. The artificiality of personhood facilitates and justifies the exclusion of people considered not fully human according to the dominant definition of humanity. The legal person and its surface variations are grounded on a permanent, univocal and stable identity in the service of the dominant socio-economic order. The legal person is too flexible and malleable an instrument to be abandoned to its moralistic alter ego. At times the link between legal and moral personality is loosened, at others strengthened. This flexibility makes it indispensable both for the moving sands of identity recognition and for the operation of late capitalism.

RIGHTS OF NON-HUMAN ENTITIES

In a famous article, Marcel Mauss concluded that the person has moved 'from a simple masquerade to a mask, from a "role" (*personage*) to a person (*personne*), to a name, to an individual; from the latter to a being possessing metaphysical and moral value; from a moral consciousness to a sacred being; from the latter to a fundamental form of thought and action – the course is accomplished.'[12] But is it?

Everyone who has tried to cross from Israel to Palestine has experienced the humiliating and scary experience at the checkpoint of the wall dividing the two.[13] It has separated families, farmers from their land, people from their place of work. The wall has been condemned by the United Nations, by the International Court of Justice and almost every human rights organisation. Israel has been accused of organising its own apartheid and has responded with threats to annex illegally part of the occupied territories. Yet the Israeli environment minister Yehudit Naot's concern was that the wall is 'harmful to the landscape, the flora and fauna, the ecological corridors and the drainage of the creeks.'[14] As the Palestinian activist Omar Barghouti observed, 'the ministry and the National Parks Protection Authority mounted diligent rescue efforts to save an affected reserve of irises by moving it to an alternative reserve. They've also created tiny passages [through the wall] for animals.'[15]

Various scientific bodies have announced that we have entered a new age, the Anthropocene, the age of the human. The term is used somewhat negatively to indicate that human intervention is changing the planet, its geology and ecosystems, in an unprecedented way. For some, there is a positive side

---

[12] Marcel Mauss, 'A category of the human mind: the notion of person; the notion of self' in Michael Carrithers, Steven Collins and Steven Lukes (eds), *The Category of the Person* (CUP 1985) 23.
[13] Ayeal Gross, *The Writing on the Wall* (CUP 2017).
[14] Quoted in Naomi Klein, 'Let Them Drown' (2016) 38:11 London Review of Books 11.
[15] Omar Bargouti, 'Resisting Israeli Apartheid' (2016) 4.2 Babylon 134.

too. The Anthropocene is also the Antropic age: the epoch when human rights, the rights of humanity, have been universally acknowledged and give our political and legal institutions their normative grounding and legitimacy. The strong message is that the humans belong to a single and unique category, that of humanity which has finally reached its peak in the formal recognition of its deserts. If the term Anthropocene is used, in part, to decry the effects of humans on the planet, the Anthropic age celebrated the achievements of this same humanity. Humanity is one and has the same rights and entitlements everywhere.

But this is not true. Slaves and women, today Palestinians and refugees, don't have the same rights, do not belong to the same humanity as the masters and men, or Israelis or citizens of countries receiving migrants. Kind-hearted western humanitarians believe that underneath their many rights privileges, they are the same humans as the Palestinians and the refugees. They believe that there is a common denominator, the soul, speaking, reason or some other unknown X that unites all humans in their common humanity. The humanist's universality is that of the company of fellow men. Despite the many power imbalances, Israelis and Palestinians are more similar than different. We are all the same. In the humanist language, humanity is both a descriptive category – all human animals – but also a normative foundation. The needs and desires of humanity prescribe the rights and entitlements that all humans deserve. Once we put in the picture class, race, gender, ethnicity, religion, sexual orientation, disability and other real characteristics, however, people stop being one. They are divided into many hierarchical subcategories. Some with full humanity and the accompanying rights, others with lesser humanity and, finally, others totally excluded. The fully human, the lesser human and the inhuman are the three broad categories to which human animals belong. Humanity rather than being a common characteristic or set of rights and expectations is a strategy of differentiation and categorisation amongst humans.

At the opposite end, the law has given legal rights and recently human rights to non-human entities, including corporations, non-human animals, natural zones of protection and even deities. Artificial entities, such as the Church, corporations and the nation state, have been given legal personhood and recently some human rights. This assignation of personhood was seen as a legal fiction that treated non-human entities as if they were human. But this fictitious character was a main attribute of personhood right from the start. As far as business is concerned[16] the extension of corporate legal and human rights

---

[16] *First National Bank of Boston v Bellotti*, 435 U.S. 765 (1978); see Nikolas Bowie, 'Corporate Democracy: How Corporations Justified Their Right to Speak in 1970s Boston' (2018) 37 Law and History Review 943.

has been moving fast. In *Citizens United* the US Supreme Court removed most limits on political campaign spending by corporations.[17] Corporations were given religious rights and protections in *Sebelius v Hobby Lobby*.[18]

Let us turn to the legal treatment of animals. Pigs, rats, leeches and insects were accused of crimes in the Middle Ages, formally summoned to courts of law, tried, convicted and punished.[19] Animals arraigned before courts included 'asses, beetles, bloodsuckers, bulls, caterpillars, chickens, cock chafers, cows, dogs, dolphins, eels, field mice, flies, goats, grasshoppers, horses, locusts, mice, moles, pigeons, pigs, rats, serpents, sheep, slugs, snails, termites, weevils, wolves, worms and miscellaneous vermin.'[20] The punishments varied from execution by burning at the stake, burial alive to strangling and imprisonment for lighter offences. In 1522, rats were acquitted in Autun of the felony of eating and wantonly destroying the barley crops.

Two legal strategies have been used to extend rights to animals. Peter Singer and Paola Cavalieri, the directors of the Great Ape Project, using the metaphysical view of personality, have argued that apes are a 'community of equals' with humans. They feel fear and happiness, they use language and tools and remember the past. Singer's utilitarian strategy aims to create sympathy and care by drawing on the similarities between humans and apes. A second strategy utilizes the difference between legal personhood and the entity behind it. Steven Wise, an animal rights campaigner and head of the Nonhuman Rights Project (NhRP), has been trying to turn apes into 'nonhuman persons' and give them basic legal protections. They have been trying to get a court to issue a writ of habeas corpus and examine the lawfulness of an animal's incarceration in a lab or zoo thus obtaining partial legal personhood. In 2014, Wise applied for habeas corpus in New York on behalf of Tommy, a privately owned chimpanzee.[21] Tommy, should be compared to a human child who 'can understand that he does not want to be imprisoned for his life in a cage,' but, unlike a human adult, cannot be held legally responsible for his actions. The judge noted that legal personhood comes with 'responsibilities';

---

[17] 558 U.S. 310 (2010).

[18] 723 F.3d 1114 (10th Cir. 2013). See the excellent analysis of this series of cases in Wendy Brown, *In the Ruins of Neoliberalism: The Rise of Anti-Democratic Politics in the West* (Columbia UP 2019).

[19] Jean Vartier, *Les procès des animaux du Moyen Age à nos jours* (Hachette 1970); Luc Ferry, *The New Ecological Order* (Carol Volk tr, University of Chicago Press 1992) ix–xvi.

[20] Gunther Teubner, 'Rights of Non-Humans? Electronic Agents and Animals as New Actors in Politics and Law' 33:4 Journal of Law & Society 497.

[21] Elizabeth Barber, 'Chimpanzees are not entitled to human rights' (2014) *Time* <http://time.com/3619581/chimpanzee-tommy-human-animal-rights/> accessed 17 August 2023.

it would be unwise 'to foist any responsibilities on this chimpanzee.' The appeal court agreed, opting for a definition of moral personality rather than legal personhood. The references to rights, responsibilities and accountability build a Kantian conception inappropriate for non-humans. However legal personhood, a constructed and artificial status, does not need to pass such stringent moral tests. It is not exclusively a question of rights but of provision of protections and security. Legal personhood without the ascription of specific rights can protect an entity from activities or practices that negate or belittle its nature.

The first victory for animal personhood came in Buenos Aires in late 2014. The court accepted that Sandra, an orangutan, should be released from the zoo. She deserved the basic rights of a 'non-human person' and she had been unlawfully deprived of her freedom.[22] At first glance, recognising Sandra not as an object but a 'nonhuman person' with basic rights such as life, liberty and freedom from torture, looks like a striking development. But the legal technique is common and well-understood. The law regulates social relations by endowing entities with a bunch of obligations and rights. The court's argument in the Tommy case 'that human beings possess the unique ability to bear legal responsibility' was wrong.[23] Legal responsibility can be borne by companies, gods, churches or nature reserves and apes as much as by natural humans. The law constructs the bearer of rights; the dividing line has been consistently elastic; sometimes extending, at others contracting, the status of legal personhood.

The American law finally started extending the line, in 2015. A Manhattan Supreme Court justice granted for the first time two chimpanzees, Hercules and Leo, the right to seek a writ of habeas corpus against unlawful imprisonment.[24] The apes were used for medical experiments at Stony Brook University. Stony Brook was asked to explain why the chimpanzees should continue to be 'unlawfully detained' instead of being transferred to a primate sanctuary in Florida. The NhRP welcome the decision, arguing that it is moving a long way towards recognizing apes as legal persons. 'Only a "legal person" may have

---

[22] Richard Lough, 'Captive orangutan has human right to freedom, Argentine court rules' (2015) *Reuters* <http://www.reuters.com/article/2014/12/21/us-argentina-orangutan-idUSKBN0JZ0Q620141221> accessed 17 August 2023.

[23] Patrick Barkham, 'Sandra the "nonhuman person" is sadly not the face of a welfare revolution' (2014) *The Guardian* <https://www.theguardian.com/commentisfree/2014/dec/22/sandra-nonhuman-orangutan-welfare-revolution-court-ruling> accessed 17 August 2023.

[24] Alan Yuhas, 'Chimpanzees granted petition to hear "legal persons" status in court' (2015) *The Guardian* <http://www.theguardian.com/world/2015/apr/21/chimpanzees-granted-legal-persons-status-unlawful-imprisonment> accessed 17 August 2023.

an order to show cause and have a writ of habeas corpus issued in his or her behalf. The court has therefore implicitly determined that Hercules and Leo are "persons".'

In July 2015, New York County Supreme Court Justice Barbara Jaffe, refused the relief 'for now', citing the Tommy precedent. However, she added:

> '"Legal personhood" is not necessarily synonymous with being human [...] Rather, the parameters of legal personhood have been and will continue to be discussed and debated by legal theorists, commentators, and courts and will not be focused on semantics or biology, even philosophy, but on the proper allocation of rights under the law, asking, in effect, who counts under our law.'[25]

'This is one step in a long, long struggle,' commented Steven Wise. Chimpanzees are intelligent, emotionally complex and self-aware enough to merit some basic human rights, such as the rights against illegal detainment and cruel treatment. In a similar case taken by Steve Wise on behalf of Tommy and Kiko, two chimpanzees held in captivity, the New York appeals court rejected the application for habeas corpus in September 2017. In a circuitous argument, the court said that the apes are not humans; they cannot be held legally accountable for their actions and granted legal personhood.

Christopher Stone argued that trees, parks and other natural objects too should be given rights, starting a major debate.[26] Greenbelt zones should become legal subjects with the power to go to court, through representatives, to protect the ecosystem from intrusion.[27] A river, waterfall and the environment have recently been recognised in some jurisdictions as persons with limited rights. In New Zealand, the Whanganui River was recognised as being a legal person with rights. The river would have a guardian that can bring cases on its behalf like the legal guardian who represents children in cases against its parents. Legal personhood has been successfully extended to environmental entities such as the Ganges River and sections of the Amazonian rain forest.[28] In the case of the Ganges, the High Court in the northern Indian state

---

[25] Michael Mountain, 'New York Justice Denies Habeas Corpus Relief for Hercules and Leo Given Precedent Set in Previous Case, "For Now"' (2015) *NhRP* <http://www.nonhumanrightsproject.org/2015/07/30/new-york-justice-denies-habeas-corpus-relief-for-hercules-and-leo-given-precedent-set-in-previous-case-for-now/> accessed 17 August 2023.

[26] Christopher Stone, 'Should Trees have Standing? Towards Legal Rights for Natural Objects' (1972) 45 Southern California Law Review 450.

[27] Marie-Angèle Hermitte, 'Le concept de diversité biologique et la création d'un statut de la nature', in *L'homme, la nature, le droit* (Bourgeois 1988).

[28] David Boyd, *The Rights of Nature: A Legal Revolution That Could Save the World* (ECW 2017).

of Uttarakhand in assigning such status determined that the river would be afforded all the 'corresponding rights, duties and liabilities of a living person' including protection from harm.[29] The Declaration of River Rights states that rivers are 'living entities that possess legal standing in a court of law' and that they shall possess, amongst others, 'the rights to flow, to perform essential functions for the ecosystem, to native biodiversity, to restoration and to be free from pollution.'

We can conclude that after the person's metaphysical transubstantiation two trajectories opened. First, the person continued its work as a technology of separation and division. The second associates the person with a metaphysical conception of human nature and insists that only humans can be legal persons. The secularist metaphysician emphasizes the person's unity, continuity over time and permanence over space as well as sentience, consciousness and conscience. The legal provenance and constructed character of the person survives, nevertheless. Legal technology no longer or exclusively divides persons from things, or free men from slaves. It redefines what it means to be human, giving personhood to animals and greenbelts, actants and hybrids, androids and replicants, computer programmes and AI robots. The epoch of the post-human is that of the revenge of the legal person against its metaphysical mimic.

LEGAL PERSONHOOD OF ROBOTS

Rights can be given and enjoyed by entities recognised by the law to legal persons. Persons exercise legal rights and are bound by legal duties. To be a person means to have rights. Legal persons with rights and duties are necessary for the operation of the law. Rights are created by rules. They are not natural properties automatically accompanying humans like arms and legs. Two normative issues have dominated the discussion about robots and AI. First, should robots be given legal and human rights? Second, how can humanity stop the inexorable evolution of AI reaching a point at which intelligent and fully autonomous robots may endanger their makers and humanity. The first is a question about the protection from harmful human actions robots should be given. The second, is about the protection humanity should be given from the harmful action of robots. Both involve the question of legal personhood.

---

[29] Michael Safi, 'Ganges and Yamuna rivers granted same legal rights as human beings' (2017) *The Guardian* <https://www.theguardian.com/world/2017/mar/21/ganges-and-yamuna-rivers-granted-same-legal-rights-as-human-beings> accessed 17 August 2023; Sudipta Sen, 'Of Holy Rivers and Human Rights: Protecting the Ganges River' (2019) <https://yalebooks.yale.edu/2019/04/25/of-holy-rivers-and-human-rights-protecting-the-ganges-by-law/> accessed 17 August 2023.

As we have seen, the law has given legal rights and recently human rights to non-human entities. The first step in the process of giving rights to an entity is its recognition as a legal person, as someone who can claim protection and be represented in a court of law. Legal personality has not been an exclusively human prerogative. Humans were given legal personality relatively late, after the creation of corporate personality. Legal personhood is constructed, a creature of political calculation and balance of power, administrative convenience and social convention. It privileges some interests and promotes particular capacities, for example the sentience and susceptibility to suffering of human animals – the paradigmatic legal persons rather than their non-human peers on the disadvantaged side of what rights scholar Steven Wise characterised as the 'thick legal wall' differentiating humans from other animal species.[30]

The extension of the categories of persons and rights to women, minoritised groups and animals shows two strategies at work. The legal recognition of great apes or ecosystems is a defensive mechanism. It aims at protecting non-human animals from the evils society and humans visit on them. The extension of personhood to women or black people is different. It includes into the 'community of personhood' humans hitherto excluded. Two separate political strategies for assigning personhood operate. Personality is, first, a border practice, a mechanism of including/excluding entities from recognition, agency and protection. Second, within the recognised and included group, personhood differentiates between those who receive full protection and rights and those with limited and defective privileges.

Similar arguments have been put forward for and against the attribution of personality to other non-human entities, such as Bruno Latour's 'actants', that is non-humans to which science has given some or full ability to act. Computer programs or other electronic means that initiate or respond interactively without action by humans fall into that category; or 'hybrids', which create associations between humans and non-humans.[31] Should robots be given citizenship with its associated civil and political entitlements? Should our existing moral codes and human rights be extended to AI and robots?

As we have seen, there are two definitions of personhood. The first is that of an entity given legal rights and duties and accepted as someone who can go to the law to ask for the protection of its interests. The second adopts the metaphysical and moral definition of personhood. Someone who has absolute value and cannot be taken as a means towards someone else's ends. This is the defi-

---

[30] Stephen Wise, 'The capacity of non-human animals for legal personhood and legal rights', in Raymond Corbey and Annette Lanjouw (eds), *The Politics of Species* (CUP 2013).
[31] Teubner (n 20).

nition that most science fiction literature and films adopt. Their robots built to look identical to humans enjoy the emotional depth and imagination associated with human dignity. In *Blade Runner*, Zhora, the bioengineered female robot whom the blade runner Rick Deckard chases and kills, is an exotic dancer. The replicant Roy's soliloquy before his 'retirement' by Deckard, is a moving eulogy. Andrew in *Bicentennial Man* falls in love with the granddaughter of his owner and asks the World Congress to recognise him as human in order to marry her. When his petition is rejected because he is immortal, Andrew decides to age with his loved one. He is recognised as human and the lovers get married at Andrew's deathbed. In *Ex Machina*, Nathan the creator of Ava, a humanoid robot, brings Caleb Smith, a programmer, to an isolated retreat and asks him to judge whether Ava has consciousness. Ava meets Turing's test, according to which if an entity behind a screen replies to questions a human asks which cannot be considered to come from a machine the entity is intelligent. Caleb falls in love with Ava who manipulates him by making accusations about Nathan and claiming that he cannot hear their conversations. Eventually it becomes clear that Ava is using Caleb to neutralise Nathan and she escapes in the helicopter meant to take home Caleb, who is left behind in the compound. When the helicopter takes her to a city, she joins the crowd as another ordinary woman.

Science fiction literature and film seems to suggest that if robots behave like persons, in the eyes of humans they are sufficiently 'human' to be seen as legal persons and given some of the rights and duties of personhood. This extension is facilitated by the similarities between robots and humans. The first requirement for a robot becoming human is personification, the assumption of a human face and characteristics. If God made humans in his image and likeness, humans make robots in their own image and likeness. As the first part argued, however, personhood is a matter of convention and convenience. Entities do not need to become human-like to acquire legal personhood and rights. Nothing stops political and legal systems extending the benefits and duties of legal personality to AI entities. Legal personhood places a mask on humans, non-human animals and other entities and turns them into legal persons by assigning them certain rights and duties. What is necessary for creating a human robot is precisely the same as for creating a legal person. Robots and persons are creations with similar characteristics. As Margaret Davies put it: 'modern Western law openly and necessarily constructs reality and has no need to *reflect* anything – hence law can deploy whatever outlandish fictions are instrumentally conducive to specific situations or contexts (if "outlandish" seems extreme, remember that a *ship* can legally be a *person*).'[32] The limited conception of personhood as a constructed bunch of (some) rights and duties, capacities and disabilities is as fully applicable to robots as it is to corporations and animals. The metaphysical and moral conception of the person-qua-human-with-dignity has been restricted, for the time being, to human animals. Furthermore, it can be argued that this dignity-based limited conception has been retreating even among humans.[33]

The legal person, deprived of the moralistic gloss of dignity, can do what it has always done: separate and divide, offer some protections to some entities and deny them to others. This is already happening and there is nothing the metaphysicians and moralists of personhood can do to stop this process. Gunther Teubner and Bruno Latour consider this dehumanisation of the legal person both historically justified and legally necessary.[34] As Miguel Vatter puts it – commenting on Teubner – 'anything that is nonhuman can still interact in a human-like fashion (and thus, in principle, be granted rights and duties) as long as it is functional to the communication occurring within the system or network about the environment that surrounds it.'[35] The answer to the question should AI robots have (what) rights is to be sought not in the definition of the human with his dignity but in the practicalities of the entity's interaction with the economic and social system. Arguments about restricting such rights must be sought in the environment of robot operation and not in the inner meaning or essence of personhood. The legal fiction which created initially the personhood of the free property-owning Roman citizen, later, that of the corporation, of animals and of the green belt, can be extended to the personhood of AI robots. There is nothing new about it. It is the logical extension of the constructed and constructing character of law.

The law can bestow (limited or full) legal personhood therefore on AI robots and androids. It is unlikely that this will be the result of an organised social and political movement as was the case with animals. The animal rights activists adopt arguments from human rights activism that derive from the metaphysical-moral status of humanity. Robot rights defenders cannot mobilise similar arguments yet. Utilitarianism offers the main normative source. The law will extend legal entitlements and duties to AI robots when it is practical to do so; in other words, when the interests of capitalist business

---

[32] Margaret Davies, 'Distributed Cognition, Distributed Being, and the Foundations of Law' in Marc de Leeuw and Sonja van Wichelen (eds), *Personhood in the Age of Biolegality: Brave New Law* (Palgrave Macmillan Cham 2020) 206.
[33] Douzinas (n 10) Chapter 4.
[34] Teubner (n 20).
[35] Miguel Vatter, 'Nature's Law or Law's Law? Community of Life, Legal Personhood and Trusts' in de Leeuw and van Wichelen (n 32) 228.

demand it. Like corporations and greenbelt zones, the rights to be assigned and protected will be decided on a case-by-case basis through a cost and benefit analysis. Questions of civil responsibility and criminal liability will gradually pass from the owners of the robots to the entities themselves. Extended AI with its benefits and dangers will hasten the process.

What about proper robot moral and legal responsibility. Isaac Asimov's three laws of robotics offer the ground rules: 'One. A robot may not injure a human being or, through inaction, allow a human being to come to harm. Two. A robot must obey the orders given it by human beings, except where such orders would conflict with the First Law. Three. A robot must protect its own existence, as long as such protection does not conflict with the First or Second Law.' Asimov later added a fourth law that completes and transcends the other three: 'A robot may not injure humankind, or, through inaction, allow humankind to come to harm.' These laws transfer to robots the main characteristics of human ethics and lawful behaviour. It is possible to foresee these limited moral injunctions programmed into robot behaviour. The question of the format through which robots will have these laws inscribed and obeyed is not part of this paper or of the competence of the author.

What about the reverse side. Do androids dream of human rights to protect them from harmful action? If we assume (something we cannot at the minute) that robots have a type of consciousness enabling them to imagine, dream and experience emotions then the answer can be found again in the extension of legal personhood. The moral ethic and legal code that protects humans from android action could also protect androids from the harmful action of other entities. This state would be reached at the completion of the process of gradual acquisition of personhood. One expects that the process of legal personhood ascription will parallel that of android acquisition of consciousness. Corporations are legally liable for their harmful activities and legally protected from several unlawful harms. We can foresee the same process of gradual extension of moral and legal rules to android behaviour. The morality and the law are there, legal personhood, the mask of the law can be easily placed on the face of androids. But do androids dream? When they do, personhood and rights will follow without great fuss. The key question therefore is about the android ability to dream and not that of enjoying rights and duties.

Index

3D scanning 197–8
Aarhus Convention 154
actants 252
actio de pauperie 36
Adorno, T.W. 187
aesthetics 105–6
Afada 122–3, 125, 129, 130, 131
affecting, flooding and 227–8, 230
affirmative biopolitics 202–4
affordance 180
Afro-Amerindian Indigenous peoples 174
Afro-descendant communities 145–8, 161
Agamben, G. 104
agency 158
agent (subject of imputation) 102
agential realism 158–60
Albert, B. 11, 223, 230–9
algal blooms, toxic 210, 219
Allen, C. 184–5
Altamira 224, 229
Amazon, the 11, 180, 223–39
    Belo Monte dam 11, 223–30, 235
    The Falling Sky 11, 223, 230–9
American Legislative Exchange Council (ALEC) 216, 217
Andean cosmologies 9, 144, 155–63
animal rights 3, 76, 109–10, 248–50
    Chucho (bear) 6–7, 20–8, 34–5, 38
    chimpanzees *see* apes
    deliberate legal equivocations 8, 118–40
    juridical existence of animals 6–7, 20–38
    residual humanism 6, 13–19
animality 13–19, 236–8
animated structuralism 169, 181–2
Anthropocene 41–4, 142, 189–90, 203, 246–7
anthropocentrism 189–90, 207–8, 219–21

anthropomorphic perspective 138
Aotearoa/New Zealand 110–11
    Whanganui River 47, 50–3, 59, 60, 63, 190, 250
apes 248–50, 252
    chimpanzees 110, 248–50
        Cecilia 8, 121, 122, 129–40
        Hercules and Leo 249–50
        Kiko 250
        Tommy 110, 248–50
    Sandra (orangutan) 8, 109–10, 121–9, 133, 134, 136–9, 249
applied ecology 150
appropriation 58–9, 61
Aquinas, T. 93, 98
Arendt, H. 14, 103, 104
Argentina court rulings 8, 118–40
    Cecilia (chimpanzee) 8, 121, 122, 129–40
    Sandra (orangutan) 8, 109–10, 121–9, 133, 134, 136–9, 249
Aristotle 98, 133
Aronowsky, L. 49
artificial intelligence (AI) 7, 66, 191, 197–8, 251–5
    US air force drone simulation 11, 240–1
    see also robot rights
artificial persons 94–6
Asaro, P. 69
Asimov, I. 255
attribution 28–9
Augustine, St 67, 94
Australia 52
auto-limitlessness 48–50, 60, 62, 65
automated vehicles 197–8
autonomous delivery robots 72

Bachofen, J.J. 37
Balibar, E. 97
Barad, K. 86, 158–60

Barghouti, O. 246
Barranquilla City Zoo 20
Bass Energy 215
bears 6–7
    cases for the jurisprudential meanings of the bear 34–8
    Chucho's case 6–7, 20–8, 34–5, 38
Bekoff, M. 15
Belo Monte hydroelectric dam 11, 223–30, 235
Benjamin, W. 187
Bermann, C. 225, 229
Berry, T. 219–20
Bertachini, G. 98
Bicentennial Man 253
big data analysis 245
biopolitics 202–4
bioprospecting 46
Birch, T. 82, 84, 86
Blade Runner 253
blockchain 198–9, 202
bodies
    encounters between bodies opening up to more-than-huma data rights 197–201
    new materialist notion of rights 195–7
body/soul dualism 94, 95, 244
Boethius 93
Bolivia 155–6, 160
    re-constitution 143, 144–7, 161, 187, 190
Borrows, J. 171, 186–7
Bourke, J. 241
Boyce, J.K. 183
Bratton, B. 198–9, 203
Brazil 10–11, 223–39
    Belo Monte dam 11, 223, 224–30, 235
    Workers Party 223, 224, 227
    Yanomami people 11, 223, 230–9
British Contagious Diseases Acts 241
British North America Act 242
British Petroleum 211
Britto, A. 230
Broadview Heights, Cleveland 213–15, 220
Bryson, J. 71
Buenos Aires City Zoo 122, 123, 128–9, 135

Burgat, F. 136–7, 138
Burgos, E. 233
Burke, E. 88, 103, 104

Canada 36–7
Čapek, K. 66, 70
capitalism 244–6
carbon trading 54–7, 60
Cavalieri, P. 248
Cecilia (chimpanzee) 8, 121, 122, 129–35, 136–7, 138–40
ceremonial gifts 176–9
42
Chandler, D. 222
chickens on blockchain 199, 202
chimpanzees *see* apes
China 199
Christianity 78, 93–4, 97–8, 243–4
Chucho (bear) 6–7, 20–8, 34–5, 38
Cicero 243
circulation 177
Citizens United case 248
class 108
clean energy 228–9
climate activism 9, 164–88
Coeckelbergh, M. 78, 85–6
Coetzee, J.M. 18
collective environmental damage 131–2
colliding cosmovisions 9, 154–61, 162–3
Colombia 111, 165–6, 187
    civil code amendments 21–2
    Constitutional Court 6–7, 20–8, 34–5, 38
    clarification of Judge Ortiz Delgado 25–8
    construction of the debate 23–5
    habeas corpus petition for Chucho 20–1
    legal background to the case 21–2
    Magdalena River 165–6, 167–8
    Papayal Island 165–6, 171–4, 183
colonialism 42, 144
commune 168–9
Community Environmental Legal Defense Fund (CELDF) 40, 45, 212, 213, 215
condictio indebiti 31–2
conflicts 195, 196–7

conflictual more-than-human rights 201–5
Confucianism 85
consciousness 101, 166–7
construction costs 229–30
context 174–5
Convention on International Trade in Endangered Species 35
Coombe, R. 46, 65
Cooper v Stuart 52
COP26 164
corporate-state alliances 209, 215–18, 221, 222
corporations 247–8
corporeality 179
Correa, R. 53–4, 55, 56
cosmovisions, colliding 9, 154–61, 162–3
counter-ethnography 11, 223, 230–9
Covid-19 pandemic 160
Cubitt, S. 200
Cusicanqui, S.R. 186
cyberneticism 7, 44, 62–4
    auto-limitlessness 48–50, 60, 62, 65
cyberspace 175–6

Daston, L. 35
data rights 10, 190–205
    conflictual more-than-human rights 201–5
    encounters between bodies opening up to more-than-human data rights 197–201
    more-than-human perspectives and new materialist Deleuzian notion of rights 194–7
David, Judge P. 133
Davies, M. 253–4
de Graaf, M. 73–4
De la Cadena, M. 106
De Libera, A. 90
de Vitoria, F. 136
decentring the human 206–10, 220–1
Deleuze, G. 29, 192–3
    new materialist Deleuzian notion of rights 194–7
Delgamuukw v British Columbia 37
deliberate legal equivocations 8, 118–40
    Cecilia (chimpanzee) 8, 121, 122, 129–40

different persons, different rights 135–40
non-human persons 125–9, 133–5, 137–9
ontological cleansing 118–20
other differences 120–2
Sandra (orangutan) 8, 121–9, 133, 134, 136–9
Derrida, J. 14
Descartes, R. 95, 101
Descola, P. 106
difference
    control of 140
    similarity/difference and the Turing test 113
digital personhood 245
digitalization *see* data rights
diplomacy for human/non-human relations 9, 164–88
Dirceu, J. 225
dispossession 169–70
Doerfler, J. 171
dogs 13–19, 238
    Stella 16, 18–19
Douzinas, C. 192
Dreamlife project 197
Drewes Farm Partnership 212
drones 11, 240
Duns Scotus, J. 99
duties/rights pairs 75–6

Earth jurisprudence 39–65, 211
    auto-limitlessness 48–50, 60, 62, 65
    Earthly legality 41–4
    ecologies of legality 45–8
    ventriloquizing nature 58–65
    Whanganui River 47, 50–3, 59, 60, 63
    Yasuní-ITT initiative 53–7, 59–60, 63
Earthly legality 41–4
ecocide 188, 223–30
ecologies of legality 45–8
economic exchanges 177–8, 181
economic meltdown 178
Ecuador 45, 152–3, 155–6, 160, 211
    re-constitution 143–7, 161, 187, 190
    Yasuní-ITT initiative 53–7, 59–60, 63
Edwards v Canada 242

Eisenberg, A. 215–16
El Quimbo hydroelectric project 168
elected guardian/steward 151–2
empathy 17–18
entanglement 17, 159–60
　ontological 115–16
entitlement 115–16
environmental activism 9, 164–88
environmental regulation 209–19
epistemic extractivism 63–4
equality, test of 115–16
equivocations *see* deliberate legal equivocations
Esposito, R. 82, 92–3, 97, 115
ethnic cleansing 228–9
ethnicity 108
EU Charter on the Fundamental Rights of Nature 9, 144, 150–63
　colliding cosmovisions on non/human relations 9, 154–61, 162–3
euphemisms 230
European Citizens' Initiative (ECI) Draft Directive for Rights of Nature 150–52
European Parliament 112–13
European Union 143–4, 148–53
Ex Machina 253
exchange 173, 176–9
　economic 177–8, 181
exclusion, inclusion through 4–5, 92–3, 243

faith 16
Fajardo Rivera, D. 23–5, 34
Falling Sky, The (Kopenawa and Albert) 11, 223, 230–9
fictitous persons 94–6
Fischer-Lescano, A. 46–7
flooding, affecting and 227–8, 230
Floridi, L. 79
Folkers, A. 56, 59
forest, self-owned 198–9, 202
forgetting 235–6
fossil modernity 56, 59–61
fossil-fuel use 42
Foucault, M. 102, 114
fracking 217
Frase, P. 3
Frater a fratre law 31–3

French Civil Code 119–20, 138
French Declaration of the Rights of Man and the Citizen 88, 104
Freud, S. 17–18
Fundación Pachamama 45
future memory 186

Gaia hypothesis 7, 42–4, 49–50, 62–3, 64
Gaius 91, 97
Ganges (Ganga) River 47–8, 190, 250–1
Garcia, J.F. 172
gifts 173, 176–9
Global Alliance for the Rights of Nature 45, 58
global governance 214
God 243–4
Gómez Maldonado, L.D. 20–1, 27–8
Gordon, J.-S. 79
grassroots environmental activism 10, 206–22
　Ohio 209–20, 222
Great Ape Project 248
　Sorocaba Sanctuary 121, 129, 130, 135, 140
great apes *see* apes
Greek *prosopon* (theatrical mask) 90–1, 242
Grotius, H. 99
Gruen, L. 17
Guaraníes, the 230
Guerrero Pérez, L.G. 23, 25, 34

habeas corpus cases 248–50
　Cecilia (chimpanzee) 121, 122, 129–35, 139–40
　Chucho (bear) 20–8
　Sandra (orangutan) 121–5
Hamilton, Colonel T. 240–1
Hampshire, M. 198
Haraway, D. 194, 203
Hart, R.D. 71
hearings 226
Heidegger, M. 107
Hercules (chimpanzee) 249–50
Hindriks, F.A. 73–4
Hindriks, K.V. 73–4
Hobbes, T. 96, 196
Hohfeld, W. 67, 75–6
'Home Rule' 40, 218

human rights 3
    Deleuze's perception of 194–5
    'existential crisis' 1
    subject of 88, 103–7
    wrongly associating robot rights
        with 66–72
human/nature relationship 153, 162–3
    colliding cosmovisions 9, 154–63
    Indigenous peoples and diplomacy
        for 9, 164–88
humanism 100, 115
humanity 11, 236–7, 247
hybrids 4, 252
hydroelectric dam projects 235
    Belo Monte 11, 223–30, 235
    El Quimbo 168
hyperboles 230
hypothecation 61

imputation 102
in dubio pro natura doctrine 153
Inayatullah, S. 69–70
incest, prohibition of 178
incidents 75
inclusion through exclusion 4–5, 92–3,
    243
India 15, 111
    Uttarakhand state 47–8, 190, 250–1
Indigenous peoples
    Brazil
        and the Belo Monte dam 224–6
        the Yanomami 11, 223, 230–9
    and diplomacy for human/
        non-human relations 9,
        164–88
    epistemic extractivism 63–4
    kinship relations 84–5
    Latin America
        Andean cosmologies and
            the EU Charter on
            Fundamental Rights of
            Nature 9, 144, 155–63
        re-constitutional processes
            143–8, 161–2
    Maori and the Whanganui River
        50–3
    technologies 182
individualism 245
    possessive 95–6
industrialization 42

injunctions 227, 229, 230
Innocent IV, Pope 94
interest theory 76–7
International Labor Organization 226
'International Mother Earth Day' 142
intra-action 159–61, 163
Israel West Bank Barrier 246

Jaffe, Justice B. 250
Japan 112
Jules and Jim 17
jural relation 30–4
juridical existence of animals 6–7, 20–38
    cases for jurisprudential meanings of
        the bear 34–8
    Chucho's case 6–7, 20–8, 34–5, 38
    Kurki's theory of legal personhood
        28–31, 33–4
    Savigny 30–4
Kant, I. 101–2
Kapferer, B. 217–18
Kayapó people 224–5
khipus 182
Kiko (chimpanzee) 250
Kim, T.W. 85
kincentric ecology 158
kinship relations 84–5
Kogi, the 174
Kolling, P. 198
Kopenawa, D. 11, 223, 225, 230–9
Kräutler, Fr E. 225
Kurki, V. 28–31, 33–4
Kyoto Protocol Clean Development
    Mechanism 57
Kyrtatos v Greece 152

Lake Erie Bill of Rights (LEBOR) 190,
    210, 212, 218, 219
Land Transfer movement 215–16
Las Pavas community, Papayal Island
    165–6, 171–4, 183
Latin America
    nature rights in plurinational states
        143–8
    see also under individual countries
Latour, B. 4, 43–4, 62–4, 252, 254
Law, J. 146, 207
Lazar, S. 222
Le Guin, U.K. 184

LeCun, Y. 71
legal personhood *see* personhood
legal relationships 30–4
legal/natural rights distinction 77–81
legality
    Earthly 41–4
    ecologies of 45–8
Leibniz, G.W. 100
Lenton, T.M. 43, 62–3
Leo (chimpanzee) 249–50
Leviathan 96
Levinas, E. 86
Lewis, J.E. 84
liberation narrative 69–71
Liberatori, Judge E. 125–8
license of partial installation 230
life rights 150
Lima, G. 73, 74
limpieza (social cleansing) 172–3
'living well' 187–8
living with a place 158, 159
loan between brothers 31–3
Locke, J. 14–15, 96, 101, 102
Loh, J. 86
Lorde, A. 82–3
love 17–18
Lovelock, J. 7, 43, 49
Lula da Silva, L.I. 224, 225, 227
lwa 17

Macpherson, C.B. 95–6
Magdalena River 165–8
Malm, A. 184
Maloney, M. 219
Manaugh, G. 197–8
Mansfield, B. 45–6
Maori people 50–3
Marguénaud, J.-P. 120, 137–9
Margulis, L. 43
Maritain, J. 103
Mármol, M. 172
Maroon communities 145–8, 161
Martínez, E. 147
Marx, J. 75, 79
Marx, K. 2, 5, 62, 88, 103, 104, 244
masculinity 108
masks 90–1, 242, 243
Mauricio, Judge M.A. 129, 131–5
Mauss, M. 90, 246
McNally, P. 69–70

medieval jurists 94–5, 99–100, 119
Meister, R. 177
Melo, A. 225
Melville, H. 13, 16
Menchú, R. 233
merchandise people 232, 234–5, 238
Merino, R. 144–5
Metuktire, R. 225, 226
military dictatorship 223, 224, 227
Miller, M. 218–19
mimetic relations 164–5
minoritised groups 252
Misael, Don 165, 166, 171, 174
mistreatment of animals 126–7
Mitchell, T. 55–6
Mitman, G. 35
moral person 243–6
moral rights (natural rights) 77–81
moral status ascription 85–6
more-than-human rights to data 10, 190–205
    conflictual more-than-human rights 201–5
    encounters between bodies opening up to 197–201
    more-than-human perspectives and new materialist Deleuzian notion of rights 194–7
Morita, A. 124
multijuridical multiperspectivism 186–7
municipalization 219–21
Muñiz, C.M. 134
Muniz Lopes, J.A. 225

Naot, Y. 246
Native communities 145–8, 161
natural gas extraction 213–15
natural legal institutions 30–1
natural persons 94–6
natural rights (moral rights) 77–80, 81
nature rights 3, 7, 39–65, 76, 141–63, 190–92, 250–1
    auto-limitlessness 48–50, 60, 62, 65
    Brazil *see* Brazil
    Earthly legality 41–4
    ecologies of legality 45–8
    EU Charter 9, 144, 150–63
        colliding cosmovisions 9, 154–63
    European countries 148–9

grassroots movements 10, 206–22
Ohio 209–20, 222
Indigenous peoples and the climate crisis 9, 164–88
nature as subject of rights 106, 110–12
plurinational states in Latin America 143–8
recognition and integration in the EU 143–4, 148–53
ventriloquizing nature 58–65
Whanganui River 47, 50–3, 59, 60, 63, 190, 250
Yasuní-ITT initiative 53–7, 59–60, 63
nature/human relationship 153
colliding cosmovisions 9, 154–63
Indigenous peoples and diplomacy for 9, 164–88
neo-extractivism 53–7
networks 175–6
new materialism 189, 194–7
new municipalism 220
New York Times debate before COP26 164
New Zealand *see* Aotearoa/New Zealand
nomos 43–4
non-human entities, rights of 246–51
non-human persons 125–9, 133–5, 137–9
non-human/human relations, diplomacy for 9, 164–88
Nonhuman Rights Project (NhRP) 24, 25, 76, 248, 249
Nonini, D. 217, 220, 221
Norte Energia 226, 229

object 98–101
O'Brien, T. 17
Ockham, William of 98
O'Dell, T. 212–13
Ohio 10, 209, 220, 221
House Bill 278 213
nature activism 209–20, 222
Ohio Department of Natural Resources (ODNR) 209, 213, 218
Ohio Valley Energy 215
oil 53–7
Omama 232–4, 238
ontological cleansing 118–20
ontological entanglement 115–16

ontological turn in anthropology 206–7, 208, 221, 222
oppression 69–71
orangutan Sandra 8, 109–10, 121–9, 133, 134, 136–9, 249
Ortiz Delgado, G.S. 25–8
Orwell, G. 83
Our Land Association (Llaka Honhat) v Argentina 187–8

Pachamama Alliance 45
Papayal Island 165–6, 171–4, 183
Parikka, J. 191
partial installation, license of 230
Pellow, D. 214
People's Congress, The 172
personal delivery devices (PDDs) 72
personhood 11–12, 20–38, 240–55
Chucho case 6–7, 20–8, 34–5, 38
digital 245
genealogical account 89–96, 107–8
history of 241–3
Kurki's theory of legal personhood 28–31, 33–4
moral person 243–6
nature 46–8
non-human persons and animal rights 125–9, 133–5, 137–9
residual humanism 6, 13–19
rights of non-human entities 246–51
robots 11–12, 251–5
Roman law 91–3, 97, 107–8, 242–3
Savigny 30–4
and subject of rights 89–103, 135–40
perspectivism 236–7
Petroamazonas 54
Petroecuador 54
place-thought 158, 159
Plaumann doctrine 152
'plurinational' states 143–8
politics 105–7, 116–17
Pontes Jr, F. 225, 228, 229
possessive individualism 95–6
posthumanist approaches 149
Pottage, A. 119
Povinelli, E. 203
power
disparities and environmental degradation 183–4

robot rights and 82–4
privilege 82–4
properties approach to moral status 78–9
property rights 42, 58–60, 132–3
prosopon (theatrical mask) 90–1, 242
protection actions 125–9, 135, 137
psychoanalysis 17–18
Pufendorf, S. 99
Pugliese, J. 192
Pulido, L. 214–15

Radbruch, B. 46
radical alterity 219–21
Rancière, J. 8, 88–90, 104–7, 108, 109, 113, 115–16
rational agent 244
Rawson, A. 45–6
real (physical) persons 94–5
reason 136
recalcitrancy 116–17
reciprocity 176–82
recognition 29, 109
re-constitutional processes 143–8, 161–2
recursivity 169–70
regulation, environmental 209–19
Reid, J. 222
relatedness 18–19
representation 62, 94–5
res (things) 91–2
residual humanism 6, 13–19
resource extraction 200–1, 203, 204
    Broadview Heights 213–15
    Yasuní National Park 53–7
responsibilities 248–9
rights/duties pairs 75–6
Rights of Nature Ordinances 40
rites 85
rivers 250–1
    Ganges 47–8, 190, 250–1
    Magdalena 165–8
    Whanganui 47, 50–3, 59, 60, 63, 190, 250
    Yamuna 47–8, 190
robot rights 3, 7–8, 66–87, 112–13
    AI *see* artificial intelligence (AI)
    alternatives and thinking otherwise 81–6
    analyzing rights 74–7
    differentiating rights 77–81
    legal personhood 11–12, 251–5

    social scientific approach 66, 67, 72–4
    Sophia (android) 11, 71, 112, 240
    wrong assumption that rights mean human rights 66–72
robotics, laws of 255
Roe v Wade 39
Rogers, N. 219
Roman law 29–30, 36, 120
    medieval reformulation of 94–5, 99–100, 119
    person 91–3, 97, 107–8, 242–3
    Savigny's system of modern Roman law 30–4
Rousseff, D. 224, 225, 227
Royal Aeronautical Society 11
Royal Dutch Shell 7, 49
Rudhyar, D. 40
Russia 199
Rylands v Fletcher 36

Sahlins, M. 181
Salmón, E. 158, 159
Sandra (orangutan) 8, 109–10, 121–9, 133, 134, 136–9, 249
Santosuosso, A. 69
Saudi Arabia 11, 71, 112, 240
Savigny, F.K. von 30–4
Schmitt, C. 43–4
science fiction literature and films 253
Sebelius v Hobby Lobby 248
second Copernican revolution 41
'Seeley Lake Medeek' 37
Seidler, P. 198
self-determination, right to 185–6
self-owned forest 198–9, 202
sentience 21–2, 109–10, 133, 136–8
Sevá, O. 225
shamans 237–8
Shaw v McCreary 36
Sierra, G. 172
similarity/difference 113
Singer, P. 109, 248
slaves 241, 242
smoke 236
social relational ethics 85–6
social relationships 30–1
Sophia (android) 11, 71, 112, 240
Sorocaba Great Apes Sanctuary 121, 129, 130, 135, 140

soul/body dualism 94, 95, 244
Sousa Santos, B. de 214
Spain 15
spectacled bears 35–6
    Chucho 6–7, 20–8, 34–5, 38
Spinoza, B. 193, 196
spirituality 179
Spivak, G.C. 61
stakeholders 214
state pre-emption bills 216–18
state-centrism 219–21
state-corporate alliances 209, 215–18, 221, 222
statuses 91
Stella (dog) 16, 18–19
Stiegler, B. 181
Stone, C. 39–42, 62, 208, 211, 250
Stony Brook University 249
Strathern, M. 49, 60, 64
Suárez, F. 99
subject of rights 8, 88–117
    genealogical account 89–96, 107–8
    human rights 88, 103–7
    meanings of subject 97–103
    (non) human rights 107–14
    and person 89–103, 135–40
subjugation 69–71
Suchman, L. 86
Summenhart, K. 99
Surrallés, A. 136
suspension of security 227
Susser, I. 217, 220, 221
Swann v Charlotte-Mecklenburg Board of Education 39

tap water crises 210, 219
Taussig, M. 165, 169, 181
Tavares, P. 144, 146–7
Taylor, T. 76–7
Te Awa Tupua (Whanganui River Claims Settlement) Act 50–3, 59, 60, 63
Te Pou Tapua 53
technical perspective 138
Teófilo 172
Teosi 234
terra0 project 198–9, 202
terraforming Earth 199–200, 202–3
Tertullian 93, 243
Teubner, G. 254

things (*res*) 91–2
thinking otherwise 86
Thomas, Y. 29–30, 93, 111, 119
Thomasius, C. 99
Tiefensee, C. 75, 79
timekeeping 182
Tiputini 53–7, 59–60, 63
Toledo, Ohio 210–12, 218–19, 220
Toledoans for Safe Water 219
Tolosa Villabona, L.A. 22
Tommy (chimpanzee) 110, 248–50
Townsend, D.L. 156
toxic algal blooms 210, 219
transference 18
transformative tactics 183–4
transitivity 184–7
transposition 169–70
true (physical) persons 94–5
Tuíra Kayapó 225
Turing test 113
Turner, J. 80, 81

Ulpian 36
United Nations Development Programme (UNDP) 54, 240
United Nations Harmony with Nature agenda 142–3
United States of America (US) 10, 15, 112, 220
    air force AI drone simulation 11, 240–1
    CELDF 40, 45, 212, 213, 215
    Environmental Protection Authority (EPA) 218–19
    'Home Rule' 40, 218
    nature activism in Ohio 209–20, 222
    personal delivery devices (PDDs) 72
    slavery 241
Universal Declaration of Human Rights 69, 103
utilitarianism 254–5
Uttarakhand state, India 47–8, 190, 250–1

Vatter, M. 254
ventriloquizing nature 58–65
verification 105–7, 109, 113
Vernadsky, V. 40
Villey, M. 92

Viveiros de Castro, E. 124, 231, 236, 237
Vizenor, G. 171, 184, 186
vodou 17

Waitangi, Treaty of 50, 51, 53
Wang, X. 199
water supply crises 210, 219
Watts, V. 158, 159
Wenar, L. 74–5, 77
Whanganui River 47, 50–3, 59, 60, 63, 190, 250
White Earth Nation Constitution 184
Wi Parata v Bishop of Wellington 52
will theory 76–7
Wise, S. 15, 248, 250, 252
Wolff, C. 100
Wollstonecraft, M. 76, 77, 82
women 76, 241–2, 252
Workers Party 223, 224, 227

'wrongful life' suits 26–7

xapiri 234, 237–8
xawara 236
Xingu River 224–30

Yamuna River 47–8, 190
Yanomami, the 11, 223, 230–9
Yaosi 234
Yasuní Guaranty Certificates 54, 55, 60
Yasuní-ITT (Ishpingo-Tambococha-Tiputini) initiative 53–7, 59–60, 63
Yusoff, K. 203, 204

Žižek, S. 81–2
Zouhary, Judge 212